# THE PARTY DECIDES

Presidential Nominations Before and After Reform

Marty Cohen, David Karol, Hans Noel,
and John Zaller

The University of Chicago Press
Chicago & London

MARTY COHEN is assistant professor of political science at James Madison University.
DAVID KAROL is assistant professor of political science at the University of California, Berkeley.
HANS NOEL is assistant professor of government at Georgetown University.
JOHN ZALLER is professor of political science at the University of California, Los Angeles. He is the author of the classic study *The Nature and Origins of Mass Opinion*.

The University of Chicago Press, Chicago 60637
The University of Chicago Press, Ltd., London
© 2008 by The University of Chicago
All rights reserved. Published 2008
Printed in the United States of America

17 16 15 14 13 12 11 10 09 08   1 2 3 4 5

ISBN-13: 978-0-226-11236-7   (cloth)
ISBN-13: 978-0-226-11237-4   (paper)
ISBN-10: 0-226-11236-5   (cloth)
ISBN-10: 0-226-11237-3   (paper)

Library of Congress Cataloging-in-Publication Data

The party decides : presidential nominations before and after reform /
    Marty Cohen . . . [et al.].
        p.   cm. — (Chicago studies in American politics)
    Includes bibliographical references and index.
    ISBN-13: 978-0-226-11236-7 (hardcover : alk. paper)
    ISBN-10: 0-226-11236-5 (hardcover : alk. paper)
    ISBN-13: 978-0-226-11237-4 (pbk. : alk. paper)
    ISBN-10: 0-226-11237-3 (pbk. : alk. paper)
    1. Presidents—United States—Nomination. 2. Primaries—United States.
    3. Political parties—United States.   I. Cohen, Marty.
JK521.P37 2008
324.273'015—dc22

                                                    2008002172

8/10/15

Pap.

Happy 70th Birthday. Sure hope I'll be as accomplished and in good shape when the Social Security checks are coming in...

The Party Decides

[signature]

CHICAGO STUDIES IN AMERICAN POLITICS

A series edited by
Benjamin I. Page, Susan Herbst, Lawrence R. Jacobs, and James Druckman

In memory of
Nelson W. Polsby

Contents

Acknowledgments

From an oversized chair in the southwest corner of his living room, Nelson W. Polsby delivered the remarks that became the basis of this and many other books by his students and grandstudents. The occasions were the informal American politics seminars that he held at his home from the late 1960s until his death in 2007. His distinguished guest, someone like David Broder or Robert Dahl, sat on the couch next to Nelson's chair; two or three Berkeley and Stanford faculty occupied the remaining seats; and graduate students sat cross-legged on the carpet. On many evenings five or ten students and faculty stood at the back of the room or in the entrance hall.

Nelson was nearly always the dominant personality. He didn't lecture or make presentations. He introduced, questioned, and gently corrected the presentations of others. It was from Nelson that the participants mostly learned. Political parties were among the many topics of discussion. Nelson was not a fan of the party reforms of the 1970s and brought in Austin Ranney, a political scientist who helped draft them, for one of his sessions. Ranney readily confessed that he had botched the job, undermining party leaders and opening the floodgates of intraparty democracy. Nelson deeply regretted this opening. He believed America needed parties to organize its disparate social groups and interests into effective electoral coalitions. The prereform parties, with their powerful national conventions, did this. The old parties brought leaders of major policy demanders into a big room and gave them the incentives and the institutional means to find common ground. With the rough edges of group demands blunted by intraparty compromise, each party could offer a presidential candidate who was acceptable not only to its own side, but to the whole nation. Nelson was deeply worried that ordinary voters, as empowered by the McGovern-Fraser reforms, could not perform this work of political integration. Other institutions, most likely the mass media and those adept at using it, would fill the vacuum, with the country being the big loser.

Learned either first- or secondhand from Nelson Polsby, this view of parties as organizers of diverse group interests is the foundation of this book. Nelson did not invent the view—it goes back to the first decades of modern political science—but he was one of a small number of political scientists who kept it current in the latter decades of the twentieth century, and he was the one who passed it on to us. Except for Nelson's influence, we probably would not have written this book.

This is not to say, however, that Nelson would agree with the book. We believe he would share much of our view of parties as coalitions of group interests and policy demanders, but would disagree with our view that presidential parties have survived the McGovern-Fraser reforms. Destruction of he traditional party nominating convention, he would probably say, is simply too great a blow. Yet Nelson took our argument seriously, assigning our manuscript to his students, inviting us to his seminars to discuss it, and even helping to hire one of us at Berkeley. So we would like to believe that, with a little more time, we could have brought him around. Probably we couldn't have, but we regret so much that we do not have the opportunity to try. For us, and we hope for others, this book will help to keep alive the memory of Nelson as a great friend, teacher, and intellect.

While our deepest debt is to Nelson, we owe thanks to many others as well. Larry Bartels, Paul Allen Beck, Kam Yi Dionne, Scott James, David Mayhew, Chloé Miller, and Byron Shafer read the complete book at various stages. Three anonymous referees for the University of Chicago Press also read it. Our gratitude to these readers is very great. They saved us from many errors—though, alas, surely not all.

We are also grateful for the specialized advice we received in three areas. Richard Ellis, Scott James, and Jeff Pasley gave the historical sections a close look. Jeff Lewis gave us extensive methodological advice, and Gary King offered a valuable critique as well. Kathy Bawn commented repeatedly and patiently on the theory chapter.

A version of this project circulated for several years. Among the scholars to whom we are grateful for critical comments are Chris Achen, Randall Adkins, Terri Bimes, Casey Dominguez, Andrew Dowdle, Wesley Hussey, Sam Kernell, Greg Koger, Paul Kellstedt, Seth Masket, Bill Mayer, Markus Prior, Sam Popkin, Alan Rozzi, Priscilla Southwell, and Wayne Steger.

We profited from research assistance across the country: Erin Brown, Kate Madden, Jenny Shin, Narbeh Shirvanian, Joanne Uy, Aja Walter, and Chantalle Zakarian at UCLA; Ala Belkina and Sarah Edwards at Berkeley; and Monica Hughes, Jonathan Leo, Mirela Missova, D. Pierce Nixon III, Marissa Siefkes, Laura Stewart, and Steven Ward at Georgetown. Several colleagues completed a questionnaire to help us construct our weighting scheme for the endorsements data in the later chapters: Ken Gaalswyk, Gregory Koger, Mark Hunt, Wesley Hussey, Seth Masket, Darrel Menthe, Joseph Doherty, and Barbara Sinclair. And we especially thank again our expert coders, Mark Hunt and Wesley Hussey.

The book benefited greatly from a book conference at Princeton University organized by Larry Bartels and featuring Byron Shafer. We are also grateful for critical comments by participants at seminars on our work at Berkeley, Fairleigh Dickinson, George Washington, Harvard, Indiana, Michigan, Pennsylvania, Princeton, Stanford, UC Riverside, UC San Diego, Vanderbilt, and Yale.

The first presentation of this project was at a panel at the Midwest Political Science Association convention in 2001. John Tryneski, our editor at University of Chicago Press, was in attendance and afterward gave us encouraging words. From then until he saw how many changes we had made at the copyediting stage, and even after that, he has remained a steadfast and helpful backer of the project. We are most grateful to him. We are grateful as well to Sandra Hazel, Rodney Powell, and especially our copy editor, Clair James, who put up with more from us than any editor should have to.

We have done our best to follow the wise advice of many friends and colleagues on this project, but our execution of their suggestions has no doubt been imperfect. We should also note that some of those who have advised us did so despite their reservations about the book's basic challenge to conventional wisdom. We therefore take responsibility for the large and small errors that, despite many people's best efforts, we have been unable to root out of the book.

The raw data used in this book are available from Marty Cohen, Department of Political Science, James Madison University (martycohen17@ gmail.com).

The Outrageous Nomination of Hubert Humphrey

In his campaign for the 1968 Democratic presidential nomination, Vice President Hubert Humphrey did not contest a single primary. He campaigned instead among party leaders, union bosses, and other insiders. Meanwhile, his competitors, Senators Eugene McCarthy and Robert Kennedy, entered every state primary they could and won the vast majority of votes in them.[1] Yet when the Democratic Party convention met to pick its nominee, Humphrey won on the first ballot. This was possible because the leaders of the Democratic Party controlled enough delegates to the nominating convention to choose whomever they wished. The opinions of voters in the primaries could be safely ignored.[2]

Roughly the same was true on the Republican side. Up until the 1970s, politicians who wished to win the Republican nomination needed to run in state primaries to prove their popularity, but the real power lay among the top politicians and activists of the regular party. These party insiders used the results of primaries to gauge the popular appeal of the leading competitors, but in the end they chose as they saw fit.

That system is a far cry from the one that exists today. In the old system, party leaders controlled outcomes by controlling state and local party conventions, most of which were either closed to the public or discouraged their participation. Today, in contrast, the voting public chooses almost all of the delegates to the national party nominating conventions. They do so by means of state-by-state primary elections and caucuses in which candidates win delegates in rough proportion to the popular vote for them in that state.[3] The reforms leading to the new system began in the Democratic Party in response to dissatisfaction with the Humphrey nomination, but spread to the Republican Party as well.

The Democratic Party activists who initiated these reforms wanted to open up presidential nominations to greater participation by rank-and-file voters—"power to the people," to use the language of the time. Many scholars agree that something like popular control actually ensued. "Nominations are fought and won among mass electorates," as Polsby, Wildavsky, and Hopkins (2007, 130) put it in a widely shared assessment. As they add, "Once upon a time, presidential nominations were won by candidates who courted the support of party leaders from the several states. . . . That system is history. Now, nominations are won by accumulating pledged delegates in a state-by-state march through primary elections and delegate-selection caucuses" (2007, 97).

In light of this widely shared view, most scholarship on presidential nominations focuses on the series of particular tasks candidates must carry out in order to successfully contest primary elections: raise money, secure favorable media coverage, build a personal campaign organization, and, ultimately, appeal to voters. Party leaders are typically peripheral actors. Some scholarship has argued that if any elites are influential in the nomination process besides the candidates themselves, it is the media elite rather than the party elite. In a fairly typical assessment, William Crotty wrote in 1985, "The new party system has witnessed a collapse in party control over its own nominating process. . . . The new power center is the media, especially television" (129). Two other scholars of the nomination process, Michael Hagen and William Mayer, write, "In the new system, effective power came to reside in [party voters] and in such non-party entities as the news media. The party organization and the party in government were almost entirely stripped of any significant voice in the decision" (Hagen and Mayer 2000, 52).

Stephen J. Wayne, in the 2000 edition of his respected textbook on presidential elections, is more cautious than other scholars but still buys the death-of-parties argument: "By promoting internal democracy, the primaries helped devitalize party organizations already weakened by new modes of campaigning and party leadership already weakened by the loss of patronage."[4]

A few scholars have suggested—usually without providing systematic evidence—that parties play a stronger role in presidential nominations than generally believed. The one scholar who does provide such evidence is Wayne Steger. Based on data and methods similar to those we use in chapter 9, he finds that "elite party elected officials appear to have a potent effect signaling the partisan electorate as to which candidate should be supported" (2007, 97). However, the dominant view is that parties play no important role in presidential nominations. This view is well expressed by Paul Allen Beck in the eighth edition of *Party Politics in America*: "The parties have devised strategies to retain some influence in the [presidential nomination] process—Democrats by selecting super delegates, Republicans by continuing some of the old rules—but the truth is that their efforts have borne little fruit. It is now difficult for the party organizations to exert much influence over the presidential nominations" (1997, 243).[5]

We argue in this book that the demise of parties has been exaggerated. Candidate-centered efforts are tremendously important, and the McGovern-Fraser reforms have certainly made it more difficult for parties to get their way. But parties remain major players in presidential nominations. They scrutinize and winnow the field before voters get involved, attempt to build coalitions behind a single preferred candidate, and sway voters to ratify their choice. In the past quarter century, the Democratic and Republican parties have always influenced and often controlled the choice of their presidential nominees.

That careful observers have failed to find much party influence in some contests is understandable. Parties did lose control of nominations in the aftermath of the McGovern-Fraser reforms. The nominations of 2008 were also cases of limited party influence. But in the nominations of Ronald Reagan, Walter Mondale, Bill Clinton, Bob Dole, Al Gore, and both Presidents Bush, party influence has been in plain view. Observers have failed to recognize it for three reasons. One is that they have been wedded to a conception of parties in which top politicians and party officers are the key players. But traditional interest groups, issue advocacy groups, and ideological activists are in long-term alignment with parties and may exert as much influence in nominations as officeholders and officials. Second is a failure to recognize that the traditional national party convention, which has been made obsolete by the McGovern-Fraser reforms, is not the only means by which parties may affect nominations. Party coalitions acting in concert can funnel resources to their most preferred candidate and also influence rank-and-file voters to follow their lead. The third is that, in focusing on candidates and their organizations as strategic players, scholars overlook the capacity of party leaders, groups, and activists for strategic behavior of their own. Or, rolling all three points into one, existing scholarship fails to recognize that, with several strong candidates vying for nomination, party coalitions can exert a decisive influence by throwing their weight behind one of them.

We do not claim that parties are juggernauts that always prevail. Indeed, the massive power of the American presidency—the most powerful office of the most powerful country in the world—finds a strange complement in the apparent weakness of the party institutions that structure presidential nominations. Yet precisely because the presidency is so powerful, it would be surprising if party leaders, aligned groups, and activists stood by and made no attempt to influence their party's choice for that office. And, indeed, they do not stand by. Parties are a systematic force in presidential nominations and a major reason that all nominees since the 1970s have been credible and at least reasonably electable representatives of their partisan traditions.

In our view, then, the history of recent reforms in presidential nominations follows the trajectory of an earlier wave of party reforms, which required parties to choose nominees for legislative office through primaries. Writing about those reforms in 1909, H. J. Ford observed:

> One continually hears the declaration that the direct primary [for legislative offices] will take power from the politicians and give it to the people. This is pure nonsense. Politics has been, is, and always will be carried on by politicians, just as art is carried on by artists, engineering by engineers, business by businessmen. All that the direct primary, or any other political reform, can do is affect the character of the politicians by altering the conditions that govern political activity, thus determining its extent and quality. The direct primary may take advantage and opportunity from one set of politicians and confer them upon another set, but politicians there will always be so long as there is politics. (Cited in Key 1965, 394–95)

These comments could just as well have been written about the McGovern-Fraser reforms, but with this fundamental caveat: The individuals who, as we argue, now control nominations include "politicians"—governors, big-city mayors, members of party committees, and legislators—but not only politicians. In opening the process to rank-and-file voters, the reforms opened it to many other players as well. These include organized interests—unions, religious organizations, civil rights groups, and business (Lengle and Shafer 1976; Shafer 1988). Also included are people whose technical skills are necessary to win mass elections, such as organizers, fund-raisers, pollsters, and media specialists. Finally, and perhaps as important as anyone else, are citizen activists who join the political fray as weekend warriors.

When these diverse party players can agree to work together for a candidate, as usually they can, they constitute a formidable political force. A governor, for example, may lend his personal organization to a candidate for the state primary. An experienced fund-raiser may mobilize a donor network of hundreds or even thousands of people. An environmental group or a church may ask its members to support a particular candidate and help in organizing them for this purpose. Thousands of citizen activists make phone calls, canvass door-to-door, and help drive voters to the polls. The party coalition does not have a monopoly on campaign resources, but it controls a large fraction of them—enough to make a critical difference. The support of party insiders helps determine which of many potential candidates become actual candidates and which of the actual candidates can mount strong campaigns.

Party insiders have also become adept at working through voters. Indeed, our evidence suggests that the power of political persuasion—a cue from partisan leaders to partisan voters—may be the most important mechanism of insider control. The need for persuasion makes control more precarious than in the old days. A few insider favorites, notably Democrat Walter Mondale in 1984 and Republican Bob Dole in 1996, nearly lost. But the overall record is one of success.

Parties also must work together in order to succeed. If the coalition splits into competing factions, each pledged to a different candidate, voters become the real power by choosing between the insider-backed candidates. This happened in 2008 but is not the modal pattern.

The nominations of George W. Bush and Al Gore in 2000 exemplify our argument. In the months prior to the start of primary voting in Iowa and New Hampshire—a period often called the invisible primary—each man won the overwhelming support of the elected officials, top fund-raisers, interest group leaders, campaign organizers, and ordinary activists in his party. On the back of this support, Bush and Gore then cruised to victory over strong opponents in the state-by-state primary contests.

The strength of losing candidates in these races deserves emphasis. John McCain, who lost to Bush in 2000, was not a noticeably weaker candidate than the man who beat him. Nor was he very different in his policy views: McCain had a strongly conservative record on most party issues, as did Bush. Perhaps the most important difference was that McCain supported campaign finance reform and Bush did not, but McCain's position was the more popular with voters. McCain also had a longer record of public service, including heroic leadership of POWs during the Vietnam conflict, and he was a strong campaigner. Yet Republican insiders—including twenty-seven of thirty-two Republican governors—favored Bush. Not a single Republican governor endorsed McCain, and few other top Republicans endorsed him either. Voters in the Republican primaries took the cue and gave the nomination to Bush.

Bill Bradley was Gore's opponent in 2000. Few would say that Bradley was an exciting campaigner, but few would say that Gore was inspirational either. Bradley had at least won fame as an All-America basketball player and NBA All-Star. In early polls of Democratic voters, Gore usually led Bradley, but not by much. The two men were also about equally liberal. Yet Gore, as the sitting vice president, was able to capture the large majority of insider endorsements and commitments of support. Eleven of seventeen Democratic governors endorsed Gore and not one endorsed Bradley. In a larger sample of Democratic leaders and activists, 82 percent supported Gore over Bradley.[6]

Several scholars have noted the success of insider-supported candidates in recent cycles (Busch 1992; Mayer 1996, 2001), but our claim in this book is larger. It is that the various leaders, activists, and interest group leaders who seek to influence presidential nominations are more than a collection of individual actors; they meet the standard definition of political parties. They are, in other words, a broad coalition aiming to control not only the presidency, but also Congress, the Supreme Court, governorships, state legislatures, city councils and county boards, and every other locus of political power in the United States.

Most scholars deny that parties play a strong role in presidential nominations on the grounds that party leaders lack formal control over the nomination. We agree on the empirical point, but maintain that parties should not be defined in terms of leadership structures. They should be understood as we have just defined them: a coalition of interest groups, social group leaders, activists, and other "policy demanders" working to gain control of government on behalf of their own goals. By that criterion, the groups that work to control presidential nominations qualify as parties.

Scholars do mainly agree that the Democratic and Republican parties are strong within Congress and many state legislatures, and they recognize that presidents are party leaders. Nonetheless, they see parties as unable to control nominations for most elective offices. We think parties do largely control presidential nominations and, though it is beyond the scope of this book, we suspect they have important influence in nominations for legislative office as well.[7]

In some theories of democracy, party competition leads to government policies that voters want—or at least that the median voter wants (Downs 1957). An important argument of this book, however, is that parties try, via the candidates they nominate and elect, to pull policy toward what their interest and activist groups want, even if that is not what most voters want. Thus, our claim about how parties work is also a claim about how democracy works. The claim, moreover, extends much beyond the contemporary period. The book examines the formation of the country's major political parties in the late eighteenth and early nineteenth centuries, and it looks as well at how parties handled presidential nominations in the middle decades of the twentieth century. The purpose is to show that, across the entire span of American history, parties behave in the same basic way—as vehicles by which the most energized segments of the population attempt to pull government policy toward their own preferences. The extent to which parties actually succeed in this goal is not, we must immediately add, what the book is about. It is about parties and presidential nominations and what parties *attempt* to accomplish through nominations for office.

To summarize: The reformers of the 1970s tried to wrest the presidential nomination away from insiders and to bestow it on rank-and-file partisans, but the people who are regularly active in party politics have regained much of the control that was lost. Control rests on their ability to reach early agreement on whom to support and to exploit two kinds of advantage—control of campaign resources (money, knowledge, labor) and the persuasive power of a united front of inside players. Insider control is not unshakable, but it has usually been sufficient to the task at hand for some two decades.

Two Big Problems We Face in This Book

Beating reform is a recurring theme in American party politics. Starting with the Constitutional Convention of 1787, the designers of our institutions have viewed parties as a dangerous influence and tried to frustrate them. "Curing the mischiefs of faction," as James Madison put it, was a central aim of the constitutional system of checks and balances and divided power. Nonetheless, parties quickly developed in the new republic, founded by the very men who designed the Constitution to contain them (Hofstadter 1970), and parties have been with us ever since. Generations of reformers, most importantly the turn-of-the-twentieth-century Progressives, have taken steps to limit parties, but with little lasting success.

Our claim that party insiders have largely beaten the reforms of the 1970s and now control most nominations will nonetheless be difficult to make in convincing fashion, for two reasons. The first is lack of solid evidence about how party actors behave. The personal qualities and abilities of the candidates, their electoral strategies, their intense efforts to raise money, the rules of the game, and the dynamics of poll support all get a good deal more attention from journalists and scholars than the activities of party insiders who, in our view, matter at least as much. For example, Emmett H. Buell, Jr., and James W. Davis open their chapter on the 1988 contests as follows: "In 1988, as in past election years, the Democratic and Republican presidential nominations were decided in the context of resources, delegate-selection rules, state laws, momentum, and what Machiavelli calls 'fortuna.' To have any prospect of success, every presidential aspirant had to formulate a plan that made sense in this strategic environment" (Buell and Davis 1991, 1).

In the remainder of their essay, Buell and Davis provide as thorough and compelling an account of the 1988 contests as one could wish for, but it is from the candidates' strategic point of view. The possibility that individuals within a political party might also be acting strategically to steer the contest toward the candidate they favor, and might succeed in doing so, is not considered. In a similar vein, a field essay in *Political Research Quarterly* by Barbara Norrander summarized the operation of the nominations process without using the word *party*: "The post-reform system involves a series of complex interactions between elites (candidates, media, large contributors), semi-elites (smaller contributors, activists) and a small, but mostly representative, group of interested voters" (1996, 900). Norrander goes on to describe what she sees as the most important gaps for future research to fill, but again does not discuss parties. Her review indicates, albeit indirectly, that most scholars and Norrander herself regard parties as virtually without influence in the current nomination process. Political journalists share the same proclivities, providing far more information about candidates and their activities than about party insiders.

The bent of existing scholarship and journalism exists for a reason. It is far easier to learn about candidates, who crave all sorts of attention, than about parties, which don't. This in turn makes it easier to tell a story about "a candidate rounding up insider support" than one about "party insiders coordinating on a preferred candidate." But the resulting lack of information about party actors makes it difficult for us to advance our thesis of party resurgence.

The second difficulty is theoretical: The traditional instrument of party control, the party nominating convention, was eviscerated by reform. Hence, party insiders must now exert themselves by informally coordinating behind a preferred candidate and providing that candidate with the support necessary to prevail in the state-by-state primaries. To political scientists accustomed to the more concrete institutions of the preform parties, informal cooperation is not recognizable as party activity. Thus, our frequent experience in presenting this research to colleagues has been that, even when we manage to convince an audience that partisan insiders dominate presidential selection, the next comment is, "But what you have described is not a real party!"

Our twin difficulties can be appreciated by contrasting the current system with the prereform party system. Through most of American history, parties did the work of choosing their presidential nominee at a national convention. The actual decision-making was not done in a completely transparent manner, but it was clear enough who was in charge. Here is how H. L. Mencken described decision-making at the party conventions of 1932:

> It is instructive to observe these great men at the solemn business of selecting a First Chief for the greatest free Republic ever seen on earth. One hears, in their speeches, such imbecilities. . . . One sees them at close range, sweating, belching, munching peanuts, chasing fleas. They parade idiotically, carrying dingy flags and macerating one another's corns. They crowd the aisles, swapping gossip, most of it untrue. . . .
>
> The average delegate never knows what is going on. The hall is in dreadful confusion, and the speeches from the platforms are mainly irrelevant and unintelligible. The real business of a national convention is done down under the stage, in dark and smelly rooms, or in hotel suites miles away. Presently a State boss fights his way out to his delegation on the floor, and tells his slaves what is to be voted on, and how they are to vote. (Cited in Hinderaker 1956, 158)

From accounts like these, which abound in party history, it is obvious that parties and strong party leaders actually existed and that they controlled presidential nominations.

Today, by contrast, national party conventions have little importance. There are no smoke-filled rooms where key decisions are made. Conventions are merely a venue for delegates chosen in state primary elections to ratify the decisions of the voters who selected them.

On the surface, it therefore appears that voters choose the nominee by choosing convention delegates in their state primaries and caucuses. But the appearance is deceiving because, as we have suggested, party insiders use the invisible primary to coordinate behind a preferred candidate and to endow that candidate with the resources and prestige necessary to prevail in the state-by-state contests.

Our challenge, then, is (1) to develop evidence of the role of the invisible primary in presidential nominations and (2) to explain how, in theory, this evidence is consistent with our thesis of party resurgence in presidential nominations.

The Evidence Problem

What, then, is the invisible primary and how exactly does it work? No universal definition exists, but Marjorie Randon Hershey provides a good overview: "Almost all serious candidates begin at least two years before the election to take polls, raise money, identify active supporters in the states with early primaries, and compete for the services of respected consultants. Their aim is to win a place for themselves in the group of candidates who are described by the media as 'front-runners' (2005, 177). Candidates often cover hundreds of thousands of miles, giving speeches, meeting donors, recruiting workers, and seeking the endorsements of party leaders. It is an incredibly grueling process. At the end of it, a small handful, often only one candidate in each party, emerges at the head of the field.

The inner workings of the invisible primary are, as the name implies, hard to see. It takes place at widely scattered places and times, has no defined set of participants, and plays out long before the public begins to take an interest in presidential politics. For these reasons, journalists make little attempt to report on it in detail, and when they do, they focus more on the visible indicators of support, such as fund-raising and polls, than on the players who may give or withhold that support. Candidates' personalities also feature prominently in the coverage. An example is journalist Sidney Blumenthal's book-length treatment of the 1988 presidential election. Blumenthal aspires, with some success, to plumb the deepest mysteries of Michael Dukakis's political character. But the following passage is the totality of the information he provides about how Dukakis emerged as a top-tier candidate in the invisible primary: "Almost from the instant that Dukakis made his decision to run, [John] Sasso demonstrated his prowess as a political manager by fielding the biggest, wealthiest, and best-staffed organization of any candidate. On this basis alone, Dukakis was immediately seen as a formidable contender" (1992, 143). Could it be so easy: Hire the right campaign manager and become an instant contender? Actually, we believe that operatives like Sasso are extremely important to success in the invisible primary, but it would be helpful to find out how exactly they work their magic. Blumenthal is typical of many journalists in providing little information about this critical part of the process.

Compounding information shortage is the complexity of the process itself. Multiple events unfold at once: Candidates try to build support, polls are taken, money is raised, stories are written, and leader endorsements are sought. The most common way of summarizing what goes on in the invisible primary is to say that it is "candidate-centered." Because candidates must assemble their own teams, raise their own money, and mount their own campaigns, this is plausible. Old-style parties are nowhere in evidence in the invisible primary, but candidates and their entourages are at the center of everything, especially news accounts. In the phrase of Alan Ehrenhalt (1991), candidates seem to "self-nominate."

But consider a comparison between presidential nominations and Olympic figure skating. The skaters are at the center of everyone's attention as they glide and leap and occasionally crash across the ice. To judge by the television accounts, the only other actors having importance in the process are coaches and family members who support the skaters. So, in one sense, the competition is dominated by the skaters. Yet the skaters do not determine the number and kinds of jumps and spins they must perform. Nor do they determine the standards of performance. Nor, above all, do they choose the judges, who are selected by the larger figuring skating community to implement the community's rules of competition and its standards of judgment. Skaters win not by pleasing themselves or their coaches or even the crowd in the arena, but by pleasing the judges and the insider community they represent. These are similar things, but not the same things.

So it is with the invisible primary, except that it is more difficult to tell who is judging and by what standards. In nomination contests, moreover, the judges are free to consult with one another, make private deals, and throw obstacles in the path of contestants they dislike. Thus, while the candidates and cheering crowds command media attention on center stage, the outcome of the contest may be determined offstage by actors who, like Olympic figure skating judges, are critically influenced by criteria other than the crowd appeal of the contestants.

We should note that some scholars favor the term *exhibition season* rather than *invisible primary*.[8] The preference is reasonable, especially as the politics of presidential selection have become more visible in recent years. However, we prefer *invisible primary* for two reasons: The process really is a competition for support rather than an exhibition, and its most important events are still difficult to observe and often invisible.

Our argument, then, is that party leaders, associated groups, activists, and other insiders are the main drivers of the invisible primary. Candidates put themselves forward, but the party coalition chooses among them, now as in the past. The following account of George W. Bush's invisible primary campaign for the 2000 nomination gives a vivid picture of a part of the dynamics we envision:

> Even before Mr. Bush emerged publicly as a candidate, the nation's Republican governors, eager for a greater say in the affairs of the national party in 2000 and privately irritated with what they regarded as Congressional Repub-

licans' bungling of public sentiment, had largely concluded that the time had come to nominate one of their own for president.

Now Mr. Bush has assembled a remarkably unified team from the ranks of the Republican governors—the chief executives of 31 states, and 8 of the 9 most populous—with whom he frequently consults for both campaign advice and policy ideas. Many of them endorsed him long before he officially jumped into the race in June, and led fund-raising drives that helped him amass more campaign money than any other presidential candidate in history. . . .

The concerted effort on Mr. Bush's part was led by several governors, including Mr. Engler, Paul Cellucci of Massachusetts and Marc Racicot of Montana, who, beginning early this year, called colleagues around the country urging them to endorse him, even as he was saying he would not make up his mind about running until after the Texas legislative session ended in May.

Gov. Bob Taft of Ohio remembers getting a call from Mr. Engler but replying that he would hold off since an Ohioan, Representative John R. Kasich, was in the race. "Then the day after John dropped out" in July, "Marc Racicot was on the phone," Mr. Taft recalled. "And it was, 'O.K., can you do it now?'"

An earlier Bush boomlet occurred in February at a meeting of the National Governors' Association, where several other governors announced for Mr. Bush. "It was the only spontaneous thing I've seen happen in R.G.A./N.G.A. politics in five years," Governor Rowland said with a laugh. (Verhovek 1999, A22)

In this account, party leaders seem to take the initiative in building support for Bush, which in our theory makes the Bush nomination party-centered rather than candidate-centered. Unmentioned in this account, however, are other kinds of Republican regulars—activists, campaign technicians, and interest groups—that we believe are also key. This is part of the evidence problem we noted earlier: Journalists naturally pay more attention to events that are easy to observe and count, such as the endorsements of governors. Much political science, we must add, is no better. Indeed, it is not clear that we ourselves can do much better, since, in the end, we cannot know much more about the inner workings of the nomination process than journalists report. Still, we state it as a conscious goal of this book to develop the full theoretical story of the nomination process, even when the data necessary to fully test it are not available.

Our claim that the party coalitions decide presidential nominations in the invisible primary is, of course, just one hypothesis. The obvious alternative is that the strongest candidate wins the invisible primary on the basis of his or her own strengths. Even with vast amounts of information—which we do not have—these opposing possibilities would be difficult to distinguish. In our theory, party insiders rally to the candidate of their choice, endowing him or her with endorsements, access to fund-raising networks, and pools of talent and volunteer labor. In the candidate-centered account, the strongest candidate manages to attract endorsements, money, and volunteer talent. The leaders, donors, and volunteers are the same in both theoretical accounts. How, then, does one tell whether the party is choosing the candidate or the candidate is capturing the party?

We attack this problem on several levels. From historical evidence, we argue that parties have been using the invisible primary to choose nominees since the 1930s and that the process did not change much in the aftermath of the McGovern-Fraser reforms. From reconstructions of important contests, we find that parties usually manage to nominate the candidate they want, often forcing seemingly strong alternative candidates out of the race at an early stage. Finally, and perhaps most importantly, we collect data on several measurable aspects of the invisible primary—endorsements, media coverage, fund-raising, poll support—and do a statistical analysis to see which factors seem to cause others to change. This analysis points again to party insiders as the principal force in nominations. But, alas, the data upon which we rely for statistical analysis are top heavy with officeholders and light on no-name group leaders and activists. Hence, much of our argument that a wide set of party insiders determines presidential nominations ends up depending heavily on nonstatistical evidence.

The Theory Problem

But demonstrating how the invisible primary works is only half of our argument. The other half is to show what the invisible primary means for our thesis of party resurgence. As noted, some scholars accept our factual claims about the invisible primary but question our conclusion of party resurgence.

We interpret the invisible primary as the analog of the smoke-filled room at prereform conventions—the venue in which the party does the real work of making up its collective mind about whom to nominate. The form, however, is very different. The invisible primary is essentially a long-running national conversation among members of each party coalition about who can best unite the party and win the next presidential election. The conversation occurs in newspapers, on Sunday morning television talk shows, among activist friends over beer, in chatter at party events and, most recently, in the blogosphere. Face-to-face meetings with candidates are an especially important part of the conversation, as party leaders, groups, and activists seek assurance that they can trust the candidate to promote their most important policy demands. Candidates actively plumb for support, as emphasized in the media. But the party conversation determines their fate.

Some people's voices obviously count for more than others in the invisible primary, but anyone can join simply by paying attention, attending party gatherings, and chiming in. The weighting of voices is determined by the resources (money, labor, expertise, prestige) the speaker can bring to party business and by the cogency of the remarks offered.[9] Politics enters as well: pressure to go along with one's group, to get on the bandwagon of the likely winner, or to repay old obligations. But the main business of the invisible primary is figuring out who can best unify the party and win the fall election. Or so we argue.

A century ago, this sort of party conversation could have occurred only at a central location. The travel and communication technology to sustain it on a national scale did not exist. Which is why, of course, parties held nominating conventions. But, as we argue, the invisible primary can now do what national nominating conventions once did—provide a mechanism for the party to coordinate on a nominee. Indeed, the invisible primary had begun to displace party conventions as the real venue of party decision-making well before the McGovern-Fraser reforms.

The fact that the invisible primary does not much resemble a traditional party convention raises the interpretive challenge. An analogy to the concept of markets in economics illustrates our view of this challenge. Early markets in Europe were created by merchants who set up stalls in the town square and bargained face-to-face with buyers over price. But today's most important markets are electronic. They do not involve stalls, town squares, or face-to-face bargaining, and for this reason might not seem like real markets. Yet electronic markets behave, in essential ways, as earlier markets did. For example, electronic markets obey the law of supply and demand, just as traditional ones did. We make a similar argument for the invisible primary. In particular, we argue that the invisible primary—with its new mix of players and its absence of bosses and meaningful conventions—performs the same tasks for political parties that the national conventions traditionally performed. By far the most important of those tasks is to coordinate on a nominee who can unite the party and win the general election.

The invisible primary is not the only institution that does not closely resemble its traditional counterpart. Parties themselves offer a new look—and therefore a fresh interpretive challenge. Hence, even analysts who recognize that the invisible primary has come to dominate the nomination process may refuse to recognize it as a *party* process. A good example is *Washington Post* reporter David Broder, who wrote in late 2003,

Something strange and important has happened to the system of picking presidential candidates. Influence that was supposed to move from political insiders to the broad public has been captured by activists, pollsters, pundits and fund-raisers—not exactly the people the reformers had in mind. . . .

Political scientists say that the whole "drama" of the primaries is a fraud—that the opposition party almost invariably nominates the candidate who raises the most money in the pre-election year and leads the field in the final polls of the year. . . .

This rush to judgment devalues the role of the party leaders and elected officials and still fails to achieve the reformers' populist goals. It comes close to being the worst way possible to pick a president.

Broder's main point here is that "political insiders" have undermined the reforms intended to deliver power over nominations to voters. We agree on that point. But Broder does not consider these insiders to be a party; indeed, he says their importance "devalues" that of party leaders. For Broder, it appears, a party is defined by its "leaders and elected officials," whom he distinguishes from "activists, pollsters, pundits and fund-raisers."

Most political scientists share that view. When they discuss parties, they focus on top leaders. In the leading theoretical work on parties, parties are the creatures of officeholders or top party officials (Reiter 1985; Aldrich 1995). And, based on this view of parties, they generally conclude that parties have lost control of presidential nominations.

But why tie parties so closely to party leadership as such? Why not view parties as larger coalitions that include not only top leaders but activists, fund-raisers, interest groups, campaign technicians, and others? Certainly the larger set of actors has great influence on party behavior.

We therefore propose to theorize parties, and to study them in practice, as coalitions of the larger set of actors. Politicians will be important but not necessarily dominant; interest groups, activists, and other policy demanders will be permitted large roles in party decisions. Our theory will focus on why diverse political actors might attempt to form parties and what kinds of candidates they might seek to nominate.

Much is riding on this theoretical issue. If one accepts our understanding of party as a working coalition of diverse players, one finds good evidence of party control of nominations. One can also explain important features of party life. But if one focuses narrowly on party leaders, one finds that parties have limited influence over presidential nominations.

Necessarily, then, this book is an argument about how best to conceptualize parties as well as a narrower argument about how presidential nominations work. It will therefore have a substantial component of pure theory—that is, reasoning about why individuals might want to form a party and how such an organization would be expected to operate. And, in order to show that parties work as our theory indicates, it will include a substantial dose of party history, beginning with the formation of the nation's first political parties in the Early Republic. By this route, the book aims to show that the party insiders who dominate today's nomination process behave in a manner that is consistent both with a plausible theory of party and with evidence of how similarly situated party actors have behaved in the past.

We would like to say that this book rigorously tests our theory of parties against the leading alternative theory—that of parties as politician- and leader-dominated organizations—but that claim is probably too strong for the analysis we have been able to do. But we do our best with the available evidence to determine which theory makes more sense.

To summarize this section: Our argument on the role of parties in presidential nominations has two main parts. First, we present evidence that a mixed coalition of party loyalists—officeholders, ideologues, fund-raisers, interest groups, and others—is the principal causal force in the emergence of front-runners in the invisible primary and in the success of those front-runners in the regular primaries and caucuses that follow. Second, we argue that this coalition should be viewed as a real political party, similar in nature to parties throughout American history, rather than a haphazard collection of special interests and unsavory characters.

Two Methodological Notes

On Our Use of Theory

Many researchers construct arguments by gathering as much factual information as possible and then developing a theory to explain the facts they have collected. This approach, often called the inductive approach, has value, but it is not the only possible approach and, for our particular problem, it carries a distinct danger. The danger is that if, as we have suggested, the bulk of the information about presidential nominations concerns highly visible but sometimes unimportant aspects of the process, constructing a theory to explain the bulk of the available information might be a bad idea. The alternative approach is to develop a theory and to actively seek out the information necessary to evaluate the theory, whether this evidence is readily available or not. The latter will be our approach in this book. To be clear: this approach does not mean looking for evidence that will *support* the theory; it means looking for evidence that will fairly *test* it.

A well-worn tale among political scientists tells about a drunk who is searching for his lost keys under a street lamp. When asked by a stranger where exactly he lost them, the drunk replies "down the street." Then why is he looking under the lamp? "Because the light is better." The moral is that researchers should look for evidence where their theory tells them to look, not simply use the evidence at hand. In taking this lesson, we shall be venturing into some very bad light, for, as we have noted, the information most critical to the evaluation of our theory—information about the internal dynamics of parties—happens to be in short supply. Journalists do not always prize it, and parties often like to keep it private. This is true not only for the current period, but for other historical periods. Yet, notwithstanding this difficulty, the burden remains on us to produce evidence that tests our views, and properly so. Our point here is simply to warn the reader of some unlikely searches ahead.

On Sources of Evidence

In making our argument, we rely on a mix of history, theoretical analysis, and quantitative and qualitative data. The last includes sometimes-lengthy quotations from journalistic sources that establish empirical conditions or facts essential to our argument. We might have condensed these quotations for the sake of brevity, but think the original language communicates information that cannot be either adequately summarized or reliably evaluated in shortened form. Just as we try to provide enough information about our quantitative analyses to allow the reader to independently assess the conclusions we draw from them, so have we tried to provide enough qualitative information for the reader to judge our inferences from that material.

A potential danger in using journalistic reports as data is, as a critic has pointed out to us, that journalists may sometimes have a point of view that would bias our analysis. This is indeed a danger, but that bias is generally in the same direction as that of most political scientists—toward a narrow focus on candidates and their strategies as against party insiders and their strategies—and therefore against the thesis we wish to examine. Naturally, we are as careful with evidence supplied by journalists as by anyone else.

Plan of the Book

The book presents a theory of political parties and empirical tests of that theory, with tests based on who leads in the formation of new political parties and how parties make presidential nominations. None of this evidence—historical, qualitative, or quantitative—is without weaknesses. Yet if taken together, we believe it provides a compelling accounting of what political parties are and how they behave, both now and in the past.

Chapter 2 presents our theory of parties. It looks past most recent theorizing about parties, which has viewed parties as the creatures of ambitious politicians, to an older tradition of theorizing by E. E. Schattschneider. They key idea is that a party is a coalition of interests that band together to nominate and elect candidates for office. They do so because it is more effective to capture politicians at the nomination stage than to bid for their support after they gain office.

Chapter 3 examines the foundational period of America's most important parties—Federalists, Jeffersonian Republicans, Jacksonian Democrats, and antislavery Republicans. It argues that, contrary to recent theorizing, social groups and activists, rather than ambitions politicians, led party foundation.

Chapters 4 and 5 examine presidential nominations in the final decades of the pre-McGovern-Fraser party system. We disagree with scholars who argue that parties were becoming weaker and more candidate-centered. We agree that the national party conventions were becoming less important, but this is because, even before the reforms, the insider-dominated invisible primary was becoming dominant.

Chapter 6 describes how parties regrouped after the McGovern-Fraser reforms opened nominations up to public participation. Chapter 7 develops tests for how one could tell whether candidates or parties dominate nominations and examines recent nominations in light of the criteria developed.

Most evidence in the book is qualitative, but chapter 8 offers a statistical analysis of the dynamics of the invisible primary. Chapter 9 then presents a statistical analysis of the end game in the nomination process—voter selection of delegates to the national party conventions. With over-time data on polls, media coverage, fund-raising, and publicly reported endorsements, we show that endorsements are at least as important as any other factor—and probably most important—in causing other developments in the invisible primary. And endorsements have at least as much effect as—and probably more effect than—any other factor in determining the outcome of the voter primaries. Both qualitative and quantitative evidence thus support the view that party insiders dominate presidential nominations.

Chapter 10 describes the current state of the presidential parties, including their performance in the invisible primary phase of the 2008 nominations.

Whose Parties?

"If I could not go to heaven but with a party," wrote Thomas Jefferson to a friend, "I would not go there at all" (cited in Rutland 1995, 3). That was in 1789, when the government of the United States was just getting started. Eleven years later, Jefferson won election to the presidency as the leader of an organized party. "Where the principle of difference [between the parties] is as substantial and as strongly pronounced as between the republicans and the monocrats of our country," he explained, "I hold it as honorable to take a firm and decided part and as immoral to pursue a middle line, as between the parties of honest men and rogues, into which every country is divided" (cited in Rutland 1995, 18).

So much for good intentions. As much as Jefferson and other Framers wanted to avoid parties, they fell quickly into them. In fact, all free countries, and many that are not free, develop political parties. Noticing the trend, political scientists largely agree with Schattschneider's claim that "modern democracy is unthinkable save in terms of parties" (Schattschneider 1942, 1).

But why exactly is this so? And what is the nature of these parties that are so unavoidable and perhaps even necessary? These questions, which have lately emerged as important in political science, are central to our analysis of party control of presidential nominations, so we now take them up. The leading contemporary view is that politicians create parties to serve their political and career needs. Our view, based on an older strain of party theory, is that parties are the creatures of interest groups, ideological activists, and others whom we call intense policy demanders. These actors organize parties to get the government policies they want.

Definition

We begin by defining what we are talking about. One classic definition of party is Burke's (1790) notion that a party is an association of persons united by common principle. Few modern writers, however, find this definition useful except as a foil. Its problem is that major parties are rarely if ever united by "common principle."

Characteristically of modern political science, John Aldrich writes, "Political parties can be seen as coalitions of elites to capture and use political office. . . . [But] a political party is . . . more than a coalition. A major political party is an institutionalized coalition, one that has adopted rules, norms, and procedures" (1995, 283–84; see also Schattschneider 1942 and Downs 1957). Aldrich's definition has four notable features. First, a party is a coalition (or alliance) of actors with different goals. Second, party coalitions aim for control of government. Third, a party is a coalition of politically active people (i.e., elites), not ordinary voters. Finally, Aldrich notes that a party is more than a collection of individual actors; the actors have some regular basis of working together. Although other definitional approaches exist, we take this general view to be the most useful and shall proceed with it.

Our next step is to develop a theoretical understanding of how parties, as just defined, work in day-to-day politics. We are especially interested to know who controls parties, a matter that cannot be solved by definition.

The Contemporary View of Parties

The modern view of parties may be traced to Joseph Schumpeter's (1942) *Capitalism, Socialism, and Democracy*. The Austrian-born economist argued that the general view of democracy—which saw it as rule by "the people"— was hopelessly romantic and vague. Trying for a realistic and clear formulation, he proposed that democracy was a system in which leaders were chosen on the basis of competition for popular support. Schumpeter discusses parties, but his focus is on politicians.

In *An Economic Theory of Democracy* (1957), Anthony Downs brings parties to the forefront. Democracy, he says, consists of competition between parties. Parties, as he defined them, are "a coalition of men seeking to control the governing apparatus by legal means." Downs's party teams have no policy preferences of their own. In competing for office, they promise and enact whatever policies maximize their chances of winning elections. The party teams were so cohesive that Downs seldom had occasion to discuss individual politicians separately from the party to which they belonged.

Today, most theoretical work on political parties views them with Downs as teams of office-seeking politicians. This view is both plausible and theoretically tractable—though, as we shall argue below, not quite right.

As the Downsian view of parties gained ascendancy in scholarship of the 1960s, parties themselves seemed to go into decline. Candidates for congressional office became more independent of parties, mounting their own campaigns and developing an "incumbent advantage" on the basis of a "personal vote" from their constituents that was independent of party (Mayhew 1974; Fiorina 1980; Cain, Ferejohn, and Fiorina 1987). The trend toward the personal vote began in the 1940s and affected a wide variety of state and national offices (Ansolabehere and Snyder 2002). Politics, it thus appeared to many scholars, was becoming candidate-centered instead of party-centered. But the politicians remained election- rather than policy-oriented. In other words, they would enact whatever policies voters wanted—or at least give verbal support to whatever voters wanted—in order to win election.

In these same decades, party control over legislative nominations weakened. The pace of decline has not been established, but in 2004 Gary Jacobson wrote in *The Politics of Congressional Elections* that the influence of parties in congressional nominations is "typically feeble." A nomination "is not something to be awarded by the party but rather a prize to be fought over . . . by freebooting political entrepreneurs" (16). Parties, he adds, once played a major role in congressional nominations, but no more. To show what a robust party looks like, Jacobson writes as follows:

> Scattered modern instances of party control over congressional nominations can still be found. When the congressman who represented the 5th District of Illinois (in Chicago) died in 1975, state representative John Fary "was called into Mayor Richard J. Daley's office. At 65, Fary had been a faithful servant of the machine; and he thought the Mayor was going to tell him it was time to retire. Instead he was told he was going to Congress." He did, declaring on the night of his special election victory, "I will go to Washington to help represent Mayor Daley. For twenty-one years I represented the Mayor in the legislature, and he was always right." When, in 1982, Fary ignored the party's request that he retire, he was crushed in the primary. (15–16)

A party, as it emerges in this description, is an institution in which a boss or perhaps some other authority controls both nominations and the behavior of politicians in office. In Downs's terms, the party is a unified team and it has a leader. Jacobson does not assert that this kind of party is the only kind that could exist, but it is the only positive example of a political party he gives. And though once important, he says it no longer is.

The story is much the same for presidential nominations. In the days when active national parties were easier to observe, scholars typically described them as alliances of county and state party organizations of the type Jacobson described. In presidential election years, the local organizations would send delegates to a national party convention to perform their only important task—the selection of a party ticket. The real choice, however, was not usually made by the individual delegates, but by the bosses or other state leaders who typically controlled them. Nominations were a bargain among the bosses and leaders.

Shortly before the McGovern-Fraser reforms were seen to fatally undermine control of presidential nominations by party leaders, V. O. Key, Jr., described parties as follows: "Viewed over the entire nation, the party organization constitutes no disciplined army. It consists rather of many state and local points of power, each with its own local following and each comparatively independent of external control. Each of the dispersed clusters of party professionals has its own concerns with state and local nominations and elections. Each has a base of existence independent of national politics. Each in fact enjoys such independence that more than a tinge of truth colors the observation that there are no national parties, only state and local parties" (1965, 329).

In *Placing Parties in American Politics*, David Mayhew (1986) made an extensive survey of local party organizations as they existed at the time Key published this account. Mayhew did not study local party organization in general, but what he calls the "Traditional Party Organization," or TPO. The Chicago organization described by Jacobson above is perhaps the most famous example of a TPO.[1] Mayhew found that TPOs had been in long-term decline and were, by the late 1960s, almost extinct.

This finding presents a puzzle, if not a problem, for the textbook account of national parties proposed by Key and others. The TPO, as characterized later by Mayhew, is the only well-developed model of party organization that existed in political science at the time Key wrote. If TPOs were nearly nonexistent in the 1960s, what was the nature of the local organizations—"state and local points of power," as Key calls them—that were at the base of national parties?

Looking at a wider swath of history, Mayhew cites Moesei Ostrogorski's 1902 estimate that, even near the heyday of TPOs around 1900, these organizations covered areas representing only about a third of the U.S. population. Mayhew comments that Ostrogorski's general survey, of which this estimate is a part, is "remarkably accurate when matched against more recent evidence of the geographic particulars at the turn of the century" (1986, 209–10). For the rest of the country, and for the country's more recent history, some other form of political party organization has prevailed. But what? If TPOs were not at the base of the nominating system, political scientists of the 1960s did not have a clear idea of what was.[2]

When political scientists wrote about national parties, they did not dwell on uncertainties about their local roots. They focused on what they could clearly see—the parade of local officials, committee members, and loyal activists who showed up at national party conventions every four years to make a presidential nomination. These party actors, whatever their form of local organization, were the national party. Hence, when, after the McGovern-Fraser reforms, these actors lost formal control of presidential nominations, most political scientists concluded that *parties* had similarly lost control. There was little else they could conclude. Some scholars went further, arguing that parties in general were in long-term decline and perhaps headed for extinction (Burnham 1982). Electoral competition was still important, but as explicated by David Mayhew in *The Electoral Connection* (1974), its main imperative was that each candidate should appeal to her own constituents, almost regardless of party.

But the ink had scarcely dried on these assessments when trends reversed. The turnaround seems to have occurred in the 1970s. Party-line voting and party organization in Congress began to rise (Rohde 1991; Cox and McCubbins 1993; Poole and Rosenthal 1997; Sinclair 2000; Jacobson 2004; Bond and Fleisher 2000; McCarty, Poole, and Rosenthal 2006), state-level party organizations became more active (Gibson et al. 1985), and voters began to vote more loyally for a preferred party (Bartels 1998; Bartels 2000; Jacobson 2004). The one area in which, according to most scholars, no revival occurred has been presidential nominations—though, as we argue in this book, parties are resurgent here as well. In the 1980s and 1990s, scholars debated whether parties were truly reviving, but, except for presidential nominations, that debate has now been largely settled in favor of party resurgence.

The revived parties, however, were not always the unified teams that Downs theorized. As analyzed in recent decades, they are parties in which individual politicians are the central players. Thus, Joseph Schlesinger writes: "In a political party it is clear enough which people have the best defined personal stake: those with ambitions for office. Their payoffs, substantial and personal, are worth the costs of organization. Office seekers are the entrepreneurs of party" (1984, 388).

Schlesinger acknowledges the weakness of formal party organization—official committees, national conventions—but maintains that "formal structure is obviously not the real organization." The real organization is a loose agglomeration of officeholders, campaign workers, donors, pollsters, and other activists who make decisions by means of "organized trial and error." "Thousands of individuals and interests seek to control the party's decisions. They push candidates, frame issues, recruit workers, make alliances, and devise campaigns. Among these competing forces choices are made, choices whose correctness is ultimately determined not by the party but by the electorate. Nevertheless, it is the party organization which assures that the right choices, i.e., those which win elections, are retained and the wrong ones are rejected" (390). "Organized trial and error," as described in this passage, means learning from electoral success and failure what kinds of candidates are most likely to win. As seekers of office, parties aim above all to find and nominate such candidates. Schlesinger's parties, thus, aim to please voters, not themselves.

Schlesinger points to the vigor of two-party competition in all regions of the United States in the 1970s as evidence that parties have been getting stronger rather than weaker. He goes so far as to argue that the McGovern-Fraser reforms strengthened the Democratic Party's role in presidential nominations. Prior to the reforms, he says, ideological purists sometimes insisted on nominees who were too extreme to have much chance of winning the general election. But with the rise of primaries following McGovern-Fraser, party nominees must survive the test of the political market before they can be nominated, thus making it more likely they will be good nominees. Presidential primaries, Schlesinger argues, have made parties more candidate-centered, but not less strong as party organizations: "the expansion of the direct primary in the presidential nominating process and the channeling of public financial support through candidates have further enhanced the inherent candidate orientation of American parties. Little in the American structure restrains candidate, and thus party, maneuverability in the search for votes" (1984, 393).

Schlesinger's view of parties is widely respected, but his notion that parties control nominations through "organized trial and error" made little impact on the textbook view of parties. As we saw earlier, Jacobson maintains that the influence of party in congressional nominations is "typically feeble." As we have seen, most of the leading writers on presidential nominations also assert that parties have little importance.

Meanwhile, scholars of legislative politics have developed theories of party that focus more narrowly on officeholders and how they use parties to keep themselves in power. In *The Efficient Secret*, Gary Cox (1987) argues that members of Parliament invented the modern mass party in Britain as a device for mobilizing voters in the newly expanded electorate of the nineteenth century. In *Legislative Leviathan* and *Setting the Agenda*, Cox and Mathew McCubbins (1993, 2005) show how members of the U.S. House of Representatives create party institutions in the interest of keeping majority control of Congress. Their argument is roughly: By controlling the policy agenda, the majority in the legislature can create a party reputation—or brand label—that will enable its side to win elections and thence continue to enjoy the perquisites of being in the majority in Congress.

The theory of Conditional Party Government, as developed by David Rohde and John Aldrich, is similar (Rohde 1991; Aldrich and Rohde 1998, 2000). In this theory, the majority party in Congress tries to enact the preferred policies of the party voters who elected them. To do this, the majority party must enact policies that represent the median position of the majority party rather than the median of the legislature as a whole (Rohde 1991). So if, for example, Democrats are the majority party, they will turn out legislation that appeals to the median Democratic legislator, rather than the median member of Congress. Republican majorities will likewise enact distinctively Republican policy. Achieving partisan rather than median policy outputs requires a high level of party organization and discipline, but majorities are happy to make the effort because they get the policies that their partisan supporters want.

The theory of party embedded in studies of congressional politics goes beyond Downs's notion of party teams to examine their inner workings. The key actors are officeholders who use party organization inside the legislature to choose policies that will maximize their chances for electoral success. Scholars working in this area have little to say about party organization that is independent of the legislature. Their parties, thus, are politician-dominated parties.

Parties research, like other political science research, tends to be narrowly specialized, with legislative parties, local party organization, presidential parties, and voter attachment to parties all studied by different scholars for different purposes. A notable exception is John Aldrich's *Why Parties?* (1995). Building on an earlier essay by Thomas Schwartz of the same title, Aldrich's book is a self-conscious effort "to develop a theoretical account of

parties that can help us make sense of the widest possibly array of empirical findings relevant to party politics" (14). Thus, *Why Parties?* is at once
a study of parties in government, parties in the electorate, and local party
organization—and of how the different parts relate to one another across
American history. From the moment of publication in 1995, *Why Parties?*
became a standard of the American politics literature.

Aldrich follows the bulk of recent theorizing about parties by putting
the ambitious officeholder at the center of party theory. Parties, as in other
recent work, are politician-centered parties. As indicated, we have reservations about this approach. Before presenting our own view, however, we
shall outline Aldrich's argument in *Why Parties?* We begin where Aldrich
began, with Thomas Schwartz's "Why Parties?"

The Schwartz-Aldrich Model

In this important but unpublished essay, Schwartz (1989) imagined how a
three-person legislature with no parties might structure its business. There
would be a great temptation, Schwartz observed, for two legislators to gang
up on the third by passing bills that help their constituents while shifting
costs to constituents of the third. Schwartz called the winning coalition
a "long coalition" to signify that it would form over a great many issues,
always to the benefit of the same majority and the detriment of the same
loser. The long coalition would be stable, because the two winning legislators would have every reason to continue cooperating over all business
of mutual advantage. Voters, for their part, would be happy to reelect the
two majority legislators because their interests would be well served by the
long coalition. Schwartz generalized his argument to a large legislature,
showing that the appeal of a "long coalition" of permanent winners would
remain strong.

The formation of a long coalition would be no boon to the minority of politicians who were not part of it. Their fate is to lose 100 percent of the time.
But politics always has winners and losers, and the politicians in the minority coalition are the losers. Yet the losing politicians may fight back, trying
to win enough support in elections to form their own majority in the legislature. When they succeed, they do not hesitate to use the powers of a
majority coalition against politicians in the former majority. Thus develops
a system of regular party competition.

Why, then, do parties form? On this account, they form because any bare
majority of politicians can get a better deal for its constituents by forming a
"minimum winning coalition" and keeping it together over all issues. Without the long coalition, these politicians would be subject to the uncertainty
of shifting majorities; as part of a long coalition, they win on every vote.

This temptation is simply too great to pass up, so some group of politicians will organize into a long coalition.

Schwartz proves his argument is internally consistent. He proves, that is, that the formation of a stable minimum winning coalition over all distributive bills in the legislature—a long coalition—is an activity in which rational legislators could engage. In his argument, the long coalition is the party.

Schwartz's account is obviously quite spare, omitting important features of party organization in elections, local communities, and, the subject of most interest to us, presidential elections. In *Why Parties?* Aldrich builds on the Schwartz framework to fill in many of these features.

The most important idea in Aldrich's *Why Parties?*—the idea that comes up over and over and drives almost everything else—is that parties can be explained in terms of the benefits they provide to the ambitious politicians who form them. This is a change from Schwartz, who assumed that politicians formed parties in order to increase the flow of benefits to their districts. Aldrich thus writes that: "the major political party is the creature of the politicians, the ambitious office seeker and the officeholder. They have created and maintained, used or abused, reformed or ignored the political party when doing so has furthered their goals and ambitions. The political party is thus an 'endogenous' institution—an institution shaped by these political actors" (1995, 4).

In a departure from the Schumpeter-Downs line of theorizing, Aldrich's ambitious office seekers are more than single-minded seekers of office: They also care about good public policy and about power and prestige within government. Yet, as Aldrich goes on to argue, politicians must win election before they can accomplish any of their other goals. Thus, Aldrich's parties, like those of Schumpeter, Downs, and Schlesinger, aim first of all to please voters.

What, then, are the benefits that politicians get from the parties they create? One of the most important is the reputation that parties develop with voters. Many voters pay too little attention to politics to learn what individual politicians stand for. By associating with a party that is well known, a politician wins the support of voters who know only the party. Parties also build electoral machinery that aids individual politicians. A party coalition thus attracts voter support in one election after another, providing politicians with a basis for long professional careers.

But before a party can develop a reputation with voters, its officeholders must somehow come together as a coalition. This does not happen easily. In a legislature that contains many points of view, there are likely to be many potential majorities rather than just one. Thus, one majority may favor B over A, and another majority may favor C over B, but then a third majority may favor A over C. In this way, one majority can beat another in a potentially endless cycle. Stopping cycling, even on different versions of the same bill, may take huge effort. But, as Aldrich points out, the formation of a long coalition—a group of legislators who vote together on many issues—saves legislators the "transaction costs" of creating stable majorities for each new bill and at the same time creates a partisan group that lasts long enough to acquire a reputation with voters.

A signature argument in *Why Parties?* is that parties serve the electoral needs of ambitious politicians in different ways now than in the past. Until about 1960, party organization consisted largely of patronage workers who mobilized voters for politicians in elections. (Patronage jobs are government jobs that are filled by followers of the winning party.) In the current period, patronage has largely disappeared, so parties help candidates through polling, training, fund-raising, and other electoral services. To use Aldrich's terminology, the "mass mobilization party" of the last century has given way to a contemporary party that is "in service" to politicians' needs. With the services thus provided, candidates create their own campaign organizations and follow their own political strategies, making for a candidate-centered style of party politics. But this difference does not seem fundamental: Neither the mass mobilization party nor the in-service party tries to constrain politicians or hold them to any particular policy position; both kinds of parties aim to help politicians do what prevailing theories say politicians want to do—get elected to office and stay in office.

The motives of party workers have also changed over time. Patronage workers of bygone years cared little about issues, but nowadays, party activists care greatly. In an incisive analysis, Aldrich explains why activists are more ideologically extreme than most voters and pressure politicians through the nomination process to take their extreme views. This seems a significant change: Rather than helping politicians to win election, activists constrain politicians in ways that can make election more difficult. The activists also provide helpful electoral resources, but the resources come at the cost of pressure that limits the flexibility of candidates to take the policy positions that will most please voters. Despite the pressure, however, Aldrich's argument remains that the modern party is "in service" to its officeholders, who are "the actual leaders of the party" (1995, 183).

We take the Schwartz-Aldrich model of politician-centered parties to be the most important contemporary treatment of American parties in the political science literature. It not only subsumes a vast amount of prior theorizing from Schumpeter to Conditional Party Government, it makes novel contributions of its own. Yet we also believe that a key feature of nearly all contemporary party theory—the central focus on the ambitious politician—is questionable. Departing from the bulk of recent theorizing, we think that a focus on group and activist demands for policy would provide a more useful starting point for theorizing about parties.

Volunteer Policy Demanders

We now commence to make that argument, beginning with an observation by Paul Allen Beck. After outlining the formal legal machinery of parties, Beck describes the role of regular party workers, as follows:

> The party organization is a grouping of people, most of them contributing their time and energy on a purely voluntary basis. Even paid professional party workers who increasingly staff the national and state offices share many of the attributes of volunteers. The statutes ignore these men and women of the party, their goals and ambitions, their interactions and relationships, the contributions they make to the organization, and the price they exact for their contributions. Yet, the activity and motivations of those men and women are closer to the real world of party politics than all the statutory paragraphs put together. (1997, 106)

A few pages later, Beck adds that "the desire to use the party as a means to achieve policy goals appears to be the major incentive attracting individuals to party work these days" (113).

We could not agree more with these observations. America has been, at least since the time of Tocqueville, a country in which citizens have flocked to voluntary civic and political institutions. Every activity that any number of people really cared about—whether social, political, religious, recreational, or self-improving—has become an object of cooperation among like-minded citizens. Some of these associations have grown into major social movements, others have remained merely local clubs. As Beck's remarks make clear, political parties are another important outlet for Americans' traditional impulse to get out and work for what they care about.

The notion that parties are, and may long have been, powered by large numbers of policy-oriented individuals does not explain why parties exist, or whether parties are organized as Traditional Party Organizations or in some other way, or what contribution activists make to parties. It is not, in short, a theory of parties. But it can be the foundation for one.

A Group-Centered Theory of Parties

The central idea in the Schwartz-Aldrich model is that officeholders form parties to organize legislative business, mobilize voters, and assure stable careers. Parties exist, in other words, because they serve the needs of the politicians who create them.

But why only politicians? What about interest groups, social movements, sectional interests, and citizen activists who are also prominent in political parties? Might these actors have needs that parties could serve? Might they wish to form parties? No one denies such groups play a big role in party politics. Yet they are absent or secondary in contemporary theorizing about party organization. The attitude seems to be that party organization can be studied separately from the political forces that underlie it. This seems mistaken. Parties are a central political institution—arguably *the* central institution—for organizing society's diverse demands and interests. The myriad political actors that care intensely about these matters do not stand idly by while politicians organize parties and choose nominees for office. To the contrary, they insert themselves into the middle of the process, trying mightily to shape every important aspect of parties and often succeeding.

Much of the energy in American politics comes from these "intense policy demanders." Examples are business and labor, slaveholders and abolitionists, feminists and religious traditionalists, greenbackers and gold bugs, farm groups, environmentalists, gun owners, civil rights workers, southern white segregationists, immigrant and ethnic organizations, and people commonly known as liberal and conservative activists. Many of the party workers described above by Beck would probably fall into this last category. Intense policy demanders agitate, organize, and work late into the night to get policies they want. Because these groups are often motivated by deep feelings of justice and moral necessity, they are not deterred by long odds.

We define intense policy demanders by three criteria. They are (1) animated by a demand or set of demands, (2) politically active on behalf of their demands, and (3) numerous enough to be influential. Formal organization is often present but not essential.

Many intense policy demanders are identifiable by social, economic, or demographic characteristics, but what is relevant for our theory is that they have the same policy demands. In some cases, intense policy demanders from the same social or demographic category make opposing demands. When this happens, we say that two (or more) groups of intense policy demanders exist. For example, most members of feminist organizations are intense policy demanders for a liberal view of women's rights. But some women do not care much about feminism, and some women actively oppose liberal feminism. In our theory, the relevant group is not "women," but "feminist women" and "traditional women." So it is with all intense policy demanders: They are defined by their demands, not their social or demographic characteristics.[3]

Having said carefully what we mean by intense policy demanders, we now wish to provide a shorthand expression for it. The shorthand is *group*. When we use the word *group* in this book, we will generally mean a *group of intense policy demanders, as defined by common demands*. The group may be a formally organized interest group, but also unorganized numbers of farmers, religious leaders, or ideological activists who make common demands.

Few if any groups of intense policy demanders are big enough to get what they want working alone. So they seek allies. But in joining party coalitions, groups do not put the good of the party ahead of their own goals. Parties are a means to an end, and the end is the group's own policy agenda. Groups cooperate in party business only insofar as cooperation serves their interests.

The most important party business is the nomination and election of office seekers *who will serve the interests of the party's intense policy demanders*. The italicized phrase marks the key difference between our theory and most other contemporary theorizing about parties. In our theory, parties—that is, the groups that constitute parties—do not care about winning for the sake of winning office. They care about the policy gains. And they make those gains not simply by the election of someone nominally affiliated with their party. They make them by the election of someone committed to the maximum feasible achievement of group goals.

In making nominations, the groups that constitute parties go beyond merely pressuring candidates to adopt positions closer to their own than most voters might prefer. They define basic party positions, decide how much electoral risk to take in pursuit of these positions, and choose which candidates to put forward under the party banner. Their purpose is to place reliable agents in government offices. Thus, intense policy demanders expect that their nominees will, if elected, provide loyal service on matters large and small. A variety of evidence indicates that they are not often disappointed in this expectation. For example, Karol (1999, 2001, 2009) shows that when groups within a party change their positions on issues, or when a new group joins a party coalition, top politicians routinely change their views to agree with the new group position. For example, when business and labor groups changed their positions on free trade around 1970, top Democratic and Republican officeholders changed with them. When social conservatives joined the Republican party in the 1980s, numerous top Republicans turned from pro-choice positions to pro-life ones. Groups did not punish this behavior as flip-flopping; they encouraged it with praise and support.

In a different but related vein, Hall and Deardorf describe how special-interest lobbyists, most of whom have close relationships with a party, approach their work: "The proximate political objective of [lobbying] is not to change legislators' minds but to assist natural allies in achieving their own, coincident objectives" (2006, 69). In other words, lobbyists mainly just fill in details for goals that they and the officeholders share.

Our argument about the centrality of group demands in party politics has roots in an older tradition of theorizing by Arthur Bentley, E. E. Schattschneider, V. O. Key, and others. But it has been several decades since mainstream political science has taken seriously a group theory of parties. We therefore see value in working more fully through its logic. That done, we shall proceed to testing, as best we can, whether the modern politician-centered or the more venerable group-centered model gives a better account of how parties behave in presidential nominations. A large part of this book is concerned with this question.

Our development of the logic for group-centered parties takes the form of the "why parties?" analysis of Schwartz and Aldrich, except that it has a different starting point—instead of an imaginary legislature made up of politicians, we begin with an imaginary society having groups of intense policy demanders as well as politicians.

Why Groups Organize Parties

In our imaginary society, government consists of a policy dictator who is elected and serves a four-year term. Society has an abundance of ambitious politicians willing to promise whatever it takes to win this office.

Groups in our stylized society form when any large number of people wants either to change the status quo through government action or defend a status quo that is under attack. The number of intense policy demanders therefore varies across time and political circumstance. Intense policy demanders are the main source of campaign donations and campaign labor.

Voters in this society often hold strong political views but do not always attend to politics. As a result, some government actions fall into an "electoral blind spot" in which policies and their effects are invisible to voters. A degree of voter blindness is central to our analysis because it creates the possibility for politicians, or groups that may influence them, to convert public policies and resources to group purposes. If, for example, voters do not follow the details of regulatory politics, officeholders can sell regulatory policy to intense policy demanders in exchange for campaign resources. Selling policy to groups is tricky, because no one can estimate what voters will notice and punish.[4] But exploitation of voter inattentiveness by groups of intense policy demanders is the principal reason groups become active in politics, whether in party politics or in other ways.

Having now outlined the main features of an imaginary society, let us figure out how its politics might work. We begin our analysis as the country is about to have its first election. With intense policy demanders controlling most campaign resources, the outcome will depend on whether they back a candidate. Would it make political sense to do so? Or would the intense policy demanders do better to wait to deploy their resources until the dictator has been chosen?

Let us suppose the groups decide to sit out the election. If, after the election, a group wants something, it will have to induce the dictator to go along. For policies that would make most voters better off, simple persuasion would be effective. But for policies the public doesn't favor and may even oppose, something more will be needed—the promise to donate money to the dictator's reelection. But the dictator may demand a high price, and if one group won't meet her price, she can do business with another group and adopt its policies instead. If the groups try to form an alliance against her, the dictator might refuse them all. Suppose, for example, a group wants extra trash pickups from the government trash service. The dictator might go along with the demand in exchange for campaign donations. Alternatively, the dictator might reassign trash workers to political duties that would help toward reelection. Either way, voters get less trash pickup for the taxes they pay, but probably not enough less to notice, and the dictator gets extra campaign support. The bottom line, then, is that an incumbent politician can drive hard bargains with groups that try to buy policy from her and may not sell on any terms.

Suppose, then, that one of the groups foresees this problem and decides to back someone in the initial election who will be friendly to its needs once she gets into office. With many politicians in the race and only one group offering campaign funds, the group has the upper hand and is almost sure to find a politician who will promise what it wants in exchange for campaign resources. Or better yet, the group may be able to find a politician with a proven record of working for the group or, in the group's ideal world, the politician may be an actual member of the group and hence share its values. Political scientists typically treat politicians as separate from the groups that back them for office, but the separation becomes somewhat artificial if, as groups might like to do, they choose politicians from their own group. A politician committed to group values will still value reelection, but she will be more likely to take initiatives and risks for the group than would one with a different background.

From this analysis, we infer that at least one group will decide to become active in the initial election by sponsoring—that is, nominating—a candidate for office. The advantages of being able to select the politician at the nomination stage, as against buying her support at the postelection stage, are simply too great to pass up. But if one group becomes active, other groups will not want to stay on the sidelines while the first group picks the policy dictator. Many groups will therefore enter the electoral fray, which will create a new problem: If each group backs its own candidate, only one group will win and the rest will lose. These are bad odds.

The groups will therefore consider forming a coalition. They will consider, that is, combining forces behind a single politician who is committed to a program that gives each of the groups what it wants. If all the groups support the same candidate, they can be almost sure of winning, and they can probably do so for relatively little cost. However, the question arises: Can all the groups work together in a coalition?

This is another tricky issue. If each group wants a policy others don't care about—for example, one wants more trash pickup, another wants looser enforcement of liquor laws—cooperation is easy. The coalition just gives each group most, though perhaps not all, of what it wants. Qualification is necessary because no group can get so much that it unduly burdens other groups, and all group benefits must remain within the voters' blind spot. For example, the group getting extra trash pickup cannot get so much service that other groups don't get their trash picked up or that voters suffer a noticeable drop in service.[5]

But conflict between groups need not be a barrier to a party coalition unless the conflict is severe.[6] Indeed, if public resources are available to underwrite party pacts, a coalition can be the means for resolving group conflict.

From this analysis, we conclude that groups can often get more from government by funneling their resources through a party coalition to nominate and elect officeholders friendly to their interests than by buying policies one at a time from independent officeholders after they have taken office.

Having decided to unite behind a nominee, the groups must choose one. Who they choose reflects who is in the coalition and who is not. Coalitions need to include enough groups to attract a majority of voters in the election, but not so many that it dilutes too much the benefits that any one group can get from being in the coalition.

A long coalition in a legislature can define itself bill by bill as it takes votes. A nominating coalition doesn't vote on individual bills, nor can it bind its nominee to any particular positions, since the nominee will be legally free to do whatever she wants once she gets into office. Hence, the parties must pick a nominee whose record or background demonstrates that the nominee can be trusted on all issues that groups in the coalition care about. In other words, the nominee must be acceptable to all members of the coalition. We go into this matter in more detail in chapter 4, where we discuss what exactly parties want out of nominees and the means by which they select them.

In our analysis, we have focused on election of a policy dictator, but our analysis would apply as well to the election of multiple officeholders. If, for example, we analyzed a case in which groups needed the support of scores of legislators as well as a president to enact policy, the efficiency gains from getting control of all these politicians at the nomination stage, when they were weak and disorganized, would be even more important than in the election of a policy dictator.

The advantage of party formation might be especially valuable to groups that sometimes come under popular attack. No group could expect an independent politician to stand up boldly for its interests when a majority is aroused against it. But if a politician has been selected to share group values, it will be individually rational for the politician to accept at least some electoral risk on behalf of the group. The problem with independent politicians is that they will jump ship in moments of danger; groups can expect greater steadfastness from politicians selected to share their values.[7]

A final advantage of forming a party coalition, especially if no other party yet exists, is the opportunity to bias electoral procedures in favor of the group's party. We are not suggesting fraud, which is failure to follow rules, but rules that have a tilt to them. For example, if the party were strongest in cities, it might require voters to cast their ballots at urban locations. By such means, the first party to get control of government can create a permanent bias for its candidates. Even better than tilting the playing field is preventing an opposition party from forming in the first place. If only one party exists, it can quietly settle group differences internally, thereby increasing the range of policies in which voters will be blind to what groups are getting. As we argue in a later chapter, America's first party saw the opportunity for one-party politics and tried to seize it. The conditions under which party competition develops or fails to develop is an important but understudied problem in party politics (see, however, Masket, in press; Mickey 2008; Trounstine 2008).

In his original "Why Parties?" argument, Schwartz assumed that losing politicians would appeal to voters to win seats to become the majority. We make a similar assumption, except for groups. We assume, that is, that some initially inactive citizens will be directly hurt or angered by policies of the first party, become active as intense policy demanders, and form an opposition party. The result will be regular competition and rotation in office among group-dominated parties. Each party resembles one of Schwartz's long coalitions—a group of actors who vote together on a long list of issues.

It is natural to think of parties in a two-party system as majoritarian. Ours, however, are not. They want to win elections, but they do not necessarily wish to represent a majority of voters. As a by-product of their wish to govern, parties must offer a degree—perhaps a large degree—of responsiveness to popular majorities, but responsiveness to voters is not why parties exist. They exist to achieve the intense policy demands of their constituent groups. One might criticize parties for lack of deference to majority will, but their groups would not much care. Intense policy demanders nearly always believe their demands are just and that it is their duty to work for these demands whether or not most voters agree with them.

The theoretical analysis reported in this section grew out of our study of presidential nominations. We observed that party insiders seemed to control presidential nominations, but we could find no contemporary theory of party that would count their influence as party influence. Our theory of party has been created to explain why we believe it really is *party* influence.

Our theory of parties has many additional implications, including implications for the role of parties in legislative elections. We explore many of these implications, and also develop a formal foundation for the theory, in a separate work, "A Theory of Political Parties" by Kathleen Bawn, Seth Masket, and the four authors of this book (2006).

Our Theory in Relation to Other Theories of Party

Before putting our theory of party to use in the study of presidential nominations, it will be helpful to compare and contrast it to other theories. That is the task of this section.

Parties and Voters
The parties we have theorized are not humble servants of democracy. In this critical respect, they are quite different from parties as theorized by Schumpeter and Downs, which care about winning elections for the sake of holding prestigious office and therefore both promise voters what voters want and do their best to deliver it.

Our parties are also markedly different from Joseph Schlesinger's version of candidate-centered parties. In his theory, the interest of politicians in winning competitive elections is the dominant party motive, which again means that satisfying voters is the highest priority.

Our parties are again different from the officeholder parties as theorized by scholars of Congress, though not markedly. For example, in the Leviathan parties of Cox and McCubbins (1993), the majority party tries by the legislation it passes to create a "brand label" that will appeal to a majority of voters, thereby keeping itself in power. Similarly in the theory of Conditional Party Government, the majority party crafts policies that appeal to the partisan majority that elected it to office.

These theoretical arguments are similar to ours, but not the same. The similarity is that congressional parties do not aim to pass consensus policies that appeal to the median voter, but partisan policies that appeal to partisan majorities. The difference is that the motive of politician-dominated parties in the Congress studies is electoral—getting and keeping power through elections—whereas the motive of parties in our group theory is to get power in order to serve constituent groups of intense policy demanders.

The Role of Politicians

Our theory of parties does not minimize the role of officeholders. Indeed, officeholders do everything in our theory of parties that they do in the politician-centered and legislature-centered theories of party. They create their own campaign organizations, organize partisan machinery in Congress, broker disagreements among the party's various groups and factions, and take initiatives they believe will benefit the fortunes of the coalition. They also care greatly about enjoying long careers in office. The differences from contemporary theories are (1) the party includes many players other than office-seeking politicians themselves, chiefly groups of policy demanders, and (2) the politicians' electoral motives are not the central concern of the party. Rather, group goals are central, and politicians work with groups to achieve them.[8] Politicians may, in fact, be viewed as agents of the groups that make up a party.[9] One might say that politicians are also agents of the voters who elect them, but our theory holds that the principal-agent relationship between politicians and groups is more binding than that between politicians and voters.

We do not claim that politicians, even politicians who are group members, prefer working as agents. At least some of the time, they might strongly prefer to put their own reelections above the wishes of intense policy demanders. Indeed, they might try to use the powers of their offices to create exactly the sort of in-service party that Aldrich describes. Politicians might also compete with groups for the control of parties and sometimes get the upper hand.[10] But if groups move first, using their resource advantage to pick reliable agents at the nomination stage, they should be able to dominate politicians. The observer of parties should then see groups and their agents, the politicians, working together in harmony to achieve group goals.

The Role of Groups

Groups of intense policy demanders play a relatively small role in contemporary theories of parties. Although it is rarely noted, this is a major departure from how leading political scientists theorized parties in most of the last century. Typical of this older work is the following statement by Charles Merriam in his 1922 textbook, *The American Party System*: "The broad basis of the party is the interests, individual or group, usually group interests, which struggle to translate themselves into types of control through government" (2). A more upbeat but similar view is offered by Pendelton Herring in his classic essay *The Politics of Democracy*: "Our party system is best explained as a rivalry between two organizations each bent on presenting as its own a view of the public interest as widely acceptable as possible. The task of the party is to achieve a working combination of sections, of interests, and also of the liberals and conservatives within its own ranks" (113).

V. O. Key, Jr. offers a statement in *Politics, Parties, and Pressure Groups* that is quite similar to our view: "When a crowd of people first foregathered and agreed to enter their support on specified candidates in an election, 'party' was born. As a corollary to nomination, party has the function of mobilizing electoral support" (314). Key continues, saying, "Party organization . . . may be usefully conceived as the problem of arranging collaboration among the political activists." These activists include party officers and officeholders, but also "business leaders, labor-union officials, editors, advertising men, suburban housewives" (344).[11]

Of the older theories, the one most similar to ours is that of E. E. Schattschneider in *Party Government*. Schattschneider saw interest groups as the "raw material of politics" and described parties as coalitions of groups. The party was defined as an organized effort by the coalition to get control of government. The central act of a party coalition, as he argued, was the formation of a "united front" to control nominations for office. "He who can make the nomination is the owner of the party" (1942, 64).

Schattschneider's theory also contains an element that is missing in most theories of party but is salient in ours: That superior organizing by party insiders yields disproportionate benefits to the organizers. He discusses, for example, an election in a boys club in which each boy votes for himself for president, except two who cooperate and thereby win the election. At another point, he discusses how two-party competition gives voters so few choices that parties reap an "unearned increment" of votes, that is, votes for which the parties do not have to offer anything (45).

Each of these older studies obviously has more parts than described here, including important roles for politicians. But all of them, as it appears to us, assign a more central role to group interests and activists than theories in the Schumpeterian line.

These theories of parties are closely related to the theory of pluralism, which is the idea that government in the United States reflects the interplay of group pressures. The pluralist literature is widely known for the upbeat tone of its assessment of American politics, and many of the group-centric studies of party shared this optimism. For example, Ivan Hinderaker, who made the interplay of groups and parties central to his *Party Politics*, opined: "The American system has shown itself to be remarkably flexible in its ability to adapt to changing needs and problems . . . fundamentally both the system and the parties themselves are as adequate as any other democratic representative alternatives in sight for meeting whatever crises lie ahead" (1956, 674–75).

Although our theory of parties has much in common with the views of Hinderaker, Key, and others who describe the close relationship between groups and parties, we do not share their upbeat tone about the overall contribution of parties to democracy. This is not to say that we are downbeat, just that we are quite different from the major party theorists. In our brief discussion of the contribution of group-centered parties to democracy in the closing chapter, we pointedly decline to offer an overall evaluation.

Reading through the older studies of parties, one sometimes has difficulty finding clear statements of cause-and-effect and careful empirical tests of key propositions. Arguments are illustrated, not demonstrated. Some language is decidedly prescientific. In these ways, the studies seem old-fashioned. But we see nothing old-fashioned about the basic theoretical claim that group interests and activists—policy demanders, as we call them—are central to the understanding of parties, and therefore see no reason why group actors should now have become such minor players in contemporary theories of party.

One other older theorist merits notice. James Madison believed that parties arose from differences in factional interests, principally between "those who hold and those who are without property," but also between people having different opinions on religion and government. A central problem of politics is to prevent these factional groups from capturing government, as they naturally wish to do. In debates over the adoption of the Constitution, Madison saw a solution in the fact that the United States would be an "extended republic" in which factions would be too numerous and too scattered "to discover their own strength, and to act in unison with each other" (*Federalist 10*). Madison was right about what factions would try to do but wrong to think they could not easily form in an extended republic: A diverse coalition of southern slaveholders, northern workingmen, and back-country farmers rather quickly discovered their strength and formed a majority party to take over government. Thus were Madison's fears and our expectations borne out.

Many other variants of party theory, centering on class, social cleavage, voting behavior, realignment, and ideology, could also be sketched. In most of them, a group or activist impulse could be shown to be important. But we think we can go directly to the main point of this section: Although our theory is a departure from most contemporary theorizing about parties, it is compatible with some recent theory and strikingly similar in outlook to a large body of older, group-centered theory. Only the theoretical line that begins with Schumpeter and continues through Schlesinger and Aldrich is seriously incompatible with ours. We do not contend that the Schumpeterian line of theories is unworthy of development and testing, only that our approach is worthy as well.

We cannot test every theoretical position in the scholarly literature on parties. We would, however, like to test as best we can a central point of theoretical difference: whether it is more useful to conceive of parties as dominated by groups and their politician-agents or as dominated by ambitious officeholders and would-be officeholders. Or, to put all this in shorthand, we will test a group-centered view of party against a politician-centered view.

Tests of the Two Theories

Despite their basic differences, both the politician-centered and the group-centered theories of party attempt to explain the same basic facts about how parties behave and must therefore end up making many of the same predictions. If, for example, groups dominate parties, the groups would want their politicians to get themselves elected, to enjoy long careers, to create electoral institutions that aid in reelection, and to build legislative organizations to control policy outputs and enhance the party's reputation with voters—which are, of course, the same things that a politician-centered theory expects politicians to do on their own.[12] Hence, we must look elsewhere for testable differences between the two theories.

We have, however, identified one area of difference between the two theories that is promising for empirical testing. In the politician-centered theory of parties, politicians are the key decision-makers. They organize campaigns, take positions on issues, and create service organizations within the party to help them. Activists may, in Aldrich's variant of politician-centered parties, pressure candidates, but the candidates remain the "actual leaders" of the party. The party is the creature of the ambitious politician. But in our group-centered theory, the party consists of groups whose aim is to get policy out of government. Acting as a coalition, groups decide which candidates to nominate for office and what positions they want them to take on issues. As full-time professionals, officeholders are often the most visible members of the party, but, to use Schattschneider's phrase, groups are the owners of the party.

One testable implication of this basic difference involves the foundation of new parties. In our group-centered view, policy-motivated groups rather than office-motivated politicians handle important party business. Among the most important decisions of any party might be, as in our analysis of party formation in an imaginary society, whether to start a party in the first place. We therefore expect that policy-oriented groups, more than office-oriented politicians, will lead in the creation of new parties. Further, because forming a party involves nominating politicians for office, and because nominations occur at the level of local politics, we should expect party formation to occur at the local level. The politician-centered theories of Schumpeter, Downs, and Schlesinger do not have a developed mechanism of party formation. However, the Schwartz-Aldrich model does: Legislative politicians, having already been elected to office, form a long coalition to make a reputation that in turn assists in mobilizing voter support. In *Why Parties?* Aldrich analyzes the origin of the Federalist and Republican parties in terms of this mechanism. Chapter 3 takes up this matter.

A second area of testable difference in the theories involves party policy change. If groups dominate parties, then changes in party policy ought to be traceable to changes in what groups want or the relative power of groups within the party coalition. If, on the other hand, politicians dominate parties, large changes in party policy ought to be traceable to changes in electoral pressures on officeholders.[13]

We have noted that groups will rationally want their politicians to compromise as necessary to win elections and remain in office, and this may involve some tweaking of party positions on issues. But we are talking here about initiatives that are so large as to change what parties stand for and hence which groups they represent. One example is the Democratic Party's adoption of a stance of racial liberalism in the 1960s after some one hundred years of support for racial segregation. A large literature on political realignments claims that party changes of this magnitude are generally due to electoral pressure (Sundquist 1983). Our theory suggests, however, that office-holding politicians, having been selected for their reliable commitment to group goals, should not generally depart from party orthodoxy in response merely to electoral pressure. From the politician-centered view of parties, by contrast, major party change should be traceable to the electoral calculations of office-holding politicians, as influenced by changes in voter preferences. Chapter 5 presents evidence bearing on this question.

A third theoretical contrast focuses narrowly on the nomination process itself. In the politician-centered view of parties, candidates manage their own nominations, with the strongest candidate winning. It has been argued, for example, that Barry Goldwater won the Republican nomination in 1964 because he was able to "outmobilize regular Republican organizations," which were "weaker" than his own politician-centered organization (Aldrich 1995, 271). Many contemporary scholars view this type of politician-centered effort as typical of the contemporary party system. If it were typical—if candidates did typically win nomination by overpowering party regulars—we agree that it would be compelling evidence for the candidate-centered model of parties. But if, on the other hand, party leaders, interest groups, and activists make largely autonomous choices among two or more strong candidates, we would take it as evidence for the group-centered view. Chapters 5, 7, 8, and 9 address this question of party-centered versus politician-centered nominations.

A fourth test centers on risk management. In the politician-theory as developed by Aldrich, activists pressure politicians to take more extreme positions, possibly in exchange for compensatory campaign resources. In our theory, groups want politicians to cede as little policy to voters as possible, which implies they also pressure candidates to take more extreme positions. So in both theories, politicians accept a certain amount of risk by the positions parties force them to take. This raises the question: Who manages the level of risk? If politicians face more or less constant pressure from activists to take risky positions and decide how to manage this risk for themselves, we would take it as evidence for the politician-centered view of parties.[14] But if party insiders make this decision, debating how much nonoptimal positioning to force their politicians to accept, or choosing the candidate with the positions they themselves judge to be optimal, we would take it as evidence for the group-centered theory of parties. We report evidence bearing on this question in chapter 5.

We have, then, identified four areas in which politician-centered and group-centered theories have contrasting and testable implications, all of which bear on presidential nominations in some way. For each, the question is: Who decides the party business—office seekers and would-be office seekers, motivated by their electoral goals, or groups of intense policy demanders, motivated by policy goals? Our basic expectation, as conveyed in the title of our book, is that the party, controlled by groups of intense policy demanders, decides all important matters of party business.

This is not to say that officeholders have no important role in party decision-making. As we have explained, groups seek to nominate and elect politicians who share their basic values and preferences, often because they are members, close associates, or former members of the group. Farmers, for example, regularly elect farmer-politicians to office; liberal activists regularly elect liberal politicians to office. Such politicians are full participants in party decisions, sharing power with intense policy demanders who are not officeholders or would-be officeholders. As full-time professionals, officeholders are the most visible members of the party, but they rarely act independent of the preferences of the extended coalition upon which their own and the party's prospects depend.

Officeholders, thus, may play a dual role in our theory as both policy demanders and agents of the larger coalition of policy demanders. We say "may" because some politicians may not truly share group goals or may shirk in pursuit of them. But our sense of officeholders, especially leading officeholders such as presidents and party leaders, is that they do play both roles.[15] Consider, for example, Salmon P. Chase, a founder of the antislavery Republican Party. For most of his early career, Chase was notable as an intense policy demander against slavery. But in 1849 he was elected to the U.S. Senate and thence took on the role of officeholder—indeed, the role of intensely ambitious officeholder. As historian William Gienapp comments,

> the sincerity of his hatred of slavery is beyond challenge. The Ohio Free Soil leader had committed himself to the antislavery movement in the 1830s when it was not respectable; he had braved anti-abolitionist mobs; he had waged a long legal struggle for black rights; and he had labored diligently for many years to form a powerful antislavery third party. As his commitment to political activity grew, however, so, too, did his ambition; he was, in the words of one Ohio politician, "as ambitious as Julius Caesar." . . . Pontificating ceaselessly about his disinterested commitment to the antislavery cause, he displayed (like many politicians) an increasing inability to distinguish between his own political fortunes and the advancement of his party. (1987, 72)[16]

From Gienapp's account, Chase is both intense policy demander and ambitious politician. His ambition for office was great, yet his dedication to policy goals came earlier and never flagged. Even after the Republican

Party won control of government, Chase was a leader of its radical wing, pushing not only for an end to slavery, but also, a much less popular cause, positive affirmation of the rights of African Americans. Chase's lifelong antislavery commitment is the basis of our classification of him as, above all, an intense policy demander.

Yet not all politicians exhibit the constancy of Chase. Consider, by way of contrast, George Corley Wallace. He began his career in Alabama as a racial moderate, but was beaten in his first race for governor by a hard-core segregationist. Vowing never again to be outflanked on race, Wallace became a hard-core segregationist, declaring famously at one point, "Segregation now, segregation tomorrow, segregation forever." After African American citizens were empowered to vote, however, Wallace backed off his stance on segregation, apologized for it, and won many votes from blacks.

Wallace acted the role of ambitious politician whether he was in office or not. Consider the following account of his early career in politics in rural Alabama:

> A farmer in Barbour county remembers, "All through [World War II], people around here had been gettin' these Christmas cards from all kinda place— Denver one year, then the next year, it'd be Guam or someplace like that— and openin' them up, they'd read, 'Merry Christmas, George C. Wallace.' I got 'em too, and I couldn't quite figger them out. I thought it was real nice of this young fella, so far away and all and yet bein' so thoughtful, but I wasn't quite sure I knew who this George Wallace was, and why he was writin' me. It seemed kinda strange. Anyway, when the war was over with and the local political races got started over the county, I was out in my field one fine spring afternoon plowin', and I happen to look up and see this young fella comin' across the plowed field from the road, like he had just popped up out of nowhere, steppin' real smart and lively across those furrows, already grinnin' and his hand already stretched out, and all of a sudden I knew why I had been gettin' them nice cards every Christmas. (cited in Chester, Hodgson, and Page 1969, 265)

From this account, Wallace is an ambitious politician much more than he is an intense policy demander.

Most politicians are, of course, more difficult to classify than Chase and Wallace. Indeed, even Wallace would have been difficult to classify except over the course of his entire, highly inconstant career. But policy demanders do nevertheless try mightily to judge who is authentically committed to their goals and who is merely pretending to be committed. If they do a good job in these judgments, the politicians they nominate will tend to be more like Chase than like Wallace, which means most will have a dual status as officeholder and policy demander.

★ ★ ★

We turn now to the historical and contemporary record of party formation, party change, and presidential nominations to conduct our four tests. We begin in the next chapter with the founding period of four major American parties, all from the late eighteenth and early nineteenth centuries. The reason we go so far back in history is that our country's most important parties were founded in this period. In our reading of the historical record, groups of intense policy demanders were major influences in the founding of all four parties and dominant in at least three of the four. Most officeholders simply watched—albeit, with great interest—as groups did the main work of organizing new parties.

3

The Creation of New Parties

Parties, as we have noted, formed quickly in the early American Republic, but they also expired quickly. The Federalists dominated the 1790s, but they never won another presidential election after the Republicans beat them in 1800 and gave up even trying to win after 1816. By 1820, the Republicans too had disappeared, dissolving into the so-called Era of Good Feelings. Almost immediately, another party division emerged, but it took two or three elections to stabilize. This system pitted Whigs against Democrats and lasted for four or perhaps five presidential elections. In the 1850s, the Whig Party fell apart and was replaced by a second Republican Party.

We have, then, several periods in which major new parties emerged: the Early Republic, the period around 1830, and the 1850s. We shall examine each to learn what we can about who forms parties and why. We shall be particularly interested to know whether the impetus came from ambitious officeholders anxious for stable careers or from policy demanders intent to capture government for policy purposes.

As always, our investigation will be hampered by the fact that evidence of internal party politics is not as abundant as we would like. Chroniclers have paid more attention to the nuances of ideological and doctrinal struggles, which are conducted in writing, than to on-the-ground details about how politics was actually organized. Yet, guided by theoretically derived expectations, we can learn a fair amount by attending carefully to such evidence of party organization as does exist.

The Nation's First Political Party

The fifty-five men chosen for the Constitutional Convention in Philadelphia in May 1787 were hardly a representative cross section of postrevolutionary America. No one expected they would be. The early United States was a class-stratified society, with a small group of gentlemen enjoying traditional rights to govern. Naturally, the Framers of the Constitution were drawn from this group. By occupation, they were mainly merchants, lawyers, shippers, large-scale farmers, and slave owners.

The country had a national government in 1787, including a congress and its president.[1] But it was a relic of the wartime Articles of Confederation and very weak. When efforts to strengthen the government failed, a group of nationalists—intense policy demanders, in our view—moved to create a whole new government through a constitutional convention. Their group demand was for a government strong enough to deal with the country's problems, especially as regards defense and commerce.

The last thing the Constitution Framers at Philadelphia would have called themselves was a political party. Yet, if the proverbial man from Mars were to examine them, he would notice they acquired a partisan name, Federalists. He would notice they were an alliance of different segments of the country. If the Martian were well read in political science, he would also notice that the Framers fit the standard definition of a party—a coalition of elites seeking to get control of the government by legal means.[2] The fact that the Framers had to first create the government they wanted to control scarcely undermines their fit with the definition.

Most of the effort at Philadelphia was to design a government with an acceptable mix of costs and benefits for coalition members, as represented by state delegations. The key issues were between large and small states, and between slaveholders and nonslaveholders. There were no fights concerning the interests of smaller farmers or slaves, since they were either underrepresented or unrepresented. Even so, the compromises were difficult to hammer out, as intraparty compromises often are. But the expected gain from cooperation was large, especially as regards commercial development. A national government strong enough to actually govern would be a major boon in achieving the Framers' vision of a Great America.

As in our analysis of party formation in an imaginary society, the Framers took seriously the danger that an opposition coalition might capture the government and use it for purposes opposed to theirs. This opposition would be, in contrast to their view of themselves, a party. Shay's Rebellion in Massachusetts, rowdy workingmen's parties in Philadelphia, and the Revolution itself had shown that large political combinations were possible in America. As Madison observed in *Federalist 10*, "Complaints are everywhere heard from our most considerate and virtuous citizens . . . that the public good is disregarded in the conflicts of rival parties, and that measures are too often decided . . . by the superior force of an interested and overbearing majority." In view of this problem, the proposed Constitution was, as Richard Hofstadter put it, a "Constitution against parties" (1970, 1).

The presidency was the most obvious target for capture by a majority coalition and was therefore the object of special attention by the Framers. "No problem caused more perplexity for the delegates than that of determining how the President should be elected," writes Richard McCormick. "They wanted a method that would be impervious to faction, intrigue, or any unwholesome form of manipulation; a method that would defy [as they saw it] politicization" (1982, 24). Through most of the convention, delegates planned for Congress to choose the president. But near the end of their deliberations, they reconsidered. "The candidate would intrigue with the Legislature, would derive his appointment from the predominant faction, and be apt to render his administration subservient to its views, argued Madison" (19). Election by Congress could thus present a convenient opportunity for the nation's far-flung factional interests—as depicted by Madison in *Federalist 10*—to combine into a majority faction. So, in keeping with Madison's argument in *Federalist 10* about the advantages of an "extended republic," their solution was to force the choice of president to be made, as far as possible, by independent actors scattered around the country and unable to coordinate with one another. Counting on the slow mail service of the day, the plan was as follows: Each state would pick presidential electors who would meet *in their respective states* where they would all cast their ballots *on the same day*. Results would be sent under seal to the president of the Senate, who would open and tally them in the presence of the assembled Congress. If any candidate had an absolute majority in the Electoral College, he would become president. But with each state deciding independently, no candidate might get a majority. In these cases, Congress would pick the winner from among the top five finishers—and would do so *immediately after the state votes were counted*, so that legislators would have no time to form coalitions.[3] With party coalitions unable (as it was hoped) to organize, Congress would have no basis for choice other than the personal character and ability of the candidates—an arrangement that would perpetually favor the particular groups that had already organized themselves as the Federalist Party. Declared Alexander Hamilton, "every practical obstacle should be opposed to cabal, intrigue, and corruption. . . . The Convention had guarded against all danger of this sort with the most provident and judicious attention." "It is impossible," said another delegate, "for human ingenuity to devise any mode of election better calculated to exclude undue influence" (McCormick 1982, 26).

The Electoral College did not work as planned for even one election. Hamilton himself led the behind-the-scenes organizing in 1788 to ensure that colleagues in each state chose electors pledged to the prearranged candidates, George Washington and John Adams, with a few votes held back from Adams to be sure he finished second to Washington. The Framers' elaborate plan is nonetheless illuminating, because it shows how they were acting as a party to create a procedure that would favor the nomination and election of their candidates over those of other potential coalitions.

The proposed Constitution was so controversial that it nearly failed to be ratified. In one state convention, a motion to demand that the Constitution be rewritten, which was tantamount to rejection, failed on a vote of 80 to 80. Opposition came from several sources. Slaveholders worried that a national government might some day seek to abolish slavery. Some citizens feared that any strong national government would invariably be captured by narrow interests and used to exploit the populace. And still others, particularly in the west, feared that creation of a national government would aid the mercantile sections of the east without doing them any good. These "anti-Federalists" mostly stayed away from the Philadelphia Convention, and from national politics generally. But the existence of a large if not always active and organized anti-Federalist opposition sharpens the image of the Framers themselves as a partisan group.

So if the Framers were a party, are they better understood as a politician-centered party or a group-centered party? There is some evidence both ways. An analyst partial to the politician-centered view of parties could point out that the Framers had extensive experience in politics and office holding. About three-quarters of them went on to serve in the new government, including several, like Washington and Hamilton, who took high posts.[4] This might suggest that the Framers created the Constitution as a vehicle to enlarge their careers as politicians.

One might further argue that attendees at the Philadelphia convention, voting almost unanimously among themselves in favor of the Constitution, constituted a sort of long coalition of diverse national interests. To be sure, not all of the country's interests were represented in Philadelphia, but a long coalition is not theoretically expected to be universal, only minimum-winning. And the closeness of the later ratification vote in the individual states demonstrates that the Federalist coalition was not much more than minimum-winning. If the Constitution was the product of ambitious office seekers, essentially unanimous among themselves across a range of issues but a bare majority within the national political elite, it would be an almost perfect fit with the politician-centered theory of party.

However, one piece of this vignette strikes us as conspicuously incorrect: the attribution of political ambition to the Framers who later held office in the new government. The Framers were ambitious men, but few needed a career boost, and most who served in the national government did so for only a term or two. Their motivation is quite unlikely to have been office holding. The Framers are, we believe, much better understood as policy demanders intent on creating and controlling a government strong enough to achieve their partisan purposes. To this basic point we would add only that, in describing the project of the Framers as partisan, we by no means demean it. As two mid-twentieth-century scholars have commented: "[The Federalists] conceived of themselves not as constituting a political party but merely as the promoters of sound government. The opposition, as they saw it, consisted of disgruntled obstructionists to good government. . . . The priceless legacy of the Federalist party to posterity was the firm establishment of the national government prescribed by the Constitution" (Binkley and Moos 1958, 180).

If the Framers are understood more as policy demanders than as ambitious would-be officeholders, the closeness of the ratification vote in the states would be consistent with our claim that policy demanders want to win elections, but not by ceding any more to public opinion than necessary. We do not insist on this point, since a vote on a national Constitution would probably have been close in any case. Yet we cannot help wondering whether a Constitution designed to appeal to the workingmen and small farmers of the interior rather than the mercantile and planter interests of the seaboard might have generated a more positive ratification vote. Of course, many of the Framers themselves would have opposed such a Constitution, but that hardly invalidates our point.

Formation of a Second Political Party

The first national elections were as staid as the Framers hoped they would be. Washington was chosen president with essentially no opposition. In elections for the House of Representatives, voters mainly chose men of local standing and reputation, men who were entirely similar to the Framers themselves in political outlook.

With a huge amount of work to do in setting up a new government, the
nation's first Congress got off to a slow start. "I think it is the most dilatory
assembly in the universe," wrote one member in his diary.[5] But appointment of Alexander Hamilton as secretary of the treasury, several months
into the session, brought an infusion of energy. The headstrong New Yorker
took the lead in developing policies and assembling the majorities to push
his measures through the House. His method was a tool familiar in colonial history, the party caucus:

> It was customary for Hamilton's followers to hold meetings of their own.
> Although the word "caucus" was not applied to these party gatherings, they
> were caucuses in all but name. It was on these occasions apparently that
> policies were determined upon, and it was doubtless the assurances obtained
> in them that enabled Hamilton to estimate the probable vote with such
> exactness. Maclay refers to "the rendezvousing of the crew of the Hamilton
> gallery," or to a "call of the gladiators this morning," or again to the statement
> of Speaker Muhlenberg that "there had been a call of the Secretary's party last
> night." These allusions are made in a perfectly matter-of-fact way, as though
> such meetings were already looked upon as familiar occurrences. (Harlow
> 1917, 144)

These caucuses, along with the policies they advanced and the opposition
they provoked, were unmistakably partisan. Division between the Hamilto-
nian Federalists and the Jeffersonian Republicans—who are not to be confused with latter-day Republicans—became sharper through the 1790s and
resulted in "the Revolution of 1800," the nation's first broadly partisan election for president. Republicans led the way in developing party machinery,
because they had to overcome the antiparty devices placed by the Federalists
in the Constitution. Tracing this process allows us to see how an opposition
party develops from scratch, at least in this particular case.

Any account of the rise of the Jeffersonian Republican party must begin
with policy conflict, of which disagreement over Hamilton's proposal for
a National Bank may stand as illustration. The bank was to be a private
institution, but it would be the repository of public funds and would have
regulatory power over state and local banks. In Hamilton's view, the bank
would provide a stable national currency, support promising business ven-
tures, and encourage foreign investment. But to congressional opponents,
the bank would be a gift of interest-free public money to the bank's private
directors and a license to exploit the rest of the banking system. And so it
went. Everything Hamilton proposed by way of commercial development
was attacked as a giveaway to well-placed friends of the Washington ad-

ministration. In many ways, these disputes were a continuation of debates between Federalists and anti-Federalists over the Constitution. The former (prominently including Hamilton) wanted a strong national government to promote development; the latter feared government would be captured by what we would now call special interests.

Party conflict had a cultural dimension as well. As noted earlier, the United States was a class-stratified society. "We were accustomed to look upon gentlefolk as being of a superior order," recalled a modestly born Connecticut farmer. "For my part, I was quite shy of them and kept off at a humble distance" (cited in Fischer 1965, 8). Common people, when they took part in public affairs, did not presume to assert their own views; rather, they supported the local gentleman or notable. This was as the Framers wanted politics to work and hoped it always would. But the norm of deference gave way in the 1790s to class resentment and to insistence by the white male working class of its right to political participation.

Hamilton was among the leading skeptics of demands for popular government. As he opined during the Constitutional Convention, "The people are turbulent and changing; they seldom judge or determine right. Give therefore to [the rich and well-born] a distinct, permanent share in the government. They will check the unsteadiness of [the people]; and as they cannot receive any advantage by change, they will therefore maintain good government" (Hamilton 1903, 401). To avoid the perils of mass politics, Hamilton argued that the president be elected for life. In the First Congress, Federalist John Adams proposed a law to bestow titles on government officers in order to increase public respect for them. The president, he suggested, should be addressed as "His Most Benign Highness."

From the other side, Thomas Jefferson wrote that "My most earnest wish is to see the republican element of popular control pushed to the maximum of its practicable exercise" (1816). Even after the excesses of the French Revolution made clear the potential harm of maximum participation, Jefferson stuck to his commitment. "The masses of people were not born with saddles on their backs" (1826), he wrote to a friend.

The popular classes—including many who had risen above humble origins but still felt snubbed by high society—exulted in Jefferson's attitude and excoriated that of the Federalists. As a not-so-humble Rhode Island man wrote of the Federalist Party:

> These men I hate 'cause they despised me
> With deep contempt—and 'cause they advis'd me
> To hold my tongue when th'was debate
> And not betray my want of wit.[6]

The Jefferson-Madison faction in Congress defeated Adams's proposal to bestow titles of nobility, but was unable to scotch a national holiday for George Washington's birthday. The opposition also attacked the purchase of fine china for the president's dinner service as offensively anti-Republican.

If we think back to the Schwartz-Aldrich theory of party, we see that this conflict was "long" in their sense of a long coalition; that is, it embraced many issues, from economic policy to cultural tone. However, Hamilton was never able to put together a stable majority coalition in Congress. He had a core group of supporters and won passage of most of his key measures, but he won them with different majorities, each assembled (as would be expected in the absence of parties) through great effort.[7] Thus, if our expectation is that a minimum-winning long coalition will emerge to stabilize legislative business, the expectation is not supported.

Yet partisanship was certainly present in Congress. In his detailed study of *The Jeffersonian Republicans: The Formation of Party Organization 1789–1801*, Nobel Cunningham provides the following description of voting in the Third Congress: "The roll calls . . . indicate that no party regularity was shown in the voting records of nearly half of the members. But the two parties nevertheless dominated the proceedings of Congress. The principal members of the House generally had identified themselves with one side or the other, and these men were more than likely to be the speakers who controlled the debates. . . . The proceedings of Congress thus gave the appearance of a more decided cleavage than the voting records of Congress reveal" (1957, 70–71). In other words, about half of the members of Congress were voting as committed partisans, but the other half refused to take sides. Even with the aid of a partisan caucus, the talented and energetic Hamilton could not create a long coalition.

Hamilton resigned his office during the Third Congress, ending regular use of the partisan caucus in the House. Loss of this institution might have been expected to bring a decline in party voting. But the opposite occurred. Party voting was stronger in the Fourth and later Congresses than it had been under Hamilton's leadership in the first three. The increase apparently began late in the Third Congress (Cunningham 1957, 71).

We see nothing in the internal politics of the House that might explain this increase, which we take as another point against a politician-centered theory. However, outside Congress—and mostly outside the hands of office-holding politicians—party building was going on and may perhaps explain the rise of party voting inside of Congress. We see three fairly distinct developments: The emergence of a Republican press to spread party propaganda; the emergence of citizen activism against the incumbent administration; and the formation of party nominating committees to coordinate electoral

activity. Together, they describe the birth of the Republican Party. We take
each in turn.

Newspapers and Party Formation

Like a tree falling in the forest with no one to hear it, the earliest partisan
debate had little impact on national opinion because no newspaper reported
it in much detail. But that changed in 1791 when Thomas Jefferson, who
may be seen as both an intense policy demander and an ambitious politician, recruited a firebrand editor to run a paper giving the Republican view
of events. This paper lasted only two years, but a second Republican paper
emerged on its own—that is, independent of Jefferson and other officeholders—and built a nationwide circulation. Meanwhile, the older *Gazette
of the United States* became more openly pro-Federalist. Partisan vitupera-
tion now spread across the nation. Even Hamilton and Madison, despite a
code of honor that frowned on engagement in public controversy, joined
the fray. As the election of 1792 approached, Madison wrote an article called
"A Candid State of Parties," in which he stated the obvious: that the country
was now divided between two parties. As he described them, the first was
a "Republican Party" that trusted the wisdom of the people and the other
was an "antirepublican party" that distrusted the people and played to the
"opulent" classes (1791). The high master of partisan mudslinging from
the other side was William Cobbett of *Porcupine's Gazette*, who described
Jeffersonian Republicans in these terms: "refuse of nations"; "yelper of the
Democratic kennels"; "vile old wretch"; "tool of a baboon"; "frog-eating, man-
eating, blooddrinking cannibals" (Warren 1931, 90–91). In calm moments,
Cobbett and other Federalists referred to Jeffersonians merely as Jacobins,
after the extremist club of the French Revolution.

Federalist papers were initially more numerous, but, in a decade of rapid
circulation growth, Republican newspapers came to predominate (Pasley
2001, 203). Republican editors were also more attuned to electoral politics
(Pasley 2001, 229–36). As a result, observers agree that the surge in partisan
journalism was a huge boon to the Republicans. "The newspapers are an
overmatch for any Government," complained a disgruntled Federalist after
Jefferson won the election of 1800. "The Jacobins [*sic*] owe their triumph to
the unceasing use of this engine" (Cunningham 1957, 167).

A newspaper was in this period the organ of its editor-printer. These editors therefore merit examination. According to a recent study by historian
Jeffrey Pasley, they were typically men of humble birth, bookish inclination,
and a steely commitment to "equal liberty." The job of eighteenth-century
editor was never lucrative, and embracing Republican politics in the 1790s
made it less so. Partisan editors risked loss of ad revenue from Federalist

merchants, physical abuse at the hands of progovernment thugs, and, in the late 1790s, prosecution under the Sedition Act of 1798, which forbade commentary tending to defame the government and was aimed squarely at leading Republican editors, several of whom wound up in jail. Yet the number of Republican papers substantially increased as the 1800 election approached. "Almost all of the post–Sedition Act papers were working parts of the Republican Party from their inception," writes Pasley (2001, 167). Men were drawn to journalism, as Pasley argues, by a basically political motive: it "gave them an outlet for expression of their personal virtue and independence, an outlet that was denied in the consensual, elite-dominated politics favored by the Federalists" (162). Many of these editors were anti-Federalist activists before they became journalists (Prince 1967, 15–16).

Among the politicians of the day, Jefferson was perhaps the most active in encouraging the Republican press, channeling both money and ideas to favorite editors. Some other Republican officeholders did so as well. However, Pasley asserts that "the phenomenal growth of the Republican press cannot be attributed to the scattered, episodic efforts of the office holding gentry, whether in person or by proxy. At the heart of it was a new breed of printer, a group of artisan politicians" (161–62). From our perspective, these ideologically driven printer-activists are another clear case of intense policy demanders trying to influence government.

The Republican editors worked together, creating a national intelligence network for good ideas and arguments. "An especially powerful political essay or paragraph could spread through the country in a matter of weeks, and an especially well-executed newspaper could gain national, target exposure far beyond its own circulation" (Pasley 2001, 173).

Activists and Party Formation

As partisan newspapers became widespread, so did activist politics. By activist politics we mean non-office-holding citizens working to affect political outcomes. The first glimmering came in 1793 with the formation of two so-called Democratic clubs in Philadelphia. Dozens more clubs followed across the country. Their agenda was the core Republican agenda, with an especially strong emphasis on popular sovereignty.

The main stated purpose of the clubs was to discuss issues of the day and increase public awareness of them. In practice, this entailed a great deal of criticism of not only the Federalist Party, but also George Washington, for their supposed monarchical tendencies. Criticizing Washington, the hero of the American Revolution, was a bold step. Equally bold, the clubs openly praised the French Revolution. They celebrated its victories, addressed one another in the French manner as "citizen," and added the

French tricolore to their ordinary dress. The clubs were therefore angered when Washington declared that the United States would remain neutral in the conflict between Britain and France, and they turned to petitions and street protests to oppose the Jay Treaty, which they deemed sympathetic to Britain. But here the activist movement discovered its limited popularity. Not only did the Senate approve the Jay Treaty, but public opinion seemed to turn against them as Federalists picked up seats in the 1796 House elections. About this time, the club movement went into decline.

At its peak, the movement consisted of some forty to fifty clubs around the country. Given that the House of Representatives had only sixty-five congressional districts, this was a large number. And the clubs took a keen interest in what their state and national legislators did. Historian Eugene Link reports "hundreds of . . . instances in which societies, individually and collectively, brought pressure to bear in legislative halls. Doubtless during their regular meetings the question of the actions elected representatives took was the most time-consuming as well as the paramount issue in most of the clubs" (1942, 150).

In his review of club activities, historian William Miller (1939) also notes six cases in which the clubs became active in congressional elections and suggests there were many others. "Wherever there was a Democratic Society, the [electoral] fight was a hard one for the federalists. For the first time they faced an organization, disciplined, practical, aflame with enthusiasm."[8] Later historiography is more cautious about the electoral involvement of the Democratic societies. The clubs often criticized congressmen with whom they disagreed and fought some of them in elections, but there is no statistical evidence that they were an influence in electoral politics.

Whatever the level of organization, Federalists abhorred the Democratic societies. Fisher Ames, a leading Federalist in Congress, reviled them as "despised by men of right minds." Yet he respected their electoral clout. "They will be as active as Macbeth's witches at the election, and we all agree the event is very doubtful" (cited in Miller 1939, 135). Washington himself publicly criticized the clubs as "self-created societies"—by which he meant they were illegitimate because outside the Constitution—and blamed them for the Whiskey Rebellion, an organized refusal to pay Hamilton's excise tax.

Office-holding politicians played little role in founding Democratic clubs. Nor did the Republican Party leadership in Congress, which never had a regular congressional caucus, exert direction. Even Jefferson kept his distance from the clubs, fearing their open sympathy for the French Revolution would "sink the Republican interest" in a public backlash (Wilentz 2005, 54). Some members of Congress were associated with the club movement, but at least in Philadelphia and New York, this was because clubs were a major force in politics and had helped to nominate or elect them.

But if officeholders did not seem to influence club formation, the pressure tactics of the clubs may have influenced officeholders. We noted earlier the surprising rise in party voting in Congress in the Second and Third Congress. This rise, we now observe, coincides with the rise of Democratic clubs. We cannot demonstrate a causal link, but other evidence suggests that party voting in legislatures can depend on external pressure from activists (Masket, in press).

However this may be, the Democratic clubs should be understood as the activity of intense policy demanders. The clubs were not particularly representative of public opinion as a whole, as we can see from their damaging dust-up with Washington. But representativeness is not a hallmark of intense policy demanders.

Partisan editors and citizen activists became, as we shall see in a moment, pillars of the new Republican Party. But what of officeholders? It is hard to imagine a political universe in which opposition politicians stand by while the elements of a mass party gather strength. And, in fact, they did not stand by. The letters of Madison, Jefferson, and other major figures are full of discussions on how to behave for maximum political impact. But strategic behavior is not the same as partisan organization. On that score, historian Sean Wilentz observes in *Rise of American Democracy* that the activities of Jefferson, Madison, and others in the early 1790s mainly involved

> the cooperation of a few leading gentlemen who would handle their affairs discreetly, more like diplomats than grubby politicians.
>
> Ideas about building permanent electoral machinery that might fuse the national leadership with the voters were nearly as alien to the Republican leaders as they were to Federalists. (2005, 50)

Activists Form Party Committees

The election of 1796, however, brought the first clear instance of what can be called party activity—that is, an organized attempt to get control of government. Consistent with Richard McCormick's (1966) analysis, it centered on the office of president; and consistent with our analysis, it was grew out of local politics. Yet, as seems always to be the case in the study of parties, key details are in short supply. We know much more about what Jefferson and Madison wrote to each other than about what happened in local communities in which Republican committees began to contest elections. But a close look at the evidence nonetheless yields a coherent picture.

The earliest on-the-ground party organization focused on an electoral device that few contemporary Americans understand, the ballot ticket. Voters would write the names of the candidates they supported on a "ticket" and bring it to the polling place. Tickets were necessary because election officials did not print ballots; they provided only a box in which to collect them. Cunningham provides the following accounts of ticket making in 1796:

- "In the New York state elections of that year there was a 'Republican Ticket' and a 'Federalist Republican Ticket' offered to the voters of New York City. Both tickets were framed at party meetings. The Republican ticket was agreed upon at a 'very large and respectable meeting of Republican citizens' held at Hunter's Hotel; the Federal Republican ticket was recommended by a similar gathering of friends to the Federal interest."
- "In Delaware, 'deputies from the several hundreds' of the county assembled at Dover, 'for the purpose of preparing a ticket, to be recommended to the Republican Citizens of Kent County, at the ensuing general election,' and recommended candidates for both Congress and state offices."
- "[In Philadelphia] 'Republican members of the State Legislature and of Congress from this State' together with 'a number of citizens from various parts of the state' drew up a slate of presidential electors, headed by Chief Justice Thomas McKean, and designated it the 'Republican Ticket.' The assembled gathering then appointed a committee 'to communicate to the citizens of Pennsylvania any information of importance on the subject of the election . . .' and selected as chair of this committee Dr. Michael Leib . . . who had been a leading organizer of the Pennsylvania Democratic Society." (1957, 110–11)

These early party meetings appear to involve a mix of partisan activists and officeholders. One must assume that officeholders and future officeholders, as leading members of their political communities, were among the leaders of the effort. But officeholders do not appear to be issuing orders from on high. Rather, they seem to be working with citizens toward a common goal. This impression—alas, only an impression—is one that we get from all of the early party proceedings.

Agreeing on slates was not, of course, the end of the process. Communicating the nominations to voters under the conditions of the day was another big challenge. A Philadelphia hatter and Democratic Club member named John Smith—a kind of anti-Adams Paul Revere—provides the following account of his efforts to disseminate the names of party-designated electors during the 1796 presidential election:

I undertook and performed a journey of 600 miles. . . . The object I had solely
in view was to make Mr. Jefferson President. . . . For upwards of three weeks
I was out, there was not one day I was not on horse back before the sun rose,
nor put up at night till after it set. In that time, I held 18 public meetings,
making it a practice at night to pay some person immediately to go through
the neighborhood [neighborhoods were more spread out in those days] and
notify the people to attend that night—at which respective meetings I addressed myself to them in a zealous language. (Pasley 1996, 554)

By this means, he and others distributed some fifty thousand handwritten
ballots to towns and villages around Pennsylvania. Such energetic activity
was unusual in 1796. In most of the country, the election still worked as
quietly as it had in Washington's two elections.

The level of insurgent effort was dramatically higher in 1800, but the
design of the Constitution continued to hinder party organization. In four
states, voters directly chose electors to the Electoral College, naming as many
electors on their ballot as their state had votes. In the other states, where legislatures chose the electors, voters could affect the presidential race only
by casting ballots for state legislators committed to their presidential candidate. Getting far-flung and often isolated pockets of voters to coordinate
on these tasks was, as the Framers intended, difficult. In Philadelphia, for
example, Republican sympathizers, including carryovers from club days,
appointed committees in each county and charged them to form slates.
In Bucks County, the committee kicked off its activity with the following
public notice in a newspaper:

The Republican committee have projected, three general meetings of the
friends of freedom in this county, to be held previously to the ensuing general
election; viz. one at Swift's tavern, in Middleton township on Sunday the 16th
inst., one at Benner's tavern, in Rockhill township on Saturday the 16th inst.,
and one at Addis's tavern in Buckingham township on Saturday the 13th of
September next. The citizens in general to meet about 11, and the members of
the committee positively by 10 o'clock of each day.

The object of these meetings is, to collect information respecting the persons proper to be chosen to the several elective offices, *and generally to condense
the rays of political light and reflect them strongly on all around.* (cited in Cunningham 1957, 160; emphasis added)

The 10 a.m. committee meetings, ahead of the general meetings, were intended to prepare recommendations for the larger group. The leading politi-

cians in the area would likely have attended. But Federalists still dominated rural Pennsylvania, so few of the organizers would have been officeholders. The larger meetings would modify or ratify the proposed ticket, sending delegates on to a higher level meeting where the slate would be finalized.

In New Jersey, a line of anti-Federalist agitation can be traced from the formation of an early democratic society in 1793 to the emergence of Republican Party nominating machinery in the election of 1800 (Prince 1967, 11–40). In April 1800, two subscribers to the Newark *Centinel of Freedom* sent a lengthy letter to the newspaper to propose a statewide plan of township and county meetings to form slates. In the next few months, the newspaper "was filled with reports of Republican meetings at which committees were appointed in accordance with the blueprint for Republican organization published earlier in the *Centinel,* and by the end of the summer, Republican township committees had made their appearance in most of the counties of the state," after which county-level meetings were held to finalize the slates (Cunningham 1957, 158). Historians agree that Aaron Kitchell, an incumbent member of Congress, played a large role in the organizational drive of 1800, but he was not nominated for reelection in that year.

So, again, we see a process involving activists and officeholders. The impression is one of a substantial contribution to party building by both groups.

With John Adams running for reelection in 1800, the outcome in his home state of Massachusetts was never in doubt. But even in this Federalist stronghold, activists challenged Federalist dominance through a homegrown Republican organization. As historian Paul Goodman describes the effort: "The party builders were not primarily national statesmen directing affairs from Philadelphia or professional politicians operating from Boston. Unlike later professional party leaders, they were generally ambitious merchants, tradesmen, capitalists, speculators, ministers, and office seekers who formed an interest and mobilized relatives, friends, acquaintances and dependents" (1964, 70).

The party battle was fiercest in New York, where party development had gone further than in any other state. As the 1800 election approached, the friends of Jefferson realized that he could probably win the presidency if he could get the state's twelve electoral votes, which had gone to Adams in 1796. New York was one of the states in which the legislature chose electors, so attention focused on the legislative elections of April 1800. "It was generally conceded," writes Cunningham, "that the thirteen members from New York City would turn the scale in favor of whichever party was successful there." Aaron Burr, a former U.S. senator who was then a state senator, managed the Republican effort; Alexander Hamilton, now a practicing

attorney, handled the Federalist campaign. Burr's strategy, says Cunningham, "lay in the plan to offer a powerful ticket which would represent all
the elements of Republican strength and contain the names of such distinguished and influential political figures that the personal weight of the
candidates and the force of their names alone would contribute greatly to
the success of the ticket" (1957, 177–78). But several key figures were uninterested in running, so Burr cajoled them into the race and steered their
nominations through the large public meetings that served as nominating
devices. All such activity was informal, because no formal or legal party
processes existed. For the campaign, Burr organized "all the young men
and ardent politicians of the city with whom he had any intercourse" into a
smoothly running machine that canvassed much of the city block by block.
When the votes were counted, the Burr ticket won every seat in what had
been a Federalist city, giving Republicans a bare majority in the state legislature and an insurmountable edge in the Electoral College.

In New York and elsewhere, the new party tickets were highly effective.
As soon as they appeared, the names they proposed took almost all offices
as voters fell quickly into the habit of party voting. Parties, it thus appears,
were not an imposition on voters, but a useful tool for making their voices
heard.[9] To make party tickets as easy to use as possible, party committees printed and circulated them along with election appeals, so that voters
needed only to sign a ticket and drop it into the ballot box. In Pennsylvania,
where printed ballots were illegal, parties circulated handwritten tickets to
voters, thereby circumventing an antiparty measure. The tickets did not
always carry an overt party label, but they carried sufficient cues that voters
could tell one ticket from the other.[10] Tickets covered all state and federal
offices that were in play in the election.

The success of party tickets in structuring the vote was immensely significant. It was, first of all, a defeat for the ideal of democracy of the Framers, who wanted elections to turn on the character of individual candidates
rather than coalition politics. The success of tickets was equally a tribute
to the newspaper wars, whose coverage made partisan division meaningful to voters. But it was, above all, a victory for the Republican Party—the
national coalition of officeholders, activists, and editors that cooperated
across numerous local, county, and state boundaries to win not only the
presidency but the House, the Senate, and key state legislatures.

The form of party organization varied by state, depending on local tradition and legal structure. In the South, officeholders, most of whom were
also slaveholders, led the formation of party committees. In New England,
where there were few Republican officeholders, citizen activists took the
lead. But party organizing of one kind or another was widespread. "Wher-

ever the two parties came into the sharpest conflict, [transition to a formal system of nomination] was well under way as early as 1800" (see Luetscher 1903, 2–3, chap. 3, chap. 4).

Unfortunately, no data have been complied on overlap between early club activists and later party activists. From areas in which records are most complete—New York and Philadelphia—even a reader of the secondary literature will notice overlap. For other areas, overlap is unknown. One must suspect, however, that the people protesting the Washington administration in the mid-1790s were at least the same kinds of people working to elect Jefferson in 1800.

The final layer of party activity was provided by the congressional parties. In both 1796 and 1800, Federalists and Republicans held caucuses of their members in Congress to nominate presidential candidates. The importance of this activity, however, is not clear. In both of these elections, Adams and Jefferson were widely assumed to be their party's standard bearers for months if not years ahead of caucus action. In 1800, Burr's New York victory preceded the action of the congressional caucus, and much other partisan activity did so as well.[11]

How the Republican caucus chose its vice presidential nominee is revealing. With Jefferson, a southerner, expected to be the party's nominee for president, there was general agreement that the vice president should be a New Yorker. But several names were possible. Hence, Albert Gallatin, the party leader in the House, was delegated to obtain "correct information of the wishes of the New York Republicans" (Cunningham 1957, 162–63) When word came back that they preferred Burr, the caucus promptly met and nominated him, and in the subsequent election, all electors who voted for Jefferson also voted for Burr. Cunningham cites the disciplined Electoral College vote as evidence of the supremacy of the Republican congressional caucus, but this episode can also be cited to show that the real power in the party lay in local parties.[12]

Who Formed the Republican Party?

What light does all of this throw on whether political parties are better explained as politician-controlled or group-controlled?

In the Schwartz-Aldrich model, one impulse to party formation is the instability of legislative coalitions. Such instability was certainly a problem for Hamilton and the Federalists in the First and Second Congresses, but it did not lead to the formation of a long Federalist coalition. But an opposition Republican Party did form and certain details of its formation are consistent with a politician-centered scenario. Most obvious is the behavior of Aaron Burr. This ambitious officeholder put himself forward for the vice presidency as early as 1792 and, by his exertions in the New York legislative elections, he succeeded in getting himself elected to that position in 1800. Another exhibit for a politician-centered theory is Thomas Jefferson, who seems to have written letters more or less continuously to friends around the country in an effort to engineer a victory in 1800. Many Republican officeholders—perhaps most of them—also contributed to the organizational effort.

Yet it would take a one-sided reading of the evidence to assert that ambitious officeholders organized or controlled the organization of the Republican Party. The political actors who arguably had the greatest career stake in a national party, members of each group's congressional delegation, did not exert collective leadership or even consistent individual leadership over the formation of party nominating committees. Initiative came from a mix of local actors whose primary motive was policy. This was most clear for the Democratic club movement, which formed more or less spontaneously and whose principal means of making policy demands were strident proclamations and protests. Editors, too, were by Pasley's account mainly motivated by political concerns. By the late 1790s, editors and activists across the country were linked in a national movement. This critical development—in effect, the formation of a long coalition out in the country rather than in the halls of Congress—was by no means organized by officeholders. It was, rather, a response of politically active citizens to the incumbent Federalist Party and its ill-organized but articulate Republican opposition in Congress. When energies eventually turned to the formation of machinery to contest elections, the picture muddies, but only somewhat. The main players were no longer pure policy demanders, but a mix of citizen activists, partisan journalists, and officeholders. Yet all continued to lay heavy stress on Republican issues and values, and it would be hard to dismiss this emphasis as window dressing. Anyone, including any officeholder, who demurred on basic Republican values would not likely have remained viable in the new party.[13] Thus, the formation of the Republican Party was more the culmination of a movement of intense policy demanders than the feat of career-minded officeholders. One could perhaps claim that officeholders gained control of a movement they did not initiate, but even that may be too strong. Officeholders gained control, if they gained control at all, by going with the flow.

Thus, the central event in party formation was not, as politician-centered theory would have it, office-holding politicians organizing themselves into a durable minimum-winning coalition and working to create a supportive electoral organization. This never happened in either the Federalist or Republican parties. Meanwhile, the key event in the life of the Republican Party was formation of a self-organized national network of policy demanders which at first merely pressured officeholders but eventually began to nominate and elect them. Officeholders contributed to this national coalition, but it was not their creature. This pattern, if we are correct in our description of it, is consistent with a group-centric view of parties.

We note in passing that as the Republican Party triumphed in state after state, legislatures switched to direct popular election of electors pledged to a particular candidate. In so doing, Republicans replaced the antipopular bias in presidential election procedures that Federalists had favored with a popular bias that Republicans expected would favor their interest.

Formation of the Democratic Party in the 1820s

After losing five straight presidential elections, the Federalist Party declined to make a nomination for president in 1820. This allowed James Monroe to cruise to reelection in a suddenly nonpartisan "Era of Good Feelings." But feelings were not all good within the ranks of the victorious party. One of the most dissatisfied was Martin Van Buren, the leader of a New York party accustomed to receiving patronage from Republican administrations in Washington. He criticized Monroe for cooperating with Federalists and urged a revival of party conflict. When Van Buren arrived in Washington in 1821 as New York's new senator, one of his first acts was to provoke a national controversy over Monroe's appointment of a former Federalist to a plum federal job in Albany. The position, he insisted, should go to a loyal Republican. The challenge was unsuccessful, but Van Buren's effort to stimulate partisanship continued and bore fruit. Within a few election cycles, struggle between two organized parties, Democrats and Whigs, had come to dominate American politics.

Van Buren, a career politician, did not single-handedly create this second generation of party conflict, but he did everything he could to help it along, and historians give him much credit for the end product. It is therefore illuminating to follow his efforts.

Our account begins with the presidential election of 1824. Four accomplished men, all claiming to be good Jeffersonian Republicans, entered the race. Each had support from his section of the country, but none had strong national support. John Quincy Adams, as the only candidate from New England, had the largest natural base; Andrew Jackson, Henry Clay, and William Crawford drew support from the southern and western parts of the nation.

In the face of this disarray, Van Buren wanted a caucus of Republican members of Congress to choose. The caucus had been making nominations since 1796 and Van Buren saw this institution as a natural base for party building. The clear expectation was that, if the caucus succeeded in electing its candidate, the distribution of patronage (and probably policy matters as well) would again become partisan. But three of the four candidates were nominated—that is, put forward as candidates—by a friendly state legislature or convention. Members of Congress whose candidate had been nominated by their section subsequently refused to go along with Van Buren's plan; many even signed a public declaration of refusal to take part in a congressional caucus. But Van Buren pushed ahead anyway. He managed to assemble a caucus of about sixty legislators, most from states that backed Crawford, and they proceeded with a caucus nomination of Crawford. But the underattended event was widely criticized and did little to concentrate support on Crawford.

We take the failed congressional caucus of 1824 as another instance in which national officeholders refused, despite strong leadership, to play a leading role in national party formation. The opportunity to form a coalition in support of a candidate with whom they could later govern in partisan fashion was laid before them, but they mostly passed on it. Further, from the evidence of who came to Van Buren's caucus and who stayed away, the most important motive was not party formation but responsiveness to local pressure.

Jackson won a plurality of the electoral vote in 1824 but lost the election to Adams in the House of Representatives. Old Hickory was furious and began his campaign for the 1828 election almost immediately. Van Buren, too, became active for Jackson early on, but not simply for Jackson. His aim was to construct a national coalition with Jackson its leader. This time, however, he focused his efforts out in the country, among state and factional leaders. As Robert Remini writes, "The making of the Democratic Party—or, more precisely, the revamping of the Republican Party—was largely the work of Martin Van Buren. While he was aided and abetted by many, . . . he alone discharged the tremendous task of reorganization. . . . It was Van Buren who joined together the different sections of the country and united the followers of Calhoun and Crawford with the rest of the Jacksonians. It was he who tried to draw the East and West closer. It was he who renewed the alliance between the North and South that lasted until 1860" (1959, 125–26).

One of Van Buren's most important converts was Thomas Ritchie, the editor of the Richmond *Enquirer*. Ritchie was the recognized leader of Virginia state politics and a good example of the kind of Republican editor who, according to Pasley, anchored antebellum party politics: "Officeholding politicians came and went, but a strong and skillful editor could command the [local] party continuously for decades. . . . Newspaper editors were the most truly professional politicians in the party system. . . . In an age when legislative sessions were short and official pay was designed to meet only the expenses of serving, editors . . . actually earned their livings from political work" (2001, 17, 15).

Ritchie, however, was not a truly independent politician. Virginia politics were dominated by slave owners, with non-slave-owning whites mainly excluded. Ritchie had the trust of slave owners but could retain it only as long as he served their interests. Thus, when Van Buren contacted Ritchie, he was, in fact, reaching out to Virginia's most important policy demanders. Van Buren's strategy was to bring his state party in New York State into an alliance with state parties in the South that would dominate national politics—a union, as he put it to Ritchie, of the "the plain Republicans of the north with Southern planters." Van Buren saw this as a revival of the old Jeffersonian alignment and told Ritchie that its effect would be to stifle "the clamor against the Southern Influence and African Slavery." As the New Yorker explained:

> Instead of the question being between a northern and Southern man, it would be whether or not the ties, which have heretofore bound together a great political party should be severed. The difference between the two questions would be found to be immense. . . .
>
> Effects would be highly salutary on your section of the union by the revival of old party distinctions. . . . If the old ones are suppressed, geographical division founded on local interests, or what is worse prejudices between free and slave holding states will inevitably take their place. (quoted in Remini 1959, 131–32)

If, in other words, the Jeffersonian union of northern and southern states were allowed to lapse, a new party tie, pitting slavery and antislavery forces against each other, might develop instead. Historians have debated whether Van Buren was proslavery or merely trying to put together a winning coalition. For our purposes, it doesn't matter. What is clear is that Van Buren, the leader of the largest northern state, was offering to southern planters an alliance that would protect them from antislavery agitation. Ritchie, though initially cool to Jackson, bought the argument. So did Crawford and John Calhoun, two southern slave owners who had national followings and were also initially cool to Jackson.[14] Van Buren made a celebrated tour of four southern states in 1827 to meet directly with leading citizens— most of them probably slaveholders—constantly pushing the line that alliance with New York would undermine sectional antagonisms and thereby safeguard their interests.

Slavery was not the only issue that a national coalition had to accommodate. Trade, manufacturing, and agriculture were expanding rapidly and the frontier was moving rapidly westward. These developments created a tangle of conflicting needs and wants that no concrete political program could possibly organize. Nonetheless, the citizen activists and Republican editors who had powered the Revolution of 1800 were still the leading actors in many states and were still devoted to what they took to be Jeffersonian principles. Van Buren was keenly aware of this ideology and wrote constantly of the need to nourish and strengthen it. As he wrote from Washington to his supporters in New York in 1826, "My language here to our friends is that we will support no man who does not come forward on the principles & in the form in which Jefferson & Madison were brought forward" (Remini 1959, 53–54).

In areas in which Jackson ran well in 1828, men who considered themselves faithful Jeffersonians were often the backbone of the campaign. For example, Van Buren's principal ally in New Hampshire was Isaac Hill, the humbly born editor of the *New-Hampshire Patriot*. The paper took upon itself the mission of aggressively defending the poor farmers of interior New Hampshire from bankers and merchants on the coast. Hill had grown wealthy from publishing and government contracts, but his Jeffersonian fire was undiminished (Cole 1970). Although full of sympathy for the white working class, Hill was not bothered by slavery. Ideologues of Hill's stripe were mainstays of Van Buren's national network of Jackson supporters. In Kentucky, a coalition of debtors, bank haters, and Jeffersonian journalists formed the nucleus of the Jackson campaign (Cole 2002, 95–100). In Pennsylvania, western debtors and Philadelphia Working Men's parties, all devotees of Jefferson, were the basis of the Jackson campaign (Wilentz 2005, 304). In the pivotal state of Ohio, old Jeffersonians were at the forefront of the Jackson campaign (Ratcliffe 2000, 304–10).[15]

From his position in the Senate, Van Buren did what coalition building he could. Perhaps his most critical effort involved the so-called Tariff of Abominations, which was working its way through Congress in the year of the election. The tariff was an especially vexing issue for a coalition of northern, western, and southern interests. Van Buren's involvement in the tariff bill was defensive, intended less to create a coalition than to keep it from flying apart (see Wilentz 2005, 298–300). In a more positive vein, Van Buren wanted, even in 1828, to use a congressional caucus to make the presidential nomination, but there was little interest and none was held.

Van Buren did most of his party-building work independently of Jackson and was brought into the candidate's inner circle rather late. Hence, it would be incorrect to say that Van Buren was simply the manager of

Jackson's candidate-centered drive for power. Van Buren played the leading role in organizing the disparate state interests that supported Jackson and became the basis of a permanent national party.

In terms of our theoretical analysis, Van Buren—known in his day as the Little Magician—stands as an almost pure case of ambitious officeholder.[16] Organizing caucuses, managing legislation, and selecting candidates was his full-time occupation in New York, where in the 1810s he was the commanding figure in the best organized state party in the nation. From his first days in Washington, Van Buren sought to do for national politics what he had done for the politics of New York. The national party he helped to build elevated him to the office of vice president in 1832 and president in 1836. All this fits extremely well the view of parties as the creatures of ambitious politicians.

It is also easy to interpret Van Buren's national organizing as an attempt to construct a reliable long coalition—that is, a set of political actors who would cooperate on all issues while excluding their opponents (Federalists and Adams's apostate Republicans) from any share of policy.[17] This coalition, anchored by the sectional powers New York and Virginia, was intended to be big enough to win all or almost all of the time. Because it was based in the Electoral College rather than a legislature, it is not the kind of coalition Schwartz had in mind in "Why Parties?" but it seems in other ways like a long coalition. Again, the fit with the Schwartz-Aldrich model is good.

Yet there is a big detail that does not fit so well. The actors that Van Buren organized into the Democratic Party coalition were not all or, especially in the South, even mostly officeholders. He tried to organize officeholders in both 1824 and 1828, offering them what would seem a clear opportunity for partisan gain, but his efforts were unavailing. His most important and novel contribution to American politics was his self-conscious effort to create a coalition among interests based in state and local communities. The resulting coalition gave the Democratic Party its distinctive character up to the Civil War and beyond.

We acknowledge that, after Van Buren's party got up and running, it attracted large numbers of ambitious politicians, who then became cogs in a national machine that placed an extremely high value on winning political office at any cost. No doubt the prospect of a national, election-oriented party was part of the party's initial appeal. But, then again, why should an intense policy demander refuse political office in a coalition that serves his policy demands? The existence of ambitious politicians within the Van Buren coalitions by no means nullifies the importance of Van Buren's founding appeal to intense policy interests. These interests certainly wanted to win elections, but even more, they wanted to win on their own propatronage, proslavery, Jeffersonian, antibank terms. Thus, when the public mood later shifted against slavery, the party did not change with this change in opinion. It did its best, even in its northern branches and through most of the 1850s, to resist the tide.

Altogether, we will take the formation of the Democratic coalition as a mixed case—assembled by an ambitious officeholder for his own purposes and including many ambitious politicians as party leaders, but based on interest groups that realized their intense policy concerns through Van Buren's coalition. To say that Van Buren succeeded by making himself the agent of these interests, most notably southern slaveholders, seems a fair description.

A salient feature of our account has been unwillingness of most national officeholders to lead in party formation. We suspect they were reticent because they lacked the political authority to take such an important initiative. This suspicion is strengthened by our final case of party formation, the antislavery Republican Party of the 1850s.

Abolitionists and the New Republican Party

In 1830, one of America's greatest evangelical preachers, Theodore Weld, began a decade-long series of passionate, religiously motivated attacks on slavery. Along with his students, he influenced tens of thousands of Americans against this inhumane institution. In 1831, William Lloyd Garrison began his antislavery newspaper, the *Liberator*. Its first issue declared, "I will be as harsh as truth, and as uncompromising as justice. . . . I am in earnest—I will not equivocate—I will not excuse—I will not retreat a single inch—and I will be heard."

In 1833, Garrison's secular and Weld's evangelical traditions came together in a new organization, the American Anti-Slavery Society. In 1839, an offshoot formed a political movement, the Liberty Party, to compete for political power. Its first campaign did not go well. Of the 2.4 million voters in the presidential election of 1840, the Liberty Party garnered about 7,000, many fewer than the number Weld and his students had preached to and seemingly converted.

From these fledgling efforts—the formation of a new party by a group of intense policy demanders—one can trace a clear path to the formation of the Republican Party as an antislavery party in the mid-1850s, the election of Republican Abraham Lincoln to the presidency in 1860, and the destruction of slavery in the Civil War that followed.

But this path, though fairly consistently forward, was anything but straight. To give but one indication of its twists and turns, the Liberty Party merged in 1848 with dissident Democrats and a few Whigs to form the Free Soil Party—with sixty-five-year-old Martin Van Buren as its presidential candidate! Van Buren was, at that point, a mere figurehead, but by the time the Republican Party took shape in the mid-1850s, the antislavery movement was thoroughly penetrated by professional politicians who were more than figureheads. Moreover, the new party was no longer strictly abolitionist, but opposed merely to the extension of slavery to new territory.

Who, then, founded the Republican Party? Professional politicians who co-opted the antislavery movement to assure continuation of their careers amidst a national crisis? Or intense policy demanders who compromised as necessary to create a majority party against slavery?

Before offering an answer, we must first provide some historical background on the period. In the Missouri Compromise of 1820, Congress prohibited slavery in new states north of latitude 36°30′. In the Kansas-Nebraska Act of 1854, a Democratic president and Congress effectively repealed the Missouri Compromise by allowing settlers in each territory to decide for themselves whether they wanted slavery. Over the next year, settlers in Kansas fought pitched battles over whether the future state would be free or slave, and the proslavery side seemed to be winning. Southern states, which had been falling behind the North in population, were encouraged by these developments, which held out the prospect of maintaining equal influence with the North and perpetuating slavery. Antislavery activists were deeply angry for the same reasons. By all historical accounts, the Kansas-Nebraska Act and the events in "Bloody Kansas" that followed were the impetus to the formation of the Republican Party.

Yet, at almost the same time, another issue roiled the country. Native-born Americans became disturbed by the large number of Catholic Irish immigrants coming into the country and formed the so-called Know Nothings to oppose them.[18] The Know Nothings were nothing if not intense. They believed the pope was sending "battalions" of his loyalists to subvert American liberty and therefore demanded limitations on the political rights of immigrants. With little initial encouragement from office-holding politicians, hundreds of thousands of Know Nothings organized themselves into an estimated ten thousand lodges. They also formed a national party called the American Party to compete in elections. In the 1854 congressional elections, Know Nothings ran a genuinely grassroots campaign that elected sixty-two members of the House of Representatives, making them the second biggest party in Congress after the Democrats.[19] At this point, the Whig party essentially dissolved as its politicians migrated to other parties or retired.[20] The Know Nothing Party also soon faded as its members became more worried about the "slave power" in the South than the pope in Rome.

From this chaos emerged the Republican Party, drawing former Whigs, some Democrats, and some Know Nothings into a major political party.

With this background, we return to our question: Who created the Republican Party and from what motive?

It is easiest to begin by saying who did not create it. Despite having an excellent opportunity to do so, national officeholders of existing major parties did little to initiate a new antislavery party. Their opportunity came during the debate of the Kansas-Nebraska Act. As southern Whigs rallied to support the act, opposition centered among northern Whigs, Free Soilers, and antislavery Democrats who would eventually form the core of the Republican Party. But as William Gienapp writes in his detailed study of *The Origins of the Republican Party, 1852–1856*: "Retaining their separate identity, Democrats opposed to the bill refused to caucus with northern Whigs. . . . The bill's opponents 'could not forget they were Whigs, they were Democrats.' . . . Free Soilers, Whigs, and anti-Nebraska Democrats voted together, but they could not work together."[21]

Once the bill was passed, about thirty congressmen met to draft a call for a new national party but adjourned without taking action. A little later, another caucus was held "to lay the foundation of a real party of Freedom," but the resulting proclamation urged no definite action, failed to include the names of the sponsoring officeholders, and produced no visible effect (Gienapp 1987, 89–91). Thus, the notion that the Republican Party originated as a coalition of officeholders has scant support.

It is also easy, as a general matter, to say where the new party did originate. As Gienapp has written, "The Republican movement grew out of national developments, but the party first took shape at the state level"(1987, 192). To understand how this happened, we must get into the nitty-gritty of state politics.

In every state in which the Republican Party was established, it was done by means of a political convention. In this traditional process—the same process, incidentally, that was used to ratify the U.S. Constitution—a notable person, newspaper, or group would publish a public call for a convention to occur at a particular time and place. Often the call would include a procedure, such as local elections, to choose convention delegates, but some calls were for "mass conventions" open to anyone. Finally, the call would give the purpose of the convention. If attendees were so inclined, they would vote on a platform, nominate candidates, set up a central committee, and by these means present themselves to fellow citizens as a party.

No state was typical of all others, but the forces at work in the formation of a Republican Party in Ohio were fairly typical. Ohio was also the third most populous state at this time and an early breakthrough for the Republican Party. The first call for an antislavery convention in Ohio was a nonstarter. It was issued from Washington by the state's two senators and two of its House members, all of whom were well-known antislavery office-holders.[22] This call, as Gienapp reports, "did not coincide with the views of the profusion leaders in the state and apparently was used only in areas of pronounced antislavery feeling" (1987, 115). A substitute call was issued by a committee of three men, none prominent.[23] The call requested Ohioans who opposed repeal of the Missouri Compromise to attend a convention in the state capital on July 13.

The committee that made the call consisted of a Democrat, a Whig, and a Free Soiler of no great fame, but this was a bit of a ruse. The real drivers were apparently three antislavery members of Congress, led by Free Soil Senator Salmon P. Chase. As we discussed in chapter 2, Chase appears to be an outstanding example of a person who is both intense policy demander and ambitious politician. The resulting convention was a large but modest gathering: "A large throng of delegates [i.e., persons elected to the convention in some manner] and unofficial participants [persons not so elected], including Whigs of various persuasions, anti-Nebraska Democrats, Free Soilers, Know Nothings, and Germans, came together at Columbus on July 13[, 1854]. . . . With none of the state's congressional leaders in attendance, leadership fell to the lesser state politicians. A number of Democrats were present, but Benjamin F. Leiter, a former speaker of the assembly, was virtually the only one who had a statewide reputation" (Gienapp 1987, 116).

Leiter had been elected to a two-year term in the state assembly for 1849–50 and served as speaker in the second year. If he was the most prominent politician present at the convention, it is hard to argue the convention was primarily a vehicle for ambitious officeholders. It appears, rather, that the state's major party officeholders were keeping a cautious distance at this stage. The convention was cautious as well: it voted an anti-Nebraska platform and nominated anti-Nebraska candidates, but did not declare itself a permanent party. Nonetheless, Ohio voters followed its lead, electing both of its nominees (which were for minor statewide offices) in preference to the regular Whig and Democrat candidates.

Far more significant were congressional elections. The state convention left nominations for these races to separate district-level conventions. Gienapp provides no information about these activities, but, in a remarkable political triumph, all twenty-one nominees of the district-level antislavery conventions won their fall elections to the House of Representatives. Once in Washington, these Ohio House members formed the largest state bloc of antislavery strength in the Congress—a bloc just big enough to give the Republican Party its greatest triumph to date, the election of a Republican Speaker of the House of Representatives in 1855.

To learn more about these critical Ohio House members, we examined their career patterns. As shown in Table 3.1, they may be grouped into three clusters:

- Six nominees were former major party incumbents (Whig or Democratic) who decided to join the new party and were elected under its banner. This is the group most likely to be using the emerging antislavery party as a vehicle of career stability. Yet they do not have the profile of careerists, since none had served more than one prior term in Congress and none stayed long in Congress after this election. All, of course, had voted against the Kansas-Nebraska Act.
- Two nominees were incumbent Free Soil House members. One of these, Joshua Giddings, was clearly a career politician. Giddings was a dedicated antislavery man, pressing antislavery measures in Congress from the first days of the political antislavery movement. When the Free Soil party founded, Giddings switched over to it. The other Free Soil incumbent, Edward Wade, held no elective office at the time of his election to Congress, though he had been a county prosecutor a decade earlier.
- The remaining thirteen nominees were nonincumbents. They are a mixed lot, but only two, John Sherman and John Bingham, have the profile of career politicians who might have profited from formation of an anti-Nebraska party. Yet even these two were essentially neophytes when first elected. The remaining eleven look like part-time and occasional politicians.

As a group, then, the candidates elected out of Ohio's anti-Nebraska conventions were scarcely a cadre of professional officeholders. The modal new member of Congress was a person with a small amount of prior office-holding experience—often far in the past—and a small amount of experience in Congress ahead. The political universe suggested (but not proven) by the data is one in which national officeholders are drawn from a large pool of activists in which office holding is common, but usually only for a brief stint in the midst of a lifetime of routine, low-scale activism. This impression, plus the lack of prominence of major officeholders at the state convention, makes it hard to argue that, at least in Ohio, the new antislavery party was anything like the creature of people ambitious to hold office and win election for its own sake.

Recall that the twenty-one antislavery members of Congress were the fruit of a state convention that did not declare itself a permanent party.

Table 3.1: Career patterns in Ohio's first class of Republican members of Congress

Name	Most recent political position	Second most recent political position	Additional terms
Incumbent Whigs or Democrats reelected with anti-Nebraska party			
John Harrison	Whig member of Congress, 1853–54	*	0
Lewis Campbell	Whig member of Congress, 1853–54	Newspaper publisher, 1831–35	2
Aaron Harlan	Whig member of Congress, 1853–54	State constitutional convention delegate, 1850	1
Matthias Nichols	Democratic member of Congress, 1853–54	County prosecutor, 1851	1
William Sapp	Whig member of Congress, 1853–54	County prosecutor, 1845	0
Edward Ball	Editor	State assembly, 1845–49	0
Incumbent Free Soilers reelected with anti-Nebraska party			
Joshua Giddings	Free Soil member of Congress, 1849–53	Whig Member of Congress, 1837–49	1
Edward Wade	Free Soil member of Congress, 1853–54	County prosecutor, 1833	3
Newly elected with anti-Nebraska party			
Timothy Day	Newspaper editor	*	0
Richard Mott	Mayor of Toledo, 1845–46		1
Jonas Emrie	County probate judge, 1851–54	State Senate, 1847–48	0
Benjamin Stanton	Whig member of Congress, 1851–52	State constitutional convention delegate, 1850	2
Cooper Watson	*	*	0
Oscar Moore	State Senate 1852–53	State assembly, 1851–52	0
Valentine Horton	*	*	2
Sam Galloway	Secretary of State, 1844	Whig National Convention, 1848	0
John Sherman	*	*	21
George Bliss	District judge, 1850	*	1
Charles Albright	Publisher	*	0
Benjamin Leiter	State assembly, 1849–50	Town mayor for 10 years	1
John Bingham	County attorney, 1846–49	*	7

Source: Biographical Directory of the United States Congress.

The next stage in the creation of the Ohio Republican Party provides a somewhat clearer view of intense policy demanders in action—in fact, two opposing sets of them.

As the 1855 elections approached, a committee put in place by the 1854 not-yet-party convention issued a call for the election of delegates to another convention to choose that year's candidates. In view of the group's success in the 1954 election, the fight to control this convention was serious. The threat came not from the Democrats and Whigs, which were both proceeding to make nominations as usual, but from Know Nothings. As they did in several states, anti-immigrant organizers sought to control the emerging Republican Party as well as their own, and, given the system of open elections for delegates to party conventions, it was quite possible they would succeed. "Why, gentlemen," wrote a Know Nothing editor in a taunt to antislavery organizers, "you can't select enough prominent 'Republicans' in Ohio to act as delegates to the convention, without having in it a majority of Know Nothings" (Gienapp 1987, 193).

This threat materialized in fact.[24] When the antislavery nominating convention convened, observers agreed that Know Nothings were a majority of elected delegates. Yet in the end, the Know Nothing favorite withdrew in favor of Chase. Chase, running now under the banner of a self-declared Republican Party, went on to win the Ohio governorship in the first such victory in the nation for the Republican Party.[25]

How exactly Chase beat the Know Nothing favorite in a convention having a majority of Know Nothing delegates is as convoluted and dramatic a story as any politics junkie could wish, but a big part is the following: Free Soil Party leaders anticipated Know Nothing influence at the antislavery convention and called a convention of their own to meet at the same time in the same city. The threat, openly discussed in the press, was that if Chase failed to get the Republican nomination, the Free Soil Party would immediately give him its nomination, which would throw Ohio politics into a state of chaos that would benefit neither side. The four hundred delegates at the Free Soil convention—demonstrating by their physical presence Chase's ability to mount a campaign if necessary—made this threat credible and gave his supporters the bargaining power to prevail over the Know Nothings inside the Republican convention.

This series of events, odd though it is, shows that the hundreds of delegates who attended these conventions were not simply ciphers. Whatever Chase's status as intense policy demander or ambitious politician, the sheer numbers at the parallel convention of antislavery activists mattered greatly. The events also fit nicely within our theoretical framework: two opposing sets of activists, one antislavery and the other anti-immigrant, struggling to control what both sides hoped would be the replacement for the Whigs as the country's second major party.[26]

Antislavery activists, we should also note, were important for more than just nominations. Nineteenth-century election campaigns were highly labor intensive. They included mass rallies, large-scale picnics and parades, door-to-door canvassing, and get-out-the-vote drives, all of which were handled by party workers. Lacking the regular organization of the established parties and powered by what could only have been antislavery activists, the new Republican Party was immediately competitive in these standard ways.

Our bottom line, then, is that while Chase was certainly an ambitious politician, the Republican Party that he helped bring into existence was anything but his personal vehicle. It was a coalition of people from diverse backgrounds working to oppose slavery, with Chase at the head of the group.

Although we see no need to go into detail, newspaper editors acting as self-appointed policy demanders played a major role in the formation of the Ohio Republican Party, as they did in the previous cases of party formation. For example, the leader who brokered Chase's nomination at the 1855 convention was Oran Follett, editor of the *Ohio State Journal* (Gienapp 1987, 198).

All of these events, of course, relate only to Ohio. The formation of the national Republican Party involved the union of many state party organizations, each with its own history. An important point is that in states in which the Whigs were stronger and antislavery forces weaker than in Ohio, the Whig Party took longer to dissolve and was able to place more of its officeholders in the emerging Republican Party. So we are not claiming officeholders were always as unimportant, or activists as important, as they were in Ohio. The argument may be summarized as follows: For several decades beginning about 1830, abolitionists and other political opponents of slavery sought to make slavery a national issue, and, beginning in 1840, some pursued this goal through a northern antislavery party. But their political efforts had limited success until the Kansas-Nebraska Act and the rise of the Know Nothings caused the existing alignment of Whigs and Democrats to lose force. When this happened, antislavery editors and activists moved quickly in many states to put up candidates (including some Whig and Democratic incumbents) who were pledged to a program of not extending slavery. Their dramatic success in a few states (including Ohio) in which they were strongest enabled antislavery officeholders to elect a Republican Speaker of the House in 1855, thereby critically accelerating the demise of the Whigs and the rise of a major antislavery party in the North.

This turn of events was exactly what most ambitious officeholders in both major parties had been resisting since Van Buren engineered the creation of the Democratic coalition in the late 1820s. It was also close enough to what politically active opponents of slavery had been working toward that, despite the considerable prominence of incumbent politicians in the new sectional party, intense policy demanders deserve more credit for creating it than the agile officeholders who came on board only after the Whig Party melted down.

Concluding Comments

The four most important new parties in this country's history have been the Federalists, the Jeffersonian Republicans, the Jacksonian Democrats, and the antislavery Republicans. In this chapter, we have tried to make sense of the foundation of these parties in terms of competing theories of why parties exist and whose interests they serve. In the politician-centered view of parties, parties exist because ambitious officeholders find them useful to achieve their career goals. If this view is correct, officeholders ought to lead in creating parties in order to achieve electoral goals. In our alternative theory, parties exist because groups of intense policy demanders find them useful for getting the policies they want. If this is right, these groups ought to play the leading role.

We do not flatter ourselves that we can definitively settle this question in this brief chapter. The question is too large and the gaps in the extant historical record are too great. Evidence about critical events at the activist base of the party system is not only rare to begin with, but few historians have shown interest in it. Yet we do believe that a considerable amount of good evidence exists and that our review makes a useful start in analyzing it. We summarize the conclusions of this effort as follows: In none of the four cases did we find ambitious officeholders working together to form new national parties. In the Schwartz-Aldrich model, officeholders form a long coalition that becomes the basis of the new party; in none of the four cases did anything like this happen. Indeed, for the cases of the Jeffersonian Republicans, the Jacksonian Democrats, and the antislavery Republicans, we found rather clear evidence that such cooperation failed to occur despite efforts by individual politicians to bring it about. Hamilton was unable to organize a long coalition in the First and Second Congresses; Van Buren was unable keep the congressional nominating caucus alive in the 1820s; antislavery officeholders in Congress declined to cooperate in creating a new antislavery party even though their common opposition to the Kansas-Nebraska Act gave them an excellent vehicle for doing so. In these three cases, some talented and energetic politicians tried to do what politician-centered theory suggests they would do, but their efforts did not succeed.

At the same time, we found evidence that individuals who seem well-described as intense policy demanders did endeavor to create parties to achieve their policy goals and seemed to succeed. We acknowledge that positive evidence of the nature and importance of their activity is less clear than the negative evidence on activities of officeholders, but it is good enough for preliminary conclusions, which we summarize as follows. Intense demanders for a strong national government, known as Federalists, organized a constitutional convention in 1787 that not only achieved their immediate policy goal but sought to provide for the group's long-term control of government. As Federalists began to use the new government as they had intended to use it, ideological activists and Republican editors at first agitated and then organized a party against them. When the first party system collapsed, the same kinds of policy demanders, prominently including slaveholders, responded to Van Buren's efforts to create a dominant party that would keep slavery permanently off the national agenda and, as many activists saw it, also keep special interests out of power. Frustrated by the long-term stability of Van Buren's coalition, antislavery activists and editors agitated for two decades before getting and seizing the opportunity to form a national antislavery party. In each case, intense policy demanders cooperated closely with officeholders or politicians who later became officeholders, but nonetheless provided the main energy in the drive to create the new party. The new parties resembled Schwartz-Aldrich long coalitions, except that they formed out in the country rather than in a legislature and were instigated by a different cast of characters than anticipated by that model.

Party formation, on this reading of party history, is primarily an activity by which intense policy demanders pursue policy goals and secondarily an activity by which professional politicians achieve careerist and electoral goals. Some policy demanders, of whom Salmon Chase is the outstanding example, do take office in the parties they create, but this does not undermine their theoretical status as intense policy demanders.

It is important to notice that new parties shape subsequent politics in ways that reflect the intent of their group founders. This is most obviously true of the Federalist Party and its antiparty Constitution—or perhaps we should say, its anti-every-party-except-the-Federalist-party Constitution. Even today, some 230 years after the Philadelphia convention, we are a nation in which political change is slow and difficult, exactly as intended by the nation's first political party. Jeffersonian Republicans likewise put their stamp on subsequent events through new electoral rules that made government more responsive to popular majorities of the kind they themselves represented. Finally, the coalitional structure of the Van Buren Democrats and antislavery Republicans determined the nature of slavery politics during the life of each party—the first kept slavery largely out of national electoral politics, the second put it at the center of national politics. Within all four of these parties, ambitious politicians came and went, some perhaps eager just to hold office, but all under the influence of party founders who valued office as a means rather than as an end.

The aim of this chapter has been to establish our group-centered theory of parties as a viable vehicle for understanding American party politics. We believe we have done that. We turn now to the role of parties in presidential nominations just before and after the McGovern-Fraser reforms of the 1970s. The role of intense policy demanders will not always be so close to the surface of politics as it has been in these cases of new parties, but we shall nonetheless be able to find much evidence of its importance.

4

Weak Structures, Strong Parties

What intense policy demanders want in a presidential nominee is obvious: a candidate who is devoted to their group's goals and who can win the election in November. What a coalition of intense policy demanders—that is, a party—wants is quite different but equally obvious: a candidate who can unify the party and win in November.

The party goal is easier to state as a glittering generality than to achieve in practice. One big problem is that the party's intense policy demanders want different and sometimes conflicting policies. Even on matters on which they largely agree, they typically have different priorities. Thus, finding a strong candidate who is acceptable to everyone on policy grounds may be difficult, sometimes impossible. Another difficulty is that intense policy demanders are, by their natures, unlikely to want what most voters want. Indeed, policy demanders may be active in politics precisely because they want policies—say, same-sex marriage, a high protective tariff, strict prohibition of abortion—that most voters do not. Thus, a candidate who fully satisfies a party's core groups may have trouble winning the general election. A nomination thus involves two compromises—one among the conflicting policies and priorities of groups inside the party, and another between preferences of the party groups and the preferences of voters.

In this chapter we examine how parties make these compromises. The
chapter has two parts. In the first, we consider in detail what kind of candidate is most likely to satisfy the party and also win the fall election. In the
second, we describe the decision-making mechanisms by which parties
have chosen such candidates. In the course of these arguments, we develop
criteria for judging from a party's nomination process whether the party
is strong or not. We shall use these criteria in later chapters to assess the
strength of parties in various nomination struggles.

The Ideal Party Nominee for President

Reflecting on the prospects for the Republican Party in 1860 and the kind of
candidate who should get its nomination, Horace Greeley, the crusading antislavery editor of the *New York Tribune*, wrote: "Now about the Presidency:
I want to succeed this time, yet I know the country is not Anti-Slavery. It
will only swallow a little Anti-Slavery in a great deal of sweetening. An Anti-
Slavery man per se cannot be elected; but a Tariff, River and Harbor, Pacific
Railroad, Free Homestead man may succeed although he is Anti-Slavery"
(Luthin 1944, 615). It is striking that even in the Republican party of 1860—
a party founded in 1854 for the purpose of opposing slavery—radical antislavery was not a winning position for a presidential nominee. Two prominent men facing this difficulty, William Seward and Salmon P. Chase, also
came up short. Each had been governor and senator of a major state and an
antislavery radical—and each proved unacceptable to the party in large part
because of the slavery issue. Meanwhile, a little-known midwestern lawyer,
whose highest position had been one term in the House of Representatives,
was quietly convincing fellow partisans that he could develop the necessary
breadth of support. As he wrote in reply to a supporter from Ohio:

> My name is new in the field; and I suppose I am not the FIRST choice of
> a very great many. Our policy then, is to give no offense to others—leaving
> them in a mood to come to us, if they shall be compelled to give up their first
> love. This, too, is dealing justly with all, and leaving us in a mood to support
> heartily whoever shall be nominated. . . . Whatever you may do for me, con-
> sistently with these suggestions, will be appreciated, and gratefully remem-
> bered. Please write me again.
>
> (signed) A. Lincoln[1]

These vignettes illustrate a major principle of American party politics.
In the multiparty systems of Europe, factional leaders can do well as party
leaders because there is often a distinct party for each major division of

society—a farmers party, a Green party, a workers party, a Catholic party, and so forth. Coalitions among these factions are formed in the legislature, after elections have taken place. But the United States, a bigger and more diverse nation than any in Europe, has only two parties. The party coalitions are forged before elections, in the nomination process. Politicians who appear to be merely factional leaders—"an anti-Slavery man per se"—have trouble capturing as much support as they need to win a major party nomination. Nominations have more often gone to someone who is no one's "first love" but has managed to "give offense to no one," thereby becoming acceptable to everyone.

Recall that, in our theoretical model, parties resemble Schwartz's long coalitions. A long coalition is one in which all actors—legislators or groups—stay together on a great number of issues, where "length" refers to the number of issues on which the coalition has agreed to cooperate. Coalitions may be more or less broad, where "breadth" refers to the number of actors. Generally, coalitions want to be as broad as they need to be in order to win, but no broader, since a broader coalition means diluting the benefits any one group can receive.

Neither in the legislature nor in a nomination does each actor in a long coalition get everything she wants. No one in politics ever does. Rather, the coalition develops an understanding that each group will get a certain amount of what it wants and then expects each member of the coalition to support *all* elements of the accepted agenda. Loyalty to the common agenda is key: Coalitions will quickly fall apart if they allow members to get the benefit of coalition support on items they like and to defect on items they dislike. Coalitions will also quickly fall apart if they deny any individual group its agreed upon share of benefits.

In the legislative setting, members of the long coalition are officeholders and vote the common agenda item by item, often fine-tuning the elements as they go, but a party choosing a nominee cannot do this. For one thing, some issues aren't known at the time of nomination; more fundamentally, the coalition of groups does not take office, its nominee does. Hence, the aim of the coalition in making a nomination is to choose someone who—by her prior record, predispositions, and group attachments—can be trusted to support the wishes of the coalition, as they may emerge over time, on every issue that arises.

As difficult as it is to judge whether a given politician can be trusted, this is what party coalitions must try to do when they make a nomination. If party actors cannot judge reasonably well which politicians can be trusted and which cannot, the party's constituent groups will be better off using their resources to buy individual pieces of legislation.

What this means in the ordinary language of politics is that nominees must be *acceptable* to all or nearly all members of the coalition rather than the choice of any small part of it. The nominee must, in other words, have *broad* support. A party that tries to force the choice of nominees who lack broad acceptability within the party quickly ceases to be a long coalition at all, becoming instead a collection of warring factions. And a party is not likely to be successful in getting its nominees elected if one faction controls nominations over the strong objections of another (Lengle 1980, 1981; Southwell 1986; Stone 1986; Kenney and Rice 1987; Wattenberg 1991; Lengle, Owen, and Sonner 1995).

Because party groups want different and even opposing policies, a big part of a president's job—perhaps the most sensitive part of it—is negotiating differences within the coalition itself, both on long-standing issues and on new issues as they arise. Each group in the party coalition can reasonably insist that the person they nominate for this position be an honest broker who is not too close to any one group—not, that is, any group's "first love." Clinton Rossiter (1960), in his account of Democratic Party politics at the time of the Kennedy nomination, captured this idea quite well when he wrote: "An unwritten law governs the proceedings of the Democratic national convention, commanding the delegates to nominate a candidate for President who is 1) a loyal son of the party, a warrior with scars, 2) not too closely identified with any of the major elements in the coalition, and 3) not openly hostile to any one of them" (205).

Yet groups of intense policy demanders do not necessarily rush to their second-choice candidate. They are more likely to approach slowly and reluctantly, prodded by party leadership and the imperatives of coalition unity. Polsby and Wildavsky (1968) provide a nice account of the flavor of this movement in this description of the nomination of Adlai Stevenson by the Democrats in 1952: "The factions working for the Stevenson nomination did not cooperate with one another to a significant degree and in fact squabbled among themselves on occasion. Yet Stevenson was nominated; his success came about because he was the second choice of an overwhelming number of delegates who could not agree on any of their first choices and the first choice of a significant number of leaders in spite of his disinclination to pursue the nomination in an organized faction" (92). This account suggests a useful way of thinking about party strength: A strong party is one that is able to identify and get agreement on a nominee who is arguably the party's best choice even though that candidate may not be any important group's first choice and perhaps even when the candidate himself is not particularly interested in the honor. By this criterion, the Democratic Party distinguished itself as a strong party in 1952. But the basis of its strength had nothing to do with the role party leaders played or failed to play in engineering the nomination; what mattered was the result—diverse groups united behind a strong candidate.

When Parties Can't Agree

In any stable party system, much of the work of political nominations is done by the structure of the party system itself. To take an obvious example: The Democratic coalition put together by Van Buren in the 1820s, a party with southern slave owners at its base, could not nominate an antislavery candidate for the presidency without tearing itself apart. The same holds for nominations today. Thus, the Democratic Party, with its base of African American activists, could not nominate a candidate who was lukewarm on a key group demand such as affirmative action—unless, of course, it were willing to see activists bolt the party.

But this is in a stable party. Although party coalitions do tend to be fairly stable from one election to the next, group demands and the relative power of groups are never completely constant, and sometimes they undergo rapid and major change. If, for these or other reasons, the essential concerns of groups have come into conflict, it may be impossible to find a presidential nominee who satisfies everyone. Or, to use the language of the previous section, everyone's second choice might not rise to the threshold of being acceptable to everyone. In such cases, it may be politically rational for the losing group to refuse to sign on with the winner, or even attempt to sabotage him. Leaders of the religious right in the Republican Party made a threat to do these things in the course of the 2008 nominating process.

This was also the situation in 1948 in the Democratic Party. African Americans from northern cities were a rising group in the party, and many liberal activists took their side of the civil rights struggle in the South. When the majority of delegates passed a strong civil rights plank at the party convention, several southern delegations walked out of the nominating convention and nominated their own candidate for president, South Carolina governor Strom Thurmond. The new "Dixiecrat" Party said what the national Democratic Party refused to say: "We stand for the segregation of the races and the racial integrity of each race." The southerners aimed by this action to show the national Democratic Party that it could not win without them and therefore needed to heed their intense concerns about race. When the Democrats did win in 1948 despite the walkout, the lesson was just the opposite.

This episode should not be taken as evidence that the Democratic Party—which, as we just saw, showed strength in 1952—was actually quite feeble just four years earlier. We suggest instead the following conclusion: Given that a party is a coalition of intense policy demanders, policy conflicts are bound to arise and become occasionally serious. When they become irreconcilable, as the one between northern blacks and southern whites had, no one should expect the party to make an amicable nomination. The strength of the Democratic Party at this point may be seen in the fact that most state delegations, even in the South, remained loyal to it and that the party was able to wage an effective and indeed winning campaign across all levels of government in the fall elections. A weak party would have splintered into numerous ineffectual pieces, either for one election or many. The Whig Party demonstrated this sort of weakness in the aftermath of the Kansas-Nebraska Act of 1854.

It is interesting to speculate why the fate of the Democratic Party was so different from that of the Whigs. Probably a big part of the reason was the greater loyalty of voters who, in 1948, had an immense commitment to the party of Franklin Roosevelt's New Deal. Even to most southern activists, the popular appeal of the Democratic label was too great a political resource to walk away from. Thus, the strength of a party may reside in its past record of successful governance. It is hard to see that the Whig Party had any such record. It won only two presidential elections and both times its man died early in his term and was succeeded by a politician judged to be weak.[2] The Whig Party's most important leader, Henry Clay, never won election as president despite numerous tries.

One can make a similar argument for the Republican Party in the aftermath of its 1912 meltdown. This was the year in which the "progressive" supporters of Theodore Roosevelt walked out of the party's nominating convention, which in this case did lead to the party's defeat in the fall elections. Roosevelt's supporters, especially in the farm states suffering the stress of an industrializing economy, wanted stronger government regulation of business. His conservative opponents championed the new industrial system and wanted government to help out when it could and otherwise keeps its hands off. One can see this conflict as created by changes in social conditions that no party should be expected to contain. Yet the Republican Party, which had a record of successful governance, rebounded well, nearly winning the next presidential election in 1916 and achieving political dominance in the one after that.

Our point, then, is that a party's strength cannot be reliably determined by whether it has difficulty in making a consensual nomination for president in a given year. Admittedly, difficulty in making nominations is not a positive indicator of party strength, but it is not a fatally negative one either. Except in a society that undergoes no social change and experiences no new issue concerns, conflict over nominations cannot always be avoided.

The test of party strength should be how well a party rebounds from any difficulty it faces and how it handles nominations in more normal times.

Party Interest versus Popular Interest
The American people may want a president who will rise above party and govern as the president of the whole nation. Parties, however, do not. Parties are composed, at least in our theory of them, of factional interests that are concerned above all to defend or advance those interests. No one, for example, would expect labor unions in the post–New Deal Democratic Party to sign off on an antiunion candidate for the sake of winning an election. Even if the public mood were extremely hostile to unions, union leaders would insist—or try to insist—that the Democratic nominee for president be at least quietly prounion. And what is true of unions is true of many other interests.

Consider the seemingly straightforward issue of political corruption. The vast majority of Americans oppose the idea that parties should fund their activities from bribes and kickbacks. Thus, all else equal, a politician who has a reputation for fighting corruption should be preferred by parties. But, as illustrated in Franklin Roosevelt's effort to win the nomination of the Democratic Party in 1932, all else is not equal in a case of this kind.

Roosevelt was the front-runner in the 1932 race, but he was by no means a shoo-in. His strongest support was in the South. In the East and Midwest, where the Democratic Party was a party of urban machines, Roosevelt faced real opposition. And for good reason: As governor of New York, he had supported anticorruption investigations, including the recent discovery of an officeholder who had managed to build up a $400,000 personal savings account on a salary of $10,000 per year. The party's urban machines feared such investigations because they routinely collected large amounts of cash by means that were at best barely legal.

As the Democratic convention approached, two well-known clergymen wrote public letters urging Roosevelt to launch investigations of two other Democratic officeholders who had amassed big bank accounts on small salaries. Roosevelt responded in a public letter of his own:

> It would perhaps be easy for me to question the good faith in which these letters were written, or to assume you care more for personal publicity than for good government. . . . I am becoming convinced by your letters that corruption in public office and unfit servants in public office are both far less abhorrent to you than they are to me. A rushing into print early and often, with extravagant and ill-considered language, causes many of our decent citizens to doubt your own reliance on law, on order, and on justice.

The time which you two gentlemen now spend in bringing charges . . .
could be more profitably spent . . . in pointing out to the electorate of New
York City that an active insistence on their part would result in better qualified and more honest and more efficient public servants. (cited in Neal 2004,
159–60)

The explanation for this self-humiliation is that Roosevelt needed the
support, or at least the acquiescence, of the party's urban machines to be
nominated. In the end—at the last possible moment—he got it. With his
candidacy stalled after four ballots at the party convention and his support beginning to unravel, the Chicago party boss, Mayor Anton Cermak,
relented and put Roosevelt over the top. Whether by agreement or not,
Roosevelt decided not to press an expected corruption case against Jimmy
Walker, the mayor of New York. Nor, despite indications of personal racial
liberalism, did Roosevelt double-cross the party members from the South,
who had been the foundation of his nomination, by confronting the evil of
southern racism.

It is normal for parties to exercise vetoes over candidates that threaten
core concerns. The various factions that make up a major political party are
active in politics precisely because they have intense preferences on certain
issues, and it is a notable feature of a strong party that party factions are
well-positioned to defend their preferences. If, as in the case of political corruption, the majority of public opinion is against group interests, it is only
more reason to screen out unacceptable nominees.

It follows that the candidate who can do best in the fall election is not
always the candidate who can best unite the party. Party members want a
winner, but they also want a nominee they can trust—a politician who is
not a maverick but a team player, someone who will work with party factions to achieve their goals and more generally strengthen the party.

Estes Kefauver, a Democratic senator from Tennessee in the 1950s with
a penchant for using television to promote his causes, was certainly a maverick in the eyes of his party. Big city Democrats distrusted him because
his televised investigations of Mafia corruption threatened to expose their
underworld ties, and southern politicians distrusted him because he was
liberal on race. Journalist T. H. White credits an urban Democratic boss
for this explanation of Kefauver's inability to win the party's nomination
for president: "Kefauver? Look, let me explain in terms of my own governor. When I decided to nominate him, I called him in and said, 'Today,
I'm the boss. But when I nominate you and you're elected, you'll be the
boss because you're governor. I'm putting a gun in your hand and you
can shoot me with it.' Now, you see, with Kefauver, you could never be

sure he wouldn't take that gun, turn around and shoot you" (White 1956, 28). In 1952, Kefauver entered fifteen primaries and won twelve. Entering the convention with most of the delegates he needed to be nominated, he nonetheless lost to Illinois's Stevenson, who had spent most of the campaign season insisting that he did not want to be nominated and who, as we saw earlier, was not the first choice of the party's key groups. But as the protégé of the Chicago Democratic machine, Stevenson was "safe" on the corruption issue, which made him acceptable to machine politicians; he was also not a crusader on the race issue, which made him acceptable to the southern wing of his party. And yet, notwithstanding his lack of crusading zeal on these major issues, Stevenson maintained the aura of a liberal idealist. These qualities made him a nearly ideal party candidate to unite the Democratic Party coalition. Stevenson had only one shortcoming: He could not beat Republican Dwight Eisenhower in the fall election. But, as we shall see later on, Eisenhower and the party that nominated him were strong players too.

Parties do not, if they have any strength at all, nominate candidates simply because they are popular with voters. Parties certainly want to win, but they endeavor to win with someone whom they can trust to safeguard their most intense concerns. At their strongest, parties are able to bottle up candidates like Kefauver and to substitute candidates like Stevenson. As we shall argue in detail in later chapters, despite many social, legal, and technological changes, today's parties retain at least some of this capacity.

Bamboozling Voters

In setting out our theory of parties in chapter 2, we assumed a citizenry that paid some, but not a great deal of, attention to politics. The effect of limited attention, as we argued, is to create a sort of "electoral blind spot" in which parties can do whatever they wish because voters are not carefully monitoring them or perhaps simply don't care what government is doing. This is a strong and important assertion, and so we wish to provide a little more explanation for it.

Political scientists have devoted enormous energy to gauging the sophistication of ordinary voters. One famous conclusion is V. O. Key's assertion that "voters are not fools." As evidence, he cited the tendency of electorates to punish poor party performance with defeat and to reward good performance with another term in office. Voters, he suggested, tend to function as the "rational god of vengeance and reward" (Key 1965, 568). We accept this view, provided it is not overstated. For it is also true that, as Larry Bartels has written, "The political ignorance of the American voter is one of the best documented features of contemporary politics." (Bartels

1996, 194). Thus, in a recent paper, Chris Achen and Larry Bartels (2002) show that, while voters do vote more for the incumbent party for president when the economy has been good than when it has been bad, they do so in an extremely myopic manner: The economy can be weak for most of a president's term, but if it comes back strong during the last six months, he will likely be reelected. Voters also appear to punish and reward politicians for random acts of nature. Thus, based on county-level data on vote for president and rainfall that was above or below normal, Achen and Bartels found that Al Gore lost about one million votes in the 2000 election due to bad weather. The title of one of these Achen-Bartels papers, "Musical Chairs," suggests a substantial amount of pure chance in the events that determine whether presidents get reelected or not (Achen and Bartels 2004). To whatever extent voters do cast their ballots for president on the basis of random events like weather or uncontrollable economic performance, it creates an incentive for parties to ignore voters' policy preferences, nominate the candidates they themselves want, and hope that chance is on their side.

Political parties are sufficiently sophisticated to know everything political scientists know and probably a lot more. It therefore seems likely that they recognize the existence of what we are calling the electoral blind spot. Intense policy demanders are also sufficiently self-interested—or, perhaps we should say, sufficiently devoted to the moral probity of their causes—to try to take advantage of voter inattentiveness. We therefore expect parties to "get away with what they can" in nominating candidates who are closer to their own preferences than voters would support if more attentive to politics.

We take the theoretical warrant for this view to be strong. It amounts to little more than a statement that parties pursue the preferences of their own intense policy demanders rather than those of ordinary voters. Yet providing empirical evidence is difficult. Parties not only do not advertise efforts to exploit voter inattention, but would adamantly deny that they would even consider doing so. We have, however, been able to develop some useful evidence on this point.

As has long been understood, the activist bases of the Democratic and Republican parties are more ideologically polarized than the electorate as a whole (McClosky, Hoffman, and O'Hara 1960). Republican activists tend to be staunchly conservative; Democratic activists are comparably liberal. If these activists were to please only themselves, they would nominate candidates far to the left or right of most Americans, who tend to be ideologically centrist. And, indeed, political scientists have demonstrated that both the Democratic and Republican parties do reliably tend to nominate candidates that are distant from the ideological center (Ansolabehere, Stewart, and

Snyder 2001; Canes-Wrone, Brady, and Cogan 2002; Fiorina 2005; Adams, Merrill, and Grofman 2005).

This evidence is weakly consistent with our view, but we can push the argument further. But first a small bit of technical background: The National Election Studies routinely asks Americans to rate their ideology on a seven-point scale running from extremely liberal to extremely conservative. And it asks them to rate the presidential candidates on this same scale. Using these ratings, plus some additional data gathered by Steven Rosenstone (1983), it is possible to rate the ideological location of presidential candidates from 1948 to 2004. Consistent with other research, the typical nominee is about 1.5 scale points (on this seven-point scale) from the center. If parties were trying to appeal to the median (or mainstream) voter, they could certainly do much better at nominating centrists.

But if, as we maintain, the goal of parties is to nominate the most extreme candidate having a good chance to win, parties should test the limits of voter tolerance. They should, in other words, occasionally nominate a candidate who is perhaps too extreme to win in order to be sure that the candidate really cannot win. Then, if the candidate does fail to win, parties should back off and nominate a more moderate standard-bearer in the next election.

Figure 4.1 suggests that parties do this. More specifically, the figure shows the ideological distance of presidential challengers from the ideological center in each election from 1948 to 2000. The units of ideological distance are derived from the survey questions referred to earlier.[3] As can be seen, the more consecutive presidential elections a party has lost, the more likely the party is to nominate a candidate who is close to the ideological center. Challengers never reach or even approach the ideological center, but electoral defeat impels them to move somewhat closer.

Scholars of presidential elections have often discussed the problem of candidate extremism in terms of a contest between purists and pragmatists. Purists are those who hold out for party principles, even at risk of defeat in November. Pragmatists and "professionals" are those most willing to compromise. The dynamics of intraparty politics are a never-ending contest between these two types (Sundquist 1983; Polsby and Wildavsky 2000). This figure is consistent with that view, but shows more. It shows that the outcome of this struggle varies from election to election, depending on how long the party has been out of the White House. This variation in outcomes is what would be expected from parties that were always testing the waters to see what they can get away with.[4]

The pattern in this figure can also be taken as evidence of strong parties. If a party were to nominate extreme candidates in election after election,

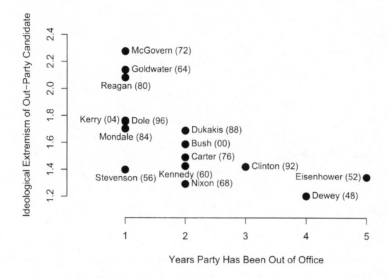

Fig. 4.1. Challenger positioning in presidential elections.

even though it was losing each time, it would be evidence of failure to respond to signals from the electorate—evidence, that is, of a weak party. Or if a party of ideologues were to nominate centrists in election after election, winning by landslides each time, it could also be taken as a sign of party weakness—the ideologues were not getting as much policy benefit from winning as they perhaps could. But the pattern we see here, which is consistent with trying to nominate the most extreme candidate who can win, is the pattern we should expect from a strong party of intense policy demanders.

Although our discussion in this section has focused on ideology, a party's intense policy demanders may want policies that have little to do with ideology. Our argument applies to any sort of policy benefit, whether colored by ideology or not.

Summary
The kind of candidate most likely to unify a party and win in the general election is a candidate who may be no group's intense first choice on policy grounds but who is acceptable to everyone and who is, despite being no group's first choice, as close to the preferences of the party's activist base as voters are likely to accept. A party is strong when it can identify and nominate a candidate having these qualities.

We must add that it may be, in practice, difficult to tell whether a given candidate is acceptable to all important groups. Certainly we cannot require that the nominations of strong parties be acceptable to every delegate at the party convention. By that standard, no party would ever be strong. The test of party unity, rather, should be whether candidates are broadly acceptable within the party and intensely objectionable to no important group.

Decision Mechanisms

Our analysis in the last section focused on the party as a coalition of intense policy demanders and sought to determine the kind of candidate that a party of such groups would ideally wish to nominate. But as John Aldrich has aptly pointed out, "a political party is . . . more than a coalition. A major political party is an institutionalized coalition, one that has adopted rules, norms, and procedures" (Aldrich 1995, 283-284). Hence, we turn in this section to the institutional means by which parties have made presidential nominations. As in the previous section, we shall discuss whether these mechanisms indicate a strong or weak party.

Of course, the principal institution for making presidential nominations has been, through most of American history, the national party convention. Whigs, Republicans, and Democrats all used it and prospered with it. If parties are a "long coalition"—as they are in either the politician-centered or group-centered theory of party—the national convention is the venue at which members renew their commitment to the principles of the coalition and choose a presidential nominee to embody those principles. Or, in the older language of V. O. Key, Jr., "In a fairly real sense, the national convention is the national party. When the means develop for uniting people in support of a nominee, the essence of party comes into being" (1965, 465).

The basic nomination procedure from 1832 until 1968 was that each state party sent delegates to a national party convention shortly before the presidential elections, where they collectively chose a presidential nominee. Particularly in the nineteenth and early twentieth centuries, the power of state leaders over their delegations was great. In many states, if you didn't vote as your state leader told you to vote, you might lose your job as public works inspector or transportation supervisor—and your cousin might lose his job too. Meeting privately for bargaining in the legendary "smoke-filled room," the state bosses would work out the result among themselves. Their power, though never absolute, was often decisive.

A party convention might take as many as ten, twenty, or even one hundred ballots to arrive at a nomination, with balloting punctuated by adjournments to give the bosses time to negotiate. If none of the more famous candidates could quite get a majority of delegates,[5] the convention would typically turn to a less known dark-horse candidate whose support might build in a "bandwagon." The idea of the bandwagon was that steady increases in a candidate's support over successive ballots would create the impression of irreversible momentum, thereby inducing more delegates to get on board. To feed the impression of momentum, candidates would withhold support on early ballots for the sake of certain progress on later ones, or they would bargain for support to materialize only in late ballots. The last thing a candidate wanted was to come close to nomination on the first ballot and to make no more progress on the next two or three. When that did happen, the candidacy would generally collapse and some other candidate would make a run.

Bandwagons, however, are created not by candidates, but by delegates, and their choice is a difficult one. Nominees "are most grateful for support that helps them win; to jump when a candidate has already been nominated is to jump too late for anything but cursory consideration. A delegate can also jump too soon, off a bandwagon only temporarily stalled, or onto one that later stops dead in its tracks, for an overall effect that is graceless. Although timing is everything, when to jump is not obvious, especially if there are many would-be bandwagon riders" (Collat, Kelley, and Rogowski 1981, 427).

These two institutions—the legendary smoke-filled room (or bargaining session) of party bosses and bandwagons on the convention floor—enabled the disparate members of party coalitions to achieve unity behind an acceptable nominee even in the absence of much particular basis for it. The 1920 Republican nomination shows the system in action. In the months ahead of the convention, three candidates "waged nationwide campaigns" in which they sought to build delegate support.[6] Among several lesser candidates was Warren G. Harding, an undistinguished senator who, as was said at the time, "looked like a president." Harding ran a low-key campaign whose strategy was to offend no one and hope for deadlock at the convention. Then, according to his campaign manager, "about eleven minutes after two, Friday morning of the convention, when fifteen or twenty weary men are sitting around a table, someone will say: 'Who will we nominate?' At that decisive time, the friends of Harding will suggest him and we can well afford to abide by the result" (Whitcomb and Whitcomb 2002, 164).

Events unfolded as the campaign manager predicted. None of the main candidates could win a majority of delegates, the chair of the convention called for recess, and a smoke-filled room of party leaders decided early on Friday morning for Harding. But, as historian Richard Bain points out, the leaders did not simply pull a rabbit out of a hat. The key was that the three main campaigns had policy differences, antagonized one another, and were therefore unable to merge forces, which left each candidate stalled well short of the support needed for nomination. Only after each had tried and failed to start a bandwagon for himself did a bandwagon for Harding, its wheels greased by the orders of party leaders to their delegations, get rolling and deliver the nomination to Harding.

This is the kind of party convention, with its dramatic internal politics, that all political scientists love and that most have in mind when they say that parties were once strong but are now weak. We, too, agree that these older style parties were strong. They could deny nominations to major political figures, bestow nominations instead on nonentities like Harding, and still manage to get their preferred candidates elected as president. We also agree that national party conventions no longer function as they did in the Harding nomination. One indication of change is that, by 1952 if not perhaps earlier, political bosses were no longer able to control the selection of convention delegates in most states and were therefore presumably unable to control the delegations.[7] Another is the decline of conventions that required multiple ballots to choose a nominee. In a sharp contrast from the nineteenth and early twentieth centuries, most conventions in the period 1928 to 1968 chose their nominee on the first ballot, and only two conventions in that period took more than a few ballots. As Howard Reiter (1985) has argued, this suggests that party conventions had become rubber stamps for decisions that were actually made elsewhere.

Because Reiter is the leading exponent of the view that parties began to weaken well ahead of the McGovern-Fraser reforms, we shall look closely at this and other arguments he makes. Reiter notes, for example, that when party bosses held tight control of their state delegations, they kept state differences in ideology out of convention politics because they wanted the best candidate, regardless of ideology. "A leader in search of an electable ticket and patronage is likely to feel the ties of culture, ideology, and demography grow weaker in his chest as the scent of victory fills his nostrils" (1985, 84). Yet Reiter shows that, beginning about 1960, ideology became a major and regular feature of convention politics. This development, he says, is consistent with the view that party leaders were no longer strong enough to suppress state differences in ideology, which in turn signals a decline in the ability of conventions to identify and nominate the best candidate.

Like most political scientists, Reiter views the decline of party-centered politics as closely linked to the rise of candidate-centered politics. He suggests the Republican nomination of Wendell Willkie in 1940 as the "earliest harbinger" of this development. In the months ahead of the party convention, the Willkie campaign held public rallies, organized petition drives, and formed local support groups in an effort to generate support. Reiter cites the following description of the sources of this development: "From its inception the Willkie preconvention movement was spearheaded by two groups which ordinarily played neither an active nor an open role in presidential primary campaigns: The Willkie-for-President Clubs, organized by Oren Root among non-party amateurs . . . and the businessmen, financiers and publishers" (1985, 55).[8] Yet, as we would observe, the significance of this evidence depends greatly on what exactly one thinks a party is. If one subscribes to the theory of politician-centered parties, one can reasonably argue that almost anything that undermines the national party's principal institution—the leader-dominated party convention—must also undermine party strength. But if one subscribes to a group-centered notion of parties, no such conclusion follows. To take the most obvious case of difference of interpretation: Big business and finance had been leading members of the Republican Party since the late nineteenth century. If these groups became more openly active in behalf of their preferred candidates, it might signal a change in power or procedures within the Republican Party, but it would not necessarily indicate that the party itself was weaker. If, in a similar vein, ideological activists were becoming more independent of party bosses, it could as likely signal invigoration of the parties as enfeeblement. For as we have shown, ideological activists were a major source of positive energy in the foundation of the Jeffersonian Republicans, Jacksonian Democrats, and the antislavery Republicans. If, moreover, Ostrogorski's estimate is accurate that patronage-based organizations covered only about a third of the country even in their peak period, ideological activists were probably important in the stable phases of these parties as well. We thus suspect that the prominence of ideological politics in the modern parties is not such a radical break from past party practice as many political scientists tend to think.

Yet, setting aside for the moment the question of what exactly constitutes a real party, it is certainly true that the mechanisms of party decision-making changed over the course of the twentieth century. Reiter is also clearly correct in arguing that much of the change occurred ahead of the McGovern-Fraser Commission. In an effort to pinpoint the time of the change as precisely as possible, we have gathered data on the number of ballots needed for conventions to settle on a nominee. Following Reiter, we take the number of ballots as an indicator of the likelihood that the convention itself was the key decision-making institution.

The raw data on the number of ballots needed to choose a nominee is presented in figure 4.2. (The data are presented in log form to reduce the visual impact of outliers.) As can be seen, multiballot conventions were the norm through most of party history but became less common at the end of the prereform period. After about 1928, most nominees were chosen on the first ballot and no nominee required more than a few ballots to win.

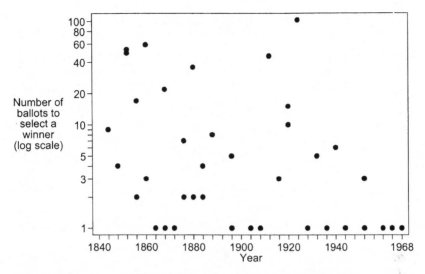

Fig. 4.2. Ballots for nomination, 1840–1968 (for open nominations only).

Figure 4.3 presents two statistical models of this time trend. The solid line on the graph is based on a model that forces change to occur over time in strictly linear fashion. The line shows a strong temporal decline. The dotted line in the figure is based on a model that allows both gradual trends over the whole period and the possibility of an abrupt shift in 1928. As can be seen, this model produces evidence of a sharp break around 1928, which is more consistent with the raw data in figure 4.2. Trial and error with alternative specifications continues to suggest a fairly sudden break in the data sometime between 1920 and 1932.[9]

If, then, the nature of national party decision-making changed around 1930 or so, what caused the change and what decision-making mechanism replaced the traditional one? We shall, for a moment, pass on the first question, but we believe we may have discovered the answer to the second. Or, rather, journalist Arthur T. Hadley discovered it. Writing in 1976, he coined the term "invisible primary" to describe the process by which presidential candidates struggled to build support in the period prior to the actual primary balloting. In seventeen of the last twenty nomination contests, he said, the candidate ahead at the time of the first primary contest was the candidate who went on to be nominated by the party convention. Thus, "the invisible primary is where the winning candidate is actually selected" (1976, xiii).

In Hadley's account, the invisible primary had been a force in presidential politics as early as the renomination of Franklin D. Roosevelt in 1936.

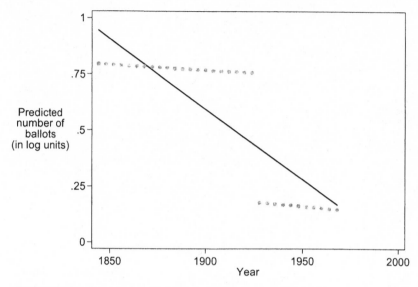

Fig. 4.3. Predicted number of convention ballots.

Broadly construed, however, it was important in the nineteenth century as well, which was before primaries even existed. For that period, it is usually called the preconvention campaign. There has never been a time in American politics when ambitious candidates and their managers failed to work to line up support well ahead of the national nominating conventions, and never a time when these efforts were lacking major importance. Lincoln's nomination in 1860 is a well-documented example. As Sean Wilentz describes his preconvention campaign:

> In 1859, Lincoln delivered political speeches all across the Midwestern states, and he followed that up in February 1860 with a major address at New York's Cooper Institute and a speaking tour of New England. . . . Lincoln's appearances won over a few Republicans completely, and established him as a viable alternative to [William] Seward [the front-runner]. . . . When Lincoln finished speaking [at Cooper], the Great Hall rang with exultation. The first newspaper reviews singled out his riveting speaking style as an unexpected sensation. ("No man," the *Tribune*'s rapturous reporter wrote, "ever made such an impression on his first appeal to a New York audience.") (2005, 760–61)

Lincoln, whose only national political office had been a single term in the House of Representatives, supplemented his two speaking tours with a regular flow of letters to political friends around the country.[10]

Efforts to build preconvention support in the nineteenth century were, however, limited by the communication and transportation technology of the time. A talented candidate could create a stir in the press and line up some support, but he could make personal contact with only a small fraction of the people whose support was needed for nomination. The rest needed to be won at the convention itself.

By the middle decades of the twentieth century, however, travel and communication had become much easier. Candidates and their surrogates began—rather suddenly, as it appears, in the 1920s—to take advantage of this development to build support and lock up the nomination ahead of the convention. Change was sharpest on the Democratic side. After a disastrous convention in 1924, in which the national convention required 103 ballots over a period of two weeks to reach a decision, the party chose Al Smith on the first ballot in 1928. The decision seems to have been worked out over the two years prior to the convention:

> All through 1927 [Smith's] allies were busy in the field. Boss Olvany made a number of trips to the South to confer with state leaders there, Mayor Frank Hague of Jersey City worked for the cause during a winter visit to Florida, and Morman Mack of Buffalo, Ed Flynn, and Thomas Chadbourne, a corporation lawyer long associated with Tammany, made pilgrimages to the provinces to seek alliances with the regional politicos.
>
> Soon favorable reports began pouring in from all quarters: Smith-for-President clubs sprang up in South Dakota, Montana, and Wisconsin; in Nebraska the maverick Republican Senator George Norris declared for Smith. . . . At about the same time mayor Rolph of San Francisco predicted that Smith would capture California, and a conference of leaders from twelve Mountain and Pacific Coast States hailed [Smith] as the party's logical choice for president.
>
> By the beginning of 1928 Smith clearly ranked as the nationwide favorite among regular Democrats (Josephson and Josephson 1969, 350–51).

A journalist observing this development referred to it as a bandwagon, noting "there is considerably more political nourishment in getting on the bandwagon than there is in standing by the curb and making faces at it as it passes by" (cited in Neal 1973, 9–10).

More, however, was involved in preconvention maneuvers than the choice of Smith as nominee. According to historian Donn C. Neal (1973), Smith's supporters worked out essential understandings among top leaders regarding the temperance issue, the party's two-thirds rule for nominations, and the site of the national convention. Hence, it seems fair to say that the nomination came about from a traditional pattern of bargaining and bandwagoning, except that both occurred out in the country rather than at the party convention. In consequence, the fractious Democratic Party enjoyed a harmonious convention, with a theme of "One big happy family."

Smith lost badly in the general election in 1928, but was interested in the nomination again in 1932, a much more propitious year in which to be the Democratic standard bearer. Yet he declined to make a preconvention effort to line up support. One reason, as he said, was that "in order to build up any great amount of support for me, somebody would have to go all over the country. It would take a lot of money—more than I could put up. And I don't want to ask my friends to do it" (Neal 2004, 116).

But Franklin Roosevelt, the Democratic governor of New York, did not lack for money. Independently wealthy, the bearer of a famous presidential name, and openly ambitious for high office for some twenty years, he dispatched his presidential campaign manager, Jim Farley, on a tour of eighteen western and midwestern states in the summer of 1931. Open campaigning for nomination must still have been taboo, because Farley did not candidly describe his tour as a campaign trip. Rather, he said that he was traveling to an Elks Convention on the West Coast and simply taking the opportunity to meet political friends along the way. As Farley has recounted: "In the next nineteen days, I was up to my ears in meetings, conferences, luncheons, dinners and 'gab fests' with Democratic leaders. Along the route, I talked to all sorts of people to learn everything I could about the public political temper. I was a sort of combination political drummer and listening post" (1948, 12). Two contemporary analysts of the 1932 campaign gave great credit to Farley as Roosevelt's organizing genius. Roy Peel and Thomas C. Donnelly wrote: "Early in the pre-convention period [Farley] had collected the names and addresses of practically every precinct committeeman in the United States, a task of no small magnitude when it is considered that there are more than 140,000 of them. These names were put on plates so that letters could be sent to all of them on short notice" (1935, 68).

If this sounds like a modern, technology-driven campaign, consider this account of the role played by the candidate in this party-centered system: "For years, Governor Roosevelt had been keeping in close touch with district leaders throughout the country. Farley also had sent them letters, talked to them on the telephone, and had even sent out phonograph records. . . . The phonograph records said, in part: 'My dear friend ____. I am a progressive. . . . I shall welcome any suggestions you may have to make and I hope to see you in person very soon'" (Peel and Donnelly 1935, 60). Farley claimed that his prenomination campaign, which pushed existing communication technology near its limit, was unprecedented. "Never in the history of politics, up to that time, was there anything like our letter writing and long distance telephone campaign," he wrote in his autobiography (1948, 9).

These efforts, plus entry into a handful of primaries, made Roosevelt the front-runner for the Democratic nomination at the start of 1932, but he was short of the two-thirds majority needed at that time for nomination. Roosevelt was able to win on the fourth ballot only through a deal with the Texas delegation to make its favorite son, John Nance Garner, his vice president—and, even so, he needed a bit more help from the Chicago machine to get over the top.

But if Roosevelt's energetic preconvention campaign did not quite achieve a first-ballot victory, it came close. It also inspired a new political principle in American politics, as captured by the acronym FRBC, or "For Roosevelt Before Chicago." FRBC stood for the fact that Roosevelt's first supporters in his campaign—those who supported him before the convention in Chicago—were also first in line when it came to patronage from and policy positions in the new administration.

This principle, plus continuing improvements in travel and communication, must then have raised a new question for party leaders and members: Why wait until the convention to decide whom to support? Why not decide before the convention and thereby attain the gratitude of the winner? This was, of course, close to the same question that party leaders had always asked before joining a bandwagon, and it carried the same obvious difficulty: Of the many candidates in the field, whose bandwagon should I join? But under the new conditions of travel and communication, the pressure to decide before the convention was stronger than in the past.

Whether for these reasons or some other, the trends in figures 4.2 and 4.3 make clear that, by the final decades of the prereform system, party conventions of the kind that nominated Warren G. Harding were dead. In their place was a "front-loaded" system in which major candidates were lining up the necessary majorities of delegates in the invisible primary and winning nomination on an early ballot in the convention, usually the first ballot. Commenting in 1968 on the decline of multiballot conventions, Richard Nixon said the reason was that "people know the game too well" (Chester, Hodgson, and Page 1969, 434) The last multiballot convention of the old system, that of the Democrats in 1952, went to three ballots only because Adlai Stevenson, the choice of the insiders, would not consent to become a candidate until the convention itself.

But was the new form of nomination process, with the invisible primary at its center, a party dominated process? Was a party that chose a nominee in the invisible primary a party at all? If, as V. O. Key maintained, "the national convention is the national party," the answers to these questions must be no. With its back-room bargaining sessions and public bandwagons, the convention was the means of uniting disparate interests behind a nominee. Anything that weakened the convention would therefore weaken or perhaps destroy the party.

We agree that a party must create unity among its disparate interests and that it needs some regularized means of doing so. But we see no reason to believe that the old-style, boss-dominated convention is the only feasible means of party decision-making. The old-style convention did work well at a time when travel and communication among party members was limited, and may have been the only institution that would have worked at that time. But under more modern conditions, another form of decision-making might handle nominations as well or perhaps better.

But what? Political science has no clear model of party decision-making except the boss-led and bandwagon-driven national party convention. In the next section, we provide an account of the process that we believe has replaced it.

Decision by Discussion

Based not on theory but on observation of how party members seem increasingly to have decided nominations since Smith's nomination in 1928, we characterize the decision-making process as follows: a long-running and widely inclusive series of interactions of party members with candidates and with each other. The interactions may occur at the convention itself, in which case they are usually called "deliberation," or on the home turf of party members, in which case they are described as the preconvention campaign or the invisible primary. Wherever they occur, these interactions amount to a huge intraparty discussion that permits decision-makers to meet and judge the candidates for themselves and to share their impressions with others. Media reports may also enter into the discussion, which runs for months, or perhaps even years, before the formal nomination. In most cases, a consensus emerges from the discussion on who should be the party nominee. The consensus is not always an overwhelming one, but it is sufficient to result in nomination.

The cast of characters in the consensus-seeking process has changed as American politics has changed. Both before and after the reforms of the early 1970s, participants appear to be a mix of officeholders, interest group leaders, and activists, but with interest groups and ideological activists a more important force in the latter period, as argued by Polsby (1983) and Shafer (1988). No precise information is available, but we suspect that a large fraction of the people who participate in presidential nominations, now as in the past, are committed to the policies of a particular ideology. Certainly, the surveys of convention delegates, which date from 1956, support this view, and there is no reason to believe that 1956 marked a sudden change (McClosky, Hoffman, and O'Hara 1960). Most participants in the nomination process are likely to be well-informed and potentially strategic players who do not need to be ordered by bosses or stampeded in a bandwagon in order to make a sensible decision for the party. Given a reasonably dense flow of relevant communication, one would expect them to be able to talk it out for themselves.

This is not to say that a party consists of members who care only about getting the best possible nominee for the party. As noted in our theoretical discussion in chapter 2, parties are not unitary actors. They consist of groups of intense policy demanders whose greatest loyalty is to their own group rather than to the party itself. Each will therefore maneuver to secure the nomination of candidates favorable to its own interests and values. Yet party members may be expected to understand the need to achieve party unity and should therefore compromise as necessary to achieve that goal.

A natural question is why party members would abandon the traditional party nominating convention as the mechanism for choosing nominees and begin—probably without conscious decision—to make decisions ahead of the convention. We offer the following conjecture. Whether on the floor of the convention or in a preconvention campaign, the choice of nominee is always to some degree a bandwagon process. Candidates and a handful of key backers launch the bandwagons, but a bandwagon succeeds according to whether enough party members see it as the most promising vehicle for achieving group goals. Party members, endlessly jostling with one another for advantage, naturally prefer to get on a potentially successful bandwagon as early as possible, both to increase their influence on which bandwagon succeeds and to increase gratitude from the winner.

As advances in communication made it possible to evaluate the likely success of bandwagons ahead of the convention, party members therefore had little reason to hesitate in committing to a candidate and more reason to make the jump. This front-loading of the decision process probably benefited some candidates over others—perhaps especially those, like New York governors Smith, Roosevelt, and Dewey, located at communication hubs—but if so, it would have similarly benefited the groups who supported those candidates.

The innermost workings of the nomination process are, as always, difficult to observe, but we get glimpses in journalistic and biographical accounts of the last conventions of the prereform period, the post–World War

II conventions. Owing to the skill of particular reporters, information about John F. Kennedy's nomination in 1960 and Richard Nixon's nomination in 1968 is unusually rich and detailed. Then, with the rise of electronic databases in the postreform period, the quality of information becomes notably better. This permits us to quantify and analyze an important part of the communication associated with nomination decisions. The rise of blogs in the most recent contests has made the invisible primary more open to observation than at any time in the past.

Not all of the communication that goes into party discussion in the invisible primary consists of words. Party professionals, campaign donors, fund-raisers, and activists who flock to one candidate and shun another are making statements that others in the process notice and take seriously. They are the modern equivalent of what used to be called party regulars— no-name people who regularly turn out to work for a party. Today's regulars are different in that they tend to be organized by candidate rather than by party structure. Yet their loyalty, as Jonathan Bernstein (2000) has shown for the important case of campaign professionals, is still primarily to a party rather than a candidate. For other regulars, such as a union or church member, loyalty could be to a group or ideology rather than a candidate. Regulars, in our use of the term, are lower-level campaign workers, including donors and fund-raisers, who routinely work for their party's candidates; following Beck (1997, 106), we assume that regulars are typically animated by a partisan, ideological, or group demand, but some may not be.[11]

Unfortunately, we have found no reliable means to study the dynamic process by which today's regulars sort themselves out between candidates in the fluid conditions of the invisible primary. As a result, we wind up mainly studying better known party actors, especially officeholders, whose actions are recorded in newspapers and other media. But when, as occasionally happens, we do get glimpses of the regulars, we shall highlight them. No-name regulars are, in our image of party politics, as important as other actors in the system, for this principal reason: Their contribution is essential to winning elections and they make their own choices about whom to support, including their nominal superiors in the party hierarchy. A shortcoming of this book is that we have little systematic evidence about no-name regulars. But the shortcoming would not be ameliorated by slighting their importance.

Throughout the period of the invisible primary, we find candidates traveling widely to build support and, as we show in later chapters, party insiders signing on to their candidacies or not. This process has less formal structure than the traditional convention, but it is not formless. It consists, above all, of dense communication among the key players over an extended period of time. We have noticed only one structural difference before and after the McGovern-Fraser reforms. In the prereform period, the leading candidate went from the invisible primary to the national party convention, where his supporters voted him the nomination. In the postreform period, the leading candidate goes from the invisible primary to the state-level primaries and caucuses, where his supporters help him win these public contests.

Is decision by discussion sufficiently regular to count as an institution? We think it is. Most serious candidates for president have known what they had to do: plunge into a nearly ceaseless round of travel and meetings in order to build support among the party's base of politically active people, from governors to campaign donors to activists. Since Franklin Roosevelt, the candidate able to mobilize the most preconvention support among these people has had a major advantage in seeking the nomination and, as our review of cases since World War II will show, has usually won it.

Political scientists and journalists have also recognized that the decision-making process we describe is a regular one. The term "preconvention campaign" can be found in scholarly studies as early as the 1950s, and in 1976 journalist Arthur Hadley gave it a flashier name, the invisible primary. Until recently, few except Hadley have attached great importance to the process, emphasizing instead the traditional party convention and its decline, but most have recognized that a regular process existed. Since the nominations of 2000, all journalists have been keenly aware of the invisible primary and cover it in considerable detail, often referring to it by this name.

A party coalition that can, by any regular means, unify itself behind a candidate with a decent chance to win the fall election has some claim to being a strong party. The form of the interactions is less important than the result—a nominee enjoying broad support within the party and capable of running well in the fall.

But one additional criterion is obviously important in evaluating party strength: whether the party itself retains control of the nomination process in the face of increasingly energetic efforts by the candidates themselves. If the rise of the preconvention campaign and invisible primary means that candidates are able to overpower party insiders—building personal organizations and popular followings that force insiders to nominate them—one would have to conclude that parties are weak. This would be so even if the candidates who win nomination are actually quite good nominees for their party. But if, on the other hand, members of the party coalition retain the upper hand in the nomination process, one should conclude that parties are strong.

The idea that a party is strong if it can unify itself around a strong candidate of its own choosing is different from what scholars usually have in mind when they ask if parties are strong, which is whether party leaders can engineer a choice of nominee through a party convention. Our criteria nonetheless derive from a plausible notion of what a party is and what it means for a party to be strong. Chapter 5 will examine whether our criteria have been met in the last nominations of the prereform system. Chapters 6 and 7 then turn to nominations in the postreform system. Chapter 10 provides further evidence from the 2008 contests involving John McCain, Barack Obama, and Hillary Clinton. These chapters provide what is, in effect, case study evidence relating to our argument.

What the reader will immediately grasp from the case evidence is that, neither now nor in the past, have parties been coolly rational, smoothly functioning decision-making bodies. Their disparate actors are always more or less distrustful of one another, reluctant to compromise any more or sooner than necessary, unsure of what voters will accept, and constrained to choose from a limited field of candidates. We therefore acknowledge at the outset that it will be difficult to tell, from the case study evidence alone, whether our criteria of party strength have been met. The strongest evidence for that argument will continue to be found in the aggregate pattern presented in figure 4.1—a pattern that holds separately within each party, both before and after the McGovern-Fraser reforms, and in at least two other countries.[12] The case studies augment this evidence by putting flesh-and-blood detail on what might otherwise seem a systematic but unpersuasive statistical claim.

5

Last Hurrahs of the Old System

Some scholars who wrote about political parties in the 1950s and 1960s saw them as weaker than they had been in past decades. One reason was the increasing importance of preconvention campaigns in presidential nominations, including the rise of polls, mass media influence, and candidate-centered campaigns. Another was the invasion of both parties by a supposedly new kind of political actor, the "amateur" activist. Together, these developments were said to have robbed party leaders of control over presidential nominations and perhaps pushed them toward extinction.

We take a markedly different view. The two parties, as we argue in this chapter, kept candidates, pollsters, journalists—the so-called forces of mass democracy—at bay throughout the final years of the old system. They faced strong challenges, but they responded effectively. We agree that parties were much influenced by their activists, but the effect was to energize rather than to weaken them. Liberal activists defeated the defenders of southern racism inside the Democratic Party, thereby making it into the vehicle of racial minorities and soon other minorities as well. Conservative activists defeated the "me-too" moderate Republicans who had been controlling postwar presidential nominations in the party, pushing it to become the anti-big-government, antitax

107

vehicle of economic conservatism that it is today. As these changes were consolidated within each party, they remade not just party competition, but American society itself. Both of the new alignments were, as we argue, due more to intense policy demanders within the party coalitions than to electoral pressure.

The plan of this chapter is as follows. First, we sketch the argument that the forces of mass democracy undermined the parties' control of presidential nominations by the middle decades of the twentieth century. We then similarly sketch the argument that "amateur" activists and ideologues invaded and weakened parties at roughly the same time. Then, in the main part of the chapter, we examine evidence on how parties functioned in this period. This evidence comes in two parts. The first is a look at internal party organization at the state level; this section is, we confess, a bit dry and perhaps interesting mainly to professional students of politics. It can be skipped without loss of continuity in our argument. The second and more important body of evidence comes next. It is called "Under the Hood in the Old System" and consists of brief but we hope incisive case studies of the major nomination battles in the period 1948 to 1968. We give particular attention to the 1948 and 1964 party conventions, which are the two contests that, as we argue, did so much to vitalize the parties in the decades that followed. The purpose of these sketches is to augment our theoretical account of how parties behave, with particular emphasis on evidence of party autonomy and strength.

Change in the Postwar Parties

The Rise of Mass Politics
In 1957, political scientist William Carleton wrote an article entitled "The Revolution in the Presidential Nominating Convention." Carleton argued that, beginning in 1928, the forces of "mass democracy" had wrought a "major transformation" in the nominating system:

> Increasingly a national nominating convention is merely choosing its nominee from among the popular national favorites; increasingly it is being forced to pick *the* national favorite. The days of the favorite son, the dark horse, the stalking horse, the smoke-filled conference room, the senatorial and congressional cabal, and the decisive trading of votes by local bigwigs are numbered, if indeed they are not already finished. "Insiders" and members of the political "club" are being cut down to size and forced to accept the leadership of those who have made successful national pre-convention campaigns and those who have become national "names" and mass celebrities. (224)

As discussed in the last chapter, the rise in first-ballot victories after 1928 did signal major change in the party nominations. Preconvention campaigns became more important and many aspects of the traditional nominating convention—smoke-filled rooms, boss control, dark-horse nominees—suffered a corresponding loss of importance. Especially in light of Howard Reiter's subsequent empirical work, Carleton's early observation of these developments seems correct. But Carleton took a big additional step when he asserted that party insiders were being "cut down to size" and "forced to accept" the candidates who emerged from the preconvention campaign, or what Hadley (1976) later called the invisible primary.

If Carleton were correct in these additional assertions, one could only conclude that parties had become weaker. Indeed, one might wonder whether anything worthy of the name party still existed. This would be true even if the eventual nominees were in other ways ideal party candidates, that is, ones who could unite the party and run strong campaigns in the fall election. Thus, Carleton's commentary emphasized the importance of autonomy as a criterion of party strength: To be considered strong, a party coalition must be able to say No as well as Yes to candidates who seek nomination. If the party gets a candidate it later likes in spite of, rather than because of, its initial preferences, the party is not strong but lucky. We shall investigate party autonomy in the main empirical sections of this chapter.

The Coming of the Amateurs

Political scientist James Q. Wilson opened his highly influential book *The Amateur Democrat* with the following statement: "Since the Second World War a new kind of politician has appeared in large numbers in several of the biggest American cities. Although they are nowhere in complete control of their parties, these new politicians . . . intend to alter fundamentally the character of the American party system" (1966, 1). The distinguishing feature of the new amateur politicians is not, says Wilson, that they are inept or dilettantish; many, he writes, "have a highly sophisticated understanding of practical politics and have proved their skills in the only way that matters—by winning at the polls" (2–3). The distinctive feature of the amateurs, rather, is their concern about issues, principles, and an abstract idea of the public good. Older style "professional" politicians, says Wilson, were obsessed by winning and losing for its own sake and would alter their strategies as necessary to win. The new amateurs, in contrast, are obsessed by winning *for their cause*. Winning has no appeal to them unless it is a victory for the correct principles and issues.

The Amateur Democrat was published in 1962 and focused on the Democratic Party. But in the 1966 edition, Wilson made clear that his notion of amateurism applied with equal force to a new breed of Republican politicians. "If I had foreseen the Goldwater nomination (who did?), this book would have been about the amateur Republican and would have said essentially the same things" (ix).

Wilson's book is important for the generality of its claims, but mainly analyzes urban rather than presidential politics. However, the *Presidential Elections* textbooks of Polsby and Wildavsky take up his major theme and apply it to their subject. Thus they note in their 1968 edition that there has been "increased amateur participation in politics" and comment: "By slow increments, the image of politicians in this country as cynical manipulators devoid of interest in public policy is giving way to a more complicated description in which practicality and patronage are mixed with idealism and issue orientation" (191). Following Wilson's notion of amateurs and professionals, Polsby and Wildavsky discuss the role of purists and pragmatists in presidential nominations. The former are party members who care intensely about issues and principles and do not want to compromise; the latter are individuals who care above all about nominating candidates who can win. Polsby and Wildavsky regret the rising influence of purists because, as they argue, the purists want only to please themselves and thereby undermine the ability of the parties to offer competitive choices to voters, thereby weakening parties. Wilson takes a similar position, arguing that democracy works best when parties are led by self-interested leaders who care more about winning office by pleasing voters than about taking morally correct positions on issues.

In a separate essay, Wildavsky went further, suggesting that the rise of Goldwater purists may, by their refusal to engage in the normal give-and-take of politics, so weaken the Republican Party as to bring about the end of two-party competition in the United States. He concluded by observing, "There appears to be little difference in style between the Goldwater purists and the leftists who constantly complain about hypocrisy in public life and how politicians sell out the people. Could it be that the United States is producing large numbers of half-educated people with college degrees who have learned that participation (passion and commitment) is good but do not understand (or cannot stand) the normal practices of democratic politics? If this is true . . . the Goldwater phenomenon, which once seemed so strange, may become a persistent feature of the American political scene" (1965, 413).

Although these authors see the coming of the amateurs as a change, we are not so sure. The Democratic clubs Wilson examined were certainly new, but the phenomenon of intensely policy-motivated individuals seeking influence within the parties was not. Indeed, Wilson observes that the amateurs reflect a "Yankee ethos" that can be found in the nineteenth century. He also notes that "throughout this century, there has always been a 'reform mentality' in American politics and in this broad sense the amateur Democrats have their forebears in the Progressive and municipal reform efforts of fifty years ago" (1966, 27–28). We suspect that, with a little investigation, a similar pedigree could be discovered for the Goldwater amateurs, perhaps among the William Howard Taft stalwarts of 1912 and certainly among the Theodore Roosevelt progressives who opposed them. The Democratic clubs of the 1790s, the Jefferson-Jackson ideologues of the 1820s, and the abolitionists of the 1840s and 50s may also be seen as precedents for the amateur activism of the post–World War II period. Amateur activists, we suspect, have been a potent force in American parties throughout U.S. history.

One reason political scientists seem to be discovering postwar activists as a new phenomenon may be that, over the course of their careers in politics, fresh-faced amateurs become battle-tested professionals. If Robert Michels's (1915) "Iron Law of Oligarchy" is right, then the more idealistic policy demanders may over time become more invested in the party itself. What Michels's law does not address is that the party may be continually infused with new, less professional activists, who pressure the leadership on policy and may also pressure it on intraparty procedure. As the relative balance of fresh faces to veterans ebbs and flows, one observes what appears to be new conflict within the party, even if that conflict reflects a recurring tension in any organization.

Still, it remains possible that this tension in the postwar period weakened the parties, undercutting control by pragmatists and damaging the ability of parties to compete for the presidency. We investigate this matter below.

Summary

The challenge raised by Carleton is whether the national parties had sufficient internal strength to resist candidate-centered organizations using the media and popular support to bully their way to nomination. The challenge raised by Wilson, Polsby, and Wildavsky is whether the parties were being overrun by amateurs and were therefore incapable of behaving as theory suggests a party should behave.

In the remainder of this chapter, we seek to answer these questions with two quite different kinds of evidence. First, we shall use an underutilized resource—a survey of how each of the nation's state parties selected delegates to their 1952 party conventions—to learn what we can about local party strength and the kinds of actors who dominated the nomination process. Second, we shall review each of the major nomination contests in the mid-century period—from Dewey and Truman in 1948 to Nixon and Humphrey in 1968—to address the same concerns at the national level, namely, the balance of power among party insiders, candidates, and so-called amateurs.

The APSA Project on the 1952 Elections

This six-page section may be skipped without loss of continuity by readers who are uninterested in the matter of state and local party organization in the pre-reform party system.

The national political parties, wrote V. O. Key in 1965, were a coalition of "many state and local points of power, each with its own local following and each comparatively independent of external control." In citing this passage in chapter 2, we noted that the nature of these "points of power" was not clear. David Mayhew's (1986) survey of party organization in that period produced a mainly negative conclusion about them: With a few exceptions, local parties did *not* include Traditional Party Organizations having strong leaders and firm control over nominations for local office.

The information necessary to say what local organization *did* consist of is not generally available. In 1952, however, the American Political Science Association sponsored a survey of how each state party organization in the country selected delegates to that year's party conventions.[1] Given our interest in this question, the study seemed worth mining. We therefore worked carefully through its five volumes and sixteen hundred pages with the purpose of classifying each state party in terms of its openness to external influence in the selection of delegates to the national conventions. Our question, in other words, was whether party insiders dominated the choice of convention delegates and hence the choice of nominee for president. Nonparty influence might come from voters, candidate organizations, top elected officials, the media, amateurs, or elsewhere.

Like everyone else who has looked closely at party politics in this period, we were struck by its diversity. Rules and procedures varied hugely, formally and informally. Actual practice was determined as much by local custom as by official rules and state law. The most common procedure of delegate selection began with caucus meetings at the precinct level that were typically attended only by party workers, perhaps only five or ten.[2] Ordinary voters might be able to attend, but in the normal absence of publicity, few would. The precinct meetings would send delegates to a congressional district convention, a state convention, or both, and these conventions would choose the delegates to the national party conventions. Sometimes the conventions would merely ratify the choices of party leaders, but in other cases delegates would debate and make the key political decisions themselves.

Consider Utah. Both parties used a state convention to select delegates to the national party convention. The Republicans also used congressional district conventions, held at the same place and time as the state convention. But top leaders appeared to dominate both forums. According to the volume, the Utah GOP delegation was "hand-picked by a closely-knit group whose campaign activities began early and reached throughout the state" (David, Moos, and Goldman 1954, 5:97). All of the major party leaders were for Taft, and they managed to get their way by setting the process in motion "before any functioning Eisenhower organization in the state was created" (86).

The Utah Democrats were more open, so that "it has been relatively easy for any active and well-known Democrat to secure a place on the delegation" to the national party convention (92). In 1952, the Democrats sent an uncommitted slate, as had been its custom. Kefauver was the keynote speaker at the state convention, but "there was no clearly defined contest in the selection of the delegation" (93). We should note, however, that anti-Kefauver Democrats in 1952 had no candidate until Adlai Stevenson agreed at the national convention itself to enter the race. Hence, the lack of a clearly defined contest in Utah may have been a device for blocking Kefauver.

Other systems were more open than either party in Utah. The Texas Republicans, described below, and the Louisiana GOP both had contentious conflicts over delegates, with an insurgent group effectively challenging the party leaders. Both states sent two delegations to Chicago, and in both cases the insurgent slate was seated.

Primary elections, where they existed, were likewise highly variable. In Oregon, for instance, voters had a choice of delegates who were pledged to a candidate, and state law required each delegate to "use his best efforts to bring about the nomination of those persons for President and Vice President of the United States who receive the most votes at the coming primary election" (5:190). In Oregon, therefore, voters called the shots in delegate selection. In other states, however, delegates were allowed to run "unpledged." If, as often happened, major party candidates avoided the state's primary, the voters had little choice but to elect the unpledged delegates. In California, rules forbade unpledged slates, but the Republican primary got around the rule by running a favorite son candidate—typically a popular senator or governor—who then controlled his own delegates. In 1952, Taft and Eisenhower followed the norm of not challenging favorite son Governor Earl Warren, who was then able to control a slate of delegates at the convention. Still other states had only "beauty contest" preference primaries, meaning voter preferences had no direct impact on delegate selection. In some states, party leaders would by custom select delegates in accordance with voter wishes despite the lack of a requirement to do so; in other states, party leaders did whatever they wanted.

Figure 5.1 presents a summary of our judgments on the openness of each delegate-selection process to external influence, as the process functioned in 1952. The appendix to this chapter presents the 104 individual coding judgments on which the summary codes are based. The interested reader may compare these judgments to the original reports in David, Moos, and Goldman (1954).

The top two categories of figure 5.1 designate delegate-selection procedures that were substantially like those in place today. In primary states, voters chose among delegates pledged to support the candidate in whose name they ran. In the second set of state parties, the delegate-selection process was open to rank-and-file partisans, so that a well-organized group of candidate enthusiasts could fight it out with the party leadership and perhaps win. (Some of these states also had beauty contest primaries.) In the Louisiana Republican Party, for instance, an Eisenhower faction that began as a bipartisan group overpowered the existing pro-Taft organization. The party sent two delegations to Chicago, and the newer faction was seated. The bottom categories of figure 5.1 are the most closed systems.

The next two categories are state parties that provided some official avenues for participation, but in practice, they were closed off or left unused by voters. Included here is the Connecticut Republican Party, where the delegates were "formally chosen at the state party convention. In practice, however, the machinery for selecting the delegates to the national convention is an undifferentiated part of the machinery which periodically makes decisions on party leadership" (2:192).

The next to last category is parties that were technically as open as the top groups, but in practice not. All fourteen parties had some sort of primary, but in practice, it was not meaningful. This could be because, as in New York, voters were given no choice in election of delegates to party conventions; as the volume comments, "rarely does the voter find more than one name listed for each of these positions, for rarely is the organization's slate challenged." Or it could be, as in Pennsylvania, that party insiders traditionally honored the preferences voters expressed in the primary, or intended to, but candidates, perhaps in deference to local leaders, did not often compete in it. In 1952, Eisenhower and Stassen entered the Republican preference primary, but Taft did not; on the Democratic side, no major candidate entered, not even Kefauver, who entered most primaries.

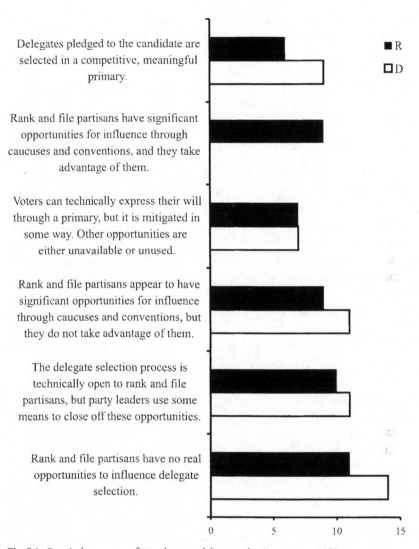

Fig. 5.1. Practical openness of state-by-state delegate-selection process, 1952.

We suspect that some of these technically open but practically closed systems could have been dominated by candidates. If candidates had the resources and incentives they now have, they might have mobilized supporters to seize control of delegate selection in caucus elections. But they didn't, and under the conditions of 1952, this left party insiders dominant.

The twenty-five state parties at the very bottom provided no opportunities for rank-and-file voters to influence the delegation on behalf of their preferred candidate. Included in this category are fifteen state parties in which the delegates were chosen directly by party officials who were themselves elected in 1950, which was well before candidates even declared interest in the presidential nomination.

Altogether, then, rank-and-file party members—and the candidates who might have appealed to voters—exercised predominant influence in about 20 percent of all party organizations. In the other 80 percent, voter influence was, in actual practice in 1952, more or less limited, and often very limited. In these cases, party insiders were apparently free to select national convention delegates and to make commitments to candidates on the basis of whatever considerations they wished.

For the large fraction of cases in which party insiders prevailed, our next question is: Who were these insiders and what motivated them? In particular, were they professional politicians or group members whose main goal was to coordinate on a candidate who could unify the party and win the fall election? Or were they more like Wildavsky's "purists" or Wilson's "amateurs"—that is, players who had no real interest in cooperating as part of a party coalition?

Our evidence relating to these questions is limited but not wholly lacking. One fairly clear point is that the dominant players were not, for the most part, stereotypical party bosses. As the authors summarize their own findings, "very few of the state political conventions of 1952 were within the grip of a recognized state political boss." Party leaders did exercise control, sometimes in the person of the governors, who "were occasionally in a position to exercise some of the powers of a political boss," but who did not continue their influence beyond their term. More often, however, party influence was widely dispersed across many actors who united in a coalition—exactly as we would describe a party: "Political oligarchies, as distinguished from one-man boss rule, were obviously present in many areas, but not as universally as may often be thought. Or, to put the point in a different way, the political oligarchy is so loosely knit in many state parties that there is a question whether it deserves the name. The federated or coalition character of such oligarchies was apparent in many states. . . . In both major parties, political power appeared to be more widely dispersed than is usually assumed to be the case" (1:170–71).

Another element largely missing from the state-by-state accounts is patronage. Without doubt, patronage was a factor in some party organizations in this period and hence a factor in selection of delegates to the national conventions as well. But there is no indication that it was a predominant influence. In most states, most party workers and even party leaders seem to have been non-office-holding "volunteers," a phrase Shafer uses to describe about half of the Democratic Party organizations in the 1960s (Shafer 1983, 281–83).

The study provides some systematic evidence about the demographics of convention delegates, but our concern is with the people who chose the convention delegates. In many accounts, the study describes the individuals who played leading roles or seemed especially influential in this process. Based on a careful reading of these accounts, we offer the following rough generalizations:

- **Professional officeholders versus activists:** Many of the political actors in 1952 seemed to make their living in politics, as high-level officeholders. Still more, however, clearly made a living in some other field, entering politics as an avocation. Lawyers, local businessmen, and union activists were more numerous than high officeholders.

- **Party regulars versus outsiders:** If most political activists were volunteers who did not make their living in politics, they were still regulars in the party. Party actors tended to have a long history of involvement. Many delegates are described as having attended several past conventions, and probably a majority held some party office at some level. Most of the actors had histories of intraparty conflicts that went back several election cycles. In thirteen of the state parties, the authors mentioned that these local political conflicts completely overshadowed the presidential nomination contests. And even where presidential politics did dominate, the players were part of a continuing political party that had its own history.

  And yet, in many of the states, an outsider or reform group challenged the old guard or regulars. In many cases, both factions were long-standing and "regular" in some way, but one group was often identified as challenging the status quo. These challenges may reflect invasion by purists, amateurs, or intense policy demanders. What is notable about these actors is that they fought within the framework of the party. Several states sent contested delegations, and the "regular" delegation was not always the one seated in Chicago. When the insurgents won, they may have remained active in the party as regulars. Some systems, as we have noted, were more open to them than others.

- **Policy versus party office:** Factional disputes were often about issues, and policy seemed behind most decisions to back one presidential candidate over another. The old guard versus outsiders sometimes seemed to be code for conservative versus liberal policies. In Georgia and Mississippi, the state Republican parties had a "lily white" faction opposed by a more

racially diverse one (called "black and tans" in Mississippi). The Virginia
Democrats were strongly in favor of southern favorite son Richard Russell,
up until the night before the state convention, when he proposed tinkering
with the Taft-Hartley Act. "Russell badges were discarded, friendly mention
of Russell was deleted from the script of the keynote speech, and the move
to endorse him quickly evaporated" (David, Moos, and Goldman 1954,
3:19). The intense conflict between those who favored Eisenhower and
those for Taft clearly had philosophical underpinnings in several instances.

Overall, then, we believe we can characterize the set of key actors in nomination politics in 1952 as exhibiting a great deal of variation, but in the end,
more volunteer than careerist, more regular than insurgent, and at least as
policy-oriented as office-oriented.

Presidential Parties at Midcentury: An Assessment

Our reading of the evidence from the APSA survey is that most party organizations were sufficiently insulated from popular pressures that the selection of delegates to the party conventions—and hence the choice of party
nominee—was dominated by insiders. Less confidently, we also conclude
that the modal party actor was a volunteer, a regular, and likely to be as
concerned about policy as about winning office. We wish the evidence for
these conclusions were more systematic. But in the absence of better evidence, we believe it is worth reporting.

This assessment firmly contradicts Carleton's assertions concerning the
forces of democracy and candidate-centered politics. Perhaps his claims
accurately capture changes from an earlier period in which parties were
even more autonomous from popular pressure, but it appears to us that
party autonomy was alive and well in 1952. Our assessment is, however,
consistent with the notion that, even in 1952, unbossed amateurs and purists were an important force in the party system. Thus, the real threat to
party strength in the 1950s, if there was one, came from the penetration of
parties by amateurs and purists who might have undermined their capacity
to function as real parties. We assess that possibility in the next section.

Under the Hood in the Old System

The sweating, belching, peanut-munching delegates described by H. L.
Mencken at the 1932 Democractic convention were fast disappearing by
midcentury. So, as we shall see in the vignettes ahead, was slavish obedi-
ence to state bosses. Convention bandwagons were also all but gone, as all
nominations were made on an early ballot, usually the first.

In this section, we ask whether parties lost power as well as color in this period. Our conclusion is that the delegates who assembled at national conventions in the postwar decades remained fully in control of their party's business. We also find that, except in the realigning conventions of 1948 and 1964, the presence of large numbers of amateurs within the parties did not prevent them from coordinating on broadly acceptable nominees.

The Last Democratic Contests

The convention that nominated Harry Truman in 1948 marks a basic turning point in Democratic Party history: For the first time, a northern majority overrode southern opposition to pass a platform that included strong and specific civil rights measures: a federal antilynching law, abolition of the poll tax, a ban on segregation in interstate commerce, desegregation of the armed services, a civil rights division in the Justice Department. When this civil rights plank won by a narrow majority, three southern delegations walked out of the convention amid boos and hisses. The party's action on civil rights was not irreversible—indeed, the intent of the southern bolt was to force a reversal—but the new position never was fully reversed, and by the early 1960s, the Democratic Party, long the bastion of southern racism, had become the party of racial liberalism. In the next few pages, we suggest why this change occurred.

Many factors contributed to the Democratic Party's emergence as the party of racial liberalism, but perhaps the most important was the migration of African Americans from southern to northern states: Each migrant decreased the electoral clout of the South and increased electoral pressure for civil rights in the North.[3]

One can imagine two distinct routes by which pressure for civil rights might have expressed itself in the Democratic Party: first, a politician-centered route in which African American voters directly pressured northern officeholders of both parties to adopt more liberal positions on civil rights; and second, a party-centered route in which new groups of intense policy demanders gained clout within the party, defeated racial conservatives, and began nominating candidates who were more favorable to civil rights. Evidence shows that both routes were important, with the party route probably more so.

As Truman's political advisors plotted his reelection strategy in 1948, they were keenly aware of the electoral clout of northern black voters. African American voters had voted overwhelmingly Democratic in recent elections to voice their approval of Roosevelt's New Deal, but few observers believed they were permanently attached to the Democratic Party. Thomas Dewey, the expected Republican candidate, was making vigorous efforts to woo African Americans, and Henry Wallace was putting together a left-liberal third-party movement that emphasized civil rights. In a famous strategy memo to Truman, Special Counsel Clark Clifford wrote in November 1947, "Unless there are new and real efforts (as distinguished from mere political gestures which are today thoroughly understood by Negro leaders), the Negro bloc . . . will go Republican." White southern voters would disapprove of any policy initiatives on civil rights, but, as Clifford wrote, "As always, the South can be considered safely Democratic, and in formulating national policy, it can be safely ignored" (cited in Sitkoff 1971, 597).

This sort of argument fits the logic of the politician-centered theory of party and does not fit our party-centered logic at all. Truman replaced Wallace as the Democratic nominee for vice president in 1944 because party leaders feared that Roosevelt would die soon and viewed Wallace as unacceptably radical. Truman, a senator from the border state of Missouri, was taken by all major factions, including the South, as an acceptable compromise of the party's liberal and conservative strains (Ferrell 1994). If Truman were to follow Clifford's advice, it would be a violation of the bargain that had brought him to the presidency. Yet Truman did follow Clifford's advice—or started to. In a special message to Congress in February 1948, he called for the passage of laws including precisely those measures that later became part of the 1948 party platform—an antilynching law, an antidiscrimination law, among other provisions. The reaction of civil rights leaders to the message was generally positive, but the white South went ballistic. Its leaders claimed that Truman's message was "a stab in the back" to the South and that his proposal would force white southerners "to crawl on their bellies through the dirt to kiss the feet of minorities." A prominent senator accused Truman of trying to bring about the "mongrelization" of the South (Sitkoff 1971, 601). In a series of regional meetings, southern leaders threatened to bolt the party unless Truman backed down.

Truman's response was to equivocate. He did not go along with the southern demand to repudiate his civil rights message, but he declined to propose a concrete legislative package to implement it. At the convention, Truman's lieutenants argued for a vaguely worded civil rights plank that suggested constitutional limitations on the power of Congress to enact civil rights legislation over objections of "states' rights."

What these events show is that candidate-centered pressures did act on Truman, but that he either sought to diffuse them with rhetorical postures or calculated that his best electoral response was to straddle. Meanwhile, decisive pressure for civil rights was building from another direction.

The death of Roosevelt and the end of the U.S. alliance with the Soviet Union in World War II left American liberalism in disarray. To regain a sense of common direction, a group of liberal anticommunists, including many labor leaders but few Democratic Party leaders, formed the Americans for Democratic Action (ADA) in early 1947. Among the first questions for the ADA was its relationship to the Democratic Party. "The consensus of opinion," Arthur Schlesinger, Jr., told the group, "seems to be that the Democratic Party presents the most likely medium for the progressives in this country." Franklin Roosevelt, Jr., added that "the surest way to make the Democratic Party a liberal party is to go into the Democratic Party" (Gillon 1987, 19). Others felt the ADA should remain aloof from partisan politics, but when the Democratic Party convention convened in 1948, 120 of the 1,200 delegates were card-carrying members of the ADA, and these ADA members caucused as a group in deciding to challenge Truman's civil rights plank as a sell-out to the South.

The ADA's final decision revealed an interesting division within the group. Hubert Humphrey, a rising liberal star who was running for the Senate in Minnesota, resisted making a civil rights challenge, fearing that a southern walkout, as was expected, would sink Truman. But under pressure from the ADA rank-and-file, Humphrey finally acquiesced at about 5 a.m. on the morning before the session to adopt the party platform. He went on to deliver one of the most famous lines in American party history, "The time has arrived in America for the Democratic Party to get out of the shadow of states rights and walk forthrightly into the sunshine of human rights" (cited in Gillon 1987, 49). But as an ambitious officeholder, he worried whether it was the right political move and would probably not have taken so bold a stand except for pressure from within the ADA.

Truman's lieutenants at the convention fought hard against the ADA plank, with the president writing in his diary that it was "a crackpot amendment" by those who wanted the South to bolt the party. He may have been right about the second point, but, even in retrospect, it is not clear what the short-term electoral implications were. Truman clearly feared a tough civil rights plank risked defeating him, but ADA members, including big-city leaders, thought it would bolster party standing in the North. Both may have been right. Certainly one reason that big labor and big-city Democratic leaders supported the ADA challenge was their belief that it would strengthen their hand with African American voters.

Given that the ADA challenge to Truman attracted much media attention—with Humphrey, not yet bald, playing the role of media darling—the episode might also be cited as an example in which "mass politics" resulted in party insiders being "cut down to size." But even if, as a result of all this, the Democratic Party ran more weakly in 1948, the ADA challenge to Truman on civil rights seems better accounted for as a straightforward case in which intense policy demanders pursued their goals through party politics. The media certainly covered the civil rights story, but we see no evidence that they created it.

We also believe that, even though electoral pressure was present, the events of 1948 are better explained as group-driven change than politician-driven or electorally driven change. Truman, responding to electoral pressure, first tried to lead on civil rights and then to straddle. In response to the straddling, the ADA, motivated primarily by its sense of moral right, pressed the issue to the conclusion that led to permanent change in the party. On this account, the electoral clout of African Americans mattered mainly as a factor in persuading big-city bosses and perhaps labor leaders to support the ADA challenge.

The point about *permanent* party change is important. The 1948 convention fight changed the terms of the coalitional pact within the Democratic Party. It showed, in particular, that no candidate could gain nomination for president without being acceptable to northern liberals on civil rights. Among the ambitious politicians to learn that lesson was Lyndon B. Johnson of Texas. He became Senate majority leader in 1955 and immediately began planning his ascent to the presidency. As part of that effort, he engineered passage of the Civil Rights Act of 1957, the first such measure since Reconstruction. Two journalists give this account of Johnson's motives:

> What neither the press nor most of his fellow legislators . . . realized was how indispensable to Johnson's national political aspirations it was to get credit for passage of the civil rights bill, and how fatal it would be for him to oppose it. If [Johnson] could transform the Eisenhower bill into the Johnson bill, he would once and for all emancipate himself from the Confederate yoke that had destroyed [Georgia Senator] Richard Russell's presidential ambitions. It would move him into the mainstream of the Democratic Party. . . . Unless he plunged into that mainstream, Johnson could not even hope for the presidential nomination in 1960—or ever. (Evans and Novak 1966, 137)

Biographer Robert A. Caro adds that Johnson persuaded southern Senators to refrain from their usual filibusters of civil rights legislation in order to boost Johnson's prestige and thereby his chances of nomination over those of Humphrey, whom southerners feared would become president if Johnson did not (Caro 2003). Thus did nominating politics drive policy-making in government. And thus did one of the party's most ambitious politicians follow his party's intense policy demanders, in this case to a position of moderation rather than extremism on the race issue.

The 1952 nomination brought the same forces into battle, with "mass politics" this time a major theme. As noted earlier, Estes Kefauver, the southern Senator who favored civil rights for blacks and opposed corruption in northern political machines, contested every presidential primary and won twelve of fifteen, losing only to "favorite sons." (A favorite son is a local politician who attempts to gain the support of his state's convention delegates, often for the purpose of bargaining at the convention.) As a result, Kefauver entered the convention with 360 of the 615 votes needed to be nominated. Stevenson, who had entered no primaries and made no other preconvention campaign, began the convention with 273 votes but went on to be nominated on the third ballot. Clearly, his nomination was no triumph for mass politics.

As described earlier in a passage from Polsby and Wildavsky, the form of decision-making on this nomination was close to what it had been in the previous century: a bargain among party leaders to break a deadlock. The ADA would have preferred Kefauver and the South would have preferred Georgia Senator Richard Russell, but Stevenson, a moderate with a flair for lofty rhetoric, was acceptable to both factions and was therefore nominated despite his disinclination to be a candidate. This outcome suggests that the Democratic Party had returned to politics as usual within the new electoral pact. Groups within the party continued to disagree, but they nonetheless managed to coordinate on a candidate acceptable to all of them. The outcome also shows that the party was willing and able to say no to a popular candidate that important factions distrusted.

Despite this, Carleton counts Kefauver as a case for the importance of mass politics. What he stresses is that Kefauver did manage to win the Democratic vice presidential nomination in 1956. But this seems a weak claim. 1956 was a year in which the popular Republican incumbent, Dwight Eisenhower, was widely expected to coast to reelection and in fact did so. No doubt Kefauver's vice presidential nomination was due to his success in the primaries, but his failure to get a presidential nomination after winning the primaries in 1952 seems more significant than a VP slot on a doomed ticket.

John Kennedy's campaign for the 1960 nomination is one of the best documented and most interesting of the period. It actually began with a loss to Kefauver in 1956 in the contest to be the Democratic vice presidential nominee. Kennedy was the conservative in that pairing and, as such, he won most of his support from southern delegates. The loss taught Kennedy a lesson about the personal touch in party politics, as in the following account of efforts to sway a Maryland delegate and his wife: "'They were entirely friendly,' said campaign manager Bobby Kennedy. 'They liked us. But Kefauver had *visited* them in their home. He had sent them Christmas cards. We couldn't shake them. Believe me, we've sent out a lot of Christmas cards since'" (White 1961, 137).

To put the point more generally, Kennedy embarked on a preconvention campaign that was probably as energetic as any other candidate's up until that time. As T. H. White wrote in his *Making of the Presidency 1960*, "Between 1956 and 1960, no Democrat . . . spoke in more states, addressed more Jefferson-Jackson Day dinners, participated in more local and mayoralty campaigns of deserving Democrats, than did John F. Kennedy. By the spring of 1960 Kennedy had not only visited every state of the union, but his intelligence files bulged with what was possibly the most complete index ever made of the power structure of any national party" (137). White's classic account of this campaign provides one of the clearest pictures we have of the terrain candidates had to navigate in the invisible primary and is, as such, worth quoting at some length:

> The laws of libel, the decencies of political reportage . . . effectively conceal the ever-changing topography of American politics. It is impossible to report publicly what world-famous governor of what state was commonly called "The Boob" by his political boss; which apparently sinister boss is only a paper tiger in the hands of other men; which labor leader can really deliver votes and money and which cannot; which great industrialist is a political eunuch while his neighbor is master of his state; which nationally eminent Negro is considered an "Uncle Tom" by his people, while some unknown kinsman really controls the wards. . . .
>
> To understand American politics is, simply, to know people, to know the relative weight of names—who are heroes, who are straw men, who controls, who does not. But to operate in American politics one must go a step further—one must build a bridge to such names, establish a warmth, a personal connection. . . . All this the Kennedys had learned in their upbringing. . . . (136)

By White's account, Kennedy won support by knowing where power lay in a vast and decentralized party system. No doubt this charming man also knew what to say to power when he met it. So the essence of the technique here was to "build a bridge" and establish a "personal connection" to the party's more active members.

> Now for three hours, broken only occasionally by a bit of information he might request of the staff, [Kennedy] proceeded, occasionally sitting, some-

times standing, to survey the entire country without map or notes. . . . "What I remember," says [Lawrence F.] O'Brien, director of organization and keeper of the political ledgers, "was his remarkable knowledge of every state, not just the Party leaders, not just the Senators in Washington, but he knew all the factions and key people in all the factions" (54–55).

The epitaph of the [Lyndon] Johnson campaign was written, for this reporter, by a Kennedy organizer who said with a flat simplicity: "Why, do you know, Lyndon actually thought Carmine DeSapio and Tammany controlled New York!" (137)

But Kennedy also ran in seven primaries and won all of them. Two of the victories stand out. In Wisconsin, JFK beat his main rival, Hubert Humphrey of Minnesota, in Humphrey's backyard. In West Virginia, a border state with presumed anti-Catholic prejudices, Kennedy demonstrated his abilities as a vote-getter in difficult terrain. In all seven of his primaries, Kennedy made heavy use of volunteers to staff his campaigns.

Journalist David Broder views the Kennedy nomination as a case of a strong candidate forcing himself on the party. JFK won the presidential nomination, Broder writes, "essentially by going outside the organization, using 'political amateurs,' to round up votes in the primaries and thus forcing the professionals in the 'cadre party' to accept him as nominee" (Broder 1972, 25).

Broder goes on to make an extremely important comment on how Kennedy's reliance on amateurs affected him: "As part of the price [Kennedy] paid for his help from the 'amateurs,' many of them previously Stevenson supporters, Kennedy accommodated himself to the liberal programs they espoused. As late as 1956, his liberalism had been suspect; the South backed him for Vice President against Kefauver. . . . But in the next four years, Kennedy gradually shifted his voting record . . . and identified himself more clearly as an advocate of civil rights and welfare measures" (25–26). Like most other political analysts, Broder here views parties as creatures of professional politicians. Hence, for him, the "amateurs" who worked for Kennedy are not really part of the party, or at least not as much a part as the "professionals in the 'cadre party.'" From our perspective, of course, they are. That Kennedy adjusted his voting record to appeal to citizen activists—raising another case in which nominating politics drives behavior in government—confirms our view of their importance. Activists would not support JFK unless he supported their view of good public policy.

We also question whether, as Broder asserts, Kennedy's success in the primaries "forced" the party to nominate him at all. T. H. White saw the matter differently. He reports that the Democratic Party's Catholic bosses actually liked JFK but felt they could not nominate him unless he demonstrated at the ballot box that his religion would not doom his candidacy: "Not until [Kennedy] showed primitive strength with the voters in strange states could he turn and deal with the bosses and the brokers in the Northeast who regarded him fondly as a fellow Catholic but, as a Catholic, hopelessly doomed to defeat" (1961, 55).

In the early editions of their textbook on presidential elections, Polsby and Wildavsky take a view similar to that of White. They express sympathy with President Harry Truman's view that primaries were "eyewash"—that is, generally unimportant—but add that primaries "do serve the useful purpose of providing politicians at the national conventions with some information about the relative popularity of candidates" (1968, 163). They cite Kennedy's victory over Humphrey in West Virginia as one of several cases in which primaries served this role.

That candidates with questionable national appeal must sometimes demonstrate vote-getting prowess to skeptical party leaders comes up in many accounts of nominations in this period and seems to have been a rule. Kennedy himself acknowledged the rule in the following comment, in which he complains that one of his opponents, Lyndon Johnson, was trying to be nominated without entering the primaries. "Could you imagine me, having entered no primaries, trying to tell the leaders that being a Catholic was no handicap? . . . In the same way, when Lyndon said he would win in the North, but could offer no concrete evidence, his claim couldn't be taken seriously. I suppose he made this mistake because he took such a flippant view of primaries, like Harry Truman. For some men, such as Lyndon and myself, primaries are not only good, they are absolutely vital" (Davis 1997, 64). We interpret the requirement of candidates to demonstrate appeal in "strange states" to be an example of how mass politics enabled parties to make wiser choices about whom to nominate. If, to everyone's surprise, Humphrey couldn't beat Kennedy either in his own backyard or in the Protestant South, isn't that information that the party would want to know and take into account?

To be sure, a fine line may exist between demonstrating electoral appeal and using the primaries to force oneself on the party. Kennedy did force himself on at least one state party, that of Ohio. The governor of that state committed to JFK only after Kennedy credibly threatened to beat him in his own state primary unless a promise of support was made.[4] But for the most part, Kennedy played to the party rather than forced it to knuckle under. If we take Kefauver as an example of someone who was

clearly trying to force himself on the party, the contrast between his behavior and JFK's is illuminating. Kefauver's most notable activity prior to
his nomination campaign was a televised probe of municipal corruption
that discomfited party powers; Kennedy's most notable activity was travel
to meet and do favors for party leaders. Kefauver entered all primaries in
an effort to collect as many delegates as possible. JFK entered only enough
primaries to prove that he was capable of running well as a national candidate, building his main delegate strength by treating with leaders. Kennedy,
then, brought less external pressure to bear on the party than Kefauver had.
Given this, and given that the party leaders rejected Kefauver, it is hard to
argue that external pressure really forced the party to accept JFK.

Any doubt that the Democratic Party of this era was able to say no to a
candidate it disliked is cleared up by the 1968 contest. In the manner of Kefauver in 1952, Minnesota Senator Eugene McCarthy challenged his party's
incumbent president, Lyndon Johnson, in the primaries. McCarthy drew
early blood: Attacking Johnson's promotion of the Vietnam War, he won
42 percent of the primary vote in New Hampshire, compared to 49 percent
for LBJ, whereupon Robert Kennedy entered the race as a second antiwar
candidate and Johnson dropped out.

McCarthy was idolized by his antiwar followers, but his professional colleagues considered him aloof, arrogant, and personally difficult—though
also witty. Consider the following remark, in which McCarthy compared
himself to the leading Democratic contenders for the 1960 nomination:
"I'm twice as liberal as Humphrey, twice as Catholic as Kennedy, and twice
as smart as Symington."[5] He might perhaps have added: And twice as disliked within the party as any of them.

Kennedy, too, had detractors in Democratic circles. As his brother's attorney general, "Bobby" showed little restraint in going after organized
crime leaders with political ties. Urban machine bosses and union leaders had reason to worry about this record. His opposition to the Vietnam
war was also unpopular with old-line party leaders, especially in the South.
Kennedy also had a reputation for putting his own view of public policy
above the interests of key party factions. Waiting to enter the presidential
race until McCarthy had shown antiwar politics to be safe fed Bobby's reputation for caring about himself above all else.

Johnson's withdrawal thus created an odd situation in which the only
Democratic candidates in the field were about as popular among insiders as
Kefauver had been 16 years earlier. But the vacuum did not last long. Over
the next twenty-four hours, Vice President Hubert Humphrey "received
more than fifty phone calls beseeching him to run" (Chester, Hodgson, and

Page 1969, 142) But Humphrey was out of the country and unable to make an immediate response. This delay gave an opening to McCarthy and especially Kennedy to scoop up support that Johnson had suddenly turned loose. So when Humphrey returned to America: "The first question [Humphrey] had asked when he stepped off the plane from Mexico was 'Has Bobby got it locked up yet?' One of Humphrey's staff said, 'Everybody expected Bobby to put on a blitz. When politicians began calling from all over the country, saying, "Bobby's pushing me [for an endorsement], I have to know whether you're going to run," we knew that the bandwagon [for Kennedy] wasn't happening. We couldn't tell them that we were running, but we were able to say, "Hold off a bit longer, and you won't be sorry"'" (142, 144).

Strikingly, most Democratic leaders did hold off committing to Kennedy, so when Humphrey sought their support, the endorsements rolled in. "Humphrey had entered no primaries . . . but the AFL/CIO [labor union] structures had delivered to him almost all of Pennsylvania, Maryland, Michigan, and Ohio [which had primaries]; Democratic governors and mayors who found Humphrey the man in the Johnson administration most sensitive to their problems, could deliver hundreds more delegates from New Jersey to Washington. The one possibly unstable element in the Humphrey coalition was the South, with its 527 [of 1,800 total] votes. [But t]he South would be firm in support of Johnson and the war and, by derivation, of Humphrey" (White 1969, 316).

No Kennedy—John, Robert, or Ted—had ever lost an election at the time Robert Kennedy declared that he was a candidate for president. Bobby blemished that record by losing the Oregon primary to McCarthy, but he bested him every other time they faced off. It is thus notable that, as Kennedy lay dying following his victory in the winner-take-all primary in California, Humphrey already had enough votes to be nominated on the first ballot at the party convention—and eventually was.[6]

The theoretically important point here is that Humphrey did not need to campaign publicly for the party support that gave him the nomination.[7] Further, in a striking violation of the script for candidate-centered politics, party insiders called him before he could call them. As in 1952, when the Democratic Party last faced a maverick, insiders wanted to make sure they had a respectable alternative to back. Thus if, by the time the Democratic convention met in the summer of 1968, the party's hands seemed tied by commitments to Humphrey, it was not because leaders had been cut down to size by the preconvention campaign. Rather, it was because many leaders actively preferred Humphrey and wanted, through commitments to him, to stop another candidate whom they opposed.

The four Democratic nominations discussed here offer little support for the notion that the decline of multiballot conventions signaled weakness in the party. In two of the cases, the party dispatched vote-getting mavericks who had campaigned hard for the nomination. In another, that of John F. Kennedy, the party nominated a vote-getting nonmaverick who campaigned hard for the nomination, but evidence that it was forced to nominate JFK is a good deal weaker than evidence of autonomy in the other two cases. Thus, the best overall verdict is one of party autonomy.

The nominations of Kennedy and Humphrey provide rather different glimpses of the decision-making procedure. In the Kennedy case, we see an ambitious politician traveling the country for years ahead of the election to build bridges and make warm contacts with his party's powers. In the Humphrey case, we observe those same powers contacting their preferred candidate, trying to support him before he even got formally into the race. What we learn from the second case—which might have looked quite different except for the accident of Humphrey's travel schedule—is that party leaders are not passive in the invisible primary. If they give their support to a candidate, even one who has actively sought it, it may be for the simple reason that they genuinely prefer that person.

The one sense in which the Democratic Party was weak in this period is that the methods used to nominate Humphrey in 1968 lacked popular legitimacy. At a time when Eugene McCarthy and Robert Kennedy were fighting for delegates in public primaries, Humphrey was making big gains in back rooms and secret caucuses where delegates were chosen in ways that were closed to the public and not ideally democratic. Even from a distance of four decades, his nomination has a bad odor. This legitimacy deficit, though having nothing to do with candidate-centered politics, can be seen as due to pressure from "mass democracy." Yet one cannot say the Democratic Party bent under that pressure; rather, it massively and successfully resisted—only to be dismantled afterward by angry reformers from the losing side. Thus we see the nomination of Humphrey as the act of a strong party with weak popular legitimacy.

Last Nominations of the Republican Party

The five open Republican conventions in this period were all one-sided affairs, but the contests were livelier and therefore more illuminating than on the Democratic side. We also see more explicit examples of how the whole party—not just top leaders—participated in the nomination decision.

Republican nominations in the post–World War II period were shaped by a stable factional division between conservatives and moderate liberals.

The first hated everything about Franklin Roosevelt's New Deal—unemployment relief, the beginnings of welfare, social security, legal guarantees for labor unions, and high taxes on the well-off—while the second grudgingly accepted the New Deal. This division was, in effect, a continuation of the Taft-Roosevelt contest of 1912, which had also pitted conservatives against moderate liberals. Not until the electoral success of conservative Ronald Reagan in 1980 did this internal struggle cease to animate Republican politics.

Through four nominations beginning in 1940, the central figures were Senator Robert A. Taft of Ohio and Governor Thomas E. Dewey of New York. This was true even of the 1940 and 1952 nominations, which were won by Wendell Willkie and Dwight Eisenhower, respectively. Taft, son of the earlier president, led the conservative wing. Dewey, like Theodore Roosevelt, had been governor of New York and led the more liberal wing of the Republican Party. He was often called a "me-too Republican" because of his willing acceptance of much of the New Deal. The nominations of 1948 and 1960 were the most similar of the five in this period, with the winning candidates—Dewey and Nixon—building up leads in the invisible primary that carried over to victory at the party conventions.

Dewey's path to the nomination was the more difficult. He had to get past Taft, who was the favorite of a large fraction of the party. But Dewey could claim to be more electable, and he knew how to campaign among party regulars for convention delegates. Here is a medley of impressions of Dewey's campaign from his biography:

> Dewey set out on his ostensibly non-political trip in July 1947. He visited [relatives in Oklahoma], where he marveled at a neighbor's automatic hay baler and spent most of his time in private huddles with Republican leaders from Texas, Oklahoma, and Arkansas. To reporters who pressed for details, Dewey said he was simply relaxing. . . . By the time he reached Kansas City, where his schedule included breakfast with 150 local Republicans and a reception for 1,500 more, the pretense was wearing thin. It was all but abandoned in Denver. . . . At the governor's conference in Salt Lake City, Dewey was the undisputed center of attention. (Smith 1982, 481)

> While Dewey carried on his own shadow campaign for the nomination, his operatives fanned out. . . . [One] was able to report a network of 376 reliable informants in 26 states. Their assignment: to learn the identities, occupations, inclinations, and personal histories of every *potential* delegate to the 1948 convention. (480; emphasis added)

"The CIA were amateurs compared to the Dewey people," recalled Ray Bliss, later national chairman of the party but in 1948 one of Taft's badly outgunned field marshals. "They knew where your bank loans were, who you did business with, who you slept with." [Dewey campaign manager Herbert] Brownell put it less melodramatically. To him, this was a logical payoff of four years of personal cultivation, of memorizing children's names and taking visiting Republicans to Yankee ballgames and Broadway plays. (494)

This was not nineteenth-century convention politics, but neither was it mass democracy. It was hard-nosed, insider politics of the kind that Farley, Kennedy, and later Richard Nixon practiced. Dewey's "Triumvirate" of top managers was famous for it in the 1940s and afterward in the way that other top political managers, like Mark Hanna and Karl Rove, have been renowned in their day.

But if not mass politics, can Dewey's hardball insider politics be aptly called candidate-centered politics? Is this, in other words, an example of a strong candidate to whom a weak party was incapable of saying no, or did Republican insiders actually want Dewey? From this one contest, it would be hard to tell. If we jump ahead to 1960, though, we get a clear verdict on the capacity of the Republican party to say no.

Like Dewey, Nixon was extremely active in the preconvention period. As T. H. White has written:

For seven years, the Vice-President [Nixon] had crisscrossed the country, delivering himself to regular party organizations, helping them at their dinners, their banquets, in their campaigns. He had done their chores and their work for six years in an administration whose President was—as they put the phrase delicately but negatively—"not politically conditioned."
 . . . . Thus, in the long civil war between regulars and liberals in the Republican Party, the regular base was [by 1959] safe for Nixon.[8] (1961, 63)

But does this mean, as Broder said of Kennedy in that same year and one might suspect of Dewey in 1948, that Nixon forced himself on the party? That Nixon, the only strong candidate in the field, was so strong that the party could not say no?

Again, we think the party could have said no if it wanted to, and here we are fortunate to have evidence. Unlike Kennedy and perhaps Dewey, Nixon did have a strong, potentially formidable opponent in the invisible primary in the person of Nelson A. Rockefeller, another liberal governor of New York. No sitting vice president since Martin Van Buren had been nominated by his party for president, whereas several New York governors had been chosen, so Nixon did not seem like a sure bet to beat Rockefeller.

Rockefeller never jumped with both feet into the race, but he showed every intention of doing so. He built a state-of-the-art campaign head-quarters, hired a large staff of writers, advance men, and publicists, and planned an ambitious schedule of travels to line up support for his candidacy. But then he dropped out. As one of Rockefeller's advisors explained, "The doors were locked, barred, and closed. . . . Here was the club, not only against Nelson because he was a liberal, but also committed to Nixon. Richard Nixon is a shrewd man; he spotted where control of the nomination lay seven years before. When he was traveling, he wasn't just making friends with State Chairmen and the regulars; he was dining with the big interests at the same time. . . . These people liked Ike. But they liked Nixon even more" (White 1961, 74).

In consequence of Rockefeller's decision to stay out of the race, Nixon had no active opponent[9] and was nominated on the first ballot—another case of a candidate who campaigned vigorously and obtained the nomination with apparent ease. Yet it makes little sense to describe this outcome in terms of either candidate-centered politics or party weakness. The governor of New York was surely Nixon's equal as a politician and most likely a better campaigner. If Rockefeller failed to fully enter the nomination contest, it was because, as White reported, Republican insiders actually wanted Nixon, probably mainly because of Nixon's relative conservatism. Recognizing this, Rockefeller stayed out of the race. That a politician of Rockefeller's stature and fierce ambition made this decision seems a clear testament to the strength of the party's control of the nomination process.

We believe that the implications of this case are extremely important and general: Scholars who believe that politics is candidate-centered often cite as evidence the emergence of a strong candidate who seems to cruise to nomination without serious obstacle. But this sort of evidence can easily mislead. It might signal weak parties and candidate-centered politics, or it might indicate just the opposite. Certainly in Nixon's case, the ease of his nomination was an indication of the strength of the party that favored him.

Of the cases examined so far, none contains much evidence that national party conventions had much life left in them. That appearance, however, is also misleading. Throughout this period, deals made in the invisible primary had to be closed at the convention where delegates could, if they wished, wiggle out of their commitments. In fact, delegates did wiggle out of their commitments in 1952 and nearly did so in 1968, thereby making clear that final power continued to reside in the convention itself.

These two conventions were mostly unbossed but yet managed to make quite reasonable decisions on their own authority. They acted, moreover, under the focused glare of the national press corps. As a result, they give us our first clear indication whether "decision by discussion" has any value for understanding party behavior.

We begin with the 1952 loser, Robert Taft. The senator from Ohio was, by all accounts, unusually intelligent, hard-working, and honest, but also extremely dull. Democrats said that he had the best mind in Washington, until he made it up. He said of himself, "While I have no difficulty talking, I don't know how to do any of the eloquence business which makes for enthusiasm or applause" (Wunderlin 1997, 271). (As professors, we can only sympathize.)

Taft's base of support lay among midwestern party activists of frequently modest means—people called "primitives" by their ideological opponents on Wall Street. To the extent Taft mounted a preconvention campaign, he campaigned mainly to them, to party professionals, and to the "rotten boroughs"[10] of the South (Smith 1982, 297). Taft ran weakly against Eisenhower in the primaries despite the fact that the general never campaigned for himself. Yet Taft was, from 1940 to 1952, the strongest candidate that the conservative wing of the party could field. He was known by his many admirers as Mr. Republican.

Taft was the early front-runner and expected winner of the 1952 Republican nomination contest. After three straight liberal Republican nominees had been beaten by Democrats in the general election, it was the conservatives' turn. But then came the New Hampshire primary, where Taft lost 50 to 39 to Dwight Eisenhower, whose name was not on the ballot. This was a blow. Yet, because Taft had the affections of the activist base and the pragmatic support of rotten boroughs in the South, he entered the convention just short of the majority he needed to be nominated.

Meanwhile, as the primaries progressed, Dewey and his lieutenants were literally pleading with Eisenhower, a popular hero from World War II, to actively seek the Republican nomination. One may suspect that Eisenhower's reticence was due to coyness, but the sense of his biographies is that the sixty-one-year-old general truly yearned for a quieter existence. In any case, Eisenhower did little to promote his candidacy. But activists of the moderate wing did. In state-level delegate-selection processes across the country, the major battles were between those who preferred Eisenhower and those who preferred Taft (David, Moos, and Goldman 1954).

Finally, in June of 1952, after the end of the primaries, Eisenhower consented to enter the nomination contest and began to campaign. He made some speeches, held press conferences, and had meetings with delegates

from numerous states, both on their home turf and at the convention itself. These meetings, much more than any smoke-filled room, are stressed
in the historical accounts (Smith 1982; Ambrose 1983). Eisenhower was
sharply questioned about his views on the New Deal, activist government,
labor, the U.S. defense posture—and even his wife's supposed drinking
problem. He answered so well that Taft at one point insisted that there
were no differences between them on foreign policy issues, only to have
Eisenhower reiterate that there were.

> [Eisenhower's] meetings [with delegates] were triumphs. There was nothing
> like the feel of the man, the firm handshake, that marvelous grin . . . the best
> way to sell General Eisenhower was to let people [i.e., convention delegates]
> meet him.
>   . . . it was an adroit campaign [but not] a complete success. Old Guard del-
> egates enjoyed meeting the general; they were impressed by him and by the
> response his foreign policy positions brought forth from their constituents;
> they were satisfied the general's domestic views were safe. But their hearts
> belonged to Taft, and if not their hearts, their pocketbooks did, because Taft
> controlled the party machinery and had been nurturing for years the party
> faithful who made up the delegates. (Ambrose 1983, 532, 535)

The forces at work to this point were typical of the period. Meeting, impressing, and lining up delegates and their leaders was critical. Controlling
the rotten boroughs of the South was a help. Taft had started years earlier and
now, despite his weakness in the primaries, was poised to be nominated.

Yet it was not to be. Even before Eisenhower agreed to become a candidate, Dewey put his famed delegate-hunting team to work for the general,
and now it pulled a rabbit out of the hat: a cleverly drawn challenge to the
credentials of enough Taft delegates to strip him of essential support.

The main challenge grew out of a party split in Texas. A minority faction
in the Texas party rode Eisenhower's popularity to elect enough delegates
to take over the state convention, but the dominant faction used its control of a party committee to lock out the Eisenhower delegates and send
a pro-Taft delegation to the national convention.[11] The Eisenhower forces
challenged the Taft delegation at the national party convention and, with
at least fifty of Taft's own national delegates voting yea, the challenge succeeded, whereupon enough disputed Taft seats changed hands to permit
Eisenhower to be nominated on the first ballot.

The key question is why some fifty Taft delegates took Eisenhower's
side in a credentials fight that was in reality a fight over who would be the

party's nominee. The challenge had a legal basis, but in a matter as important as a presidential nomination, political reasons would be expected to trump legal arguments.

One of those reasons may be found at a national governor's convention in Houston on the weekend before the Republican convention. All twenty-three Republican governors at the conference issued a statement urging—perhaps implicitly instructing—support for the Eisenhower credentials challenge.[12] Most governors then came to the convention itself where, presumably, they pushed the same line. "This is the way I want it," said Pennsylvania Governor John Fine to his delegation as the key vote approached. Dewey, who was still governor of New York and still controlled some patronage, promised to strip jobs from any New York delegate who opposed the Eisenhower challenge. "If you think that Taft has a steamroller," Dewey said, "wait until you see our steamroller operate." The support for Eisenhower's credentials challenge thus seems clearly due to leadership pressure (Smith 1982, 590). To be sure, not everyone was persuaded: When, after the general's first-ballot nomination, a leader moved to make the choice of Eisenhower unanimous, "he was turned back by furious die-hard Taft supporters, who screamed 'No!'" (Ambrose 1983, 541). But enough were persuaded to make a nomination.

Of all the conventions of this period, 1952 is the one in which voter appeal—Taft's lack of it, Eisenhower's gift of it—seems most important. But nominating a war hero over a party workhorse after five straight presidential losses is scarcely evidence of internal party weakness. The history of American party politics has multiple examples of strong parties nominating war heroes to get themselves out of tight fixes. Even less can Eisenhower's nomination be told as one of candidate-centered politics, since Eisenhower was drawn into the campaign by a major faction of the party and had his entire campaign managed by the professionals and the activists of this faction.[13]

A more plausible summing up would be as follows: the minority (liberal) wing of the party, having no strong candidate of its own, recruited a strong vote-getter of broadly acceptable views, squeezed as much delegate support as possible from its own strongholds, and then persuaded swing elements of the majority (conservative) wing to vote with their heads instead of their hearts for their second-choice candidate.

The unanimous statement of the party's governors was no doubt the turning point in the nomination. One might take the press conference at which the governors announced their view as the new form of boss domination, but with this difference: Few of the governors had any direct authority over their delegations. Hence, another factor entered the equation, the views of the delegates themselves. We see no other reason that Eisenhower, in a departure from the pattern of old-style conventions, spent so much time wooing delegates except that their views had importance. The extent to which most delegates were fully independent of their governors was surely limited, but it was sufficiently great that Eisenhower paid attention to them. Eisenhower's personal skill in successfully managing these meetings was then important as well. Thus, we see this convention as one in which "decision by discussion" was an important part of the nomination process. The new procedure—*persuading* delegates of the leaders' choice—was probably different from the one that led to the nomination of Harding just thirty-two years earlier, but it was no less an internal party decision and no less a successful adaptation to the situation in which the party found itself.

Skipping for the moment the 1964 Republican nomination, which was an entirely different kind of case, we turn now to the 1968 Republican contest, which again enables us to glimpse a party making up its own collective mind about whom to nominate. On the surface, the nomination of Richard Nixon for his second run at the presidency looks typical for its period; beneath the surface, the politics were intense and revealing. No contest before or since permits us a better view of the decision-making by discussion that we believe now dominates presidential nominations.

Nixon's nomination was made on the first ballot and reflected, above all, support in the party that he had built up from years of effort. Despite his promise to reporters after losing the California gubernatorial race in 1962 that "you won't have Dick Nixon to kick around any more," the former vice president remained active in party politics and worked energetically for Goldwater in 1964. Perhaps most notably, Nixon also traveled extensively on behalf of Republican candidates in the 1966 congressional elections. In all, he traveled thirty thousand miles and visited 82 (!) congressional districts (White 1969, 58). The credit thus earned made him viable for the 1968 presidential nomination, and when the liberal Republican candidate of that year (Governor George Romney of Michigan) folded, Nixon became the front-runner. Many professionals had doubts about Nixon's abilities as a vote-getter, so, like Kennedy and other candidates whose electoral viability was in question, he had to prove himself in the primaries. Nixon was lucky to face weak opposition, won several races easily, skillfully converted his success into committed delegates, and thereby entered the convention with enough locked-in support to be nominated.[14]

Yet many of the 1968 delegates, especially those from the South, were deeply conservative and therefore suspicious of Nixon. Nixon had been brought to the vice presidency by Dewey and, like the New York governor, had positioned himself as a moderate on civil rights. The conservative favorite was Ronald Reagan, who had been elected governor of California in 1966 and, much more relevantly for presidential politics, had just spent more than a decade traveling the country to speak on political themes. Many of his engagements were as a motivational speaker for the General Electric Corporation, but increasingly he spoke at Republican events. He had campaigned for Goldwater during the 1964 California primary and gave a well-received nationally televised speech for the Arizona senator in the fall. Thus, Reagan was not only known to a large number of Republican delegates, but liked and admired by conservatives. "I love that man," said Senator Strom Thurmond, the most respected leader of southern delegates. "He's the best hope we've got" (Chester, Hodgson, and Page 1969, 434).

Yet Thurmond was for Nixon. With other southern admirers of Reagan, he feared that if Reagan broke up the Nixon coalition, Rockefeller, who had more first-ballot pledges than Reagan, might pick up the pieces. Or, if Reagan won the nomination, he might fail to unite the party for the November election. Or, finally, Reagan might carry too much baggage from his close association with Goldwater to be viable in the general election. Meanwhile, Nixon was a candidate who was both acceptable to all factions of the party and probably able to beat the Democrats in November.

But if Thurmond and other conservative leaders saw Nixon as the best bet in 1968, ordinary delegates were another matter. A notable feature of this convention is that, as in 1952, many party regulars were free to make up their own minds and favored a staunch conservative as their strong first choice. Getting sufficient numbers of them to stick with Nixon was the biggest story of the convention, and it was mainly a story of decision by discussion. This was how Thurmond put the matter to the South Carolina delegation: "A vote for Reagan is a vote for Rockefeller. . . . . We have no choice, if we want to win, except to vote for Nixon [for nomination]. . . . We must quit using our hearts and start using our heads. . . . I have been down this road, so I know. I am laying my prestige, my record of forty years in public life, I am laying it all on the line this time. . . . Believe me, I love Reagan, but Nixon's the one" (Chester, Hodgson, and Page 1969, 447–48). After hearing this speech, the South Carolina delegation switched from 22–0 for Reagan to 22–0 for Nixon.

Meanwhile, Reagan was also making the rounds of the state delegations and, after years of practice, he knew how to move an audience. "There is nothing more impressive than Ronnie Reagan behind closed doors," said one of Reagan's admirers who was nonetheless a Nixon backer (Chester, Hodgson, and Page 1969, 454). But coming right behind Reagan as chief fireman for the Nixon camp was Thurmond. By the accounts of White and of Chester, Hodgson, and Page, his exertions were crucial.

The following passages give a flavor of the myriad forces at work in this convention:

At noon, [Reagan] entertained sixteen of the Florida people in his suite at the Deauville. The flames started to leap again. When the Florida delegates assembled for their final private caucus at two o'clock in their club, they were in a highly emotional state. The room was not so much smoke-filled as tearstained. . . . [State chair Bill] Murfin threatened to resign if they did not come into line [for Nixon]. Several of the women were weeping openly. [The delegation later voted 32 for Nixon and one for Reagan.]

To hold the South against Reagan raiders . . . Nixon needed to make at least one successful foray of his own into the heart of the urban, industrial North. . . . New Jersey was much the most vulnerable. . . . The governor of New Jersey was not a Republican, so the role of favorite son was taken over by the state's highly respected liberal Senator, Clifford Case. This in itself made discipline precarious: a Senator lacks a governor's invaluable control over jobs and offices. Case had to rely on his personality to keep a hold on his delegates; for some of them, his personality was too liberal by half. [New Jersey later gave 12 votes to Nixon].

Jim Martin, the boss of the Nixon faction in the Alabama delegation, was frantic about the mood of his colleagues. At one point, he told a Nixon contact that they might, after all, have to cast a ballot for Reagan. If Alabama did not show at least token support for the one true conservative in the nomination, there might be dire consequences—"We could get lynched when we get home." [The delegation later voted 14 for Nixon and 12 for Reagan.]

When asked about the possibility of Rockefeller strength in his delegation, Louie Nunn, Governor of Kentucky, replied, "An awful lot of our delegates know that if they voted for Rockefeller down here they wouldn't be allowed off the plane back home." [Two Kentucky delegates did, as it happens, vote for Rockefeller and still contrived to return safely.]

Michigan's favorite son was its governor George Romney, and its allegiance was fairly deep-rooted. He had, after all, been a viable candidate at the turn of the year. Now he was, by his own admission, "a dead duck"; it would have been an excessively harsh fate to lose even the token kudos of a favorite-son candidacy [i.e., support from his own state's delegates]. Four stubborn conservatives from Grosse Point were untouched by the sad saga of Romney's presidential aspirations and broke away to Nixon. But the rest of the delegation stayed behind Romney.

On Sunday, [Reagan] was well received by Alabama, Georgia, Mississippi, Montana, Utah and Wyoming—but still experienced some setbacks. Utah's tiny eight-member delegation decided, after a near commitment to him, to avoid controversy on the first ballot by going for Romney. . . . It was a futile gesture, but a safe one; no one in Salt Lake City could quarrel publicly with a vote for a fellow Mormon. (Chester, Hodgson, and Page 1969, 469, 471, 458, 454, 470, 449)

The first three passages refer to leadership, but leadership based more on persuasion than orders. The latter passages refer to parochial concerns and pressures, which show that, even in a convention torn by ideology, much politics was still local. But the balance of forces was what mattered, and it favored Nixon—but just barely. Reagan's campaign manager, who was seen by journalists as an outstanding vote counter, believed at several points that he was just one delegation short of cracking the convention wide open. But the big fissure never quite opened.

As the roll call of the states began on the convention floor, Thurmond told a reporter, "The South loves Reagan, but it won't break" (Chester, Hodgson, and Page 1969, 474). He was right. Nixon got 300 of the South's 348 votes, by far his largest block of regional support. Without that block—without, in other words, the ability of Thurmond and other leaders to get a large group of delegates to vote for their second choice—Nixon would probably not have been nominated on the first ballot and perhaps not at all.

The main new lesson to be drawn from this case is that large numbers of highly ideological activists are quite capable of acting as strategic politicians for their cause rather than as blind zealots. With such people at its base, an unbossed and bandwagon-free party can be a strong party. Or, as we would like to conclude, decision by discussion can be an effective party device.

Our final case is the 1964 nomination of Barry Goldwater. This contest bears some similarity to 1952, in that Goldwater, like Eisenhower, refused to spearhead his own candidacy. Rather, he watched from the sidelines as a dissident faction of the party worked for two years to build support for him, offering occasional encouragement but refusing to commit himself. By the time the senator finally entered the race, the Draft Goldwater Committee "had state chairmen and an organization down to the congressional district or county level in 40 states" (Kessel 1968, 42). A candidate-centered nomination this was not.

The Goldwater nomination is the Republican analog of the civil rights platform fight at the Democratic convention of 1948: a victory of one set of intense policy demanders over another that drove the losers out of the party, thereby permanently changing what the party stood for and what kinds of candidates it would nominate. The events of 1964, like those of 1948, continue even today to define party competition in the United States. For this reason, we give them a close look.

As we have seen, the Taft wing of the Republican party had been chafing for two decades under the party's tradition of nominating moderates for president, but an incident at the 1960 party convention put them over the top and, according to Theodore White, led to the launch of a movement to take over the party on behalf of conservative principles.

The precipitating incident was the so-called Compact of Fifth Avenue. When the initial draft of the party's 1960 platform was too conservative to suit Nelson Rockefeller, the governor threatened a fight on the floor of the convention to change it. Facing a difficult fight against Kennedy in the fall, Nixon was desperate to avoid such a public spectacle and flew to New York to meet privately with Rockefeller in the latter's Fifth Avenue apartment. There the two men worked late into the night on a fourteen-point statement of principles known as the Compact of Fifth Avenue. The compact was notably more moderate than the draft Republican platform, particularly on civil rights and government medical care for the elderly (later called Medicare). As titular head of the party, Nixon directed that its principles be written into the party platform.

Nixon's order provoked fury among the more conservative members of the party. The party's nominee, as it seemed to them, was attempting to change what their party stood for. "One could almost fix the moment of [the] birth" of the Goldwater movement, says White, to Nixon's action. "From Saturday of the compact to Wednesday of the balloting [on the platform], a procession of men pressed a mission on Goldwater—he must lead a revolt. They promised him 300 votes on the convention floor if he would voice the principles they shared. To them Goldwater said simply, 'Get me three hundred names of delegates on paper. Show me'" (1965, 88–89). The dissidents came up with only thirty-seven names, but they kept at it when they returned home, bringing in hundreds or perhaps thousands of fresh faces at the base of the Republican Party. The principal agent of this movement was a former Dewey operative named F. Clinton White. White worked loyally for Eisenhower in 1952 and Nixon in 1960, but became disgusted by the "me-too Republicanism" of those leaders.[15] And he had the skill, personal contacts, and financial independence to do something about it.

Late in 1961, White convened the first national meeting of his group and opened it with these words: "We're going to take over the Republican Party . . . and make it the conservative instrument of American politics" (Middendorf 2006, 15). An early memo gives the flavor of their efforts. It began:

> There are four months left in 1962. Many important and significant things will happen in these four months. We have several encouraging signs which have already developed. . . .
>
> In Illinois, Hayes Robertson has become Chairman of Cook County and is doing a tremendous job to insure the county and state being with us in 1964. I had an excellent meeting with Hayes and Charlie Barr [an executive with Standard Oil of Indiana] earlier this month.
>
> Tad Smith [Texas state party chair] had a regional meeting for his area in Phoenix, Arizona, on August 18 and 19, which I attended. This was a highly successful meeting, all states in the region being represented by key people and commitments made to fulfill the 1962 objectives.
>
> We have just had the election of a conservative County Chairman in Allegheny County (Pittsburgh). I am meeting with him right after Labor Day to discuss his work and association with us. (Novak 1964, 118–19)

In these cases, the insurgent conservative movement could take over existing organizations. But in much of the South, activists had to start from scratch. Theodore White, in the second of his classic *Making of the Presidency* books, describes how one southern activist got his start in Republican Party politics in 1960 by sending members of his small Young Republicans club to work with a bag of coins: "You start with twelve people in phone booths," he said, "and you locate two or three people in each precinct, and you go on from there. I went to forty-four precinct meetings in forty days that year, and we called some of our meetings in drugstores. For three years I traveled the state five nights a week, talking to two or three people in each county to get one leader and then train him" (1965, 136).

None of this had anything to do with the forces of mass democracy as William Carleton characterized them. It was also completely independent of the candidate himself. Goldwater was a popular Republican speaker at party gatherings around the country and might have been in a position to win the nomination on the basis of a traditional preconvention campaign. But, with his senate seat in Arizona coming up for reelection in 1964, he put out the word that he would be supporting Rockefeller in that year's contest. The Clifton White group nonetheless kept up its efforts, and Goldwater eventually agreed to run (Novak 1964). Although the Goldwater candidacy is sometimes described as candidate-centered, we see little basis for this classification. Goldwater was, in effect, drafted by the Clifton White group. Our analysis is essentially that of the *New York Times* reporter who wrote Clifton White's obituary in 1993: "The Goldwater movement germinated in 1961, when Mr. White gathered a cadre of conservatives for a private meeting at a Chicago motel. They decided to seek ideological control of the party and chose Senator Goldwater of Arizona as their nominee, although he initially spurned the idea" (Lambert 1993, A34).[16]

When Goldwater did finally announce his candidacy, one of his first moves was to marginalize Clifton White and most of the leadership of the Draft Goldwater group. "Goldwater was uncomfortable with people he didn't know well," wrote a member of that group afterward (Middendorf 2006, 68). In its place, Goldwater created a campaign team made up of a so-called Arizona mafia of long-time associates. From here on, the Goldwater campaign was indeed candidate-centered—it raised its own money, hired its own pollsters, scheduled its own campaign events. But the primary building block of that campaign—the source of most of the delegates that would eventually nominate Goldwater—remained the forty state-level organizations that had been built up by Clifton White and his operatives.

Yet the organization Goldwater inherited was not strong enough to win the nomination outright. The party had many "strong Republican state organizations that were not so easily penetrated by radical conservative activists. . . . [Here, the] prejudice and instincts of party professionals (such as Ray Bliss) to look for a candidate who could win the general election meant that Goldwater . . . had to demonstrate that he could win a contested primary in a state heavy with Electoral College votes" (Rae 1989, 56–57). Like Taft, Goldwater did not run well even in Republican primaries, but when he finally managed to edge Rockefeller in the winner-take-all California primary, much of the formerly Taft-ite Midwest wing of the party rallied to him, making him all but impossible to stop. Dewey and his lieutenants, still active in the party, nonetheless made a last-ditch effort. As T. H. White writes: "A list of delegates committed to Goldwater who might just possibly be swayed was prepared [by Dewey operatives]; and the eminent leaders did indeed try. 'But it was,' said someone familiar with the operation, 'just incredible. We called all the old names; but they weren't there any longer, or they weren't in politics any longer. It was as if the Goldwater people had rewired the switchboard of the Party and the numbers we had were all dead.' Within two weeks Dewey had decided it was hopeless" (White 1965, 158).

So the conservatives at last got their turn. It did them no good in the short term, as Goldwater suffered a disastrous defeat in the fall election. But many of the fresh faces of the Goldwater insurgency—or rather, the F. Clifton White insurgency—stayed around, especially in the West and South. "Republican organizations in the South were no longer the 'rotten Boroughs'" but conservative strongholds (Rae 1989, 64). When grafted on to Taft's midwestern base, they gave the Republican Party, which had long leaned toward conservatism, a still more solidly conservative flavor and, far more importantly, a geographical foundation for future growth.

We therefore see the Goldwater nomination as a case of intense policy demanders creating party change. Conservatives were probably the larger of the party's two main factions for some decades, perhaps since the defeat of the Roosevelt wing of the party in 1912, but they bolstered their numbers and asserted their preferences in 1964. What they wanted was not a united front behind a broadly acceptable candidate, but a basic change in what the party stood for. In an exceptionally rowdy convention that produced a black eye for their cause and significant defections among defeated moderates, they got the realignment they wanted.[17]

Contemporary accounts of the Goldwater candidacy often refer to the new arrivals as "amateurs" because of their impatient and extreme policy demands, but this sells them short in three ways. First, as noted, many stuck around to permanently change the party. Analysts often trace the rise of the Republican Party in the 1980s and 1990s to the organizational foundation laid down by the "amateurs" of 1964. If, as we suggest above, there is an ebb and flow of amateurs and veterans, 1964 represents an influx of new faces who were more ideologically stringent. But they became the veterans of the next generation. Second, as the 1968 convention and later events would show, many of the new recruits were quite able and willing to play a strategic political game when the conditions seemed to require it. Third, there was nothing obviously amateurish about wanting the Republican Party to nominate an extremist or—to put it more neutrally—a staunch conservative in 1964. Not since 1928, or perhaps even 1924, had the conservative wing of the Republican Party tested the limits of voters' appetite for conservatism. (See figure 4.1 and associated discussion.) There were valid political reasons why, as we have emphasized, the Republican Party remained the "me too" party for so long. But with memories of the New Deal fading and the Democratic Party suffering internal division over civil rights for African Americans, a plausible case could be made that 1964 was a good year for the Republican Party to try running a real conservative. That case—invoking the idea of what turned out to be a nonexistent silent majority of Americans yearning

for conservative leadership—has been discredited by sound academic analysis. But, except in hindsight, political science has no greater claim to authority on this matter than the architect of the Goldwater movement, F. Clifton
White, who thought otherwise. Periodic efforts to realign parties are part of
party politics, not an exception to it—and especially so in cases like this one,
in which the realigned party later gains power.

Concluding Remarks

We have made a series of intertwined arguments in this chapter, making
whatever theoretical point was most salient in the particular nomination
under study. A summary of the key arguments may therefore be useful:

1. Mass democracy did not undermine the decision-making process. In none
   of the cases was a party forced by strong candidates with large popular
   followings to choose a nominee it didn't want. The nearest exception was
   the 1952 Republican race, but Eisenhower's candidacy was above all due
   to the exertions of a major faction of the Republican Party itself, which recruited the reluctant war hero and ran his campaign. Party autonomy, we
   conclude, is equally clear on the Democratic side, where party conventions
   twice turned down ambitious mavericks who campaigned vigorously for
   the nomination and won significant popular support. Some party insiders
   were "cut down to size" in some of the contests we examined, but they
   were more often beaten by factional opponents within the party, not the
   forces of mass democracy.
2. So-called amateurs played important roles in several nomination contests,
   but the amateurs generally behaved as serious party players. This was
   most observably true in the 1968 Republican convention, when activists
   passed on their first-choice candidate, Ronald Reagan, in favor of someone
   they thought would be more electable. We give high marks for partisan
   seriousness to the activists of the Goldwater movement as well. For one
   thing, many came back four years later and showed they could compromise when compromise was indicated. For another, their nomination of
   a staunch conservative in 1964 after two decades of me-too Republicanism was a plausible party move. The Democratic "amateurs" of 1948—for
   so we count them—were another group of serious party players. A party
   whose members do not take occasional risks for their most preferred policies is not acting consistently with our sense of party rationality.

   One theoretical question here is how politicians position themselves
   for election. By the politician-centered theory of party, candidates must be
   sufficiently extreme to make their activists happy, and yet not so extreme

as to risk losing the general election. Our empirical accounts support a different view: Parties, not candidates, make the key choice about how far from the center their candidates will be. Parties make this decision based on their preferences and their estimate of the electoral consequences. Parties do not so much pressure candidates to be extreme—though, to be sure, this happens too—as choose them to be extreme.

3. With the exception of the Republicans in 1964 and the Democrats in 1968, parties consistently attempted to find candidates who were broadly acceptable to party groups and able to compete well in the general election. The Goldwater nomination was a case of party change, as discussed. The difficulty for the Democratic Party in 1968 was due to the sudden rise of a contentious new issue, Vietnam; American parties have never been able to absorb this kind of shock and, given their nature as largely voluntary coalitions, should not be expected to. Of the other regular nominations, that of Eisenhower in 1952 was the most contentious, but even here, the key to his victory was attracting delegates initially attached to his opponent. The unanimous support of the party's governors, and late vote changes to Eisenhower by many delegates, are further testament to the breadth of Eisenhower's appeal.

4. Lack of traditional convention decision-making structures was not an impediment to party coordination on an acceptable candidate. In two of the cases, the Republican nominations of 1952 and 1968, we find evidence of unbossed delegates deliberating independently about whom to nominate. In these cases, "decision by discussion" turned on how to balance the policy preferences of most party members with the need to win the general election, and in both cases the latter consideration was given decisive weight. Leaders were important in both conventions, but persuasion rather than command was the main basis of their influence. We suspect that decision by discussion was important in many nominations besides the 1952 and 1968 cases, but because decision in other cases was effectively made prior to the convention and merely ratified there, we were not able to observe it. Most of the nominees of this period—Dewey, Kennedy, Nixon, Humphrey—traveled extensively ahead of the convention in order to build the majorities that later nominated them. Yet in none of these cases, most obviously those of Nixon in 1960 and Humphrey in 1968, were candidates forcing the hand of the party; rather, party insiders were choosing them over rivals who also wanted to be nominated. Extensive campaigning by the winning candidate does not imply that the candidate has self-nominated.

5. Most importantly, both parties underwent important internal realignments in this period. Liberal activists successfully pressured the Democratic Party in 1948 to take a stand against southern racism, a change of

historical importance for the party and for the nation. Conservative activists turned the Republican Party in 1964 toward the staunch economic conservatism that permeates it today. In each case, more battles remained to be fought and won, but the activists who forced these turns remained engaged, extending and deepening their initial achievements. Neither development was due primarily to electoral pressure; indeed, the party actors most sensitive to electoral pressure tended to resist them. Change was due mainly to the pressures of intense policy demanders, the key actors in our theory of political parties.

A vital part of the story of party change that we have not examined is where, if not from ordinary voters, new activist agendas came from. Or, because activist agendas are essentially ideological agendas: What is the relationship between ideological change and party change? One of us, Hans Noel (2006), has investigated this question. He finds that, over the period 1830 to 1990, ideological agendas tend to appear first in the writings of pundits and political intellectuals and are later carried by activists into party politics. For example, leading liberal writers took up the issue of racial equality by 1930, some two decades ahead of the ADA activists who pressed the Democratic party on this issue in the 1940s. Leading conservative writers began to oppose abortion as early as the 1950s. This was at a time when the Democratic Party, because of its Catholic supporters, was the party more opposed to abortion, and also long before religious activists took up the issue. This pattern of change is important to our study of parties because it suggests again, but in a deeper way, how party change is a response to the views of intense policy demanders.

The main conclusions of this chapter have not been based on new evidence. Yet able analysts, looking at the same evidence, have sometimes reached opposite conclusions than ours—that parties in this period were weakening and perhaps dying. The difference is almost wholly due to differences in conceptions about parties. To most analysts, a party is not a party unless it is dominated by strong leaders and ambitious politicians. For us, parties can be strong in the absence of leader domination if their members can effectively work together to maximize the party's chances of getting from government the policies its members want. Another contrast is that, in this period as in other periods of American history, we view ideological activists, with their intense demands and extreme energy, as a source of strength rather than weakness in parties. Their role in shaping electoral coalitions is among the most important roles in democratic politics.

✦

APPENDIX TO CHAPTER 5
STATE PARTIES IN 1952

In chapter 5, we summarized the descriptions of the state parties in 1952 from David, Moos, and Goldman (1954). Table 5A.2 provides more detail for that summary, including some notes on features of the states. More details about this summary, as well as an electronic version of this table, will be available at www9.georgetown.edu/faculty/hcn4/.

Table 5A.1: Variable descriptions

Variable	Code	Description
Voters (openness to ordinary voters)	0	No opportunities for voters.
	1	Technically open to voters, but essentially manipulated away.
	2	Primaries could be useful avenue, but not enough candidates participate, or results are not binding.
	3	Primaries open to voters and with significant impact on delegates.
Unbossed (openness to unbossed activists)	0	No real avenues for outsiders.
	1	Few avenues, mostly in theory, and in reality blocked or unrealized.
	2	Significant opportunities, mostly unrealized.
	3	Significant opportunities, incompletely realized.
	4	Significant opportunities, widely taken advantage of.
	5	Essentially unbossed and open to outsider participation.
Candidates (efforts made by candidates)	0	Candidates are not involved.
	1	
	2	
	3	
	4	Candidates intensely campaigning.
Local issues dominate	1	If the authors explicitly indicate that local issues far outweighed national candidate concerns in choosing a delegates.
	0	Otherwise.
Openness		Summary, as in fig. 5.1. Guided by other variables. See fig. 5.1 for a complete description.
Volunteer (Democrats only; from Shafer 1983, 282)	1	Volunteer.
	0	Organization.
Delegate selection method		As summarized by report authors.

Table 5A.2: State Parties in 1952

State	Party	Voters	Unbossed	Candidates	Local	Openness	Volunteer	Delegate selection method	Notes
Alabama	D	1	2	1	0	4	1	Primary for delegates	Slate on ballot limited by party.
Alabama	R	0	1	2	0	2		District and state conventions	
Alaska	D	0	0	0	0	1		Territorial convention	
Alaska	R	0	0	0	1	1	1	Territorial party central committee	Internal fight used Ike's name, but may have been about local issues.
Arizona	D	0	1	0	1	1	1	State committee in session as a "state convention"	Untimely.
Arizona	R	0	0	2	0	1		State committee in session as a "state convention"	Untimely.
Arkansas	D	0	0	0	0	1	0	State committee	Untimely. Dominated by governor (always a Democrat).
Arkansas	R	0	2	0	0	3		District and state conventions	"Although it would be difficult, a grass-roots movement for a particular presidential aspirant could surge up through the Republican delegate conventions and 'mass meetings' much more easily than a similar movement could drive its way through the involuted primary-convention-state-committee-'lame duck'-governor procedure followed by the Democrats" (262).

State	Party							Selection method	
California	D	3	4	4	0	6	1	Primary of pledged delegate slates	"Under the operation of the primary law, it is quite easy for a would-be presidential candidate to secure a slate of delegates pledged to his support.... It is likewise relatively simple for a factional leader within the state to get together a slate of delegates" (224).
California	R	3	3	1	0	4		Primary of pledged delegate slates	Candidates don't run against favorite son.
Colorado	D	0	2	1	0	3		Congressional district and state conventions	
Colorado	R	0	4	3	0	5		Congressional district and state conventions	
Connecticut	D	0	1	0	0	2	0	State convention	
Connecticut	R	0	1	3	0	2		District and state conventions	Delegates "formally chosen at the state party convention. In practice, however, the machinery for selecting the delegates to the national convention is an undifferentiated part of the machinery which periodically makes decisions on party leadership."
Delaware	D	0	0	0	0	1	0	State convention	Slate prepared in advance.
Delaware	R	0	2	0	0	2		State convention	Slate prepared in advance. One faction complains it was "steamrollered," but little was done.
District of Columbia	D	3	3	1	0	6	1	Preference primary	Binding preference primary
District of Columbia	R	0	1	2	0	2		"State" convention	Precinct chairmen could register voters (for convention) in private.
Florida	D	3	5	4	0	6	1	Presidential preference poll, followed by primary for delegates, usually pledged	
Florida	R	0	0	0	1	1		State executive committee	Delegation chosen by state party committee.
Georgia	D	0	0	0	1	1		State executive committee	Delegation chosen by state party committee.

(continued on next page)

Table 5A.2 (continued)

State	Party	Voters	Unbossed	Candidates	Local	Openness	Volunteer	Delegate selection method	Notes
Georgia	R	0	2	2	0	3	0	District and state conventions	Meetings often not held, etc., but some efforts to limit participation are over-turned. Incomplete.
Hawaii	D	0	1	0	0	2		Territorial convention	
Hawaii	R	0	0	0	0	1		Territorial convention	
Idaho	D	0	0	0	0	1	1	State convention	Untimely.
Idaho	R	0	0	0	0	1		State convention	Untimely.
Illinois	D	2	3	2	0	4	0	Primary for delegates; at-large at convention; advisory write-in preference poll	Preference primary is nonbinding.
Illinois	R	2	3	3	0	4		Primary for delegates; at-large at convention; advisory write-in preference poll	
Indiana	D	0	1	0	1	2	0	State conventions and district caucuses	
Indiana	R	0	2	0	0	3		State conventions and district caucuses	
Iowa	D	0	3	2	0	3	1	State conventions and district caucuses	Some caucuses well-attended, but little conflict, often informal.
Iowa	R	0	3	2	0	5	0	State conventions and district caucuses	"Most bitterly contested convention in recent history." Helped Eisenhower.
Kansas	D	0	1	0	1	2	0	District and state conventions	
Kansas	R	0	2	2	0	3		District and state conventions	Outsiders not present in district conventions.
Kentucky	D	0	1	0	0	2	0	State convention	County conventions were formalities. Not large enough to be representative.
Kentucky	R	0	3	2	0	3		District and state conventions	
Louisiana	D	0	0	0	0	1	0	District delegates by district committee/at large by state committee	Untimely.

State	Party							Method	Comments
Louisiana	R	0	4	4	0	5		District and state conventions	Rival, originally bipartisan Eisenhower faction raids conventions, wins. Control of slate.
Maine	D	1	1	1	0	2	1	State convention	
Maine	R	1	3	2	0	3		District and state conventions	
Maryland	D	1	2	1	0	3	0	State convention/beauty contest	Unequal apportionment, indifference to the primary, some maneuvers by bosses.
Maryland	R	1	2	0	1	3		State conventions and district caucuses/beauty contest	Unequal apportionment, indifference to the primary, some maneuvers by bosses; unpublicized meetings.
Massachusetts	D	2	2	3	0	4	1	Primary for delegates; advisory write-in preference poll	Preference primary is nonbinding.
Massachusetts	R	2	2	3	0	4		Primary for delegates; advisory write-in preference poll	Not binding; no preference slate from party leaders
Michigan	D	0	1	0	0	1	1	State convention	Untimely.
Michigan	R	0	1	0	0	1		State convention	Untimely.
Minnesota	D	3	4	2	0	6	1	Delegates by primary; some at-large by primary, some by state convention; bound by preference primary	
Minnesota	R	2	2	2	0	6		Delegates by primary; some at-large by primary, some by state convention; bound by preference primary	
Mississippi	D	0	3	1	0	3	1	State conventions and district caucuses	"The one tactic, however, that was most conspicuously missing from the situation in both parties in Mississippi in 1952 was any broad attempt by the dissidents to win their point at the grass roots by organizing lawful majorities in the meetings." Many meetings had small numbers.

(continued on next page)

Table 5A.2 (continued)

State	Party	Voters	Unbossed	Candidates	Local	Openness	Volunteer	Delegate selection method	Notes
Mississippi	R	1	4	0	0	5	0	State conventions and district caucuses	Conflict among Lily Whites, Black and Tans, and new pro-Eisenhower faction.
Missouri	D	0	1	0	0	2	0	District caucuses and state convention	Local meetings controlled by leadership.
Missouri	R	0	1	4	0	2	0	District and state conventions	In some cases, local areas made choices without any meetings at all.
Montana	D	0	0	1	0	1	1	State convention	Untimely.
Montana	R	0	0	1	0	1	1	State convention	Untimely.
Nebraska	D	3	3	4	0	6	1	Primary for delegates	
Nebraska	R	3	3	1	0	6	1	Primary for delegates	
Nevada	D	0	1	0	0	2	1	State convention	District meetings poorly advertised or not even held.
Nevada	R	0	3	3	0	3	1	State convention	Precinct meetings drew a lot of attention, but local issues dominated.
New Hampshire	D	3	3	2	0	6	1	Primary for delegates	
New Hampshire	R	3	3	2	0	6	1	Primary for delegates	
New Jersey	D	2	2	2	0	4	0	Primary, nonbinding preference poll	Preference primary is nonbinding.
New Jersey	R	2	2	2	0	4	0	Primary, nonbinding preference poll	Preference primary nonbinding; slate chosen by leaders
New Mexico	D	0	2	0	0	3	0	State convention	Resolutions committee's recommendations accepted without conflict.

New Mexico	R	0	3	3	0	5	State convention	Floor battle between Eisenhower and Taft forces.
New York	D	2	1	2	1	4	Delegates by primary; at-large by newly elected 300-person committee	No choice on ballot.
New York	R	2	1	2	0	4	Delegates by primary; at-large by newly elected 300-person committee	No choice on ballot.
North Carolina	D	0	2	3	0	3	State convention	Attendance low.
North Carolina	R	0	2	3	0	2	District and state conventions	District meetings not held. Many seats empty.
North Dakota	D	0	1	1	1	1	State convention	Untimely.
North Dakota	R	0	0	0	1	1	State convention	Untimely.
Ohio	D	1	1	2	0	2	Primary for delegates; each delegate pledged to 1st/2nd choices	Parties have procedural advantages in slate-making
Ohio	R	1	1	2	0	2	Primary for delegates; each delegate pledged to 1st/2nd choices	Parties have procedural advantages in slate-making.
Oklahoma	D	0	2	0	1	3	State convention	County meetings open, but no evidence of campaigning.
Oklahoma	R	0	2	2	0	3	District and state conventions	Eisenhower forces move too slowly.
Oregon	D	3	5	4	0	6	Preference poll for candidates; primary for delegates pledged to the results of the preference poll	
Oregon	R	3	5	4	0	6	Preference poll for candidates; primary for delegates pledged to the results of the preference poll	
Pennsylvania	D	2	3	2	0	4	Primary for delegates; at-large by state committee; advisory preference poll	Delegates can "promise to support" a candidate, but usually don't, or don't get elected.
Pennsylvania	R	2	3	2	0	4	Primary for delegates; at-large by state committee; advisory preference poll	Delegates can "promise to support" a candidate, but usually don't, or don't get elected.
Puerto Rico	D	0	0	0	0	1	State central committee	All decisions in committee.

(continued on next page)

State	Party	Voters	Unbossed	Candidates	Local	Openness	Volunteer	Delegate selection method	Notes
Puerto Rico	R	0	4	0	0	5	0	State convention	Untimely.
Rhode Island	D	0	0	0	0	1	0	State convention	Untimely.
Rhode Island	R	0	3	1	0	1	0	District and state conventions	Party leaders and governor choose delegates. States' rights faction dominates.
South Carolina	D	0	1	0	0	2	0	District caucuses and state convention	Rival faction is "read out" of party.
South Carolina	R	0	2	0	1	2	1	State convention	
South Dakota	D	3	4	3	0	6	1	Primary for delegate slates	
South Dakota	R	2	5	3	0	6	1	Primary for delegate slates	
Tennessee	D	0	1	1	0	2	1	District caucuses and state convention	Seated rival delegations, managed conflict. Unit Rule.
Tennessee	R	0	3	3	0	5		District and state conventions	Convention was over in three hours, pro-Taft insiders win every move. But gave considerable opportunities to the Eisenhower people, who had no complaints.
Texas	D	0	3	0	1	3	0	State convention	Fight over general loyalty, not nominations.
Texas	R	0	4	4	0	5		State convention	Eisenhower outsiders capture control of convention.
Utah	D	0	3	0	0	3	1	State convention	Open, but no interest. Few Democrats in state.
Utah	R	0	1	2	0	2		Seemingly autonomous district conventions held in conjunction with state	Party leaders set agenda before outsiders could act.

State	Party							Selection method	Comments
Vermont	D	1	2	0	0	3	1	State convention	Few Democrats, little interest. Many people don't even show up.
Vermont	R	1	3	4	0	5	1	State convention	Eisenhower forces in procedural command. Felt constrained to make open.
Virginia	D	0	2	1	0	3	0	District and state conventions	Byrd machine, some resistance unsuccessful.
Virginia	R	0	2	2	0	2	0	District and state conventions	Eisenhower forces walk out, but cannot do more.
Washington	D	0	1	0	0	1	0	District caucuses and state convention	Hierarchical, large role of local committee elected much earlier; causal attitude toward holding proper meetings.
Washington	R	0	0	0	0	1	1	District and state conventions	Untimely.
West Virginia	D	1	4	2	0	4	0	Primary for delegates; advisory preference poll	Early filing date.
West Virginia	R	1	4	2	1	4	0	Primary for delegates; advisory preference poll	Early filing date.
Wisconsin	D	3	4	4	0	6	1	Primary; candidate must sign declaration	
Wisconsin	R	3	4	4	0	6		Primary; candidate must sign declaration	
Wyoming	D	0	0	1	0	1	0	State convention	Untimely.
Wyoming	R	0	0	0	0	1	0	State convention	Untimely.

Mastering the Postreform System

The circumstances under which Hubert Horatio Humphrey entered the contest for the 1968 Democratic nomination were extraordinary. The incumbent president, Lyndon Johnson, shocked the nation by announcing on March 31 that he would not seek reelection. Humphrey, the incumbent vice president, was ambitious for the top job, but by the time of Johnson's withdrawal, the deadlines for entering most primaries had passed. If he had wished to do so, Humphrey could have competed for voter support at the head of slates entered in Johnson's name, but he did not. Johnson had quit the race under pressure from antiwar insurgents, and Humphrey, who inherited responsibility for Johnson's war policies, had no wish to confront them in a popular election. As his campaign's top spokesman bluntly told a journalist, "We are not going to be trapped into any manufactured confrontation. We are not in the primaries, we are not going in [and] we do not have to go in" (United Press International 1968). Humphrey avoided even giving speeches in states that were holding primaries.

Humphrey's strategy was feasible because party insiders favored him and, as we saw in the previous chapter, they controlled the bulk of delegates to the party nominating convention. But

Humphrey faced a rebellion by supporters of the antiwar candidates, who challenged the legitimacy of the insider-dominated nomination process. In a concession he hoped would unify the party, Humphrey agreed to a reform commission to revamp the party's nominating system for the next election. This body, known informally as the McGovern-Fraser Commission, recommended that the selection of delegates to the party nominating convention be opened up to full and timely participation by ordinary voters. The Democratic National Committee accepted the reform and, for reasons described below, change spread quickly to the Republican Party.

This was fundamental change. Through all previous party history, most delegates to party nominating conventions were effectively controlled by party insiders—old-style bosses in machine states, more ideologically oriented activists in nonmachine areas, or some combination of the two kinds of party players. The introduction of primaries early in the twentieth century by Progressives scarcely dented insider domination.

But in the aftermath of the McGovern-Fraser reforms, many party leaders and activists were suddenly on the outside looking in. Voters, not party insiders, were in charge. Some party leaders were unable even to attend the next party convention. At one point in the 1976 Democratic nomination contest, W. Averell Harriman, an old Democratic warhorse, was told of Carter's success in the primaries and the likelihood that he would be nominated. "Jimmy Carter? How can that be?" declared Harriman. "I don't even know Jimmy Carter, and as far as I know, none of my friends know him, either" (Matthews 1989, 155). Many scholars questioned, with good reason, whether parties still existed at that point, at least as regards presidential nominations. A party that cannot control its nominations is not, in our theory of parties, really a party at all.

But the presidency of the United States is an extremely important office, setting policy on scores of subjects that politically active people care deeply about. It is therefore unsurprising that the intense policy demanders who inhabit the Democratic and Republican parties—including new groups whose power was enhanced by the reforms—were not content to stand aside and let rank-and-file voters choose their nominee. So they studied the nomination process, figured out its dynamics, adjusted the rules, formulated clever strategies, and—faster than you can say "President Ronald Reagan"—they were back in the game. By 1980 party leaders and activists had learned to control the new nomination process not as fully as Progressive-era bosses had learned to control the primaries of their day, but much more successfully than most scholarship on presidential nominations has recognized.

The new parties, however, had a new mix of players. Prereform party conventions were dominated by party regulars—that is, men and women who had worked for years or even decades within their local party organizations and were often most concerned about state or local politics. With the selection of convention delegates now open to public participation, new actors flooded in. These new actors were intense policy demanders, as were the old actors, but they were demanders who had less access to the older nominating system. They were often most interested in national politics, and they were often more loyal to group or ideological goals than to the party itself. The combination of new and old players produced some rocky moments, but by the 1980s, both parties were back on an even keel and effectively controlling the nomination process.

In this chapter we begin to lay out the evidence for this argument. The initial task is simply to describe how the reformed nominating system worked and what candidates and leading party players did to cope with the challenges it presented.

What the Reforms Did and Why They Mattered

The McGovern-Fraser reforms did not create any new institutions or proscribe any old ones. State parties could continue to select delegates through primary elections, precinct caucuses, or party conventions, as they wished. But important details were now set by the national Democratic Party. If a state party opted to use a primary to select delegates to the party nominating convention, the delegates had to be awarded to candidates on the basis of voter support for that candidate. The change here was that, in the past, voter participation in some states had been limited to "beauty contest" primaries that did not actually choose any delegates. In other primaries, voters got a choice among obscure activists whose presidential preference might be unknown. The new rules banned delegate selection by either method as insufficiently open to voter influence.

If a state party opted to use a system of precinct caucuses or state conventions to select national convention delegates, the process had to be completely open to participation by ordinary voters, and if upper-level county or state conventions were used to make the final choice of convention delegates, the result had to be tied to the preferences of party members at the precinct level. The change here was that many states had, as we saw in chapter 5, blocked or informally undermined voter participation in precinct elections and party conventions. All such restrictions were now forbidden. States that held caucuses were required to publicize the meeting times, which they had sometimes chosen not to do, and to hold the caucuses in the calendar year of the presidential election rather than, as some had done, one or even two years ahead of it.

One way to summarize these changes is to think back to figure 5.1 in the last chapter, which showed that about 20 percent of local party systems in the Democratic Party in the 1950s were fully open to voter influence. As a result of the McGovern-Fraser reforms, this figure shot up to 100 percent.

Opening up the delegate-selection process to control by ordinary party voters transformed the logic of campaigning for presidential nomination. In the old system, candidates directed their main efforts toward the party insiders and activists because they controlled selection of delegates to the national convention. Presidential candidates might try to swamp the precinct caucuses at the base of the selection process—as Eisenhower forces did in Texas in 1952 and the Goldwater forces did in 1964—but this was unusual on the Democratic side. Most major candidates accepted precinct elections as beyond their power to influence and worked instead to win over the individuals who came out of them. Locally elected party leaders and activists were thus an independent force in presidential nominations.

In the new system, precinct elections were fully open to voter influence—and, via voters, to candidate influence as well. As some candidates began seeking to mobilize support in the caucuses, all candidates were compelled to follow. In the old system, candidates worked through the party regulars who habitually attended a caucus; in the new system, candidates tried to flood party caucuses with their own people.

Primary elections were likewise transformed. In the old system, candidates entered them mainly to demonstrate vote-getting prowess to party leaders. Some primaries didn't even award delegates to the winning candidate. Hence candidates were free to skip most or even all of them. In the new system, candidates won convention delegates in relation to popular support. In addition, the number of primaries increased in 1972 and again in 1976. The result was that no candidate could win nomination without entering most or all primaries.

Convention delegates chosen under the new rules were no longer independent agents; they were required to vote at the convention for the candidate that local voters had instructed them to support. As a consequence, the national party convention began to choose nominees almost as mechanically as the Electoral College chooses presidents. The real decision was made in the selection of delegates in primaries and caucuses.

We should add that members of the McGovern-Fraser commission did not fully intend the change that their reforms engendered (see Ranney 1975, 203–9; Shafer 1983; Polsby 1983). They expected somewhat greater popular participation, but did not foresee the associated marginalization of the traditional party leadership.

Subsequent Democratic reform commissions have made further changes in the rules. Perhaps the most important was a decision in 1982 that about 20 percent of convention delegates would be party leaders and office holders not pledged to any candidate. These independent delegates, called super delegates, may have been decisive in the nomination of Walter Mondale in 1984 and conceivably could again be critical in 2008. (The 2008 Democratic nomination is undecided as this book goes to press.) Parties have also adjusted rules on the timing of primaries and caucuses. How these and other post-McGovern-Fraser rules have affected nominations is a large and complex subject, but one that is largely independent of the themes of this book.[1] Hence we shall focus on what we and most other scholars take to be the main impact of the first wave of reform: the creation of a nomination process in which ordinary party members are sovereign.

First Contests in the Reformed System

In January of 1972, as a field of eleven candidates prepared to run for the first time under the new McGovern-Fraser rules, the race seemed as predictable as the one-ballot contests at the end of the old system: One candidate, Senator Edmund Muskie of Maine, had campaigned energetically through the previous year and appeared to have the nomination locked up. He was far and away the front-runner in the polls, fund-raising, and endorsements of party politicians. As a staff member recalled later, "The money was flowing in fairly well in keeping with Muskie's standing in the polls. I figured that all we had to do was sit and wait, and that it was only a matter of a few months before Muskie would win the nomination. Journalists felt the same way."[2] "For journalists like this writer," wrote T. H. White, "there was only the annoying problem of how to . . . spin excitement out of a nomination story which [Muskie] had apparently foreclosed" (White 1973, 78).

But almost nothing went as expected. It was a new game, and the leading candidates played it badly. One example of poor play was Muskie's response to a harsh newspaper attack in New Hampshire.[3] As David Broder described it:

> With tears streaming down his face and his voice choked with emotion, Senator Edmund S. Muskie (D-Maine) stood in the snow outside the Manchester *Union Leader* this morning and accused its publisher of making vicious attacks on him and his wife, Jane.
>
> The Democratic presidential candidate called publisher William Loeb "a gutless coward" for involving Mrs. Muskie in the campaign and said four times that Loeb had lied in charging that Muskie had condoned a slur on Americans of French-Canadian descent.
>
> In defending his wife, Muskie broke down three times in as many minutes—uttering a few words and then standing silent in the near blizzard, rubbing at his face, his shoulders heaving, while he attempted to regain his composure sufficiently to speak. (Broder 1972b)

Images of an apparently sobbing Muskie were to haunt him for the rest of the campaign.[4]

Muskie's breakdown could be seen as a freak occurrence, but he and others believed that it was related to the pressures of competing in the new system. As Muskie explained:

> That previous week [before the collapse], I'd been down to Florida, then I flew to Idaho, then I flew to California, then I flew back to Washington to vote in the Senate, and I flew back to California [where he was sick], and then I flew into Manchester and I was hit with this [story]. I'm tough physically, but no one could do that—it was a bitch of a day. The staff thought I should go down to the *Union Leader* to reply to that story. If I was going to do it again, I'd look for a campaign manager, a genius, a schedule-maker who has veto power over a candidate's own decisions. You got to have a czar. For Christ's sake, you got to pace yourself. I was just goddamned mad and choked up over my anger. (White 1973, 85)

Nor was this Muskie's only mistake in dealing with the media. His strategy, which his staff shared with reporters, was to wrap up the nomination in the first four primaries, beginning with a commanding win in the New Hampshire. A staff member told reporters that if Muskie did not get 50 percent of the vote in New Hampshire, dire consequences would follow. But Muskie spent little time in New Hampshire and wound up getting "only" 48 percent of the vote. Because this was below the campaign's own goal for itself, the media played the victory as a moral loss.

As R. W. Apple wrote in the *New York Times*, "the candidate himself, in private conversations before the balloting, had said he would have to beat his nearest competitor, Senator George McGovern of South Dakota, by a 2-1 margin if he were to help himself. He came nowhere close to that" (March 9, 1972, 32). With this sort of coverage at his back, Muskie moved on to the Florida primary the next week, where he really did lose, finishing fourth behind George Wallace, Hubert Humphrey, and Senator Henry Jackson of Washington.

The Muskie campaign did, however, make some good moves. One was to spend the year prior to New Hampshire traveling the country to line up the endorsements of party officials. As we show below, early endorsements have become the key to the nomination process, and Muskie was successful in getting them. "By January of 1972," as T. H. White wrote, "the parade of endorsements from the established leadership of the party had become so crowded that one of the chief problems was sequencing their dates with enough separation to get the maximum impact" (1973, 82). By our count, some 46 percent of party leaders who made preprimary public endorsements supported Muskie, with the rest scattered across a half-dozen candidates. (We describe the methodology by which we arrived at this number below.)

But Muskie was shy on union support. Labor had worked closely with Democratic Party leaders in presidential nominations since the 1940s and would do so again in the 1980s. In 1972, however, key union leaders refused to join in support of Muskie despite his acceptable record on labor issues. Instead, labor backed Humphrey in critical contests in Florida, Wisconsin, and Pennsylvania, thereby contributing to the final demise of Muskie.[5] With Muskie out of the race, McGovern emerged from the pack and eventually won. But he was a candidate so unacceptable to labor that many unions failed to endorse him even in the general election against Richard Nixon. So here was a lesson for labor: Holding out for your first choice means risking a vastly worse outcome. In the future, labor would be more careful. Rather than contributing to the problems of consensus candidates like Muskie, it would help nurse them through the rough spots in the primaries.

Another politician who did not play a good game in the new system was Humphrey. As late as fall 1971, he still thought it would be possible to sit out all of the primary contests except the last one, California's. Later he allowed that "whoever gets the nomination will have to be in the primaries, a representative sample of them" (Solberg 1984, 428). So Humphrey entered and, with help from labor, won several big ones, but he needlessly failed to compete for delegates in several others. Nor did he compete hard for delegates in the states that chose convention delegates in big neighborhood meetings called caucuses. "I don't think that we [thought through the reforms] in the Humphrey campaign—not filing in New York [for the primary], for example," said one operative afterward (May and Fraser 1973, 41). Humphrey's strategy was to show strength in the primaries and then appeal for the support of independent party leaders at the national convention. Too late he realized that independent party leaders no longer existed in significant numbers. Even the powerful Democratic mayor of Chicago, Richard J. Daley, would be denied seating at the party convention.

The one candidate who did play a smart game was Senator George McGovern of South Dakota. Like Muskie, McGovern recognized the incentive to compete for delegates in all fifty states, but unlike Muskie, he did not exhaust himself by trying to be personally present in too many places. Rather, he concentrated first on New Hampshire, spending more time there than anyone else, while at the same time downplaying his expectations for success. Thus, when McGovern finished second to Muskie with 37 percent of the vote, the media gave him credit for a moral victory because, in contrast to Muskie, he had done better than expected. Downplaying one's chances in New Hampshire while going all out to do better than expected was to become a staple strategy of later contests, and McGovern milked it for all it was worth in 1972. The moral victory in New Hampshire enabled him to secure a niche position as the semiofficial "candidate of the left" in the nomination contest. In the aftermath of the turbulent 1960s, this was a good niche to occupy in the Democratic Party.

McGovern, who had helped to write the new rules, also saw possibilities that others did not. In particular, many states in 1972 still chose their convention delegates through a caucus system. But the openness of caucuses under the new McGovern-Fraser rules made them vulnerable to takeover by candidates. As *Wall Street Journal* reporter Norman Miller wrote:

> The McGovern organization's effective exploitation of the reform rules has been most striking in little-noticed contests in the [caucus] states. Time and again, bands of McGovern backers have "blitzed" precinct-level caucuses and seized power to name delegates from outnumbered regulars, who have either backed another candidate or *wanted to remain uncommitted*. The tactics have insured Sen. McGovern delegates from a number of unlikely states—Texas, Virginia, and Oklahoma, to name a few—enough that it now seems likely he'll attain his goal of 300 delegates from non-primary states.

> Not even organized labor has been able to deliver reliably under the new rules. In many places, observes one political operative close to the unions, labor has "let a bunch of long-hairs and college kids beat them." He adds glumly, "The new rules ruined the unions—absolutely ruined them." (emphasis added)[6]

We highlight McGovern's success in forcing the choice of committed rather than uncommitted delegates to the national convention. The latter were the basis of Humphrey's hope that a deadlocked convention might turn to him, but McGovern nabbed these delegates at the selection stage. Waiting until the convention to put together one's coalition was a losing strategy in the new system.

McGovern had the advantage of support from large numbers of college students angry over the continuing war in Vietnam. They arrived by the hundreds every weekend of the New Hampshire campaign to work for their champion, and they also powered his successful blitzes in the caucus states. McCarthy and Kennedy had enjoyed similar support in the 1968 race, but it did them less good because party insiders still controlled delegate selection. In the new system, delegates were chosen in an open process in which committed volunteer support could make more of a difference.

If McGovern was the factional candidate of the left, George Wallace was the factional candidate of the right. He came onto the national stage in 1963 when, as Governor of Alabama, he pledged "segregation now, segregation tomorrow, segregation forever." By the time of his 1972 presidential campaign, he had scrubbed racist language from his speeches and was directing his most colorful attacks against "pointy-headed" Washington bureaucrats and college professors who couldn't "even park their bicycles straight." But Wallace did attack busing to achieve school integration, which, in case there had been any doubt, made clear which side of the racial divide Wallace was on.

Wallace was a fiery campaigner with a strong base of support not only in the South but in white working-class areas of the North. But because the mainstream of the Democratic Party would never willingly accept Wallace as the party's nominee, his only chance was to compete for every possible delegate in the hope of getting a majority pledged to him personally. This Wallace failed to do. He passed on several important primaries and failed to match McGovern's efforts in caucus states. Said a Wallace staffer afterward: "I think the reason that he did not go more heavily into the non-primary states was because of a lack of knowledge about the reform rules" (May and Fraser 1973, 100).

As it turned out, Wallace was forced from the race by an assassination attempt. With Muskie beaten by that time, the contest narrowed to Mc-Govern versus Humphrey, which McGovern won.

The 1972 nomination shows how treacherous and unpredictable a sequence of fifty state primaries and caucuses can be. If a candidate as initially strong and well-positioned in his party as Muskie could lose, anyone could lose. If a candidate as far from the mainstream as McGovern could win, just about anyone could win. A slip in the media or a wrong strategic turn or a boost from enthusiastic volunteers could make all the difference.

Scholars of presidential nominations have had relatively little to say about the 1972 nomination, and probably wisely so, since the decisive factors may have been idiosyncratic to that contest. Yet three points of general significance should be noted. First, the nomination process was completely beyond the control of party leaders. The two strongest candidates, McGovern and Wallace, were from the ideological fringes of the party and would not have stood a chance of success under the old system. Muskie, the candidate favored by the party establishment, was the first to collapse. Second, media coverage seemed to play an important role—provoking Muskie to tears and setting performance expectations that affected the dynamics of the race. Third, the winner of the voter-dominated process was unable to unify his party. Mayor Daley, a major figure in the prereform party, sat on his hands through much of the campaign, and the AFL-CIO labor federation never endorsed McGovern's candidacy. The result was a landslide defeat for the Democratic Party in 1972.

The nomination contest in 1976 produced an equally unexpected result—the nomination of Jimmy Carter, a previously obscure one-term governor of Georgia. In the scholarly studies that followed, the Carter campaign became, by contrast, the archetype of the new system and is still sometimes invoked as typical. We view the Carter nomination as illuminating but atypical.

First off, in contrast to other successful candidates in recent decades, Carter did *not* spend the bulk of his time traveling around the country to meet party leaders and seek their support. Instead, he traveled around Iowa, the location of the first public contest, to build support there. His aim was to gain national media attention by doing better than expected in Iowa and to parlay that success into national success. And this is exactly what happened. Carter didn't win outright—the highest vote was for "uncommitted"—but Carter won more support than any other actual candidate. This gave him a shot of media coverage and a boost in fund-raising as he went on to the next contest, which was in New Hampshire, where he won with 28 percent of the vote compared to 23 percent for his nearest opponent, Morris Udall, a member of the House of Representatives from Arizona. This victory, modest as it was, propelled Carter to further victories in later primaries, as winning begot more winning. With each early contest, Carter picked up money and support that made him harder to stop. By the time reporters began asking "Jimmy Who?" and voters had begun to absorb some of the answers, Carter was too far ahead of the pack to be caught (Patterson 1980). As his principal opponent, Mo Udall, complained: "It's like a football game, in which you say to the first team that makes a first down with ten yards, 'Hereafter your team has a special rule. Your first downs are five yards. And if you make three of those you get a two-yard first down. And we're going to let your first touchdown count twenty-one points. Now the rest of you bastards play catch-up under the regular rules'" (cited in Bartels 1988, 4).[7]

Democratic Party leaders were as flummoxed by Carter's success as by McGovern's four years earlier. But at least party leaders were personally acquainted with McGovern; many had to learn about Carter the same way as everyone else did—by reading the newspapers.

One of the most impressive aspects of Carter's victory in 1976 was that he and his principal strategist, Hamilton Jordan, were not simply lucky. Carter and Jordan figured out how the nomination process would work and called almost every shot right. In early memos, Jordan foresaw that the media would give heavy coverage to Iowa, which had been neglected in the past; foresaw that a win in Iowa could build publicity toward a win in New Hampshire; and foresaw that a New Hampshire win could be parlayed into more media coverage, a surge in the polls, and a boost in fund-raising that would carry all the way to the nominating convention.[8] Correctly appreciating all this, Carter spent much more time than the other candidates in Iowa—and was duly rewarded. Journalist Jules Witcover documents all this in his book on the 1976 campaign, *Marathon* (1977).

In 1976, Carter's people were the only team that grasped the new dynamic of media-driven momentum. Henry Jackson, the strongest of the insider candidates, skipped Iowa and New Hampshire to concentrate on Massachusetts, which came third in the sequence of contests. According to a biographer, Jackson viewed George Wallace as his main opponent and wanted to conserve strength for the struggle against the Alabama firebrand in the bigger states (Kaufman 2000, 318–19). Jackson also felt that Massachusetts "was the kind of state that would provide the kind of acceleration . . . that would more than offset not going into New Hampshire" (Witcover 1977, 191). Wallace, confined to a wheelchair, also kept a low profile in Iowa and New Hampshire. Finally, Hubert Humphrey was also interested in the nomination but skipped the primaries and worked for a draft at the party convention. These strategic miscalculations by his best-known opponents left Carter free to score big wins, and reap major publicity, in a field lacking his strongest potential rivals.[9] The heavy media coverage that attended these wins—appearances on the morning television news shows, breathless reportage on the network news, getting onto the covers of *Time* and *Newsweek*—enabled "Jimmy Who?" to burst onto the national scene as the man to beat for the Democratic nomination.

What this thumbnail analysis shows is that, beneath the train wrecks that were the 1972 and 1976 Democratic nominations, strategy mattered, and the correct strategy was to compete in all primaries and caucuses. It shows as well the importance of the national media as a force in presidential nominations. Finally, it shows that the Democratic Party had essentially no control over its presidential nomination process. Even the media mattered more.

This analysis also raises an obvious question: How long would it take for all candidates to catch on to the correct strategy? The 1972 race was so full of idiosyncrasy that savvy players might be forgiven for missing the importance of competing in all contests, but after 1976 this lesson should have been obvious to everyone—and, as we shall see, it did become obvious to almost everyone. We return to this point below, but first a few words on reform and the Republican Party.

The McGovern-Fraser Commission was a Democratic body that had no direct authority over the Republican nomination process. But it nonetheless had two important indirect effects. The first was an increase in the number of presidential primaries. When state Democratic leaders realized that, under the McGovern-Fraser rules, ordinary voters would flood their precinct and state conventions to support their favorite presidential candidate, many chose to switch to a presidential primary as a means of insulating themselves from national politics. The state legislatures that created the new primaries were mostly controlled by Democrats and tended to feel that what was good for Democrats would be fine for Republicans too. The upshot was that the GOP got a dozen new primaries in the course of the 1970s, which made its nomination process as top heavy with primaries as the Democratic one (Polsby 1983, 53–59).[10]

The second spillover effect was even more indirect, the power of example. Democratic nomination contests in 1972 and 1976 were much more intensely fought than in the past. Every primary and every caucus was contested by someone. The national media, led by television, paid close attention as the fight continued from February until the last primaries in June. With their new primaries and the Democrats as role models, it was straightforward for GOP candidates to get into nomination brawls too. And brawl they did. When Ronald Reagan challenged incumbent President Gerald Ford for the 1976 nomination, the two candidates fought tooth-and-nail for every delegate in every corner of the country. When Ford prevailed by only 117 convention delegates—a verdict that could have been reversed by any of several state delegations—it was clear there would be no turning back from the new, all-out style of campaigning for presidential nomination. The Republicans would probably have arrived soon enough at the new style of national campaigning, but the example of 1972 gave them a nudge. In consequence, the unreformed Republican nomination contests came to closely resemble the reformed Democratic ones.

Learning from Carter

In 1980, a year in which the Republican nomination was wide open, most of the field was hustling for the early advantage that Carter had gotten from Iowa in 1976. As David Broder wrote in January 1979: "The example [Carter] set four years ago by declaring his candidacy almost two years in advance of election day, and campaigning at breakneck speed for over a year in the states with early delegate contests, has convinced his GOP rivals that this is the way to go" (Broder 1979). James Baker, who was George Bush's campaign manager in 1980, candidly admitted that his candidate had simply commandeered the Carter game plan: "The truth of the matter is we haven't changed our strategy one whit. It was never an original strategy. It's what you read in [Witcover's] *Marathon* about Jimmy Carter. We read that book. Damn carefully" (Hendrickson 1980). Thus, by 1980, candidates of all stripes knew what only Carter had clearly realized in 1976. The one campaign that hadn't quite learned—or perhaps simply refused to accept—the lesson was Ronald Reagan's. His campaign manager believed that that Reagan "should present himself as a front-runner, above the pack, beyond the pack" (White 1982, 250). Hence Reagan minimized his campaigning in Iowa, which had been Carter's launching pad in 1976. In earlier years, a candidate as strong as Reagan might have been able to get away with that strategy, when few candidates made a major effort in Iowa. But now that everyone—except Reagan—saw Iowa as their launching pad, Reagan's measured campaign effort was insufficient. So George Bush, who went all-out and won the Iowa caucuses, set Reagan on his heels by capturing, as Bush put it, "Big Mo." But Reagan was not so foolish as to neglect New Hampshire, and he was a sufficiently strong candidate that he could recover from his error in Iowa.

When all candidates, rather than only one, understand the game, it makes it a different game. No longer did the strongest candidates wait to enter the primaries at their strategic convenience.[11] They *all* organized in the year prior to the election, entered the first contests, and tried to build on their early success. In this system, politically marginal but strategically savvy candidates like McGovern and Carter had no special advantage. Weaker candidates could still hope that a "surprisingly" good showing in an early primary would create momentum for them, as occurred for underdog Gary Hart in the 1984 Democratic contest. But with the leading contenders now playing the correct strategy, the strongest candidates tended naturally to win. Hence, we are in agreement with Mayer's (2001) observation, "Thirty years after a series of reforms that were supposed to 'open up the parties' and 'level the playing field,' the American presidential nominating process has become, if anything, even more hostile to outsiders than the system that preceded it. If the 1996 nomination contests went a considerable way towards establishing this proposition, the 2000 races should remove any lingering doubt" (12).

We would, indeed, make the proposition stronger. Starting with the nomination of Ronald Reagan in 1980, insider candidates have won *every* contest through 2000 and, as we argue in the next chapter, possibly 2004 as well. And the winners have been more than just insiders; they have been *party insiders,* the chosen favorites of a party establishment. How did parties, which had almost no control of presidential nominations on the Democratic side and a bare grip on control on the Republican side, get so quickly back into the business of making nominations?

The Incentive for an Invisible Primary

We begin with this central fact: by 1980, candidates for presidential nomination in both parties recognized the need to campaign for delegate support in every state in the nation, often at the level of counties or congressional districts. But this is a vast, vast undertaking. No presidential candidate has the staff, financial resources, or know-how to conduct what are, in effect, scores of campaigns all around the country. Hence, the new campaign process virtually required serious candidates to build alliances with fellow partisans around the country. Even iconoclast Jerry Brown, the former California governor immortalized by Columnist Mike Royko as Governor Moonbeam, conformed to this law of politics: "One of the first things Brown did [when he entered the 1976 contest] was to contact [Hubert] Humphrey. 'He came to see me,' Humphrey recalled. 'He told me he wanted to run in Maryland first. He said, 'Who do you know?

Who are the people over there?' And I told him" (Witcover 1977, 333). Of course, most candidates make such inquiries well ahead of the point of entering the nomination contest. They spend many months, often many years, building the support necessary to mount a serious national campaign. During this time, they behave much as John Kennedy and Richard Nixon did, seeking out local party members on their home turf and trying to win them over. As Byron Shafer has observed in *Quiet Revolution*: "Once the institutional structure of delegate selection had changed so that the regular party did not have an automatic claim on the nomination process, and once regular party officials could not be courted as the logical route to a nomination, candidates were automatically encouraged to build campaign organizations of their own. Indeed, the creation of open arenas for delegate selection in almost every state, where any candidate could build a campaign in principle, meant that every candidate needed to do so in actual practice" (1983, 531).

The human building blocks for these candidate organizations came from several sources: individual activists, often strongly motivated by ideology or a salient issue (e.g., abortion, the Vietnam War); older interest groups, such as unions, farm organizations, business groups; and new or newly active interests, such as environmental, women's, and church groups. In states that still used local caucus elections to choose convention delegates, candidates relied heavily on these activists and interest groups to mobilize voters for the caucuses and to turn out in heavy numbers themselves. In states that held primary elections, candidates relied on local activists and interests for canvassing and for their prestige with voters.

Nothing, of course, is ever free in politics. In exchange for their labor in campaigns, interest groups and activists expected candidates to support them on issues they cared about. As Shafer explains in a later book, *Bifurcated Politics*: "groups and organizations had a long history of attempting to influence presidential selection. Presidents, after all, were likely to be able to make major contributions to their interests or causes. But before reforms, these groups . . . had been forced to operate through the political parties. . . . After reform . . . they could put themselves directly in the service of one or more presidential contenders and demand policy responses to accompany their support" (1988, 115).

These observations bring us to the invisible primary, the huge intraparty decision process that, as we argue, has been at the heart of the presidential nomination process since at least the 1940s and that continues to be centrally important in the postreform nomination process. We summarize the logic of the invisible primary as it played out in the reformed nomination system as follows:

- Faced with the need to compete in fifty state primaries and caucuses, presidential candidates have no choice but to enlist help. They also have relatively little choice about where to get it, namely, the assortment of individuals who are active in politics: local leaders and party regulars, as in the prereform system, and also nationally oriented interest groups, issue activists, ideologues, fund-raisers, and campaign technicians. Candidates also seek the help of personal and professional friends, and some are successful in bringing large numbers of fresh faces into politics. But candidates mostly rely for support on people regularly active in politics.

- Faced with multiple candidates beseeching them for support, party insiders—from governors to weekend activists—have a lot of choice. But they cannot hope to control the outcome of the state primaries and caucuses unless they coordinate on someone acceptable to all. So, after meeting the candidates, party leaders and activists discuss and deliberate over who can best represent their own concerns, unify the party, and win the general election in the fall. This deliberative process is spread out over the entire nation. By the time of the first voter contest in Iowa, a national party consensus has emerged, and party members form a united front in support of that candidate.

This, at any rate, is our argument. But it is not obvious at first blush that it is correct. In the prereform system, the players in the invisible primary were, for the most part, locally oriented leaders and regulars. They cared about national politics, but many cared more about controlling the governor's mansion or the city council than the presidency. Prereform players in the invisible primary were also a fairly small group that operated through a highly structured set of party rules, as described at the beginning of chapter 5. It was one thing for this group of party regulars to reach and enforce a national party consensus on a presidential candidate and quite another for the actors in the postreform invisible primary to do so. The postreform players are a larger group. They include more people who are outside any formal organization and a larger fraction of ideologues and issue activists—the same "amateurs" and "purists" whose supposedly uncompromising stance toward politics was discussed in chapter 5.

Among those who have not found it plausible that party insiders can coordinate on a national choice in the invisible primary is the late Nelson Polsby. In a trenchant analysis of *The Consequences of Party Reform* (1983), Polsby argued that political systems need "coalition-forcing institutions" to impel their many groups to band together in working majorities. Polsby held that party reform brought high-demand new groups into the nomination process while at the same time stripping party leaders of their coalition-forcing institutions—especially the old leader-dominated national convention. Worse, the new system created positive incentives for factional as against coalitional behavior.

The incentive for factional behavior arose from the combination of media-driven momentum and the sequence of state-level contests for delegate selection. What a candidate must do in this system, Polsby argued, is to finish as well as possible in the early contest, especially Iowa or New Hampshire. This is because winning early contests attracts the media attention and money necessary to continue competing and winning. But finishing well in an early contest doesn't require anything like majority support—or, therefore, anything like broad appeal. Simply getting, say, 29 percent of the vote (as Carter did in the 1976 New Hampshire primary) rather than 23 percent (as Udall did) may make all the difference. "The candidate's best strategy is therefore to differentiate himself from the others in the race and persuade more of his supporters to come out and vote. A premium is placed on building a personal organization and . . . hoping that the field becomes crowded with rivals who cluster at some other part of the ideological spectrum or who, for some other reason manage to divide up into too-small pieces the natural constituencies of the primary electorate" (1983, 67–68). In such a system, a candidate who is acceptable to all factions of the party but the first choice of none will fail. Instead, the factional candidate who happens to finish first in the early primaries will, with the aid of the media attention that goes to top finishers, go on to the nomination even though he or she is acceptable neither to the party as a whole nor to the general electorate.

We agree with much of Polsby's analysis. The influx of new actors into the nomination process, the end of the traditional party convention as a coalition-forcing mechanism, and the tendency of early primary victories to create momentum are all quite real consequences of party reform. We also agree that their joint effect is, as Polsby argued, to make it more difficult for party groups to form a united front behind a candidate acceptable to all factions of the party.

Yet the incentives for factional behavior in Polsby's argument would seem to be stronger for candidates than for party leaders, interest groups, and activists. For candidates, especially those lacking broad support within the party, the incentive may well be to appeal to a narrow faction and hope that a surprise victory in New Hampshire will generate national media attention. But party insiders need not be helpless spectators. Unless they are short-sighted or unsophisticated—which would be hard to argue—they should appreciate the advantage of forming a united front and trying to control the outcome of the primaries.

Since the inception of primary elections in the Progressive Era, party leaders have regularly intervened in them and regularly won. Indeed, one scholar has argued that, in many states, machine leaders preferred primaries because they thought they would be easier to control than caucuses or conventions (Reynolds 2006). So if, as Polsby argues, the media are likely to play up the results of early contests in New Hampshire and thereby magnify their importance, it only increases pressure on party insiders to make sure the winner is someone who is acceptable to them. Polsby is correct that voter control over delegate selection weakened the national party convention as a coalition-forcing institution, but party players still face the fundamental party incentive to form a united front behind a candidate who can win in November. If the reforms destroyed the national party convention as a coalition-forcing mechanism, parties leaders should develop a replacement. Party reform changed many rules, but it did not alter the imperatives of coalition politics.

The need for party members to make public endorsements is a complicating factor for our argument. Consider an officeholder whose base is some factional group—a religious or racial group, a union, a political movement like the nuclear freeze of the early 1980s, or an ideological wing of a party. This politician can support the candidate favored or perhaps even revered by members of her political base—someone, for example, with the standing of the Rev. Jesse Jackson in the African American community—or she can support a candidate more likely to unite the party. If she goes with her group's candidate, few members of her group are likely to complain. Even if the factional candidate flops in the primary contests, no one can blame her if she has been on the correct side.[12] If, on the other hand, the politician supports the candidate with broad acceptability within the party as whole, she may be accused of being a turncoat or disloyal to the group, an outcome that could endanger her standing with her political base. So there may be risk to individual politicians in joining a party's united front. But there is also the benefit of increasing the chances of party victory in November.

Measuring Party Leader Support

We have, then, competing theoretical arguments. To see which is empirically correct, we investigated how party insiders have actually behaved during the invisible primary. More specifically, we gathered data on their public endorsements of presidential candidates. If the party incentive is stronger, we should find that, by the endorsements they make, party insiders use the invisible primary to form a united front behind a broadly acceptable candidate. If the incentive for factional behavior is stronger, we should find that, in the absence of a coalition-forcing institution, party insiders generally split their endorsements among numerous factional favorites.

Figure 6.1 presents this endorsement data for major Democratic and Republican presidential candidates from 1972 to 2004. The endorsements tallied in this figure—a total of about 5,600 over all contests across these years—are from the year *prior* to the voter primaries and caucuses, which begin with the Iowa caucuses. For example, endorsements for the 1972 Democratic nomination were made from the beginning of 1971 to the eve of the Iowa caucuses, which were held at the end of January 1972. We do not claim that the period of the invisible primary precisely coincides with this particular thirteen-month window; in fact, it begins much earlier. But the last year or so of the process is the most visible part and therefore the part we study.

The endorsement count in figure 6.1 is based on a search of major national and regional publications, such as the *New York Times*, the *Los Angeles Times*, and the *Chicago Tribune*, plus any magazines that follow presidential politics. The percentages in the graphs are each candidate's share of endorsements made in the given nomination contest, as weighted by the political importance of the endorser. (The weighting scheme and other technical matters are discussed in the appendix at the end of this chapter. The appendix may be skipped without loss of continuity in our argument, but is nonetheless important for assessing the validity of the argument.)

The data in figure 6.1 show that, even in the chaotic 1970s, party insiders managed to form a united front in the invisible primary in two of the three contested nominations. But in only one of those cases, that of incumbent President Gerald Ford in 1976, did the insider favorite manage to win nomination. From 1980 on—the period in which, as we argue, insiders have largely regained control of the process—the record is notably stronger. In eight out of ten cases, party insiders were able to form a solid united front behind a preferred candidate, and in all eight cases their preferred candidate won nomination. In the ninth case, Michael Dukakis was a less-than-solid plurality winner of his party's invisible primary but was still able to win nomination. Only in 2004 did the party fail to form a united front and see their favorite through to nomination.

We admit that eight or nine successes in ten nominations since 1980 is not a perfect record, but it is far from the factional nightmare that Polsby's argument anticipates. Later chapters will examine this result

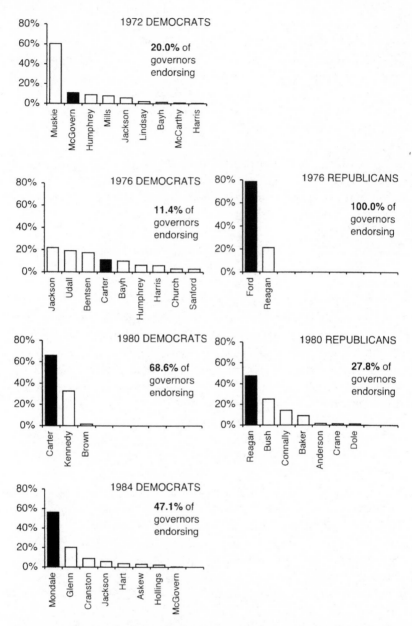

Fig. 6.1. Distribution of endorsements by contest. Distribution of politically weighted endorsements before the Iowa caucus for presidential nominations, 1972–2004. Eventual nominee in black.

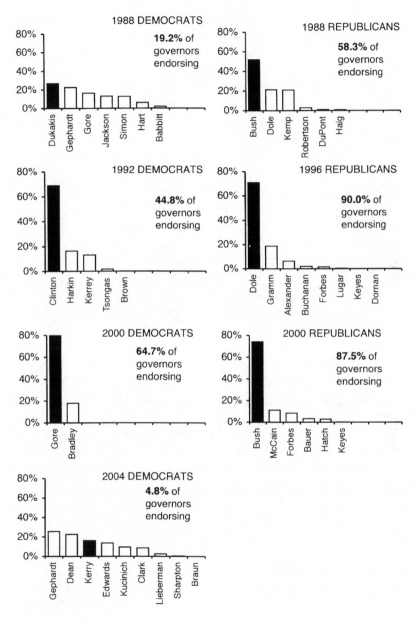

Fig. 6.1 (*continued*)

in more detail. As we will discuss in chapter 8, the winning candidates tended, all else equal, to have greater breadth of appeal than the candidates they vanquished. We shall also see that when parties failed to form a united front prior to the Iowa caucuses, it was not because party insiders had gone over to the logic of factional or candidate-centered politics; it was because they faced internal problems that were difficult to resolve. For this kind of case, Polsby was right that parties would probably have done better with a consensus-forcing mechanism.

The data in figure 6.1, as simple as they are, provide evidence that parties are back in control of presidential nominations at least most of the time. They suggest, in particular, that insiders are able to form united fronts ahead of the primaries and (by means that are not yet clear) assist their candidates through the difficult new system of delegate selection. The McGovern-Fraser rules still guarantee that voters in the state-by-state contests have the final word in choosing nominees. But the first word of party insiders in the invisible primary seems to be the word that matters most.

But what, one might wonder, became of those uncompromising purists and amateurs whose devotion to principle made them resistant to the united front even in the prereform system? Why did these supposed zealots not work mischief in the new party system as they are said to have undermined the old?

The answer, according to most research of the postreform party system, is that the so-called purists may have always been more willing to compromise than scholarship of the 1960s had allowed. Based on a survey of some seventeen thousand party activists, Walter Stone and Alan Abramowitz concluded that party activists favored "ideological purity over electability in the abstract," but favored electability over ideology in their actual choice of candidates (1983, 946). A subsequent study of activists from the 1988 cycle reached the same conclusion (Abramowitz, Rapoport, and Stone 1991). In a similar vein, a recent paper argues that party activists over the period 1972 to 2000 have increasingly become "professional ideologues"—that is, strongly interested both in issues and in candidates who can win elections with those issues (Carsey et al. 2003). In a nice summary of the viewpoint of these studies, James McCann wrote: "Those who select presidential candidates are . . . prone to think in ideological terms. But [they] do not necessarily act on these tendencies. Instead, such activists generally understand that they are not like 'average voters,' and they appear willing to vote against their own immediate concerns in the interest of choosing a contestant who will fare well in the general election" (2000, 98–99).[13]

But this is all quite general. Given our argument, it is essential to understand what exactly happens in the invisible primary. Our suggestion that the invisible primary operates as an intraparty decision-making mechanism is one possibility. An obvious alternative is that party insiders, hoping to gain the gratitude of the candidate who is likely to win anyway, jump on the winning bandwagon. In so doing, the insiders create the impression that they are dominating the action when really they are just camp followers. We are, then, still a good ways from demonstrating the thesis that is proclaimed in the title to this chapter—that party insiders have mastered the new system.

———— ★ ————

APPENDIX TO CHAPTER 6
A CLOSER LOOK AT THE ENDORSEMENT DATA

The Weight of Names

Party leaders arrive at judgments and make endorsements behind closed doors, but the endorsements do not usually remain secret. In fact, news reports of endorsements are a salient feature of the invisible primary. When, for example, Al Gore endorsed Howard Dean in the 2004 invisible primary, it was front page news in the *New York Times, Washington Post*, and many other newspapers. Yet journalists, even though reporting endorsements in considerable detail, often ridicule them as meaningless, as in the following commentary by Dana Milbank in the *New Republic*:

> the Gore campaign [has begun] circulating names of every Tom, Dick, and Harry for Gore. On September 21, the campaign, after announcing some endorsements from congressmen, sent out a press release declaring that "more than 100 Long Island leaders" endorsed Gore. Who are these leaders? Well, there's Steve Goldberg, Long Beach deputy zone leader, and Lynne Bizzarro, senior assistant attorney for some unspecified town. Bizzarro indeed. Does it really make a difference whether Irvin Toliver, director of human services for the town of Huntington, is a Gore man? Or how about Dolores Otter, listed on Gore's press release without a title? You can practically hear the buzz sweeping the nation: "Well, if Dolores Otter is on board, count me in." (1999, 17)

As we shall see, endorsements are an important determinant of success in nomination campaigns. Yet, precisely because they do convey information about political strength, politicians sometimes go into over-achievement mode in collecting and publicizing endorsements that have little value. Recognizing this, we do not count all endorsements equally. To repeat a comment from journalist T. H. White, "To understand American politics is, simply, to know people, to know the relative weight of names" (White 1961, 136). Thus, for example, Senator Al D'Amato could, through most of the 1990s, make things happen in New York. Lynne Bizzarro probably never could.[14] We have taken two steps to take account for this. First, we have used expert judges to create a weighting scale for the various kinds of people who show up in our endorsements sample.[15] This scale runs from 1 (current president of the United States) to .1, local officeholder or nonpolitical celebrity. In a number of cases, we have given extra weight to particular individuals known to be more important than their official position would indicate. For example, party figures from New Hampshire or Iowa got an automatic extra .1 points on the scale. Our coders also determined that a reference to a bloc of unnamed endorsers connotes less weight than the same individuals mentioned by name. The full set of weights we use to weight the endorsements is available from the authors on request. This scale gives due credit to big players while also giving some weight to the cumulative mass of large hauls of minions.[16] Table 6A.1 gives the full set of weights.

We must admit that we are not entirely satisfied that our weighting scheme has properly captured "the weight of names" and groups. Some senators—D'Amato, for example—have much more influence in their bailiwicks than others; some union endorsements mean a lot more than others. We are also concerned about changes in the over-time frequency of media reports on endorsements. In the early 1980s, our endorsement lists were top-heavy with big names, such as governors and senators, because only the more prominent endorsements were reported. In the current period, we have the same number of governors and senators but a much larger number of less important names, and the weights only partially control for this change. Campaigns also vary across candidates and years in their tendency to round up and puff endorsements. Candidates and political organizations now often place lists of endorsements on Web sites. We distrust such lists, preferring to rely on criteria that we can control and try to keep constant across time, but our ability to maintain such continuity is not as great as we would like. All of this creates error in our measure. This error is not likely to inflate the ability of the endorsements measure to explain other facets of the nomination process—to the contrary, it will dampen it. The crudeness of the measure is nonetheless worrisome and leaves much opportunity for improvement.

The Timing of Endorsements

Our data collection records the earliest date for which each endorsement was reported. This allows us to break the data into quarters, beginning in January of the year before the election and ending on the day before the Iowa caucuses. Figure 6A.1 shows this temporal breakdown. It shows, that is, the percentage of all endorsements, weighted by our importance scale, that were made in each calendar quarter of the preelection year, with the extra endorsements from the election year added to the fourth quarter.

Because our study includes only ten nomination contests—six for Democrats and four for Republicans—we are reluctant to make very much of the varied patterns that exist in figure 6A.1. Still, some of the patterns are worth noting.

One apparent pattern is that the Democratic endorsement derby usually runs more slowly, with more endorsers holding off to the final quarter. This was especially true in the nominations between 1980 and 1992, when most endorsements came at the end of the process. The typical Republican contest proceeds more quickly.

We believe that these and other differences in temporal pace tell us something about the invisible primaries in the various years. The generally slower pace of the Democratic contests may, for example, be due to their more fractious nature—because Democrats are more divided and less orderly, they need longer to decide. The 1992 Democratic contest was particularly slow, as we discuss in detail in the next chapter.

The slow pace of the 1988 Republican process stands out from the other Republican cases but is hard to explain. George H. W. Bush, as the incumbent vice president, might have been expected to wrap up the support of party insiders early on, but the big guns in the Republican Party held back, perhaps for the reason suggested in this news item in the *Washington Post:*

> Meanwhile, another big-state GOP governor, James R. Thompson of Illinois, has asked his top political advisers not to become involved with any of the presidential candidates for the immediate future.
>
> Some had suggested that Thompson, who had considered running, would endorse Bush. But Illinois GOP sources said Thompson has held off,

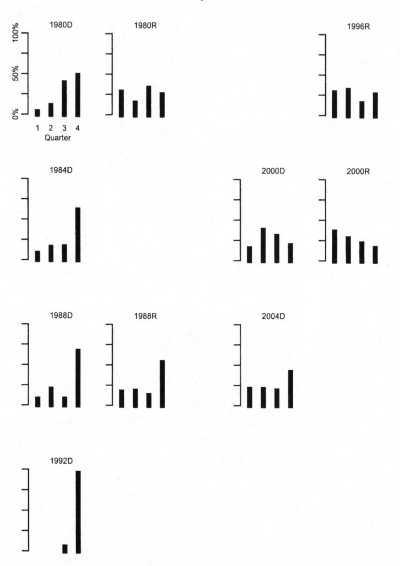

Fig. 6A.1. Pace of endorsements. Percentage of all weighted endorsements made in each quarter of each contest.

concerned about fallout from the Iran-Contra hearings on the vice president's candidacy.

To assuage that concern, Bush held a series of meetings with Republican political leaders in the state. Illinois GOP Chairman Don Adams said Bush assured everyone that, as far as his involvement is concerned, there were "no more shoes to drop." (Schwartz 1987, A5)

The 2000 Republican race was, by contrast, the fastest moving, as GOP insiders converged quickly and with a high degree of consensus on George W. Bush. Easy decisions, as this suggests, are made quickly.

This interpretation does not, however, apply to the 2004 Democratic race, which, at first glance, appears to have proceeded more quickly than other Democratic races. The 2004 invisible primary produced less consensus than any other Democratic contest in this period, as we shall show in a moment. And it did not proceed quickly: More governors held back from making an endorsement than in any other invisible primary, and the total number of recorded endorsements is appears to be lower than in most other years. What seems to have happened is that the surge of late endorsements that is typical for Democratic nominations failed to materialize in 2004 because the party insiders never managed to agree on an acceptable candidate.

In a variety of ways, then, the pace of the invisible primary is set by political considerations. Or, to put it differently, the invisible primary proceeds in political rather than calendar time.

Incomplete Measurement of Endorsements

Given that our search procedures focused on major national media like the *Times* and *Post* and important regional newspapers like the *Los Angeles Times* and *Des Moines Register,* we believe that we have picked up a high fraction of high-profile national endorsements. In the case of gubernatorial endorsements, in particular, we searched systematically on the name of each governor and believe we found most of these.[17] However, the likelihood of recording endorsements from less important figures declines at some unknown rate as the prominence of the endorser declines. Our weighting system may partly—but, as noted earlier, only partly—compensate for the fact that we most likely missed more names in the early part of our study due to the state of electronic databases at that time. To test the effect of incomplete searching near the end of our period, we used the 2000 invisible primary as a test case and searched every available media outlet on the Web. In table 6A.1 is a comparison of the results of the intensive search with the results of our standard search procedures. As can be seen, differences exist, but they are not large, especially between columns one and three, which is the most important comparison.

The more serious problem of incompleteness in the data is that we have only the endorsements of those party players who actually make endorsements; we do not know, in most cases, how many were prepared to make an endorsement if an acceptable candidate were available but abstained because none was. We do not, in other words, have a proper

Table 6A.1: Endorsements from regular and augmented searching

	Normal search rules	From additional searching	Total
Democrats			
Bradley	17.7	30.5	23.9
Gore	82.3	69.5	76.1
Unweighted N	592	683	1,275
Republicans			
Alexander	3.0	2.6	2.8
Bauer	2.7	0.8	1.6
Buchanan	0.4	0	0.2
Bush	65.2	72.0	69.0
Dole	3.9	5.5	4.8
Forbes	7.2	5.6	6.3
Hatch	2.4	0.1	1.1
Kasich	2.7	3.1	2.9
Keyes	0.2	0.1	0.1
McCain	9.4	5.8	7.4
Quayle	3.2	4.3	3.8
Unweighted N	428	706	1,134

Table 6A.2: Endorsement rates of governors

	Number of governors in party	1st quarter	2nd quarter	3rd quarter	4th quarter	Percentage who endorsed any candidate	Percentage who endorsed nominee
1972D	30	2	2	0	2	20	0
1976D	35	1	2	1	0	11	0
1976R	13	1	0	11	1	100	85
1980D	31	20	1	0	1	71	68
1980R	19	1	0	1	2	21	5
1984D	34	10	3	1	2	47	29
1988D	25	2	1	1	1	20	4
1988R	24	3	2	9	0	58	50
1992D	29	3	1	4	5	45	41
1996R	31	3	6	6	12	87	71
2000D	18	4	2	2	4	67	61
2000R	30	19	5	3	1	93	70
2004D	22	2	1	0	0	14	0

denominator for calculating the percentage of party insiders who support a given candidate.

One important group for whom we can calculate endorsement rates as well as nonendorsement rates is each party's contingent of sitting governors. As can be seen in table 6A.2, these rates vary considerably from contest to contest. The lowest rates of endorsement—that is, highest rates of abstention—are in the Democratic contests of 1988 and 2004. By contrast, the 2000 Republican contest has a notably high rate of early endorsements. We interpret such differences as evidence of the ease or difficulty of party insiders in making a choice and shall refer to this evidence in the next chapter.

Why Exactly Should We Care about Endorsements?

We turn now to the *theoretical status* of the endorsement data: What exactly do such data tell us? What are the pitfalls in using them to gain understanding of presidential nominations? The answers are not at all obvious.

If nothing else, a candidate's ability to generate endorsements indicates whether the candidate is broadly acceptable within the party. Given the fractious nature of political parties, a candidate who is broadly acceptable to the majority of party players has a leg up on the competition.

Public endorsements also represent a political resource in two ways. First, an endorsement is a cue to rank-and-file party voters as to who party insiders want. Our analysis shows that those attached to a party take this cue, supporting the candidate with the most insider support at much higher rates than those candidates who call themselves independent. Second, an endorsement is a promise to work for the candidate. If, at one extreme, the endorser is a governor or an interest group leader, it is a commitment of an organization. If, at the other extreme, an endorser is a mere activist, it is a promise to knock on doors, make phone calls, drive voters to the polls, or whatever needs to be done.

In sum, a candidate who has a majority of endorsements is likely to be more widely acceptable to party leaders and the voters who follow them, and better endowed with campaign resources, than any other candidate.

7

The Invisible Primary: Theory and Evidence

The invisible primary is the principal institutional means by which party members decide the person they want to be their nominee—the equivalent of bargaining at party conventions in the old system. In this chapter, the first of two on the invisible primary, we try to understand how this institution works. We begin with a rough model of how hundreds of party members, all observing the candidates in action and announcing endorsements as they make them, could create an information stream that would enable party members to coordinate on a widely acceptable choice. Next, we consider how to determine whether the invisible primary is (as we claim) party-centered or (as others believe) candidate-centered. The question is not an easy one. Finally, we sketch each of the ten contested nominations of the period from 1980 to 2004, assessing our key theoretical propositions about the invisible primary. In the next chapter, we develop statistical tests of some of these propositions.

A Model of Party Decision-Making in the Invisible Primary

The party members who make endorsements in the invisible primary differ in their preferences and are therefore likely to differ in their first choice of candidates. Yet, as experienced party players, they must know that factional favorites are a poor bet to unify the party. They may therefore be expected to support a candidate who is acceptable to key groups in the party. But which candidate this might be is not always easy to tell at the start of the process.

Estimating the national appeal of candidates presents another dilemma. Most candidates in the invisible primary are new to national politics. They typically have won elections in their home state, but the country is so diverse that local success often fails to translate into national appeal. Public opinion polls about candidates who have never run in national politics are not much guide. Figuring out who will flourish on the national stage and who will bomb is much more art and instinct than science.

In this situation of very imperfect information, party insiders must somehow coordinate on a nominee. Game theorists have studied a variety of such situations as coordination games. Here is a simple example: An experimenter offers to pay two randomly chosen New Yorkers a million dollars each if they can meet within two hours at some location in New York City. The individuals don't even know what the other looks like, but if they think about it, they may nonetheless win the prize. A natural solution would be for each to go to some obvious place—called a focal point—and hope that the other makes the same obvious choice. A natural focal point here would be Grand Central Station, which is a famous landmark and also centrally located.

Coordination on a presidential nominee has many differences from this example. One is that, given the million dollar payoff in the New York experiment, no one cares whether the focal point is Grand Central Station or the Empire State Building; in a presidential nomination, people care where they meet. Another difference is that, in the experiment, the players could not communicate; but the party members trying to coordinate in the invisible primary can communicate. Finally, the experiment involved only two players; in the invisible primary, thousands of participants choose. But the invisible primary is still a kind of coordination game.

Here, then, is a coordination game that better captures what may happen in the invisible primary. We call it the restaurant game. Imagine that a large number of people are trying to coordinate on a place to eat and that, if a majority manage to go to the same restaurant, they will get some benefit, such as a price discount. At the same time, all want a restaurant that matches their culinary preferences, which differ. Some diners, whom we may call purists, are more finicky than others.

In this game, diners make their choice of restaurant one at a time. No one can taste any food until everyone has chosen, but diners have three pieces of information: They can inspect each restaurant's menu; they observe each diner's choice as it is made; and they know each diner's preference for meat, fish, vegetarian, or whatever. A few diners have a connoisseur's knowledge of restaurants, because they pay a lot more attention than the rest, but no one is completely sure who is a connoisseur and who is not.

Suppose the available restaurants are a vegetarian restaurant, a steak house, a fish place, and Denny's. One might suspect that the nonspecialty restaurant, Denny's, would be the common choice, and it might well be. But suppose early deciders favor the fish house, and that they are a diverse crowd of vegetarians, families with children, fish lovers, and Texans. The remaining diners might suspect that the early deciders know something nonobvious, perhaps because they are connoisseurs. The presence of vegetarians at a fish house would be especially informative, since it could not reflect an intense preference for fish. If, as diners continue making choices, the fish house continues to draw a large and diverse crowd, even some diners with intense preferences for food other than fish might conclude that they can get a decent meal at the fish place—and earn the group discount as well.

This restaurant game would play out differently in different conditions. If the diners are very hungry, they might converge more quickly than if they had just feasted. It would also matter if the town has only one good restaurant, many good restaurants, or none. If it has only one, all diners would probably converge on it quickly, eager for a good table and knowing that everyone else will choose it. If the town has many excellent restaurants, the choice among good ones might be almost random, depending on which happened to become a focal point, perhaps because of central location. And if all restaurants are bad, diners might be slow to choose, hoping for a better choice to emerge.

The invisible primary has the properties of this game, including the incentive for participants to converge on a choice that can unify the group. An especially important common feature is that individuals of diverse preferences—here ideological preferences—must converge on a choice that might not be many people's ideal choice. Also as in the restaurant game, the sequential revelation of endorsements in the invisible primary enables decision-makers to make their choices in light of the preferences of others and the information of connoisseurs. The connoisseurs' information could involve both the depth of candidates' commitment to party values and their likely national appeal.

The restaurant game has three implications for understanding the invisible primary. The first is that party players who are motivated to converge on a common choice will be able to do so, even when none of the choices is particularly good. This is important because it means that an institutional replacement for the old-style party convention—a process of information-sharing and coordination through sequential choice—is potentially present in the structure of the invisible primary. The second is that agreement may be easier to achieve for some choice sets than others. And the third is that, in difficult cases, agreement may depend on arbitrary factors, such as a focal point.

The restaurant game does not guarantee that players will converge on the best possible choice. Potential for nonoptimal choice follows from the fact that focal points can be arbitrary and can determine outcomes. Yet it would be hard to argue that old-style party conventions, with their staged bandwagons, made choices that were more optimal. Defense of both institutions must be more modest: Both the convention system and the invisible primary are probably good at coordinating on an outstanding candidate when one exists—and at coordinating on a merely acceptable candidate when no outstanding candidate is available.

Candidate-Centered Politics?

The restaurant game is a model of a party-centered process. It is party-centered because decision-makers (party players) choose, and the objects of choice (candidates) do nothing except try to make themselves seem attractive. Many scholars, however, believe that presidential nominations are a candidate-centered process. Let us, therefore, consider what it would mean to have a candidate-centered nomination system and how such a system can be empirically distinguished from one that is party-centered.

An invisible primary that is candidate centered would be one in which the efforts of candidates dominate the process. In the context of the invisible primary, this would mean candidates building so much public support and raising so much campaign money that party insiders—officeholders, activists, interest group leaders—have no choice but to jump on the bandwagon. Party insiders would have no capacity to say no to a popular or well-financed candidate they dislike; rather, they would flock, as if having no will of their own, to the strongest of the candidates contending for their support.

Of course, candidates do make ardent efforts to win over party insiders by building poll support and raising huge amounts of campaign cash. Yet the fact that candidates make these efforts does not mean they succeed. Party insiders might sit back, survey the field, and coolly follow their own counsel.

Another metaphor may be helpful here. Suppose that garnering insider endorsements in the invisible primary is like a competition among fishermen to catch the most fish. If competitors are fishing in something as big as an ocean, and if the number of fish they catch depends on their skill in manipulating the fish to take their bait, the contest would properly be called fisherman-centered. But suppose that competitors are fishing in a small pond having only a few fish. And suppose each fish carefully examines each fisherman's bait and deliberates with other fish about whose bait to take. One would call this a fish-centered contest, since the fish are deciding the outcome on the basis of their own collective preferences. The fishermen might be trying just as hard as in the first scenario, but the fish would be in control.

The main point here is that casual bystanders, by looking at fishermen alone, could easily form an incorrect impression about the dynamics of the process. This is because it would be easier to observe the contestants working hard to land their catch than the beneath-the-surface machinations that might be present. The same could be true of the role of candidates in the invisible primary. Observation that candidates work hard to get endorsements is not definitive evidence that they dominate the process.

Whether the invisible primary is dominated by candidates or party insiders is critical to our analysis. In our view of parties, intense policy demanders form party coalitions precisely in order to get the upper hand over candidates. So if candidates dominate the invisible primary, and if the invisible primary determines presidential nominations, our group-centric view of parties is wrong.

How, then, can one tell which group—candidates or party insiders—is actually in the driver's seat of the invisible primary? One approach would be to peer beneath surface events to observe whether candidates are overpowering the endorsers or, alternatively, the endorsers seem to be making up their own minds. Direct observation is not the strongest methodological tool, but for a case in which we have little sure knowledge about what is going on, it makes a good starting point. We therefore propose to go through each nomination contest since 1980 in order to answer as best we can each of the following questions:

- **Free Will or Forced Choice?** Do party insiders make endorsements because they actually favor the given candidate, or because the candidate is so strong that party endorsers simply capitulate to him?
- **Small Pond or Vast Ocean?** Do candidates go trolling for support in a small pool of ideological and party regulars, or do they build their campaign from a larger pool of one-time activists and persons loyal to them personally?[1]
- **United Front or Factional Favorite?** Do groups make decisions in light of the likely preferences of other groups and the need to win the fall election,

or does each group support its own first-choice candidate, regardless of party considerations?

Our theoretical expectation is that most candidate support comes from a small pond of party leaders and regulars who make free choices to form a united front. On the other hand, we do not expect candidates to rely primarily on first-time activists, succeed with factional appeals, or force endorsers to knuckle under to their pressures.

These matters are not easy to determine. Still, as we shall see in the remainder of this chapter, some illuminating evidence does exist. For example, we shall see several cases in which party insiders clearly do resist the pressures of strong candidates. We shall also see some instances in which candidates tried to build their campaigns within the small world of party regulars and other instances in which they went outside regular party networks to seek support.

The advantage of this "look and see" examination of individual cases is that we can pick up whatever seems important, whether we anticipated it or not and whether we can systematically measure it or not. The disadvantage of the method is that our observations will be unsystematic and susceptible to interpretive bias. The next chapter will therefore go on to quantitative tests of our three propositions. If this statistical analysis reaches the same conclusions as our qualitative analysis in this chapter, we may begin to feel confident we understand what is going on.

Under the Hood in the New System

In the following pages, we provide descriptive accounts of the invisible primary of each recent nomination. As in chapter 5, where we sketched the last contests of the old system, we do not aspire to complete histories. We aim, rather, to focus on details that indicate whether nominations are candidate- or party-centered.

Republicans in 1980: The Right Candidate Wins
In the early 1950s Ronald Reagan began traveling the country for General Electric to make motivational speeches in company plants. Gradually those speeches became more political and then more partisan. In 1964 he gave a nationally televised speech for Barry Goldwater that raised $600,000—about $3.7 million in current dollars—for the senator's struggling campaign. But more important for our purposes, the speech demonstrated Reagan's national appeal. Reagan continued to raise money for the party, and when he became California governor in 1966, fund-raising speeches were "done on

a virtually any-time, any-place basis" (Chester, Hodgson, and Page 1969, 196). The heavy travel schedule continued after he left office in 1974, with most of the money he raised donated to worthy conservative candidates.

Reagan's 1980 campaign for president actually began almost immediately upon the conclusion of his 1976 campaign and involved revisiting friends and supporters he had made over some twenty years as a popular speaker on the Republican Party's "rubber chicken" circuit. A syndicated newspaper column and a weekly radio show made him continuously visible to those interested in him. The result, as David Broder wrote in early 1980, was that Reagan "has the advantage of the most extensive intraparty organizational network, built on the loyalty of his 1976 supporters and maintained for the past two years by his interim political organization, Citizens for the Republic, one of the biggest spending political action committees in the 1978 campaign."

Reagan was the recognized leader of the largest faction in the party, the conservative group that had fought for Taft and Goldwater but also accepted the need to compromise when necessary. However, the conservative wing of the party saw little need to compromise this year—nor should it have. Its candidate had won the governorship of the largest state in the union against a popular Democrat and been reelected handily. Reagan had also demonstrated that he could play on the national stage. In 1968, only two years past the end of his acting career, Reagan came close to beating party warhorse Richard Nixon for the Republican nomination. In 1976 he came even closer to beating incumbent President Gerald Ford in a drawn-out primaries fight.

Thus, by the time the curtain went up on the invisible primary for the 1980 nomination, Reagan had toiled longer in the field, earned more debts of gratitude in the party, and honed his campaign skills more finely than any politician of his generation. Except for Gerald Ford, who did not enter the race, Reagan also had the strongest poll numbers of any candidate. Reagan was not like Robert Taft, a favorite of the conservatives but a terrible campaigner; he was a favorite of the conservatives and a terrific campaigner. As Andrew Busch observed, "Reagan's success was, in essence, the logical fruit of the organizational dominance won by the conservatives in 1964" (1992, 539).

Yet Reagan did not dominate the invisible primary. By our endorsement count, he got just 48 percent of all publicly reported endorsements, many from the same party organizations that were taken over or founded by Goldwater supporters in 1964. Bob Dole, a candidate with weaker conservative credentials and weaker campaign skills, would get 68 percent of party endorsements in 1996,[2] and Al Gore, also a weak candidate, would get 82 percent in 2000.³ Despite Reagan's long work for the party and his political strengths, he was not the runaway winner of the invisible primary.

The main reason for resistance to Reagan was the widespread belief that, as ex-president Gerald Ford put it, "A very conservative Republican cannot win in a national election" (*Time* 1980). But Reagan's managers recognized this problem and sought to reach out. Reagan announced his candidacy in the liberal capital of America, New York City; he made a showy visit to Capitol Hill for the purpose of welcoming national support; and his campaign gave guidance to journalists that "Reagan is . . . trying to reposition himself, not as the factional favorite of GOP conservatives but as the 'natural standard bearer' for Republicans of all stripes" (Broder 1979, A1).

But the party's moderate wing didn't buy it. For them, the only question was: Who would be the candidate of the moderates?

One possibility was former president Ford. As titular head of the party, he spoke at many party events in the late 1970s and ran well in Republican preference polls. But Ford generated no excitement among party insiders and never formally entered the race. Another moderate possibility was George Herbert Walker Bush of Texas. Bush's record as a vote-getter was weak. He won two terms in the House of Representatives but lost twice running for the Senate. Following the second Senate loss, Presidents Nixon and Ford appointed him to a series of high jobs: U.S. representative to China, ambassador to the United Nations, chair of the Republican National Committee, and director of the Central Intelligence Agency (CIA). These appointments gave Bush what may have been the best resume of any presidential candidate since John Quincy Adams. He was virtually unknown to the public at the start of the race, but threw himself into campaigning around the country. Like Jimmy Carter, upon whom he modeled his campaign, Bush spent much time campaigning "out in the country," especially the early primary states of Iowa and New Hampshire.

The more promising pick to emerge as the champion of the moderates was the Republican minority leader in the Senate, Howard Baker of Tennessee. Baker was a respected figure in Washington, articulate and telegenic, and favorably remembered (except perhaps in conservative Republican circles) for his performance in the Senate Watergate investigation. As a result, he was second to Reagan in most polls measuring the preferences of ordinary Republicans for the party nomination. Baker's campaign developed as follows:

> throughout the spring and summer [of 1979], while agents for George Bush won commitments from leading Republican moderates in Iowa, the Baker campaign was largely invisible. The candidate himself stayed on the job

as minority leader of the Senate. The decision on the new Strategic Arms Limitation Treaty [SALT] was supposed to be coming to the floor [of the Senate], and Baker and his lieutenants were convinced it would be the center of a major national debate over foreign policy . . . and if he was on those nightly network news programs leading the opposition to SALT II, so much the better for his campaign. (Germond and Witcover 1981, 104)

Baker's standing in Washington politics and in the polls might have made him a focal point in the contest for centrist support. Yet it was Bush who, by campaigning hard in Iowa while Baker campaigned hard in Washington, emerged as the alternative to Reagan (see figure 5.1). Indeed, Bush actually managed more endorsements in Iowa than Reagan did, which helps explain why Bush could beat Reagan in the Iowa caucuses and then claim that "big mo" (momentum) would now propel him to the nomination.

A party's sitting governors are sometimes a force in the invisible primary, but not so in the 1980 Republican race (see table 5.2). Most governors were moderates and wary of Reagan for that reason. Yet, according to Germond and Witcover, GOP governors were reluctant to endorse Bush because he lacked "force of personality" and seemed more generally a poor campaigner (118). Thus, as the Reagan bandwagon picked up speed, Republican governors neither jumped onto it nor lay down in front of it. Watchful waiting was their stance. When Bush eventually lost to Reagan in the voter primaries, the governors found it easy to accept the California governor as the party standard bearer.

Former Texas Governor John Connally is also worth mentioning. The phrase *strong candidate* could have been invented simply to describe him. Tall, handsome, and well-built, Connally was a forceful personality, a charismatic campaigner, a solid conservative, and a superb fund-raiser. If anyone could stop the Reagan juggernaut, one might expect it would be Connally. But he had shallow roots in the GOP—he had been a Democrat until 1973—and had done little to connect to the party's conservative activists. Connally raised more money than anyone else in the invisible primary, mostly from fellow Texans, but won only 13 percent of endorsements. In the end, he spent $11 million and won only one convention delegate. Connally had been tarnished by scandal, but what his spectacular failure mainly shows, in our view, is that the invisible primary is a partisan rather than a candidate-dominated affair, and the voter primaries are dominated more by party favorites than by big spenders.

To summarize: The invisible primary was won by the leader of the party's largest faction, a proven vote-getter who spent decades building support in the party. Reagan did not, however, run as a factional leader; from the start, he recognized factional support as a problem and sought to surmount it. At the same time, party insiders were not steamrolled by Reagan. The most important of his natural opponents—moderate governors—adopted a wait-and-see attitude, and other moderates backed a candidate of their own. The choice of the moderates was not Washington power broker and media star Howard Baker; it was George Bush, who had a record as a weak vote-getter but who took the trouble to campaign to party regulars out in the country. Every element of this nomination contest—Reagan's deep ties to party regulars, his attempt to bridge factional divisions, the dominance of party regulars over media politics in the rise of Bush over Baker, the collapse of the campaign of the big-spending and personally charismatic but newly Republican John Connally—suggests that the process was party- rather than candidate-centered. As a final touch, Bush later joined Reagan's ticket as his vice president, thereby achieving the united front to which parties aspire.

Democrats in 1980: Jimmy Carter, Party Man

Politicians commonly acknowledge groups they "owe" for their election. But when Jimmy Carter took office, he made a point of saying that he owed his election to no one. Traditional party groups could hardly argue, but it is a good bet they were not happy about it. Nor were they likely pleased with Carter's "curious neutrality" toward their preferences as he created a cabinet packed with technocrats rather than interest-group ambassadors (Polsby 1983, 103). Nor again were Democratic leaders in Congress likely pleased when Carter attacked their pet spending projects as wasteful "pork." This was the behavior of a maverick, not a party man.

So when Carter's presidency got into trouble, as presidencies often do, these groups did not all rush to prop up the party leader. Some rushed instead to back Senator Ted Kennedy of Massachusetts as an insurgent for the Democratic Party nomination in 1980. A number of those who made statements of support for Kennedy in the invisible primary for the 1980 nomination are listed in table 7.1.

These endorsements are notable for two reasons. First, they come from some of the key power centers in the Democratic coalition. Second, they were all made before Kennedy announced his candidacy on November 3 or, in many cases, before the Massachusetts senator had even made up his mind, which was apparently in late summer.[4] We underscore these points because the Kennedy challenge could be taken as evidence of candidate-centered politics. Kennedy was, after all, a strong candidate who challenged the leader of his party. But, like Eisenhower in 1952, Goldwater in 1964, and McCarthy in 1968, he launched his campaign only after an important faction of his party signaled strong support.

Table 7.1: Endorsements for Kennedy in 1980

Name	Group	Date of report
Cardiss Collins	Chair, Congressional Black Caucus	February 14
Andrew Stein	Borough president	February 18
Bill Fenton	President, International Machinists Union	March 17
Paul O'Dwyer	Former city council president	March 26
Ralph Nader	Consumer advocate	May 8
NAACP	Civil rights organization	June 25
Americans for Democratic Action	Liberal interest group	June 25
William Winpisinger	President, Machinists Union	July 6
Michael Harrington	Author (socialist)	August 5
George Poulin	Vice president, Machinists Union	August 5
Edmund Muskie	U.S. senator	September 26
AFL-CIO	Labor union	September 29
Margaret Costanza	Former aide to Jimmy Carter	October 16
Joseph Brennan	Governor	October 19
George McGovern	U.S. senator	October 19
Morris Dees, Jr.	Former fundraiser for Jimmy Carter	October 25
International Chemical Workers	Labor union	October 27
Painters and Allied Trades Union	Labor union	October 27
Dominic Fornaro	President, state AFL-CIO	October 27
David Wilson	State labor leader	October 27
Frank Martino	President, United Rubber Workers	October 27
Jane Byrne	Mayor of Chicago	October 28
Arnold Miller	President, United Mine Workers	October 30

But if Kennedy had strong support in the Democratic Party, Carter had more, including some from liberal groups. Although an outsider, he eventually discovered that he couldn't govern without the support of his party's leading officeholders and began reaching out to the party establishment. Thus, by our count, Carter won some 65 percent of endorsements, with most of the rest going to Kennedy. The most notable feature of Carter's support is that it was top-heavy with governors: twenty-one of thirty-one endorsed Carter, mostly in the early months of the invisible primary; Kennedy garnered only one, with the rest staying on the sidelines (see table 6A.2).

Because the media anticipated a run by Kennedy, they reported numerous polls on the preferences of Democratic voters for Kennedy versus Carter throughout the invisible primary year of 1979. These polls typically favored Kennedy by about 2 to 1, until the Iran hostage crisis broke in November. At that point, the public rallied strongly to Carter. The pattern of insider endorsements was not, however, much affected by these polls. Most party insiders favored Carter when he was unpopular with Democratic voters and continued to favor him at about the same rate when his popularity improved. The insiders who rallied to Carter were not simply heeding public opinion; resisting public opinion would be a better description.

Reagan's nearly successful challenge of Ford in the 1976 primary highlighted the potential for factional groups to challenge presidents they disliked. The strong support of party insiders for Carter seems, in this light, notable. Though some party groups and much of the party rank-and-file were prepared to dump Carter, most party insiders remained loyal to the leader. Party insiders thus acted more like a party than a collection of factions.

Democrats in 1984: The Insider versus the Outsiders

The 1984 Democratic contest turned on three separate campaigns, each in its own way illuminating. The nominee was Walter Mondale, who had been Jimmy Carter's vice president. Mondale won 56 percent of insider support in the invisible primary and yet almost lost in the voter primaries to Senator Gary Hart of Colorado, who won only 4 percent of insider endorsements. That someone like Hart could nearly upend the party favorite shows the tenuousness of insider influence over the voter primaries. So, in another way, does the success of Jesse Jackson, the second African American to run for president.[5] Jackson had little chance of winning the nomination, but nonetheless won 10 percent of the delegates in the primaries and in other ways affected the dynamics of the race. Yet the bottom line is that, despite Hart and despite Jackson, party insiders rallied to Mondale in the invisible primary, and Mondale won the nomination in the voter primaries.

So let us begin with Mondale. A cardinal principle of campaigning in the invisible primary is that the candidate must please key party groups on the issues they care most about. This was a principle that Mondale, when he was campaigning for the 1976 nomination, had not quite mastered, as shown in this account of his solicitation of a donation from a millionaire heiress: "In her lakeside living room, Mrs. Benton rises to ask Mondale if he favors income redistribution to aid the poor. Mondale has been briefed that she always asks this question and that a 'sock-it-to-the-rich' answer would unlock bank vaults for him. Instead, he gives a thoughtful and straightforward exposition of the problems and difficulties of welfare reform. 'I won't stand there in a two-million-dollar house and do a liberal two-step for them,' he tells staff later" (Hadley 1976, 33). Shortly afterward, Mondale dropped out of the invisible primary for the 1976 election. "He didn't like what the campaign was doing to him," Mondale told an aide (35).

In 1983, however, Mondale was back in the game, and on this run for the nomination he had no difficulty telling important people what they wanted to hear. In fact, Mondale came under criticism as the tool of special interests, promising everything to everyone. At one point, Governor Mario Cuomo of New York met with Mondale and

> urged him to take the lead in confronting . . . runaway spending on programs such as Medicare that was contributing so much to the deficit.
> "I told him," Cuomo reported the next day, "that he needed to show that he could say no to somebody."
> "What did he say?" Cuomo was asked.
> "He said no to me," Cuomo replied. (Germond and Witcover 1985, 60)

As the candidate who would not say no to his party's key constituencies, Mondale won their endorsements by the bushel. Mondale also won the endorsements of sixteen of the party's thirty-four governors, compared to zero endorsements for the rest of the field together. The Mondale campaign prized endorsements for a clear reason: "If you signed up a governor, a mayor, a labor leader, it was his organization you were after, not his name or his personal following, and you moved in swiftly to secure it. His organization became yours; you simply preempted it and chalked up one less place you would have to flood with your own time, talent, and money" (Goldman and Fuller 1985, 56).

The most coveted endorsement in the Democratic Party is a union endorsement. Unions have some direct capacity to sway their members, but they also have expertise in the art of political campaigns—use of phone banks, neighborhood canvassing, and election day transportation to the polls. The president of the AFL-CIO, Lane Kirkland, was determined to be proactive in the 1984 contest. "If we're not in it," Kirkland said, "if we wait until the convention is over, then we are stuck with other people's choices [for nominee] one more time. Why should we be stuck with other people's choices . . . ?" (Dark 2004, 181). Hence, Kirkland set out to unify the labor movement around a single candidate and make an early endorsement that would shape the direction of the contest. He never used the term *focal point*, but he seems to have had that idea in mind.

Because Kirkland made no secret of his strategy of early endorsement, all of the major candidates sought AFL-CIO backing. "Hart wanted labor's favor, badly enough to *beg* Kirkland for it over lunch. . . . [Candidate John] Glenn wanted it, too. One of his operatives had guessed the worth of the endorsement to be $20 million. . . . [Candidate Alan] Cranston, the senior senator from California, was the most ardent suitor of all. . . . [A young union official] was genuinely fond of Cranston and didn't have the heart to tell him what he was thinking: *Alan, you're crazy*" (Goldman and Fuller 1985, 58). What made Cranston crazy was that labor had its deepest and strongest ties to Mondale and was not about to give its support to anyone else.[6] Besides serving labor causes for some two decades, Mondale was a close personal friend of Kirkland. But Hart was, if anything, crazier. Cranston was at least a reliable supporter of labor; Hart sought labor's support despite his advocacy of free-trade policies that were anathema to the AFL-CIO.

Labor also worked with officials from the Democratic National Committee to change the schedule of primaries to the benefit of insider candidates. The idea, as proposed by a reform commission, was to compress the schedule of primaries—to "front load" them—so that outsider candidates like Carter would no longer have time to build momentum through early victories. The primaries would come so fast after one another that only a candidate who built a strong organization ahead of the primaries would be able to succeed. The effect, as journalists Goldman and Fuller wrote, would be to "rig the game against outsiders and for . . . men like Mondale and Kennedy, with national names and connections" (55–56). As David Broder added, "When the Hunt Commission was meeting, in the aftermath of Carter's defeat, there was a 'never again' feeling about such outsider candidates. Mondale and Kennedy supporters and AFL-CIO operatives were influential in the commission decisions, as were elected officials anxious to reclaim their place of influence in the convention hall" (Broder 1983, 2).

With party insiders thus committed to Mondale,[7] Gary Hart plotted an outsider strategy. He believe that, despite the Hunt Commission's attempt to front-load the system, it was still possible, in the fashion of Carter, to do better than expected in Iowa by finishing second behind Mondale, ride the publicity to a big win in New Hampshire, and coast to the nomination. Hart shared his strategy with anyone who would listen, including the media. When asked if he wasn't simply copying Carter's strategy from 1976, Hart replied that "Carter followed *my* strategy" (Goldman and Fuller 1985, 88). The comment was fair: Hart had been McGovern's campaign manager in 1972 and helped engineer the better-than-expected showing in New Hampshire that had been critical to McGovern's success.

To score his first victory in Iowa, Hart needed some people power, and for that he turned not to leaders but to volunteers, as described in this passage: "A campaign was concentric circles, [Hart] argued tirelessly. You started with small cells of activists, meeting in a café or a living room with a sign-up sheet at the door, and kept expanding outward, circle upon circle, until your message had reached tens of thousands of people" (90).

As the Hart campaign swung into action in Iowa's main population centers, it found itself in competition with the stronger campaigns, especially Mondale's. Hart's response was inspired. He took his campaign to rural areas where it would face little competition. The ploy worked. Gary Hart captured enough votes in the Iowa countryside to finish second to Mondale, a showing that impressed pundits and won him the publicity he needed to fight the next race in New Hampshire. Hart won that contest by a wide margin and went on to give Mondale a serious run in the string of state-by-state contests.

The third major candidate in the race was Jackson, who was both a factional candidate and an astute politician. Like many African Americans, Jackson believed that the Democratic Party took the votes of blacks for granted. As a Chicagoan, he was particularly upset when Mondale refused to support Harold Washington's attempt to become the first black mayor of Chicago. As Jackson and early supporters pondered an entry by Jackson into the race for the Democratic nomination, "Getting elected [president] was never seriously part of the picture. . . . The campaign was conceived instead as a kind of protracted civil-rights demonstration raised to a higher plane" (Goldman and Fuller, 107).

In early 1983, a gathering of national black leaders debated whether a black leader, whether Jackson or someone else, should run for president. It was a hard question for them. Some worried that a black candidacy would simply throw the nomination to a candidate who was less friendly to black causes than Mondale. Others worried that it would hurt black candidates with biracial coalitions. But others "argued that the risks were worth taking for the payoff in heightened attention to black concerns and increased participation in politics" (Goldman and Fuller, 109).

These are, of course, the concerns that any faction faces as it jostles for position within its party coalition. The Dixiecrats of 1948 and the Goldwater supporters of 1964 faced them as well. When Jackson did finally enter the race, his entry forced black leaders to choose. Of the fifty African Americans in our sample of endorsers, thirty-six supported Jackson and fourteen supported Mondale. But the black support Mondale got was important. An especially important black leader for Mondale was Mayor Richard Arrington of Birmingham, Alabama. He was newly elected and the head of a well-oiled local machine. As Arrington explained to his constituents:

> I have not lost my racial pride, but I have to deal with the reality of Ronald Reagan bearing down on us. . . .
>
> So we come to the point of a tough decision. . . . No matter how strongly we feel about Jesse Jackson, the reality is that this is not a race between Jesse

Jackson and Ronald Reagan. Reagan has put more people in soup lines, more people out of work and tried to do the unthinkable of turning back our hard-won gains. We have to avoid illusions, and we can't afford an emotional binge because we aren't going to feel very good if after a good emotional high we wind up with Reagan. (Smothers 1984, B9)

Arrington made his commitment to Mondale early on and told him to announce it when it best suited his purposes. The time Mondale chose was when Jackson scored a media coup by going to Syria to win the release of an American fighter pilot who had been shot down over Lebanon. The announcement of Arrington's support gave Mondale a media presence in the middle of Jackson's big news week. In the big Super Tuesday primary, blacks in Birmingham voted 2 to 1 for Mondale, a better rate than in other parts of the state. As Arrington observed before the vote, "Blacks here are experiencing a situation of having their first black mayor, and they want me to succeed and are willing to go the extra mile with me to help me" (Smothers 1984, B9).

The Mondale and Hart campaigns exemplify strategies of party-centered and candidate-centered politics, respectively. Mondale courted established party groups who supported him on the basis of long and faithful service to their causes. These groups were so much part of the Democratic establishment that they could change the rules to make Mondale's nomination more likely. Mondale's ability to garner support from some leading black politicians is an indication of the breadth of his insider support. Hart worked through volunteers he personally recruited and relied on a strategy of impressing the media to propel his campaign. His strategy was a carbon copy of Carter's from 1976. If Hart rather than Mondale had won the nomination, we would take it as evidence that party insiders were still unable to control the nomination process. However, Mondale did win.

Jackson's candidacy was different from Mondale's and Hart's in that it had little chance of winning. But Jackson was nonetheless playing a party game, because his goal was to pressure the Democratic Party to pay more attention to the policy concerns of African Americans. Whether this strategy succeeded is unclear.

The 1964 Republicans and 1972 Democrats have often been criticized—though not in this book—for nominating candidates who pleased intense policy demanders within the party but were unelectable. A variant on this complaint might be made against the 1984 Democrats. Mondale was strongly favored by labor and by top officeholders in the party, but he lacked both personal charisma and substantive appeal to suburban and southern

Democrats. If the party insiders really wanted to win the fall election, they might have swung to Hart, who began leading Mondale in national polls after Hart's early primary victories. But, of course, parties do not care only about winning; they want to win, but only with a candidate whom they can trust to protect their most important concerns. Since they did not trust Hart, they went with a candidate they did trust.

Democrats in 1988: Gary Hart and the Seven Dwarfs

Gary Hart was not any more popular with party insiders when he entered the contest for the 1988 nomination than he had been in 1984. But, on the basis of publicity won by nearly beating Mondale in 1984, he consistently led opinion polls in which Democratic voters were asked their preferences in the contest, and this made him a focal point. Seven other candidates entered the race, but a common view was that the field consisted of "Gary Hart and the Seven Dwarfs."[8]

Hart continued to play his new ideas theme, and it continued to be unpopular among the old Democrats who continued to dominate the Democratic Party. Ronald Brownstein (1987) wrote in the *National Journal*:

> In February, he attended the AFL-CIO meeting in Florida and said he would welcome labor's endorsement in 1988. . . . But so far, he doesn't have much to show for his solicitousness.
> . . ."He has spent a lot of time trying to make friends with labor, seeing people one-on-one; then he comes back and tells people who've lost half of their members that he isn't going to do anything for them on trade," said Vic Fingerhut, a labor pollster. "That's not a hard sell; it's an impossible sell. People walk out of the room with Hart just shaking their heads."

Brownstein segues from Hart's trouble with endorsements to his trouble raising money. "In the short term," he wrote

> money may be the more pressing problem. . . . Since 1984, Hart has signed up several first-tier Democratic fund raisers. . . . But there's been no rush of the big money givers toward Hart, and few in his camp expect him to raise as much money as quickly as Mondale did [in 1984]. "We are being kept alive by direct mail," [a Hart campaign official] said.

Although Brownstein does not explicitly link endorsements and fund-raising, it is hard to believe that a Democratic candidate who left union leaders "just shaking their heads" wouldn't have trouble with fund-raisers precisely for that reason. Moreover, Hart had trouble getting any sort of insider support. As Paul Taylor of the *Washington Post* wrote:

> [Senator Gary Hart] is campaigning [in 1988] as a lonely front-runner. Aside from Jesse L. Jackson, no Democrat registered within 40 percentage points of him in a nationwide Washington Post/ABC News Poll completed last weekend. But Hart hasn't collected endorsements commensurate with his poll standing—nor, by his calculation, is he likely to.
>
> Some of his opponents are spoiling to turn that disparity into an indictment of Hart's ability to govern. Building from questions raised about Hart in 1984, they will portray him as aloof, unable even in this ripe moment to line up backing because he remains uncomfortable with fellow politicians and political transactions.
>
> "How can you lead the country if you can't lead your peers?" asked Christopher Mathews, a Democratic public policy analyst, who predicted that question will frame an "anybody but Hart" movement he expects to take shape within the party in the year ahead. (Taylor 1987, A4)

Hart's status as "lonely front-runner" suggests that voter support is by no means sufficient to ensure success in the invisible primary. Candidates must also be acceptable to core party groups and leaders, and Hart was not.

As it turned out, Hart dropped out of the presidential race shortly after these stories were written. A media firestorm erupted after Hart stated that he was engaged in no extramarital affairs but was caught by reporters spending the night with a woman who was not his wife. Except for this incident, Hart would surely have gone on—with or without party support—to compete in the regular primaries in 1988 as he had in 1984, and this prospect would have put party insiders under pressure to support him.[9]

Hart's departure from the race spared insiders this dilemma—while also depriving us of the opportunity to see how they would resolve it—but it did not solve the problem of whom to select as their preferred candidate. One of the so-called dwarfs was Jesse Jackson, who did not lack stature but did lack broad electoral appeal. In this invisible primary, fifty-seven of sixty African American leaders in the data we collected supported his candidacy, but, despite Jackson's efforts to build a "rainbow coalition," few important nonblack insiders did. Jackson is, therefore, an example of a factional candidacy.

Four of the other dwarfs—Michael Dukakis, Al Gore, Richard Gephardt, and Paul Simon—were probably acceptable within the party on policy grounds, but none proved to be a strong vote-getter in later elections. The party did have one seasoned politician who was both broadly acceptable within the party and a charismatic campaigner, namely, Governor Mario Cuomo of New York, but he refused to enter the race.

What ought a wise and nimble party to do in such circumstances? In the very old days, it might have engineered a backroom deal for someone who "looked like a president" and was broadly acceptable within the party. Dukakis, Gephardt, or Gore would have been plausible candidates for this dubious honor.

In the new system, insiders seemed simply to bide their time. For labor, this was a conscious decision in response to a weak field.[10] For others, including governors who mostly refrained from endorsing anyone, we infer the same. "Many of the party leaders are simply waiting for one of the remaining candidates to prove himself," wrote Jonathan Wollman (1987) of the Associated Press in late November 1987. Even for those who did make endorsements, the pace was slower than in most years (see figure 5.2).

The role of top fund-raisers in this "wait-and-see" contest is noteworthy. Here is an account of how one top Democratic fund-raiser experienced the contest:

Some aspirants for the 1988 Democratic Presidential nomination have apparently concluded that it would help to have E. William Crotty on their side.

In recent days, Mr. Crotty has fielded phone calls from Representative Richard A. Gephardt of Missouri, who announced his candidacy this week, and former Gov. Bruce Babbitt of Arizona, who plans to announce next month.

Senator Joseph R. Biden Jr. of Delaware flew to Mr. Crotty's Florida home for dinner Sunday night. And on Monday Mr. Crotty met in Washington with Senator Dale Bumpers of Arkansas, who is expected to announce formation of an exploratory committee shortly. That night he was invited to a retreat in Colorado sponsored by former Senator Gary Hart but could not make it.

On Wednesday Mr. Crotty had lunch with Senator Albert Gore Jr. of Tennessee, who might be a long shot for 1988 but an attractive candidate in the future.

Mr. Crotty is senior partner in a Daytona Beach law firm. More to the point, he is a top Democratic fund-raiser and therefore a potentially key player in the 1988 contest.

Now that the early field has been thinned by Governor Cuomo's decision not to run and by Senator Sam Nunn's announcement that he will put his bid on hold, Mr. Crotty and other Democratic fund-raisers are finding themselves besieged.

"I feel a little embarrassed about it, really," Mr. Crotty said of the attention he is getting.

He said he expected to decide in the next few weeks but was not leaning toward anyone. "I'm sort of waiting," he said. (Berke 1987a, A24)

This account does not fit the story of candidate-centered politics. It seems, rather, a story in which a small number of big fish are very important. But, even in the stalled Democratic contest for the 1988 nomination, big donors did not appear to be independently important. This, at least, is the inference we draw from a self-conscious effort by top Democratic fund-raisers to set themselves up as king-makers. About forty of them formed a group called Impac '88, shared lavish meals at posh hotels, and met with and interviewed leading political figures in an effort to form a united front of their own. But no agreement developed and the wannabe kingmakers began going their separate ways. Finally, seventeen of the original forty coordinated on Al Gore and pledged to raise $250,000 each for their man, or $4.25 million. But as the primaries approached, they delivered only $320,000. This made Impac '88 the butt of many jokes (Berke 1987b, A30). In this invisible primary as in others, money could not drive the outcome, even when it faced no real competition.

With no commanding figure in sight, 27 percent of endorsements in the invisible primary went to Dukakis, with 22 percent to Gephardt as runner-up. However, the overall results obscure an interesting difference. A large fraction of Gephardt's support came from national politicians, mostly members of the House of Representatives, of which Gephardt was a party leader. Thus, among federal officeholders and former officeholders, Gephardt led Dukakis by a margin of 44 percent to 14 percent. But "out in the country," where far more endorsements were made, party sentiment ran the other way: Dukakis bested Gephardt by a margin of 40 percent to 7 percent. Given that delegates are won in contests out in the country rather than in Washington, this endorsement pattern probably gave Dukakis an advantage.

When voting by rank-and-file Democrats got under way, Gephardt won Iowa and Dukakis won New Hampshire, leaving the contest stuck in neutral. Party leaders now took another look at the race, but decided the time was still not quite ripe for jumping in. As David Broder (1988) wrote,

Ohio Gov. Richard F. Celeste, who backed Glenn and then Mondale in 1984 only to see Hart win the Ohio primary, said, "A lot of us moved ahead of our own supporters last time, so there's an inclination to lay back this time."
   Celeste and a number of others regarded as potential Dukakis allies indicated that they are inclined to make a public choice after Super Tuesday, presuming Dukakis avoids a shellacking that day. "I told Mike [Dukakis] he's

got to show he can get votes in the South before most of us in the West will be ready to make a choice," said Idaho Gov. Cecil Andrus.

[New York Governor] Cuomo took a similar stance yesterday. "Super Tuesday will tell us a lot," he said, adding that he hopes to make an endorsement before his state's April 19 primary.

These comments suggest that the governors were thinking about the primaries in somewhat the same way as party leaders in the prereform system, when demonstration of vote-getting ability was often critical to nomination. As the voter primaries continued, Dukakis lost South Dakota, but won Florida, Texas, Maryland, and Rhode Island, and this, perhaps especially the southern wins, told in his favor with party leaders. Dukakis got twenty-two new publicly reported endorsements after Iowa, while Gephardt got none. Dukakis also raised $6.9 million in the two months following Iowa and New Hampshire, but Gephardt only $2.6 million (Brown, Powell, and Wilcox 1995, table 2.2).

This is surely a breed of momentum, driven not by the effect of the media on voters but, as it appears, the effect of new information on party insiders.[11] Meanwhile, Jesse Jackson was running better than he had in 1984 and was in a virtual tie with Dukakis in the delegate hunt.[12] So when Dukakis outpolled Gephardt by about 28 percent to 14 percent in contests through Super Tuesday, Democratic leaders apparently saw no point in prolonging the decision. They closed ranks around Dukakis, leaving Gephardt unable to raise money and soon thereafter unable to run campaigns either (Gleckman 1988; Germond and Witcover 1989; Taylor 1988).[13]

One might suspect that, in a country with as many ambitious politicians as the United States, it would always be easy for parties to find someone with both broad acceptability among insiders and appeal as a vote-getter. The 1988 Democratic nomination shows otherwise. The party had a choice of two able campaigners (Hart and Jackson) and at least four candidates who were acceptable on policy grounds (Dukakis, Gephardt, Gore, Simon), but the two sets did not overlap. Mario Cuomo would probably have satisfied most Democrats on both grounds, but he stayed out of the race.

Hence, our analysis is that the Democrats failed to form a unified front in the invisible primary of 1988 because they had no candidate satisfying the two key criteria for a party nominee. They waited for the primaries to generate evidence on which candidate had stronger vote-getting appeal, and when that information came in, they made a choice. Several details of the case—the seven dwarfs epithet, the wait-and-and-see pace of endorsements, the reticence of labor and governors, the direct observations of journalists, and the later history of the candidates—fit this interpretation.

A nomination in which the party fails to reach a consensus prior to Iowa cannot in the end provide strong support for our theory of strong parties. One part of the narrative does, however, provide solid support: The reticence of party insiders to rally behind Hart, a politician unpalatable to labor, when he was the leading candidate in the race. Although the party had difficulty saying yes in 1988, it was able to say no. A party saying no to its most popular candidate does not fit the story of candidate-centered politics.

Republicans in 1988: An Inside Job

As Ronald Reagan's vice president, George Herbert Walker Bush coasted to a victory in the invisible primary of 1988 with 48 percent of all endorsements. Bush won almost exactly Reagan's percentage in 1980 and was well ahead of his nearest competitors, Bob Dole and Jack Kemp, who each had about 20 percent. Dole was the party's vice presidential nominee in 1976 and minority leader of the Senate. Kemp was a prominent member of the House of Representatives.

That Bush finished so far ahead of Kemp is notable and perhaps surprising. A handsome ex-professional football player, Kemp was outspokenly antitax, antigovernment, and anticommunist, and also uncommonly sunny and warm. Except that Reagan had been an actor rather than an athlete, the two were quite similar. Kemp was a favorite of the party's conservative base, making hundreds of speeches around the country and raising large sums of campaign money for the party. "When it came to conservative orthodoxy," wrote Germond and Witcover, "many on the New Right saw Kemp as more Catholic than the ideological Pope who spoke ex cathedra from the Oval Office" (1989, 67).

Bush, meanwhile, was not a conservative favorite. He had been brought into national politics by Nixon, who was identified as a Dewey man, and Bush had campaigned against Reagan in 1980 as a moderate. Bush worked hard to make up for past sins, traveling to numerous conservative events, but he was not fully convincing. "Where was he when he didn't need us," asked one conservative insider (72). Conservative columnist George Will wrote, "The unpleasant sound Bush is emitting as he traipses from one conservative gathering to another is a thin, tinny 'arf'—the sound of a lapdog" (Will 1986). We mention these nasty remarks because our theory would suggest that, in a perfectly efficient party system, someone like Kemp (favored by the policy-demanding base) would beat someone like Bush (an unpopular but well-positioned politician) in the invisible primary. But it didn't turn out that way, so we note the disconnect.

Yet there is no shortage of explanations for Bush's success. One is poll support for the nomination among rank-and-file Republicans. Bush usually got support in the range of 30 to 40 percent; Kemp did well to get out of single digits. We do not think polls are important in the invisible primary, but, again, we note the evidence.

A bigger factor is Reagan's personal support. By all accounts, Reagan appreciated Bush's loyal service as vice president and came to like his one-time opponent. Although Reagan never formally endorsed Bush, his high opinion probably mattered in party circles.

The factor to which we attach the greatest importance is that White House political staff rallied to Bush, most conspicuously a young operative named Lee Atwater. We complained earlier that it is hard to get information about political operatives, but Atwater was sufficiently notable that reporters have recorded his actions. We suspect—though, to be clear, we do not really know—that individuals like Atwater sometimes have great influence in the new system. Super politicians like Ronald Reagan would probably make their way to the top of any system, but for most of the rest, it may matter a great deal whether someone like Atwater is managing the campaign. So let us pause over Atwater.

Germond and Witcover mention Atwater in passing in their account of the 1980 campaign: "In South Carolina a skilled young professional named Lee Atwater, later to serve in Reagan's White House, had been pressed by Senator Strom Thurmond to run Connally's campaign there, but had refused for just that reason. On the basis of a study of eighty polls involving various candidates, Atwater had formulated a rule that no one could succeed if he had 'negatives' of 35 percent or higher, unless his 'positives' were at least 15 percentage points better. And thirteen polls on Connally, taken in a variety of states, had shown 'negatives' of 37 percent, 'positives' of only 26" (Germond and Witcover 1989, 107). Data crunchers in today's data-rich political system may now be able to formulate better rules of thumb, but in 1979 that was good analysis.

In 1985, Atwater agreed to work for Bush as the director of his political action committee. As Germond and Witcover comment in their 1989 volume, "The recruitment in itself was a signal to the party's most conservative elements that Bush had found a home on the right" (70). But Atwater had been looking out for Bush's interests longer than that. As early as 1982, Atwater wondered who would come after Reagan and "saw in [Bush] a potential that eluded many other political professionals in and out of Republican ranks." Hence, "in scheduling White House events, Atwater made sure that [Bush] . . . met the key political players." Atwater believed that the candidate who could get an early lock on the South would be in an especially strong position, so "Atwater proceeded to sow Bush seeds across Dixie, in state after state where he had been involved as a consultant or campaign manager in Republican primary elections. Atwater knew most of the hundred or so individuals who constituted the activist core in each state and he set about bringing them aboard the embryo Bush campaign" (70).

Another journalist quoted an unnamed "Bush organizer," who might have been Atwater himself, on the effect of Atwater's early recruiting on another contender for the nomination: "There are only 10 or 15 guys in these southern states who know how to run a campaign, and another tier of about 80 [to] 90 good campaign workers. If you get them, there's nothing left for the opposition. . . . That's why [Bob] Dole could never get organized here because there was nothing for him" (Edsall 1988, A29). To put it in our language: the support needed to mount a campaign came from a small pond, not an ocean.

Getting a political operative on your side who was as well-regarded and who had as many political friends as Atwater seems like it would be worth far more than fund-raising prowess—but would, of course, attract campaign money as well. Bush also attracted other top talent to his team, including James Baker, Roger Ailes, and Robert Teeter. With a powerhouse team like that, even a so-so candidate could win the invisible primary and then the nomination.

A final point that should not be overlooked: Bush had long since abandoned the moderate positions on taxes and social issues that had been the basis of his 1980 campaign in the invisible primary, becoming a consistent supporter of the stronger form of conservatism that triumphed in the Republican Party in the 1980s. So, although conservatives distrusted Bush, they had no particular complaint against him beyond the fact that he had come late to the Reagan Revolution. If he had not come at all, it is unlikely he would have won the invisible primary.

The success of vice presidents in winning presidential nominations is striking. Walter Mondale, George H. W. Bush, and Al Gore each took this route to nomination in the reformed party system. Richard Nixon and Hubert Humphrey did so in the old system.

A big part of the vice president's job is to travel the country as a speaker at fund-raising events, presidential ambassador, fence mender, and perhaps dispenser of federal largesse. This puts the vice president in an excellent position to make friends, create obligations, and make himself, more generally, the center of attention. Eight years in the office of vice president also gives party members a great deal of information—more, perhaps, than about any other candidate—about how that official is likely to behave in the top office. So if a qualified vice president is among the choices that party leaders can make, he is generally a safe choice as well.

But what should we make of the dissatisfaction of many conservatives with the choice of Bush? Could one argue that Bush was a strong candidate who forced party insiders, against their will, to knuckle under and support him?

It is fair to say that Bush forced his candidacy on some insiders. We should also note that two of the advisors who helped Bush in the invisible primary, Baker and Teeter, were members of Bush's 1980 campaign team and might therefore be considered Bush loyalists rather than party loyalists.

But it seems unfair to argue that Bush won the invisible primary because of his strengths *as a candidate*. Bush was, after all, the vice president, the second highest official in the Republican Party. When a party leader gets himself nominated over other strong candidates on the basis of strengths derived from his position as party leader, one can scarcely argue that candidate-centered politics has trumped party.

We also observe that the nomination of vice presidents is not automatic. Dan Quayle, who was George Bush's vice president, performed the usual chores of the office, but was never able to overcome the impression that he was a lightweight. In one famous incident, he became a national laughingstock when, in overseeing a spelling bee, he coached a young student to add an *e* to the end of *potato*. So when Quayle entered the invisible primaries of 1996 and 2000, insiders did not flock to him. As a journalist reported in 1995, Quayle "received discouraging responses as he sounded out potential political and financial backers around the country over the last several weeks" (Brownstein 1995, A1). The same happened in Quayle's second run, with the result that, in both nomination contests, he dropped out before the first contest in Iowa.

Thus, if vice presidents usually do well when they run for the top job, it is not because the party cannot say no in the invisible primary. It is because the party usually has no strong reason to say no to its vice presidents and former vice presidents.

We earlier expressed surprise that Bush was able to beat Kemp, but we should also note that Kemp "tested the waters" for another presidential run in 1996 and again decided to stay out—and again despite what seemed a so-so field. So the conservative favorite that Bush beat was not a powerhouse politician, but a merely promising one. The other candidate that Bush beat in the 1988 invisible primary from his perch as vice president was Bob Dole, whose losing campaign against Bill Clinton in a weak economy in 1996 suggests he was not a super politician either.

Bush himself was neither an outstanding vote-getter nor a favorite of party activists, but performed well enough as vice president and positioned himself (with help from Atwater and others) to be acceptable on all key party issues. These minimal qualifications, plus the opportunity to campaign for the nomination that his party position gave him, were the keys to his success in the invisible primary. Bush might not have been able to win the invisible primary against a strong field—against, for example, a field that included someone like Ronald Reagan—but in a normal field, the assets of the vice presidency can make the difference. If a party has a top leader who's probably as good as any other candidate, and especially if the party's top campaign talent has decided he's their best bet, why would the party coalition not go along?

Democrats in 1992: The Man Would Not Play

As it had been four years earlier, the big story through most of the 1992 invisible primary was whether Mario Cuomo would enter the race. Cuomo gave himself deadlines to decide but kept missing them. Political insiders around the country made fun of the indecisive New York governor, calling him "Hamlet on the Hudson." But the consequences for the Democratic Party were serious. As late as October 1991, "The threat of a Cuomo candidacy was freezing Democratic activists and contributors who by this point might have been choosing another candidate to support." Complained Ron Brown, chair of the Democratic Party: "There was a major national force hovering and it kept people from focusing" (Germond and Witcover 1993, 118–19).

When, at one point, a rumor that Cuomo was about to declare his candidacy reached New Hampshire, it spread quickly through the state's community of political activists, who began telephoning the man expected to be Cuomo's state director. The list reached eighty people, including some of the top politicians in the state. But Cuomo held back, leaving his supporters in New Hampshire and elsewhere on a limb. Cuomo's troops, said a leader in another state, are "concerned about how long they have to wait. . . . They'd prefer it to be him, but if not, it's kind of, 'Let my people go'" (Toner 1991, B7).

Our data are consistent with reports of a frozen field, as the rate of endorsements in the 1992 invisible primary was by far the slowest of any contest. Only 5 percent of all endorsements made in that cycle were made by

October 1, and 95 percent were made after that date. By contrast, in typical nomination contests, 50 percent of endorsements were made by October 1 of the year prior to the election.

Because Cuomo never did enter the race, we cannot be sure that party insiders really were waiting for him. But because much evidence points to that conclusion, we shall assume it is correct and consider its significance.

What the party's wait on Cuomo shows is that many of the "fish" in the Democratic Party had wills of their own and had decided they wanted to be caught by Cuomo rather than by the other candidates. If the exertions of candidates determine presidential nominations, one of the other eight active candidates should have been able to round up insider support. Certainly the two more factional candidates—Tom Harkin, who was intensely favored by labor, and Bill Clinton, the self-avowed New Democrat of this contest—should have been able to get going. But the party said no to the other candidates and "pretty please" to the noncandidate of its choice. In a system that, according to most scholars is bereft of party influence, the party was, in effect, attempting to draft an unwilling nominee. It's as if the fish in a small pond were ignoring the hooks of the fishermen trying to catch them but imploring one who had stayed home, "Come on out and compete—we'll bite for you."

The attempted draft is more notable for the fact that Cuomo never engaged in the kind of extensive, countrywide campaigning that almost all other candidates engaged in. The primary basis of his support was the keynote address he made at the 1984 party convention. The speech was a stirring appeal to the traditional Democratic vision of activist government trying to improve citizens' lives. Many in the party believed Cuomo's manner of articulating this vision would bring independent and weakly attached Democratic voters back to the party fold.

This belief, however, must have been largely independent of national polls. In eleven surveys in the period in which Cuomo was deciding whether to enter the race, an average of about 22 percent of Democratic voters supported him for the nomination. These were better numbers than other candidates in the race, but scarcely commanding. If many party insiders believed that Cuomo would be a powerhouse candidate, it must have been based more on their judgment than on the candidate's demonstrated support.

Cuomo kept the door open for a possible candidacy until December 20, the last day on which to file papers for the New Hampshire primary. About a month before that, candidate Bill Clinton began moving up in the pack. Clinton did campaign hard for the nomination, but many were suspicious that he, like Gary Hart, was insufficiently committed to party principles.

But unlike Hart, Clinton resolved to tell party insiders what they wanted to hear:

> Late on the morning of Nov. 23, after Arkansas Gov. Bill Clinton finished an address to the Association of State Democratic Chairs in Chicago, Karen Marchioro rose to ask about criticism that Clinton was little more than a warmed-over Republican.
>
> The seemingly hostile question caused no anxiety among Clinton's staff. They had done everything they could to prepare the Democratic presidential candidate. They had caucused with Clinton on the speech, established their goals, salted the hotel ballroom with boisterous friends—and even encouraged hostile questions from the audience.
>
> Marchioro, the Democratic chairman from Washington State, gave Clinton an opportunity to confront publicly his doubters among party liberals. She said she had spoken with her friend and Clinton adviser Stephanie Solien earlier that day.
>
> "They wanted the question answered," Marchioro said. . . .
>
> Clinton's response, which evoked his grandfather's near-religious devotion to Franklin D. Roosevelt, drew strong applause. Clinton had cleared a major hurdle in his path to the Democratic nomination. (Balz and Dionne 1992)

Balz and Dionne point out that clearing this hurdle was more than symbolic; it paid some quite tangible benefits:

> Until Chicago, fund-raising had been slack. But when the reviews came in, the fax machines at Clinton headquarters worked overtime to distribute the clips to potential contributors. Between mid-November and the end of 1991, Clinton raised roughly $ 2.5 million, according to the campaign. The effort was led by finance director Rahm Emanuel, who put together 27 events in 20 days, and Robert Farmer, who was Dukakis's chief fund-raiser in 1988.

Thus, we again see a link between a successful political appeal and success in fund-raising. At least in the invisible primary, candidates do not simply ask for money; they ask for money in order to advance political goals, and potential donors give them money for that purpose.

Not all of the Democrats who rallied to Clinton were thrilled to do so. The ambivalence was especially great for African Americans who, once again, had to choose between a candidate who inspired them and one who was only acceptable. As Thomas Edsall (1992) of the *Washington Post* described the calculations of one of these figures:

"I'm tired of betting on the damn loser," [said South Carolina State Senator Kay Patterson].

Earlier this year, Harkin came to South Carolina and announced that Jesse L. Jackson's "Rainbow Coalition is my agenda. Tell blacks not to read my lips, read my record of 17 years. The Rainbow Coalition, that's my agenda."

Patterson, now a Clinton backer, said he liked to hear Harkin "spouting all these liberal ideas. But hell, ain't nobody going to vote for him. You can't win appealing just to black people. There ain't enough to win an election. You have to appeal to white folks."

The same sort of dilemma presented itself to union groups in the Democratic Party. Iowa Senator Tom Harkin was the natural favorite of many union leaders and activists, but their endorsements went mainly to Bill Clinton. A story from the *St. Louis Post-Dispatch* captures the sentiment among many union leaders:

Head or heart? That question is splitting the labor movement as trade unionists ponder which of two Democrats to support in the presidential race. Many political observers expected organized labor to overwhelmingly back Sen. Tom Harkin of Iowa, given his long pro-union record and his stand with labor on the key issue of trade. But that's not happening; instead, Arkansas Gov. Bill Clinton is holding his own. . . . In Illinois, for instance, AFL-CIO spokeswoman Sue Altman sees many of Illinois labor's heavy hitters going with Clinton. "It surprised us all here that Clinton could get as much as he has, because for Harkin, that's his appeal—to working people," Altman said. "I think a lot of people believe that Clinton is the most winnable candidate, and we all feel that we have got to get (President George) Bush out of the White House or working people are done for in this country." Yet, she notes, many unionists feel Harkin could be "another Franklin Delano Roosevelt, if there is a way to get him elected." That dilemma—success vs. sentiment— plagues labor nationwide. Rick Scott, political director for the 1.3-million-member American Federation of State, County and Municipal Employees, said his members were "evaluating electability along with issues." "They'd rather have someone who says some things they may not agree with 100 percent but who will get into the White House," Scott said. Such talk infuriates Sam Dawson, political director of the 650,000-member United Steelworkers of America. "I'm from Texas, and as (ex-Texas football coach) Darrell Royal says, 'You dance with who brung you'—and that's what I think you need to do in politics." . . . "Labor people are ready to put their egos away," said Duke McVey, president of the 500,000-member Missouri AFL-CIO. "Our people want a winner." (Dine 1992, 1A)

Harkin was naturally frustrated by this development, but tried to put the best face on it. "I've never said that every union is going to support me," he said. But he also said he hoped the big unions would endorse him, and added, "I wish they'd hurry up" (Berke 1992, A1). But they never did.

Taylor E. Dark (1999, 191) sees strong parallels between the way labor responded to John Kennedy in 1960 and the way it responded to Clinton in 1992.

> In 1960 Hubert Humphrey played a role comparable to that of Tom Harkin in 1992: the traditional heart-throb of the liberals—an ardent defender of the old-time religion, but an unlikely victor in the general election. John F. Kennedy in contrast, was not as close to the labor movement and was deemed more unreliable in his politics, but union leaders still swung their support behind his candidacy after the early primaries showed that he was the most electable choice. In similar fashion, Clinton garnered more union support as he succeeded in the primaries, despite his mixed record on union issues in Arkansas. And in both elections the most distrusted of the candidates— Lyndon Johnson in 1960 and Paul Tsongas in 1992—were forced out of the race as serious contenders well before the convention.
>
> Also common to both periods was that the union leaders were more inter- ested in supporting an electable Democrat than in securing the nominee who was the most "correct" on union issues. As one AFSCME leader put it, "We believe that we need to be about winning in 1992. . . . If we went for Harkin we probably could get 90% of our agenda. If we went for Clinton we probably could get 85% of our agenda. But it's Clinton who, in my opinion, can get us to the White House." This kind of pragmatic bargaining stance was familiar, having guided unions in 1960 and earlier years, and it now produced a simi- lar result: the nomination of a mainstream Democrat willing to support labor on most of its key issues.

These observations, though anecdotal, constitute evidence that Demo- cratic insiders were well aware of the imperative to shun factional favorites for the sake of a united front behind a candidate who could win in November.

According to several journalistic accounts, Clinton's Chicago speech embracing traditional party values and one or two others at about the same time marked the take-off point in his drive for the nomination (Germond and Witcover 1993, 160; Goldman et al. 1994, 82–83). He ended up with 65 percent of the endorsements in an eight-man field, with almost all of the endorsements coming in the two months following the November speech. The rush to the Arkansas governor at the end of the invisible primary was so rapid that, except for the long hesitation over Cuomo, it might have seemed the party had no ability to resist a politician who subsequently proved his mettle as a vote-getting champion. But thanks to Hamlet on the Hudson, and the long hesitation over the Seven Dwarfs of 1988, we can see that the choice of Clinton was a genuine choice, not a capitulation.

Republicans in 1996: Focal Point Politics

In their first fully open nomination since Ronald Reagan's in 1980, the Republicans suffered a dearth of good candidates. The candidate with the deepest pockets was Malcolm "Steve" Forbes, a millionaire publisher who shelled out $25 million of his own money to fund his run for the presidency. Forbes, along with his signature issue, the Flat Tax, attracted substantial media attention but not much else. He won only 1.5 percent of insider endorsements and was an early dropout from the voter primaries.

Another candidate who plotted a money-centered strategy was Senator Phil Gramm of Texas. According to a profile in *Texas Monthly* (Burka 1995), Gramm's staff noticed that the candidate who was most successful in pre-Iowa fund-raising had won all recent nominations. With this in mind, Gramm took the chairmanship of the National Republican Senatorial Committee (NRSC) for the 1992 and 1994 elections. This enabled him to travel around the country at party expense, making friends with the party's biggest donors. In launching his presidential campaign in 1995, he tapped into the same party networks, raising nearly twice as much money as his next nearest competitor in the first quarter of 1995. Gramm also made a concerted effort to gain early endorsements and did a reasonably good job.

With this flurry of early success, Gramm made a bid to become the focal point of a generally unexciting field. Gramm, we might add, is an academic economist who is likely to have an expert's understanding that an early focal point in a coordination game can dominate the process.

There was, however, another focal point in the contest. Senate Majority Leader Bob Dole had been the vice presidential nominee in 1976, the second-place finisher for the presidential nomination in 1988, and the most visible national media presence of any candidate in the race. Moreover, he was not shy about asserting that "It's my turn" for the nomination, which may be loosely translated as, "If there are no outstanding choices, I'm the focal point." Early public opinion polls also favored him over Gramm.

The invisible primary thus opened as a contest of Gramm versus Dole. In the first round of endorsements, Gramm outpaced Dole by a margin of eighteen to four. In another conspicuous display of early strength, friends of Gramm staged straw polls in states friendly to his ideological coloration, which Gramm won.

However, the focal point stratagem failed. If Gramm used his Senate leadership position to build his fund-raising network, so did Dole in his role of Senate Majority leader. As Dan Balz wrote in the *Washington Post:*

> Dole reached out to governors immediately after the 1994 elections, prom-
> ising to make relief from federal government mandates his first order of
> business in the Senate and encouraging them to become partners with con-
> gressional Republicans in reforming welfare, Medicaid and other domestic
> programs. Even before he had announced his candidacy, Ohio Gov. George
> V. Voinovich had announced his support.
>
>   [Dole's] recruitment of governors mirrors the strategy George Bush used
> to win the 1988 nomination, and he has used their support not only to build a
> national political organization *but also as the backbone of a fund-raising machine
> that has outdistanced competitors.*
>
>   Dole's campaign has carefully choreographed the gubernatorial endorse-
> ments, then followed them up with a fund-raiser in the state a month
> later. Those fund-raising events raised $3.4 million in New York, $800,000
> each in California and Ohio, $700,000 in Pennsylvania, almost $600,000 in
> Illinois.
>
>   "The governors are incredibly important in their own states, in getting the
> best people and raising the money and helping to win the states," said Robert
> Teeter, who managed Bush's campaign in 1992 and served as a senior strate-
> gist in 1988. (Balz 1995, A1; emphasis added)

Twenty-seven of the party's thirty-one governors made pre-Iowa endorsements of Dole, most toward the end of the invisible primary. As in other
invisible primaries, this political support was, as Balz emphasizes, closely
tied to financial support (A1).

The invisible primary was thus fought by two of the Republican Party's
top leaders, each of whom used his position in the party to build support
among other party insiders. Either candidate could therefore win without
endangering our thesis of party resurgence. As it turned out, the more
highly ranked leader won in a landslide with 68 percent of insider endorsements in a twelve-candidate field. Gramm, who got most of his support at
the start of the invisible primary, finished second with 18 percent.

Meanwhile, Patrick Buchanan, a social conservative, was mounting another kind of campaign, an outsider campaign. In 1992, he had taken on
incumbent President George Bush in the state-by-state primaries, winning
38 percent of the vote in New Hampshire and making respectable showings in several other states. That fact that he had no chance to win did not
faze him.

With no Republican incumbent president in 1996, Buchanan's prospects seemed brighter. His performance in 1992 suggested that he had a natural base of support of 20 to 30 percent of the Republican vote in a good number of states. If he could win the first primary in New Hampshire—as, in fact, he did in 1996—he might generate a powerful wave of momentum that would garner him considerably more support. Moreover, the first contest after New Hampshire was in South Carolina, the kind of socially conservative state where Buchanan ought to do especially well. And if Buchanan could win South Carolina after winning New Hampshire, he might really be off to the races. His chances of nomination were probably still not high, but he could certainly make a mess of the Republican primaries, and who could know what might emerge from the confusion?

Both campaigns recognized the potential importance of South Carolina and worked to line up endorsements in the Palmetto State. By our count, Dole won this skirmish easily, with twenty endorsements to Buchanan's zero. Many of Dole's endorsements, moreover, came from top party and religious figures, who worked closely with the state Republican Party. Thomas Edsall (1996a) gives the following account of the factional struggle on the eve of the vote:

> Citing the support of many county chairmen of the South Carolina Christian Coalition, such Dole backers as Gov. David M. Beasley and former governor Carroll A. Campbell Jr. are banking on winning enough of the Christian right to combine with a plurality of other voters to win overall [in the primary].
>
> Roberta Combs, chairman of the South Carolina Christian Coalition, is publicly neutral, but Dole supporters openly boast of the help she is providing and note that her husband has endorsed the Kansas senator.
>
> "We've got a lot of support there. In our internal polling, we win the right-to-life vote, we win the Christian Coalition vote," said Warren Tompkins, Dole's southern strategist.
>
> He said the only weakness is what he called the "Bob Jones strain of religious conservatives," referring to the fundamentalist Bob Jones University in Greenville.

The fact that Dole, who was pro-life but not outspokenly so, could hold the support of the state's religious establishment against the outspoken social conservatism of Buchanan is notable. It shows that, consistent with our notion of party resurgence, key Republican groups were resisting the impulse to faction and were instead pulling together as a party.

As it turned out, Dole scored a solid victory over Buchanan in the South Carolina primary, thereby putting an end to the latter's momentum in a state Buchanan might well have won. But South Carolina leaders may have paid a price for their role in Dole's success, for as Edsall also noted:

> Interviews with voters at a Thursday night Christian Coalition "God and Country" rally showed overwhelming support for Buchanan, and very little for Dole. The support for Dole among South Carolina Christian Coalition leaders has provoked some resentment.
>
> Robert Taylor, dean of the school of business administration at Bob Jones University, said some Christian Coalition leaders have adopted a relationship with GOP leaders of "I'll scratch your back if you'll scratch mine." He warned that some of these leaders "might be in jeopardy, might find they are no longer leaders."

The theoretical point here is that important leaders were willing to play their role in creating a united party front even when it was not in their interest as factional leaders to do so.

The storyline in 1996 is in the end very simple: Bob Dole won the invisible primary because leading members of his party rallied to him as the leader of the party. Even some religious leaders who might have been expected to back the more socially conservative Buchanan wound up backing Dole. It would be hard to argue that Dole was an especially strong candidate, or even a strong leader, but party insiders mostly rallied to him anyway. His most serious opponent in the voter primaries, Buchanan, made notably few inroads in Dole's support in the invisible primary.

The Democrats in 2000: Same Old Same Old
Vice president Al Gore beat former Senator Bill Bradley of New Jersey in endorsements in the invisible primary by 82 percent to 18 percent—a margin vastly greater than the amount, if any, by which Gore was actually a stronger candidate than Bradley. Gore did this by exploiting the advantages of the job of vice president. Unlike his predecessor, he avoided major gaffes and burnished his credentials as a serious politician by writing a book that was well-received in his ideological camp.

Despite Gore's advantage in political support, Bradley raised nearly as much campaign cash—the only candidate in this period to run even with the winner of the invisible primary in fund-raising. Journalists attributed this feat to contacts he developed as a leading member of the Senate Finance Committee.

Bottom line: Party leader uses position in party to get presidential nomination. His opponent raises lots of campaign cash, but it makes little difference.

The Republicans in 2000: Two Strong Candidates, One Big Winner
George W. Bush did in 2000 what Mario Cuomo would probably have done in 1992 if he had entered that race: Win the invisible primary without breaking a sweat. Bush skipped many of the candidate forums and waited to make his first campaign trip to Iowa until June 1999. He did much of his campaigning from the governor's mansion in Austin, to which party leaders and well-heeled donors traveled to listen to him speak, exchange a few words, and offer support. As reporter Dan Balz wrote,

> Politicians from Iowa, whose precinct caucuses kick off the presidential nominating process, normally wait for candidates to come to them. But [Iowa State Representative Chuck Larson] was one of a dozen Iowa legislators who chartered two planes that day to fly to Austin, and he didn't leave disappointed.
>
> "We have had an opportunity to meet (candidates) Steve Forbes and Dan Quayle and the others, and they're all very sharp and competent and capable," Mr. Larson said. "But after meeting George Bush, you know that if he runs, he will be the next president of the United States."
>
> The Texas capital is in the grip of a phenomenon that may be unique in the annals of presidential campaign startups. As a slew of other Republican candidates make pilgrimages to Iowa and New Hampshire and struggle for money, media attention and political support, the world is rushing to Mr. Bush's door in what has become the information age equivalent of William McKinley's front-porch campaign of 1896. (Balz 1999, A1)

Wealthy donors were prominent among those making the pilgrimage to Austin. Bush was so popular with them that, well into the invisible primary, he had not "had to spend one minute on the telephone pleading for donations—a luxury not enjoyed by most other candidates. 'Pick up the phone and dial for contributions?' Mr. Bush asked in an interview on Friday. 'Not at all.' Mr. Bush simply shows up at fund-raising events" (Berke 1999b, A13).

Bush's most enthusiastic support came from the office-holding wing of the Republican party, especially its governors. Republican governors meet annually, and the one from Texas made a good impression on his peers. Earlier than in any other invisible primary, governors signed on to the Bush campaign (see table 6A.2), and they quickly became major factors in his fund-raising efforts. Half of the GOP's governors were working for him by early 1999. As *Washington Post* reporter Susan Glasser (1999) added:

> The 13 governors who have endorsed Bush are also key to the money chase. Michigan's Engler, for example, "has launched full bore into a major fund-raising

effort on behalf of Bush," said his spokesman. "He is doing a significant number of phone calls."

In Massachusetts, Gov. Paul Cellucci has put his political team on the Bush assignment, and they rounded up 16 key Bay State fund-raising types to send to Texas 10 days ago, including former governor Bill Weld. The 1 1/2-hour lunch at Shoreline Grill in Austin featured a pep talk from Bush. "I expect 95 percent of the key Massachusetts Republican fund-raisers will be nailed down for Bush," said Cellucci adviser Rob Gray. *"Our organization is transferable."*

Bush's allies have turned the airport in Austin into a hub for prospective fund-raisers. Almost every day, delegations like those from Massachusetts arrive. (emphasis added)

That the financial resources of governors—as well, one must suspect, as the resources of former governors and other locally important politicians— may be "transferable" to presidential candidates is a point of utmost importance. It indicates that the money that leading candidates raise is, in some significant part, a party resource rather than a mere candidate resource.

Journalistic accounts make clear, however, that party officials are not the only source of funds. Private citizens, ranging from wealthy industrialists to persons described in newspapers as "professional fund-raisers," are also important. Yet such people are not lone rangers; they are partisan, strategic, and often hierarchically organized. In short, they are best understood as an arm of the contemporary political party. Consider the following excerpts from a description of George W. Bush's money-raising operation:

> The fund-raising structure Bush's advisers are assembling is a pyramid—"the air gets thinner as you go up," is how Sheldon Kamins, a Potomac developer who will help lead the Maryland fund-raising, put it.
>
> At the top are a few fund-raisers with national networks of their own— Bush money veterans such as Washington business consultants Wayne L. Berman and Peter Terpeluk Jr. and Michigan businessman Heinz C. Prechter.
>
> In the battle for what one Bush veteran called "the name brand people" in GOP fund-raising, the Texan hasn't won every round. Several of the biggest Rolodexes in New York, for example, are holding back as Bush and his top advisers negotiate with Gov. George E. Pataki, who has been floating his own presidential hopes of late. . . . "It far transcends the Washington establishment," said one former senior White House adviser to Bush. "It's certainly one part Bush family, one part Republican diehards and it's one big part Texas."
>
> The Bush mobilization has featured a procession of more than 400 fund-raisers—a who's who of the Republican rich and powerful—flying to Austin to hear his pitch.

[Even Bush's] opponents concede they can't compete with Bush for the key fund-raisers. "He's done a superb job in locking up the party establishment," said Ari Fleischer, spokesman for Elizabeth Dole (Glasser 1999, A1).[14]

The notion that there are "brand names" in a "Republican establishment" of big campaign donors is, once again, a point of significance. It indicates that some part—we suspect a rather large part—of what is often derogated as "fat cat" or "private" money is, rather, a form of organized *party* support.

Journalists often described the Bush campaign as "assembling" and "locking up" support of various individuals. But were the individuals thus "assembled" entirely passive in the matter? Were they "locked up" by some involuntary means? Were they incapable of saying no, as union officials said to Gary Hart? Were these Republican elites somehow unable to instead say yes to Dan Quayle, Elizabeth Dole, Orrin Hatch, Lamar Alexander, or any of several other prominent Republicans who tested the political waters in 2000 but did not actually enter the primaries? One assumes not. The party officials who turned the airport in Austin into "a hub for prospective [Bush] fund-raisers" had many choices. That they lined up behind Bush indicates that they were choosing to support him at least as much as he was choosing to "assemble" them. This difference in emphasis is important, because it is the difference between a candidate-centered and a party-centered view of presidential nominations.

But while Bush was a powerhouse candidate, he was not so powerful that he could ignore his party's intense policy demanders. Even economic conservatives were initially wary of him, recalling that the elder Bush had raised taxes and that the younger Bush called himself a "compassionate conservative." "We don't know yet [about Bush]," said David Keene, chairman of the American Conservative Union in fall 1998 (Romano 1998, B1). Economic conservatives attach particular attention to candidates' willingness to sign the anti-tax-increase pledge of Grover Norquist, president of Americans for Tax Reform. Bush at first refused, citing a long-standing policy of avoiding pledges of advocacy groups. But in June 1999, he signed the Norquist pledge anyway, and this seems to have satisfied the economic right. Later in the campaign, when other Republican candidates attacked Bush's tax program as insufficient, Norquist came to his defense.

Social conservatives within the party also felt that the elder Bush had betrayed them and were wary of being twice burned by the Bush family. At a 1998 meeting of fifteen conservative leaders, some favored a third-party candidate in 2000 if the Republican party failed to satisfy them. According to a newspaper report,

California Gov. Pete Wilson was generally viewed as unacceptable by this
group, and there were some present who described Texas Gov. George W.
Bush in the same category as Wilson, according to sources who attended. An-
drea Sheldon, executive director of the Traditional Values Coalition, said the
danger of a George W. Bush presidency is that "like father like son." President Bush "gave us [Supreme Court] Justice [David] Souter. Souter turned out
to be a real disaster," she said. (Edsall 1999)

By the following spring, however, many religious conservative leaders were
rallying to Bush. Under the headline "Conservatives Shield Bush's Abortion
Stand from Right Wing," *Washington Post* reporter Thomas Edsall wrote,

> Key leaders of the conservative establishment have begun an aggressive
> defense of George W. Bush's abortion stand in an effort to blunt attacks on
> the Texas governor's presidential campaign from the Republican Party's right
> wing.
>
> Just as such candidates as conservative activist Gary Bauer, publish-
> ing heir Malcolm S. "Steve" Forbes and television commentator Patrick J.
> Buchanan are beginning to gear up to use abortion to slow the momentum
> behind Bush, such antiabortion luminaries as Christian Coalition chairman
> Pat Robertson and David N. O'Steen, executive director of the National Right
> to Life Committee, have stepped in to defend Bush's abortion position.
>
> "Governor Bush has a pro-life record and has taken a pro-life position,"
> O'Steen said in a statement. (Edsall 1999, 4)

But some social conservatives accepted Bush without embracing him.
The problem they faced was a standard one in party politics. Two candidates in the race, Pat Buchanan and Gary Bauer, fully and enthusiastically
embraced their agenda. At the same time, Bush refused to promise an antiabortion litmus test in judicial appointments. In order to remain attractive
to centrist voters, Bush would promise only to appoint judges who would
follow the Constitution. The implication was that the nominees would be
solidly pro-life, but Bush would not say so.

Eventually, conservative leaders decided to take Bush at his implied
word and to rally their supporters. According to Richard Berke of the *New
York Times*,

> In appeals to the politically active members of their groups . . . the conserva-
> tive leaders make clear that they believe Mr. Bush can win the election if he is
> left politically unfettered on the issues—and that he will support their causes
> once in office.

David N. O'Steen, executive director of the National Right to Life Committee, said Mr. Bush "would be as effective a pro-life president as anyone seeking the office." He said his group was contacting members in its 3,000 chapters to counter "other Republican candidates who will go after the front-runner—that's not helpful to the pro-life movement. . . ."

One of the most influential conservative voices, James C. Dobson, leader of Focus on the Family, whose daily radio show draws five million listeners, has stayed silent for months. . . . Dr. Dobson has for years been particularly close to Mr. Bauer but has not endorsed him despite pleas from the Bauer campaign. (Berke 1999b, A1)

The implied deal between Bush and the religious right was not brokered in a smoke-filled room, but it was much like an old-fashioned backroom deal. And Bush appeared to keep his side of it. When, several years later, two openings came up on the Supreme Court, President Bush came through with nominations that, by initial indications, were as good as the religious right could have hoped for.[15] Bush also vetoed a bill that would have expanded public funding of stem cell research, another important issue for the religious right. This was a party system working as intense policy demanders want it to work.

At the end of the invisible primary, Bush had the support of all but one Republican governor and 65 percent of other public endorsements in a field of six active candidates—a victory as lopsided as any politician could hope for. The runner-up, Senator John McCain, got only 10 percent of endorsements.

That Bush ran in the invisible primary so far ahead of McCain, a media star and charismatic campaigner in his own right, seems notable. Bush was, to be sure, the bearer of a famous name, and in a competition in which becoming the focal point can matter, perhaps the Bush name is a sufficient explanation for all that happened. But more seems to have been involved. McCain was, as we observed earlier, a maverick. His signature issue was campaign finance reform, which he pursued despite the possibility that it might, if enacted, deprive the Republican Party of its fundraising advantage over the Democrats. His campaign finance proposals also alarmed important Republican interest groups, such as the National Rifle Association, which feared that their ability to make big contributions to the party would be undermined. McCain also made a point of forcing Senate roll-call votes on legislative provisions that he considers "pork"— that is, measures that benefit the local supporters of members of Congress but are not economically justified—and on the privileges ("perks") of the Senate as a whole, such as free parking at city airports. By forcing senators to vote publicly to maintain their privileges, he embarrassed them while making himself look good to voters. McCain's tactics played well in the media—one conservative columnist has referred to the Arizona Senator as "McCain (R–Media)"—but contribute to his reputation as a nonteam player. Republicans might rationally prefer to lose the presidency for one term rather than elect someone who might permanently undermine the party's competitive edge.[16]

In sum, Bush had not only the advantage of his family name, but the advantage of being a party man in what we take to be a strong party system. From examination of this case alone, we can't be sure which factor was more important.

What we can see, however, is that Bush did not have to fight hard for the bulk of the invisible primary support that enabled him to defeat McCain in the state-by-state primaries. The party mainly came to Bush on its own initiative in what we take to be the mark of a party-centered rather than candidate-centered system. Even religious conservatives, who supported Bush despite preferring other candidates, played the party game. We can also see evidence of implicit bargaining between Bush and the party's religious conservatives.

The Democrats in 2004: A Candidate-Centered Contest

If polls could make a nominee, Al Gore would have been the runaway Democratic choice in 2004. A CNN poll in late 2002 found that 38 percent of Democrats favored him for the nomination, with the next candidate, Joe Lieberman, far down in the pecking order with 13 percent support. Gore, moreover, seemed interested in the job. He traveled extensively in 2002, lost weight, shaved his beard, wrote two more books about political issues, built the nucleus of a campaign organization, made a guest appearance on *Saturday Night Live*—and then stunned the political world by withdrawing. As *Washington Post* reporter Dan Balz wrote,

> Many party insiders blamed Gore personally for losing in 2000 and did not want him to run again, believing the party would be better off with a fresh face. Many of his advisers from the 2000 campaign had decided not to work for him again, and some already had signed on with several of his potential rivals.
>
> Gore alluded to these problems last night. Noting that "the last campaign was an extremely difficult one," he added, "I think that there are a lot of people within the Democratic Party who felt exhausted by that, who felt like, 'Okay, I don't want to go through that again.' And I'm frankly sensitive to that, to that feeling." (Balz 2002, A1)

Gore's decision to withdraw was no doubt a complex one. But it is difficult to believe, in light of his extensive political activities in 2002, that he would have dropped out if party insiders were eager to have him back rather than, as many indicated, being reluctant or opposed. We thus view his withdrawal as a party decision as much as a candidate decision.

For those remaining in the race, the central political issue was Iraq. With the quick defeat of Saddam Hussein, the war was popular with the public through the early months of 2003, but it was extremely unpopular with the Democratic activists and donors who dominate the invisible primary. As a result, "the Democratic candidates are struggling to balance their desire to appeal to next year's primary voters—a majority of whom oppose going to war with Iraq—and their determination to establish their credentials as future commanders in chief. . . . No one wants to be against a successful war, but no one can ignore the voters who will pick the party's next presidential nominee" (Balz 2003a, 1).

The most prominent of the Democratic candidates—John Kerry, Joe Lieberman, John Edwards, and Richard Gephardt—had voted for the war in Congress and continued in varying degrees to support it. Of these, Kerry was often cited as the early front-runner, (Nagourney 2003, 14.), but his support for the war limited his appeal. This created an opening for Howard Dean, the little-known former governor of Vermont. "We told him," recalled one of his consultants, "he could run like John Kerry, or he could run like someone different. But it couldn't be a mainstream campaign, because the mainstream space was already taken" (Farhi 2003, 2).

Dean took the advice, turning against the Iraq war with a bitterness that went beyond normal discourse. "What were these people in the White House smoking?" he asked. Yet he reserved some of his harshest attacks for Democrats who supported the war. His party's elected officials, he suggested, were "cockroaches" who were not true Democrats. President Bush, he asserted, was conducting diplomacy by "petulance" and had "no understanding of defense." "Mr. President, if you'll pardon me, I'll teach you a little about defense," Dean offered (Kurtz 2003, 6).

This rhetoric drew an enthusiastic response from Democratic activists. Throughout the invisible primary, he drew the biggest crowds, raised the most money, attracted the most media coverage, and, at the end of 2003, emerged with the most support in national surveys of the Democratic rank-and-file. As the first voter contests approached, Dean led in state polls in Iowa and New Hampshire and was growing "stronger by the week" (VanderHei and Balz 2003, 1).

A central feature of the Dean campaign was use of the Internet to find, organize, and solicit people who opposed the Iraq war but had not previously been active in politics. As Michael Barone has aptly observed, "Peace candidates in the past had an easy time finding supporters in university towns and high-income professional neighborhoods but had a hard time finding them anywhere else. Using Meetup.com and MoveOn.org, the Dean campaign located Iraq war opponents and Bush haters in every part of the country. It encouraged these supporters to find others and bring them into highly cohesive electronically connected communities" (*U.S. News and World Report* 2004, 36).

Meetup.com is an Internet venture that enables like-minded people to find one another and "meet up"; it was designed for hobbyists, but the Dean campaign became its top client. MoveOn is an online advocacy group that formed during the Clinton impeachment—the idea was to "move on" from the Lewinsky mess—but remained active in liberal causes. After Dean won a poll of its 41,000 members, MoveOn leaders permitted Dean to raise money through its Web site. The Dean campaign also created blogs and chat groups to discuss events and challenge fellow "Deaniacs" to give more money. By these unconventional means, the unconventional Dean raised $41 million in campaign funds, which was more than any candidate in party history, including Al Gore and Bill Clinton.

The response of party insiders to Dean's success was mixed. Part of the Democratic donor base actually joined the Deaniac surge. The Democratic Leadership Council, however, took the unusual step of open criticism. Dean, it said, stood for "weakness abroad and elitist, interest group liberalism at home" (Lambro 2004). "The Democratic Party is in danger of being taken over by the far left," said Senator Evan Bayh, a DLC member (Nagourney 2003).

Most Democratic leaders were neutral to negative on Dean, fretting anonymously to journalists that he would lead the party to disaster but taking few concrete steps to stop him. As the *Wall Street Journal* reported at the midpoint of the invisible primary, "There is no doubt that many establishment Democrats would like to knock Mr. Dean down, or out entirely. But to try to do that now, rival camps have decided, risks a boomerang effect boosting Mr. Dean's outsider appeal" (Calmes and Schlesinger 2003). Another journalist wrote, "there is general agreement that the party establishment is not capable of mounting a stop-Dean movement. 'What establishment?' one Democrat said sarcastically" (Balz 2003b).

The principal means by which party insiders control nominations is to throw their collective weight behind a candidate able to compete in the primaries. So, when none of the declared candidates appeared able to stop Dean, a group of party insiders centering on former President Bill Clinton urged a new candidate into the race, General Wesley Clark. Clark got some quick endorsements, rose briefly to the top of the polls, but committed a series of gaffes and fell back into the pack.

With Dean the commanding front-runner at the end of the invisible primary, Al Gore and some other prominent Democrats endorsed him, saying it was time to close ranks behind the party's likely nominee. But only one of twenty-two Democratic governors and a handful of U.S. senators made endorsements, for Dean or anyone else.[17] This was the lowest rate of endorsements by top officeholders in either party over the period of our study. So while Dean won the invisible primary, he did not win it in the manner we claim is normal—by uniting the party behind his candidacy. Dean's success does, however, fit Polsby's model of a factional candidate—a candidate who seeks to parlay the intense support of one segment of the party into the party nomination.

In a period of about three weeks of intense campaigning in Iowa, however, Dean's factional campaign collapsed. Kerry, whose efforts to appeal to a wide segment of the party bore little fruit through most of the invisible primary, jumped into the lead, trounced Dean 38 to 18 on election night, and coasted easily to the nomination. Dean never won a primary or caucus except in his home state of Vermont.[18]

Other front-runners have stumbled in Iowa, but none lost as badly or faded as fast as Dean. What is to be learned from all of this?

One lesson is that there is no necessary connection between the invisible primary and the voter contests that follow. They involve different audiences, different appeals, and different skills. Blasting away at the establishments of both parties, Dean could excite activists, but he was much less adept at running a mass campaign for voters who were not zealots. As two *Wall Street Journal* reporters observed:

> While Mr. Dean's sharp-tongued attacks on Mr. Bush and Democratic opponents originally propelled his candidacy, they might have turned off as many voters [in Iowa] as they have attracted. The candidate drew loud cheers when he lashed out on Jan. 11 at an elderly Bush supporter who interrupted one of his rallies in the town of Oelwein. "You sit down, you've had your say, now I'm going to have my say!" Mr. Dean yelled. But Laree Randall, a 53-year old store owner in the audience, didn't join in the chorus, and wondered afterward about Mr. Dean's style. "Shouldn't it be toned down?" she asked. (Schlesinger and Harwood 2004)

This incident, one of several Dean gaffes in Iowa, was captured on tape and quickly turned into an anti-Dean television spot.

Dean recognized the need to soften his image, but his attempts to entice moderate voters and "guys with Confederate flags in their pickup trucks" mainly brought him grief. As caucus day approached, he gave up on the center and returned to his strident rhetoric (Calmes 2004).[19] But after defeat, Dean suggested to reporters that he would "ease up on his year-long crusade to change the Democratic party." He would also be "softening the tone of his speeches and eliminating high-voltage campaign rallies in favor of dignified appearances where he would present himself as a mature ex-governor with a command of health care and the economy" (VandeHei 2004, 1; Nagourney and Wilgoren 2004, 1). But the mature Dean lacked the excitement of the rebel Dean and fared no better with voters than he had in Iowa.

What all this suggests is that Dean was never as strong with the Democratic rank-and-file as his record fund-raising and campaign-trail crowds suggested. Even when on top of the polls, he was not as strong as previous front-runners had been. Given this, it was likely that he would stumble in the primaries and that an "Anyone But Dean" option would emerge to test and quite possibly defeat him. Kerry captured that role, but others might have taken it.[20]

It also seems quite possible that if Democratic insiders had been a little more adept, they might have rallied to an "anyone but Dean" alternative earlier than they did and gotten that person—possibly Kerry—nominated. As it was, the party took a risk. Dean had enough money and momentum that, with slightly better luck, he might have gone on to be nominated, thereby potentially saddling the party with a nominee who was more stridently opposed to the war than the public was ready to accept. Perhaps Dean would have been another George McGovern, whose leftist positions as Democratic nominee in 1972 were embarrassing to the party for decades afterward.

A final lesson from the rise and quick decline of Howard Dean is the fragility of insider control of nominations. If parties are coalitions of intense policy demanders, then new groups of intense policy demanders are always a threat to enter and disrupt the party system. Much like the Vietnam war in the 1960s or the revolt against gold in the 1890s, the Iraq war furnished a wave of new policy demanders in 2004, and they did what new demanders would be expected to do. Dean, shopping for a viable niche, was as much their creature as they were his. Thus, now as in the past, party control of nominations is not likely to be much stronger than the party coalition is stable. But, by this argument, the Dean campaign provides, in itself, little reason to doubt the efficacy of party control in more normal circumstances.

Overall Conclusions

Our accounts of the ten contested nominations since 1980 have been guided by three questions, to which we will now suggest answers:

1. *Do party insiders make endorsements because they actually favor the given candidate, or because the candidate is so strong that party endorsers simply capitulate to him?* We found some, but not a great deal, of evidence suggesting capitulation. The most important case was in 1988, when many Republican conservatives had reservations about George H. W. Bush but went along anyway. So this might be called a case of candidate domination. Yet Bush was the party's vice president, he seemed to have the blessing of the party's revered leader, and the conservatives had no strong champion to run against Bush. If, as our analysis in this chapter suggests, the 1988 Republican contest is the best case for candidate domination, the argument is weak.

   The evidence of party resistance to candidate-centered pressure is not voluminous, but there is some. One case was the 1988 Democratic nomination, when Gary Hart had good poll support and, even more important, a record from 1984 showing that he was a strong national campaigner who might win whether insiders got on his bandwagon or not. Yet party groups distrusted him, which left him a "lonely front-runner" who could not raise money or endorsements. The other case was the 2004 Democratic nomination. Howard Dean achieved a commanding lead in both poll support and campaign donations, but failed to pull ahead on endorsements. The party's top officeholders were, as our data on both overall and gubernatorial endorsements show, notable in their failure to rally to this apparently strong candidate.

   Meanwhile, a series of weaker candidates, notably Walter Mondale in 1984 and Bob Dole in 1996, did achieve commanding insider support. And genuinely strong candidates, notably Bill Clinton in 1992 and George W. Bush in 2000, also achieved high levels of support from party insiders whose support, from our reading of the evidence, was in most cases genuine.

   Altogether, then, we find that no candidate lacking a preexisting position in the party succeeded in forcing large numbers of party insiders onto his bandwagon and, on the other hand, some clear evidence that such candidates could not succeed.

2. *Do candidates go trolling for support in a small pool of regular party activists, or do they build their campaign from a larger pool of one-time activists and persons loyal to them personally?* Two candidates achieved notable success in the invisible primary by building strong support among one-time activists and volunteers. These were Gary Hart and Howard Dean, but, as noted, they failed to get party insiders to go along with their candidate-centered efforts and failed also to get the party's nomination. A few other candidates—John Connally in 1980 and Pat Robertson in 1988—tried to build candidate-centered organizations but achieved even less success.[21]

3. *Do groups make decisions in light of the likely preferences of other groups and the need to win the fall election, or does each group support its own first-choice candidate, regardless of party considerations?* A factional candidate, in our use of the term, is one who tries to parlay support within a relatively narrow part of the party into nomination. Gary Hart in 1984 and Pat Buchanan in 1996 are perhaps the best examples of such candidates. Lacking broad insider support, they hoped to do better than expected in the early primaries and ride a wave of momentum to nomination. The question is whether party insiders sympathetic to their views will sign on to their campaigns, or will instead join with other candidates to create a united front.

We find only limited evidence of insider support for such factional candidates. Most notably, most religiously conservative leaders never supported a factional candidate of their persuasion despite several opportunities to do so. Labor unions mainly supported Clinton in 1992 over their factional favorite, Tom Harkin. In 1984, most African American leaders supported Jackson, but a significant group—Coretta Scott King, Andrew Young, Charles Rangel—stayed with the more broadly acceptable Mondale. In 1988, however, nearly all African American leaders in our endorsement sample gave their support to Jackson. Since Jackson had little more chance of proving broadly acceptable within the party than he did in 1984, we view this support as the one case in which intense policy demanders did predominantly rally to a factional candidate.

Although we have said that Democratic insiders mainly failed to support Howard Dean in 2004, some did, including two former high officials, Al Gore and Bill Bradley. The insider support that Dean got—about 27 percent of all endorsements in a year in which many insiders abstained from any endorsement—was mostly staunchly antiwar and hence factional. This support constitutes the most important evidence of insiders rallying to a factional candidate.

Overall, then, we take the bulk of our evidence to support the view that party insiders have largely controlled the outcome of nine of the last ten party nominations, with the exceptional case being 2004. And even in 2004, the outsider challenge to party insiders failed.

An important feature of our theoretical analysis is that, in coordination games such as we take the invisible primary to be, some candidates can win simply by getting out in front of the field and making themselves the focal point. We find an interesting mix of evidence on this point. Certainly the parties resisted some candidates who made themselves salient in weak fields—most notably Gary Hart in 1988 and Phil Gramm in 1996. We also take the support of moderates for Bush in 1980 as resistance to the more salient Howard Baker. So one cannot say that parties generally fall into line behind the first candidate to get a little bit out in front. On the other hand, parties did go along with Walter Mondale in 1984, George H. W. Bush in 1988, Bob Dole in 1996, and Al Gore in 2000, each of whom we view as weak candidates in weak fields and each of whom launched his campaign from a position of party leadership. Although many factors contributed to their success, we view their wins in the invisible primary as consistent with the notion of focal-point politics.

An interesting question is whether some kinds of party insiders have more influence than others in the invisible primary. Suppose, for the sake of discussion, that we specify five types of party players: Top officeholders, group and ideological leaders, campaign donors, rank-and-file party activists, and campaign technicians (pollsters, professional fund-raisers). Which of these groups is most influential?

The first point to make is that the question is misleading in that it assumes a more hard-and-fast division than actually exists. Many party insiders, and perhaps most, entered politics as low-level activists working to elect their party's candidates. Some go on to play higher level roles— fund-raiser, campaign manager, officeholder—but this does not mean they cease to care about the party and ideological principles that led to their initial involvement. So perhaps it is better to ask: Which of the five group *roles* affords greatest opportunity for influence?

Even as qualified, the question may not have a strong answer. Low-level officials and rank-and-file party workers seemed the backbone of Ronald Reagan's candidacy, with governors coming along much later. But governors led the way in George W. Bush's nomination. Organized labor was probably the most important player in the nomination of Walter Mondale, but merely accepted Bill Clinton. Campaign technicians were perhaps the main force in the nomination of George H. W. Bush, but, from what journalists report, do not so clearly seem to have influenced any other win in the invisible primary. Many interest groups—labor, feminists, and civil rights groups in the Democratic party; religious and economic conservatives, as well as the National Rifle Association, on the Republican side—can probably veto any candidate they strongly oppose, but still cannot do a great deal to enable the candidates they most prefer to win the invisible primary.

Based on these salient examples, our tentative conclusion is that different types of players are influential in the invisible primary at different times, depending on the circumstances. Although our qualitative analysis in this chapter gives us reason to be dubious of the independent importance of campaign donors—and our quantitative analysis in the next chapter will give us more reason for doubt—we do not count even them out of the power game. The strongest statement we can make is that, as regards presidential nominations, a party is a coalition of many different actors and interests jostling for position, with no one group consistently able to dominate.

Anatomy of a Conversation

A central claim of this study is that parties decide whom to nominate for president in a long-running national conversation in
which party members—officeholders, interest groups, activists,
donors—discuss who can best unite the party coalition and win
the general election. The claim is difficult to prove, because we
obviously cannot specify who exactly in our huge country speaks
to whom, when, and with what effect. We nonetheless think the
metaphor of a national conversation is an apt one, and in this
chapter, we shall provide as much specificity as we can. We begin
with anecdotal examples of how we imagine the party conversation works. We do not intend these examples as evidence, but as
illustrations of what may lie at the heart of the invisible primary.
They are intended to put some additional flesh-and-blood on the
bare-bones outline of the restaurant game and the metaphor of
the fishing contest from the previous chapter. Having thus created a relatively full image of the invisible primary, we turn to
several focused tests of our general argument.

Snippets of Early Conversation

The most important part of the party conversation in the invisible primary is the public announcement of support for a candidate by a prominent individual or group. These endorsements are the best possible information about who is acceptable to whom in the party and which candidates seem to be making the greatest headway.

Endorsements are a commitment of reputation and often resources and are, therefore, not lightly given. No one wants to waste an endorsement on someone who doesn't have a chance to be nominated, and it is hard for a candidate to go all the way without being broadly acceptable in the party. Thus, before the invisible primary becomes thick with endorsements, participants seek information about its likely direction.

In this section, we will give examples to illustrate how this information may be generated and diffused in the invisible primary. Our contention—not completely provable, but we hope at least clear—is that discussion among political insiders of the sort illustrated in this section is the basis of decision-making in the invisible primary. In most but not all years, the discussion aggregates into a consensus on whom the party should nominate. We focus here on the early phases of this discussion that are most difficult to capture except in short bits and pieces.

Regulars Talk in the 1976 Invisible Primary

The single most common set of activities in the invisible primary is that a candidate will travel to an important party meeting or fund-raising center, give a speech, answer questions from an audience of party and ideological regulars, and mix with the crowd afterward. Most candidates engage in this basic ritual over and over in the invisible primary. Even candidates who campaign very little make at least a few of these trips. They do so because it is the best means of winning support among a far-flung party elite. Party members, for their part, appreciate the opportunity to acquire firsthand information about potential party nominees.

In the following passage, Arthur Hadley describes how two major politicians, Walter Mondale and Mo Udall, handled this central campaign task in the course of their efforts to enlist the support of New Hampshire activists in that state's 1976 primary:

> Udall got up, looked over the roomful of bored Democrats, and began: "You may think Senator Mondale and I are here because there is a presidential election in 1976. That is not true. We are here to visit museums and the habitat of the purple finch." The audience broke up. . . .

Udall slipped in some serious bits about conservation, energy, and the economy and his record on these, but mostly he kept the audience rocking. Then Mondale got up and delivered a head-nodder about his record in the Senate. After the meeting was over, Mondale's staff had him scheduled to leave in a hurry, while Udall stayed around until one in the morning shaking hands and making friends. The next day Marie Carrier, the Democratic National Committeewoman and one of the handful of de facto Democratic leaders in New Hampshire, got on the phone with her other activist friends. They decided to unite behind Udall. It was that simple. And that deadly for Mondale. (Hadley 1976, 36)

Several elements in this account recur in many we have read. Most obviously, the successful candidate must pledge fealty to the party's core principles. Yet to judge by the performance of the more successful candidate, insiders don't always want to wallow in the details. They do want someone who can speak in an engaging fashion. Udall seems, in fact, to have devoted the greater part of his speech to essentially nonpolitical material that suggested his prowess as an entertaining speaker. If the aim of activists is to identify someone who can unite the party and win in the fall, activists are right to want a candidate who can speak engagingly about party principles.

Another notable element is that Udall, and not Mondale, stayed around to mingle with the crowd. Most good politicians enjoy meeting party regulars, and party regulars obviously enjoy meeting candidates. But we see a deeper purpose. One-on-one exchanges with candidates are a means by which party members can assess the depth of candidate commitments to the causes they care about. In meetings too large for one-on-one interactions, questions to the candidate from the audience can be a substitute means of judging candidate commitments.

The final element in Hadley's account is, of course, the conversation among political friends that followed the event. At least in this case, the decisions of the New Hampshire activists to back Udall were not strictly individual decisions. They talked it over and decided together. We believe—without, we admit, being able to prove it—that conversations like these among political friends are among the very most important events in the invisible primary.

George W. Bush Scores an Easy Win

For the first time in fifty years in the Republican party, wrote columnist Gloria Bolger in 1997, "It's nobody's turn to be president" (cited in Kurtz 1997, C1). Nonetheless, George W. Bush won the invisible primary in a walk. It's worth a look at how this happened.

The walk began shortly after Bush's election as governor of Texas in 1994. Although he had never held public office, his win set tongues to wagging. Wrote the *Washington Post*: "The big news in Texas was the bruising victory of George W. Bush (R) over popular incumbent Gov. Ann Richards (D). The success of the former president's son in exploiting the continuing shift toward conservatism of such a large and important state immediately marked him as a potentially influential player on the national political scene" (Goshko and Phillips 1994, A42). This was just media speculation, but Republican insiders were impressed too. At the 1996 Republican convention, Bush was one of a half-dozen candidates who attracted attention as potential nominees in the next contest. And within this select group, wrote David Broder, "None, perhaps, has been the focus of more attention than Bush." "He pushed all the right buttons," said one of Broder's sources (1996).

This was more than journalistic speculation, and it continued. Two weeks after the inauguration of Bill Clinton in early 1997, Ronald Brownstein wrote, "The great mentioners scoping out potential GOP candidates for the year 2000 already have their eyes on at least half a dozen governors. Everyone's list starts with Bush" (Brownstein 1997). Bush's strengths, the article notes, are his popularity in Texas, his success in cutting taxes, and his emphasis on a popular issue, education.

Polls at this point did not favor Bush. In a survey of Republicans in late 1996, 37 percent favored Colin Powell for the 2000 nomination, with Jack Kemp at 20 percent and Bush at 19. A poll early in early 1997 found that Bush had slipped into fourth place, behind Dan Quayle, with only 7 percent of Republicans favoring him (Mayer 2003, 95). But insider interest in Bush continued to grow. In February 1997 Brownstein reported that "the pre-presidential maneuvering in GOP circles has begun unusually early this time. Almost every day, some prominent Republican calls Karl Rove, Bush's chief political strategist, offering to enlist for 2000 as soon as the governor gives the word" (1997, A5).

Such proffers of support were not premature. Trolling had already begun for one of the bigger fish in the Republican pond, Ralph Reed, then-executive director of the Christian Coalition. This particular fish, as Richard Berke reported in the *New York Times* in May 1997,

> has been besieged by prospective contenders since he announced last month that he plans to resign and become a political consultant. "There is already a remarkable level of jockeying," Mr. Reed said. "I've had conversations with a number of the prospective candidates who have expressed interest in my

involvement. Some have asked how soon I could start. But I think it's premature right now."

Even as they feel out possible advisers in private, many candidates are publicly lying low. Gov. George W. Bush of Texas, for one, has not set foot in New Hampshire this year, and he insists that his focus is on winning re-election next year. That has not stopped him from holding private meetings with Mr. Reed and others to discuss 2000. (Berke 1997a, A19)

Then came a setback. At the end of the summer—still just seven months into Bill Clinton's term and thirty months before the Iowa caucuses—Bush spoke to a large party gathering in Indianapolis amid high expectations.

The top billing, and the coveted Saturday night speaking slot . . . went to George W. Bush, the Governor from Texas who in his first term has rapidly burst into the political stratosphere as the hottest figure among major players in Republican circles. Despite the most open field in years, many political professionals are declaring, embarrassingly early, that Mr. Bush is the Republican to beat for the Presidential nomination in 2000. The buzz only intensified on Saturday when Mr. Bush, despite his protestations that his only concern is his re-election next year, made a rare foray into national politics, coming to this meeting, which showcased Presidential hopefuls. (Berke 1997b)

But Bush talked about arcane details of Texas politics and refused to take a stand on a controversial recent deal between Clinton and the Republican Congress. Richard Berke of the *New York Times* said that the speech was stiffly delivered and that several potential rivals—millionaire Malcolm "Steve" Forbes, Dan Quayle, and Senator Fred Thompson—performed better. Conservative columnist Robert Novak went further. "[Bush] generated less fervor than any presidential possibility who spoke earlier in the conference," wrote Novak (1997). "I'd say George was the dullest knife in the pantry," said one of Novak's sources. "Still," added Berke, "many in the audience said that one off night for Mr. Bush did not detract from his overall appeal" (Berke 1997b). Bush was not the Republican front-runner, asserted Novak, but was still a contender.

After this brief foray into presidential politics, Bush returned to Texas and concentrated on succeeding as governor. But he continued to be an object of interest. "Fund-raisers, strategists, party insiders—all the Republicans who stand to gain either power or employment from a presidential run—have been watching him since the moment he took the oath of office in Austin in January 1995," wrote Julia Reed in the *Weekly Standard* (1997). Her own review was quite positive. Despite his wayward youth, she described him as an authentic conservative with popular appeal. "There is something admirable when someone like George W. Bush actually grows up, if only because so many men like him never really do." More substantively, Fred Barnes, the executive editor of the *Weekly Standard*, wrote in late 1998 that

> He's conservative by instinct. On taxes and limiting government, he sounds semi-Reaganesque. The Cato Institute, in its rating of governors, called him "admirably tightfisted." . . .[1]
>
> The provocative part of Bush's spiel is his cultural conservatism. He's not a conventional social conservative. He doesn't mention abortion, homosexuality, or school prayer. But all of his speeches feature a conservative rap on the culture. (Barnes 1998)

A minor incident in 1998 showed up the delicacy of Bush's efforts to unite the party behind his candidacy. His father had never been a favorite of conservatives and had in fact greatly angered them by breaking his pledge against raising taxes. Wanting conservative support, the younger Bush therefore faced a need to distinguish himself from his father. In his interview with the *Weekly Standard*, he handled this problem by noting that his father "was educated at Greenwich Country Day" but that "I was educated at San Jacinto Junior High in Midland, Texas. I am a Texan and a westerner and a southerner" (Reed 1997, 10). But in June, one of the elder Bush's supporters circulated a letter suggesting that the son would be relying on the same circle of advisors as the father. Robert Novak described the fallout as follows: "Alarm bells went off nationwide. Despite talk of 2000 promising the most open race for the GOP presidential nomination since 1940, the party establishment made its choice months ago: George W. Bush. But the question is: Does the bright, likable and conservative younger Bush carry the unwanted baggage of politicians and advisers associated with his father's dreadful campaign of 1992?" (Novak 1998). Novak reports that the letter writer was "scolded by someone close to the governor" and forced to apologize. Novak further noted that the "son's supporters around the country don't welcome his father's retainers" and listed several that were suspect, including the senior Bush's national security advisor, Brent Scowcroft. Novak further reported that when David Keene, chairman of the American Conservative Union wrote that the younger Bush should avoid "the old Bush organization," Keene was "quickly called by a Bush associate in Austin urging him to keep it up."

At this point in 1998, Bush still had no official endorsements because he was still not officially a candidate. As well, media coverage of his campaign was minimal, in part because the campaign wanted it that way: When the governor came to Washington to meet with party leaders in 1998, his campaign refused to release a schedule of his meetings and, as is common in both parties, barred reporters from what events they might discover.

But elements of signaling and countersignaling were clearly visible in the media, along with indications of much more extensive discussion beyond the purview of the media. Some of this discussion involved other candidates, with much less reported about the many unsuccessful campaigns than about Bush's successful one. This, too, was a signal. Thus, by the time the invisible primary became more publicly visible, no one plugged into national politics would be surprised by the *National Review*'s characterization of the race: "[Bush] has the name and will have the money; the race is his to lose" (Miller and Ponnuru 1998). In fact, even the public had gotten the message. Bush began moving up in the polls in spring 1997 and was the clear poll front-runner from 1998 on (Mayer 2003, 95–96).

John McCain Woos the Republican Establishment in 2008

In his campaign for the 2000 Republican nomination, John McCain essentially gave up on getting the support of Republican activists. Most had been locked up before he committed to entering the race. McCain therefore settled in 2000 on an outsider strategy that laid heavy stress on communicating with voters through the media on his campaign bus, the so-called Straight Talk Express. Along the way, McCain denounced key religious figures as "agents of intolerance" for attacking his record. "I am a prolife, profamily fiscal conservative, an advocate of a strong defense, and yet Pat Robertson, Jerry Falwell, and a few Washington leaders of the prolife movement call me an unacceptable presidential candidate. They distort my prolife positions and smear the reputations of my supporters" (McCain 2000).

This attack on Republican insiders not only failed to win McCain the nomination in 2000, it also created resentments that were remembered eight years later when he began his run for the 2008 Republican nomination. But McCain signaled that he would run this time as an insider. "George Bush defeated me in the primary [in 2000] because he had the entire Republican establishment behind him," McCain told a journalist.

"He had worked very hard to gain that support" (West 2006). So McCain set out to gain that support for himself, starting with the religious right. He retracted the view that Falwell and Robertson were agents of intolerance, gave a speech at Falwell's Liberty University, and praised the role of religious conservatives in the party. "I believe that the . . . 'Christian right' has a major role to play in the Republican Party. One reason is, is because they're so active, and their followers are. And I believe they have a right to be a part of our party. I don't have to agree with everything they stand for" (*Meet the Press* 2006). Afterward, Falwell warmly praised McCain, saying that "the ilk of John McCain is very scarce, very small." All this set the political world abuzz. As a journalist observed, "Most political observers see the commencement speech as a major fence-mending exercise between the front-runner for the 2008 Republican nomination and the aging televangelist" (Savage 2006, A1).

Was there any other way to see it? But not everyone on the religious right believed that the fence-mending exercise had been successful. Gary Bauer, the religious conservative who ran for president in 2000, said, "It's one speech, and I think the jury is out as to whether it will lead to anything broader or more lasting" (Balz 2006b). Dr. James Dobson declined to be interviewed, but "knowledgeable social conservatives" reported that he was unimpressed. Pat Robertson did not back off his earlier remark that "McCain I'd vote against under any circumstance" (*Hotline* 2005).

Even in the midst of courting the religious right, McCain would not fully embrace its agenda. Though he steadfastly opposed abortion and favored the teaching of intelligent design in public schools, he opposed a constitutional amendment against same-sex marriage, favoring state-level prohibition instead. "If he doesn't change his mind and support this amendment, he will have a virtually impossible task to win the Republican nomination," said Richard Land, president of the Ethics & Religious Liberty Commission, the public policy arm of the Southern Baptist Convention, the largest U.S. Protestant denomination. "There won't be a social conservative in the Republican Party who [won't] remember that" (Hook and Barabak 2006, 1). Despite the warning, McCain voted in the Senate against an anti-same-sex marriage amendment to the Constitution.

McCain also had trouble with economic conservatives. He voted against President Bush's first round of tax cuts in 2001 on the ground that they would create too large a budget deficit, and although he later accepted them, the initial vote was not forgotten. "It's like an alcoholic not drinking for a day," said Norquist of McCain's turnaround. "No one trusts that this is something he is going to stick with" (Hook and Barabak 2006). As the invisible primary for the 2008 nomination heated up, McCain skipped the annual conferences of two important groups of conservatives, the Conservative Political Action Conference and the Club for Growth—an unusual action since both featured straw polls of member preference for Republican presidential nominee. McCain would have been unlikely to do well in those polls if he had attended, but skipping the conferences was a clear negative signal concerning his acceptability within the party.

An important part of McCain's strategy was to tap into George W. Bush's network of Republican activists. His initial forays generated some positive signals but no strong support. Following a closed-door meeting in 2006 between McCain and a group of South Carolina Bush supporters, one of those present offered the following assessment: " 'For people who were really strong for Bush, I feel like this was a dating meeting,' said Barry Wynn, Bush's state finance co-chairman in 2000 and 2004 and a Pioneer for Bush both times, meaning he raised $100,000 for each campaign. 'He's not quite ready to ask us to go steady. But I was a little surprised at the reaction, including my own reaction. I was much more positive than I thought I'd be going to the meeting' " (Balz 2006a).

Despite these remarks, the bulk of the Republican party's conversation about McCain in the invisible primary made clear that, despite McCain strengths as a campaigner, he was far down on the list of broadly acceptable candidates within the party—if, indeed, he was on that list at all.

★ ★ ★

These sketches are, as we have said, only suggestive. Due to the limits of media coverage, we have too little information about who talks to whom and with what effect in the invisible primary to offer a confident sketch of its inner workings. Yet, for the final phase of the invisible primary, media reports of endorsements begin to appear with increasing frequency. These endorsements, as we shall now see, afford us a markedly different but nonetheless convergent view of the process.

A Small Pond or a Vast Ocean?

In 2000, basketball player Michael Jordan and his mother both endorsed a candidate for the Democratic nomination. He supported Bradley, and she favored Gore. These endorsements generated a modest amount of favorable publicity but little else. Also in 2000, former senator Alfonse D'Amato of New York endorsed George W. Bush for the Republican nomination. His endorsement, along with that of Gov. George Pataki and others, meant that the New York Republican Party was committed to Bush and would likely deliver the greater share of the state's seventy-five convention delegates to him.

A central claim in our study is that presidential nominations are dominated by a group of party insiders who are generally active in party politics. Alfonse D'Amato is part of that group, and Michael Jordan is not.

The population of party insiders in whom we are interested is not defined by any particular position or act, but by ongoing efforts to elect candidates of one's party to as many offices as possible. The presidency is obviously the most important of these offices, but still only one among many. Electioneering efforts may involve anything from managing a campaign to donating money to knocking on doors in a neighborhood canvass. Different players make different contributions toward the common goal.

Our window into this party activity consists, for purposes of the statistical analyses in this chapter, of presidential endorsements in the invisible primary that have been reported in the news media. The assumption in using these endorsements as measures of party activity is that the journalists who record them, many of whom specialize in political reporting, can be relied upon to pick out the most important players in any given situation.

The assumption is not perfect. Journalists do not make news judgments with the idea of testing the theories of political scientists. Yet, because most of the stories from which we gleaned names are less "headline news" than "inside poop," we think the stories are, as a group, likely to contain much of the information we care about—at least insofar as that information is publicly available.

A principal concern in using these data to understand party activity is that, particularly among lower echelon players, the endorsers who make it into our sample are probably a very incomplete sampling of active persons. It is, for example, common for newspapers to report on a dinner or speech at which a governor or other top officeholder announces support for a candidate. These stories sometimes, but not always, include a survey of support among less important personages at the event or in the state as a whole. As a result, we may get a story reporting just one endorsement, a handful, or a large number, depending on the interests of the particular reporter. Because we know the names of governors and can search on them, we nearly always find the stories with top endorsers; our ability to pick up support among the lesser figures is spotty.

With these concerns in mind, we turn to our data to determine the extent to which the endorsers in the invisible primary constitute something like a small pond of regular partisan players or, instead, a candidate-specific sample from a vast sea of potential support. Our measure of regularity is whether an endorser has been active in two or more presidential contests.

In our sample of nearly six thousand individual endorsements in the period 1980 to 2004, 15.2 percent of the names come up in more than one contest, sometimes several contests. The fact that some names appear multiple times means that, in any given year, they contribute more than 15 percent of endorsements. In fact, in any given year, some 37 percent of the endorsers are from the "small world" of repeat endorsers.

These two numbers may not seem consistent, but consider this example. Suppose we have a set of four elections with one hundred endorsements each. Fifty of the endorsers make an endorsement in all four elections—thus qualifying as regular players—while the remaining individuals endorse in one election only. Hence there are fifty nonrepeaters per election and two hundred nonrepeaters over all four elections. Given these numbers, the repeaters would constitute 50 percent of endorsers in each election but only 20 percent of all individuals (50/250) who make an endorsement. In the real data, the repeaters do not usually repeat four times, but they repeat often enough that the 15 percent of names in the sample who are repeaters make up 37 percent of all endorsers in any given election.

Thirty-seven percent is not an impressively high number. However, some endorsers in each cycle are people like basketball player Michael Jordan, who have no permanent connection to politics and a scant contribution to make to any candidate's fortunes. Often, they are merely celebrity friends of the candidate. An even larger number are low-level politicians, such as state legislators and city councilors, whose inclusion in news stories might be, as indicated earlier, partly accidental. If we examine only endorsers who score above .4 on our power index—this is, someone active at or above the level of statewide politics (see table 6A.1)—the percentage of candidates who are repeat endorsers in any given year is notably higher, 59 percent. This we take to be a fairly high number.

But why not still higher? Why not a number closer to 100 percent?

The reason is a combination of three facts. (1) Most politicians occupy top positions for short periods, (2) open presidential nominations occur only once or twice in any eight-year period, and (3) political factors often keep power players on the sidelines.

Consider Governor Bill Clinton of Arkansas. He was first elected governor of his state in 1978 and endorsed Carter in 1980. In 1984, however, he was involved in a high-profile spat with the National Educational Association and declined to endorse their candidate, front-runner Walter

Mondale, perhaps to preserve his own credentials as a moderate. The possibility that fellow Arkansan Dale Bumpers would enter the race may also have helped keep Clinton on the sidelines. In 1988 Clinton was a major player in national politics, but, like the other governors we saw in chapter 7, Clinton waited until the primaries had tested the field before announcing his support for Michael Dukakis. Thus, despite twelve years as a nationally prominent governor, Clinton does not show up in our files as a repeat endorser at the time he ran for president in 1992.

Or consider another power broker, Alfonse D'Amato. He made no presidential endorsement in 1980, when he won his first election to the Senate. He also made no endorsement in 1984 or 1992, because his party had incumbent presidents in those years. And in 2000 he was out of office. Thus, in his eighteen-year career as a top officeholder, D'Amato had opportunities to make only two endorsements, in 1988 and 1996. Many politicians with shorter careers in top offices might have only one good opportunity.

In view of these and other complications, we maintain our view that 59 percent is a fairly high rate of repeat endorsements among top officeholders.[2]

Another and arguably more reliable way to get a sense of whether endorsements come from a stable pool of party players is to simply examine the political and occupational attachments of those who make them. Is the typical endorser a political novice having no long-term commitment to a party? Or do most endorsers exhibit evidence of long-term involvement?

To see what is typical, we took a random sample of twenty-five endorsements from our sample of all endorsements made over the period 1980 to 2000. We chose twenty-five because it is a big enough number to capture the diversity of the pool and small enough to be grasped whole. From a glance at the names in table 8.1, one can see that most have a history of party activism. Three, for example, are current or former members of the U.S. House. A former cochair of the Republican National Committee and current cochair of Pete Wilson's campaign, a former executive director of the New Hampshire state Republican party, a former chair of the Texas Democratic party, and a current president of the Maine State Senate are obviously regular players in party politics as well. Playboy publisher Christine Hefner, though never an officeholder, is a regular Democratic fund-raiser, blogger, and intense demander of First Amendment protection. Altogether, 76 percent of the sample manifests some indication of ongoing party activity. Several other endorsers—the two unions, the Phoenix lobbyist, and the health-care activist (who lived in New Hampshire but was interviewed in Iowa where he was working in a campaign)—might also have been part of a party network, though we

Table 8.1: A random sample of presidential endorsers, 1980 to 2000

	Position	Repeater	Regular party member
Bruce Caputo	Former U.S. representative, New York	—	Yes
David Dreier	U.S. representative, California; influential conservative	Yes	Yes
Richard "Digger" Phelps	Notre Dame basketball coach	—	—
William Scherle	Former U.S. representative, Iowa; active 20 years after loss in reelection	—	Yes
Grover Norquist	President, Americans for Tax Reform; 169 hits in *Washington Post*	—	Yes
Christy Hefner	*Playboy* publisher; daughter of Hugh	—	Yes
Dorothy S. McDiarmid	Virginia state legislator	—	Yes
Larry Smith	U.S. representative, Florida	—	Yes
Jeanie Austin	Former co-chair of RNC; Pete Wilson campaign cochair	—	Yes
Daniel Patrick Moynihan	U.S. senator, New York	Yes	Yes
John Doerr	Venture capitalist; ran campaign fund, fund-raiser for Gore 2000	Yes	Yes
Gertrude Stein Democratic Club	Leading gay group in District of Columbia	Yes	Yes
Calvin Guest	Former Texas state Democratic Party chair	—	Yes
Marine Engineers Union		—	—
Haley Barbour	Former RNC chair	Yes	Yes
Jack B. Johnson	Prince George's state's attorney	—	Yes
Solomon Ortiz	U.S. representative, Texas	Yes	Yes
Steve Gorin	Health care activist	—	—
Alfredo Guitierrez	Phoenix lobbyist	—	—
Bob Anderson	Iowa lt. governor	—	Yes
IBEW Local 2320, Manchester, NH		—	—
Christine Jones	Maryland state legislator; African American politician; supported Mondale in '84	—	Yes
Paul Young	Former executive director, New Hampshire state GOP	—	Yes
Julian Robertson, Jr.	Tiger Management, investment adviser	—	—
Joseph Sewall	Maine state senate president	—	Yes
Repeat endorsers (%)		24	
Ongoing party activity (%)			76

cannot be certain. Only Digger Phelps, the basketball coach, lacks any discernible motive for ongoing political activity. Yet he later received two low-level presidential appointments from President George H. W. Bush, the candidate whom he endorsed against Ronald Reagan in 1980; so perhaps even Phelps had some long-term involvement in politics. Thus, the somewhat low rate of repeat endorsement stands in contrast to other information suggesting that all or nearly all of the endorsers were regularly active in party politics.

The single most common occupation of the endorsers appears to be that of officeholder or former officeholder. Eleven of twenty-five, or almost half, of endorsers fall into this category.[3] If, however, this figure suggests that endorsements come mainly from professional politicians, the suggestion is misleading. Only five of the eleven are full-time officeholders; the other six are either members of part-time legislatures or former officeholders. It is also interesting that our sample contains three former party officials.

As we noted in chapter 2, it is difficult to tell whether a given officeholder should be understood as an intense policy demander, an ambitious politician, or both. The data in table 8.1 do not resolve that uncertainty. Taken altogether, however, the data do not give an impression of a nomination process that is dominated either by ambitious politicians or political novices. The indication, rather, is of a nomination process powered by a mix of players, but mainly ongoing partisan volunteers and policy demanders of one kind or another. And, by any accounting, it represents something more like a small pond of regular party players than a vast sea of potential supporters.

The combination of repeat involvement by top officeholders and a supporting cast of ongoing party actors is consistent with our view of the nomination process, but these data only go so far. Their main limitation is that they do not show how these politically active individuals make up their minds about whom to support or what impact their support has. If, despite their ongoing party activity, these endorsers—whether governors, low-level officeholders, or activists—simply flock to the presidential candidate who was likely to be nominated with or without insider support, the nomination process would have to be viewed as candidate-centered. If, on the other hand, endorsers exhibit a substantial degree of political free will, and if their endorsements affect who actually gets nominated, the process should be considered party-centered. We therefore turn to an analysis of the national political conversation by which, as we claim, party insiders arrive at decisions about whom to back for nomination.

A Conversation in Four Measurements

The dynamics of party decision-making over ten nominations would be hard enough to analyze if all ten decisions were made in a smoke-filled room with a C-SPAN camera broadcasting every gesture, speech, deal, and vote. And, of course, we have dramatically less information about party conversations in the invisible primary.

What we have, more specifically, are quantitative measures of four components of the invisible primary as it unfolds over time. These are political endorsements (as discussed earlier), media coverage, candidate support in public opinion polls, and fund-raising.[4] Each of the four components may be reasonably viewed as a measure of how one part of the political system speaks to another. And because all four can be measured at different points in time, we can test how they affect one another across time. If, for example, media coverage seems to be a leading indicator for changes in other variables, we can conclude that media coverage *causes* changes in the other variables and thereby drives the process. If, on the other hand, polls change early in the invisible primary and other measures follow, we may conclude that polls—that is, the reactions of voters to the candidates as measured in polls—are the principal driving force in the invisible primary.

This kind of evidence will give us a quite different view into the invisible primary than we have had so far. It will not give us a full test of the logic of the restaurant game, as discussed in chapter 7. What it will show is discussed in the next section.

Setting Up a Test of Free Choice

Even the most energetic candidate cannot meet any more than a tiny fraction of the American electorate. Yet, as we have seen, most serious candidates for presidential nomination do a great deal of traveling—an amount that journalists routinely denominate in the hundreds of thousands of miles.[5] At this level of effort, candidates can make personal contact with tens of thousands of people, a number that may constitute a substantial fraction of their party's most important officials, donors, interest-group leaders, and campaign workers. These party insiders are in turn connected with one another, whether through personal relationships, organizational membership, fax, or, nowadays, the Internet. The limited number and high connectedness of the activists that candidates seek to mobilize suggest another point: much of the communication that drives the invisible primary *could* be largely independent of the mainstream news media.

This does not imply that the mainstream news media would be unimportant, but the media could well be less important, or important in different ways, than in a mass election.

Yet the news media are certainly involved in the invisible primary. Newspapers cover local events, and the national newsmagazines, as we shall see, provide a sufficient amount of coverage to significantly affect candidates' standing in public opinion polls. And if news coverage can affect ordinary citizens, who pay little attention to politics, it could also affect party leaders, activists, and donors, who pay much more attention. Thus, media coverage *could* drive poll support, fund-raising, and ultimately even the endorsement decisions of political insiders.

Thus, for the sake of argument, we offer two hypothetical scenarios of the dynamics of the invisible primary. In the first, which we shall call the Free Choice scenario, party insiders make their endorsement decisions on the basis of personal communication—either direct contact with the candidates or their contact with one another or some combination. The decisions of donors are likewise based on meeting the candidate or dealing with someone who has. Media coverage may affect public opinion, but neither public opinion nor media coverage itself affects the intraparty process. The key feature of this scenario is that the invisible primary is a wholly insider phenomenon.

In the second scenario, which we call the Mass Politics scenario, media coverage of candidate activity drives the process, both directly and indirectly. Coverage affects the process directly by its impact on the decisions of party insiders and donors, who gravitate toward candidates favored by the media. Media coverage may also have an indirect effect through public opinion as measured in polls: the public responds to the media, and the insiders then respond to the polls.

These competing scenarios have been framed (not by accident) in terms of the four measurable variables discussed a moment ago. Hence, the question of Free Choice versus Mass Politics in the invisible primary can be resolved by statistical analysis of the effect of these variables on one another.

We shall undertake that analysis shortly. First, however, we must describe the key variables and how we have measured them. We have, of course, already discussed the endorsement variable, but the media, money, and poll variables require some introduction.

Media Coverage
National network news pays little attention to the invisible primary, and local television news pays even less. If, as in some domains of politics, partici-

pants got most of their information from television news, and if candidacies lived or died by that coverage, most would die. Or rather, whatever happened in the invisible primary would be independent of media influence.

However, a handful of newspapers, notably the *New York Times* and *Washington Post*, do regularly cover the invisible primary, and many newspapers, especially those centered in a state capital, provide good coverage of happenings in their bailiwicks. Much of what we learn about the invisible primary we learn from these two elite papers and their state-level counterparts.

Yet little of this coverage reaches the nation as a whole, and much is locally or regionally focused. We have, therefore, turned to the national newsmagazines *Time* and *Newsweek*.[6] These national newsmagazines are the only real source of general coverage of the invisible primary over the entire period of our study that also reaches a national audience and is therefore capable of influencing it. The magazine coverage is based on original reporting and is probably best understood as the voice of the national elite media. It is likely that local newspaper and national television coverage, insofar as it exists, is in rough sync with newsmagazine coverage.

Our measure of media coverage was obtained by counting—sentence by sentence and phrase by phrase—all reporting of the presidential nomination contest in *Time* magazine from January of the year prior to the election to the last issue before the Iowa caucus, over the period 1980 to 2004. A candidate's percentage share of all coverage is his or her score on the media variable.

This measurement strategy nicely captures a universally acknowledged feature of media coverage—front-runners get lots of media attention, a second echelon of also-ran candidates get modest coverage, and long shots get almost none (Davis 1997). This measure will enable us to see if more extensive coverage helps candidates to do better in the invisible primary.

It is not obvious that it will. Journalists may cover candidates who are doing well in the money primary, the endorsement derby, and public opinion polls and then simply ignore the rest of the field. If so, media coverage may contribute little to a candidate's success beyond what the candidate already has. Moreover, much media coverage is negative and unlikely to do a candidate much good. For a candidate struggling to build a mass following, however, any media coverage may be better than no media coverage.[7]

Figure 8.1 gives the distribution of shares of media coverage for all sixty-one candidates who ran in the invisible primary in the period 1980 to 2004. "Shares" refer to the percentage of all newsmagazine coverage that a given candidate received. So if, for example, five candidates were running in

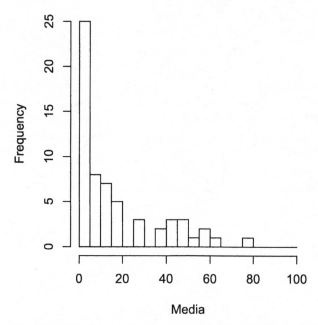

Fig. 8.1. Distribution of media coverage. Media is the candidate's share of all mentions of any candidate in *Time* or *Newsweek* in the year prior to the primaries.

a given year, and if each got an equal amount of media coverage, each would get a 20 percent share of the coverage. As figure 8.1 shows, however, most candidates received very low shares and a few candidates got very large shares—in some cases, as much as 75 percent of all coverage. Thus, media coverage was unevenly distributed, with some candidates getting very little and a few getting a great deal.[8] The most heavily covered candidate was George W. Bush in the invisible primary of 2000. For example, George W. Bush got 67 percent of all coverage, McCain 17 percent, and the ten other candidates shared the remaining 16 percent of coverage. Media coverage tends, thus, to be highly skewed.

The rule determining the coverage seems to be: Cover those who are already well-known and doing well and forget about the rest. Thus, as Buell remarks, reporting often "reinforces inequalities among candidates apparent in the national polls" (1996, 32). Figure 8.2 both illustrates this rule and shows a handful of exceptions. The *x*-axis shows candidate poll support early in the year prior to the election, which we take to be a measure of a candidate's initial standing with the public. The *y*-axis shows the candidate's share of news coverage in the year that follows this poll.

As can be seen, the vast majority of candidates are at the lower left—no standing in public opinion at the start of the contest and ignored by the media in the contest to follow. At the upper right are candidates in the opposite situation—popular with the public to start and covered relatively heavily by the media in the race that follows.

The trend line in the graph shows what would happen if every candidate's media share were equal to his or her poll standing. It might therefore be called the "fair-share line." Candidates whose scores fall right on the line, such as George Bush in 1988 receive a share of media coverage that is equal to their poll standing, which seems fair. Walter Mondale in 1984 also received a share of coverage roughly equal to his poll standing, as did Ted Kennedy in 1980. Candidates below the fair-share line, such as Jerry Brown in 1992, would seem to have grounds for complaint. Their media share falls below their share of public support. Polls show they are known and liked by the public, yet the media ignore them. Candidates above the line, such as Clinton in 1992 or Howard Dean in 2004, are the lucky ones. They manage to attract heavy coverage despite weak initial standing in the polls.

Still there is tendency in these data for candidates who do better in the polls to get larger shares of media coverage. In this sense, figure 8.2

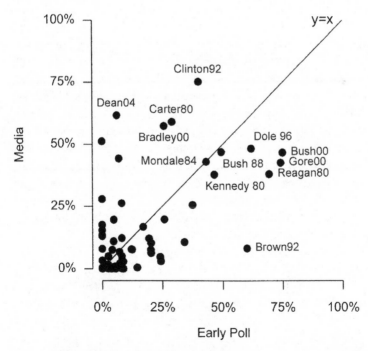

Fig. 8.2. Media versus polls. Early Poll is the candidate's share of respondents, excluding undecideds, in a poll in January the year before election year. Media is the candidate's share of all mentions of any candidate in *Time* or *Newsweek* in the year prior to the primaries.

shows that most candidates get an amount of coverage that may be roughly "fair"—meaning that most get ignored because the public doesn't care about them, and a few get heavily covered because the public does care. But a handful manage to do better or worse than "deserved."

These generalizations from the data in figure 8.2 tell us little about the autonomous role of the media in the invisible primary. The fact that reporters cover candidates who are already doing well suggests—correctly, as it will turn out—that the media reinforce the status quo more than they change it. But that is not clear from the data in figure 8.2. The reason, for example, that George W. Bush was already strong in the polls in early 1999 was that the media had already covered him extensively. Hence, we have a classic chicken-and-egg problem: Does media coverage create front-runners in the invisible primary, or does media coverage flow to candidates who are front-runners independent of the media? Our statistical analysis below provides an answer to this question.

Public Opinion Polls
Nothing of importance in American politics can be done without polls, and certainly the invisible primary cannot be done without polls—lots of them. These polls begin as soon as the dust settles after the previous presidential election and continue until the new nominees are chosen. The polls ask the partisans of each party to pick from a list of currently active candidates the one candidate they would prefer to get their party's nomination. Because polls are conducted months or years before any actual election, they may not have much value as forecasting devices. Nonetheless, leadership in the polls conveys prestige, and it may also influence other actors in the invisible primary. For example, a party member who wants simply to get on the bandwagon of the winner might use polls as a guide to decision. Later, in the primaries themselves, voters who wish to coordinate on a candidate who is "viable" may pay attention to polls. Importantly, polls also give analysts like us the ability to track the rise and fall of candidate support over time, which is an aid in seeking to unpack the dynamics of the invisible primary.

Perhaps the most striking feature of the available poll data is its general stability. Some candidates make gains or losses, but most end up roughly where they started. To show this, figure 8.3 presents a scatterplot of poll support at the beginning of our invisible primary and poll support a year later, just before the Iowa caucuses.

The line on the graph is, once again, the "fair-share" line: It shows what the data would look like if every candidate got the same public support in the late poll as in the early poll. As is apparent, most cases fall fairly near

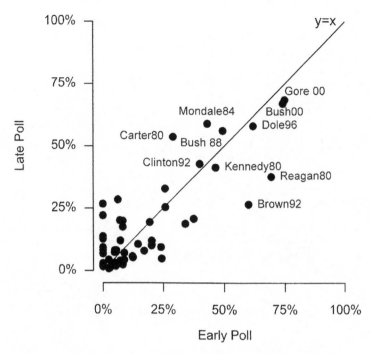

Fig. 8.3. Stability in polls. Early Poll is the candidate's share of respondents, excluding undecideds, in a poll in January the year before election year. Late Poll is the candidate's share of respondents, excluding undecideds, in a poll in January of election year.

the line. However, the off-diagonal cases are interesting. We saw in figure 8.2 above that Clinton and Dean got more media coverage than would be "deserved" on the basis of their early poll standing alone, and we see here that their poll standing rose as well. Brown, notable for getting less media coverage than he might have deserved on the basis of initial poll support, stands out here for having lost support in the polls.

Eyeball inspection of the data thus suggests that media coverage may affect a candidate's poll standing. Yet, before reaching any conclusion as to what is causing what, we will need to expand our analysis. Given the long time spans involved, it is possible that poll standing causes media coverage as much as the other way around.

Fund-Raising

By some accounts, money, more than anything else, drives American politics. "Money is the mother's milk of politics," as one successful politician put it.[9] To observers of the participants in the invisible primary, this notion would not seem far-fetched. Nearly all successful candidates—George

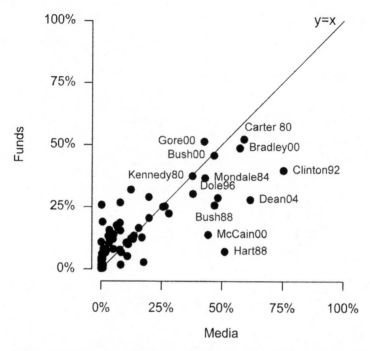

Fig. 8.4. Fund-raising versus media. Funds is the percentage of all money raised in the year prior to the primaries. Media is the candidate's share of all mentions of any candidate in Time or Newsweek in the year prior to the primaries.

W. Bush seems to be the main exception—spend enormous time at fundraisers and on the phone to donors. Those who fail at fund-raising fail in the invisible primary and quit the race, often with a blast at the baneful influence of money in politics. Successful candidates complain almost as bitterly about the amount of time they must devote to fund-raising.

Scholars disagree on the impact of money. Corrado and Gouvea (2003) and Goff (2004) argue that it is important, especially in the early stages of the invisible primary. Others believe that money can buy recognition and attention, but not the nomination (Robinson, Wilcox, and Marshall 1989; Norrander 1993; Wayne 2000). Our analysis will come out on the latter side, but not unequivocally so.

To give a sense of the raw data, figure 8.4 presents the relationship between share of media coverage and share of fund-raising. Note that the line shown in the graph is once again the "fair share" line, meaning that it shows the pattern that would exist if each candidate got exactly the same shares of media coverage and campaign donations. The extent of clustering on this line is impressive. Media and money raising are indeed closely linked. As always, though, we must be wary of making causal attributions on the basis of a simple scatterplot. Media coverage might drive fund-raising, but it is equally plausible that journalists follow rather than lead the money trail, lavishing coverage on those they expect to do well.

One Thing We Don't Measure

One factor we would especially like to measure, but cannot, is candidates' success in recruiting top professional staff. All accounts of the invisible primary note their importance. Thus, we saw a moment ago that one skilled professional, Ralph Reed, was "besieged by prospective contenders" more than three years before the start of the regular primaries.[10] Lee Atwater, as noted in chapter 7, was a major catch for George H. W. Bush in the 1988 invisible primary. There is no doubt that the candidates who can recruit the best staff have an important advantage. Not only do staff manage both the visible and invisible primary campaigns, they can also, by their prestige, attract endorsements. However, reports on candidates' success in recruitment of staff are rare in the media, which is what makes measurement infeasible.

Perhaps the main loss from our inability to directly measure top staff is that it leaves us unable to apportion influence among different types of party insiders. If we could measure candidates' ability to recruit top staff separately from other kinds of support, we could tell whether professional support, which is mostly but not entirely technical, is more or less support than political support, such as the endorsement of a governor or former president.

The Problem of Selection Bias

The invisible primary has no fixed field of candidates. Some candidates enter the race early and run until the last primary ballot is cast. Pat Buchanan in 1992 is an example. He never came close to winning a primary but nonetheless campaigned in every contest from start to finish. Other candidates, however, stay in the race only so long as they think they have a chance to win. Dan Quayle in 1996 is an example of this. He announced that he was setting up an exploratory committee to run for president in January 1995, but dropped out just a few weeks later. Quayle was, as his aides explained, "frustrated in trying to recruit leading fund-raisers and party loyalists for his campaign" (Berke 1996, A14). Thus, Quayle did not compete in a single primary or caucus.

We wish more candidates had the determination of Buchanan. His long, unsuccessful march through the primaries makes it possible for us to know exactly how much political support he had. With Quayle, it is not clear. The former vice president may have been correct in his estimate that he could not win the nomination, but he would have won some support, and our analysis of the nomination process would be stronger if we had this information.

Many more presidential aspirants are like Quayle than like Buchanan. In every open nomination, some ten to fifteen public figures either formally enter the contest for nomination or otherwise seriously test the waters in the invisible primary. But by the time of the Iowa caucuses, the field of active candidates is usually narrowed to five or six or even fewer. A handful, like Gerald Ford in 1980, Mario Cuomo in 1992, and Colin Powell in 1995, are truly major figures who are seriously interested in the race. Former president Ford, in particular, traveled some 250,000 miles on the "rubber chicken" circuit during the early invisible primary, yet, as we noted earlier, he never formally entered the race.[11] Many other dropouts are less well known to ordinary Americans, but still quite estimable figures with significant insider support. So many candidates entering the invisible primary but dropping out before we can learn their true potential makes it difficult for analysts like ourselves to tell what is really going on. The problem is called selection bias.

We can illustrate this problem of selection bias with the example of Bill Frist. Frist was elected to the Senate from Tennessee in 1994 and rose to become the Republican majority leader in 2002. This was the same position from which Bob Dole launched his successful campaign for the Republican nomination in 1996, and Frist seemed headed down the same path. Handsome, conservative, rich, and close to the Bush White House, Frist expressed interest in running for the Republican nomination in 2008 and was widely considered a strong candidate. But his tenure as majority leader did not go well. He angered conservative activists for failing to secure Senate confirmation of conservative judges and for supporting stem cell research. As one journalist reported: "Irate that the Senate majority leader had broken with President Bush on the volatile issue of human embryonic stem cell research, conservative Republicans denounced him on Friday, warning that his support for the work could cost him the Republican presidential nomination should he seek it in 2008" (Stolberg 2005, 11). In 2006, Frist announced that he needed time off from politics and would not run for president. But journalists noted that his campaign had lost steam after his stem cell vote.

We do not know all of the reasons Frist quit the race, but for purposes of analysis, let us assume that he dropped out precisely because he lacked support of party insiders. And let us further assume that this lack of activist support is a frequent reason that candidates drop out. If so, candidates who stay in the race would consist mainly of people who do have activist support—and herein lies the problem. If most active candidates have the support of activists, then activist support cannot predict which succeed.

Suppose, even worse, that a few candidates lack insider support but enter the race anyway because they have some other outstanding quality—say, strong support in the polls—that they believe will enable them to triumph despite lack of insider support. And suppose they are right. Then it will appear that polls make all the difference in presidential nominations and activist support makes no difference—which, given the way we set up our hypothetical scenario, would be wrong. Activist support mattered in our scenario, but its effect was hard to observe because candidates who lacked it would drop out before we could learn about them.

The problem of selection bias is a plague on social science. It arises whenever actors anticipate their likely fate and select out of a process or into a process for that reason.[12] It is a particular problem for analysis of the invisible primary because most candidates who consider running for president drop out early or never enter the race at all. In the appendix to this chapter, we discuss selection bias as it affects our argument in this chapter. Our conclusion is that it may be a problem, but probably a small one. Insofar as it does affect our analysis, the effect is likely to be to bias our results against finding an effect for endorsements. We do, as it turns out, find endorsement effects—but these effects are in spite of rather than because of any selection bias problem that likely exists.

★ ★ ★

With our reader, as we hope, now familiar with the nature of and potential problems with the four measures we intend to use in our analysis of the invisible primary, we are ready for the analysis itself.

Statistical Analysis

The invisible primary, as we conceive it in our statistical analysis, has four components—endorsements, media coverage, poll support, and campaign donations. Our question is how much each of them affects the others. We especially want to know whether insider endorsements are largely determined by polls and the media or whether insider endorsements are due mainly to the autonomous judgments of insiders themselves.

To answer this question, we partition our data into different time periods to see how early changes in the four components affect other components later on in the invisible primary. We would like to divide our data into numerous time periods, but our data, especially in the 1980s, are too

Table 8.2: Causes of success in the invisible primary

	Polls$_{t-2}$	Endorse$_{t-2}$	Funds$_{t-2}$	Media$_{t-2}$
10 percentage point change in Polls$_{t-1}$ predicts	**4.9**	0.5	0.4	1.9
10 percentage point change in Endorsements$_{t-1}$ predicts	0.8	**8.8**	3.0	0.3
10 percentage point change in Funds$_{t-1}$ predicts	0.2	0.3	**2.5**	−0.8
10 percentage point change in Media$_{t-1}$ predicts	**3.5**	−0.2	−1.1	**8.1**

Coefficients in boldface are statistically significant at the .05 level, one-tailed.

limited to sustain many divisions, so we divide them into only two time periods,[13] which we call Time 1 ($t = 1$) and Time 2 ($t = 2$).[14]

Having done this, we can observe how measurements made at Time 1 affect each other variable at Time 2. Table 8.2 summarizes the results of this statistical analysis, showing the most important effects in boldface. (Our criterion for boldfacing is a *p*-value of .05 or less, one-tailed. See the chapter appendix for more technical details and actual coefficients and standard errors.)

Let us begin with the first column, which shows the apparent causes of poll support at Time 2. As can be seen, each 10 percentage point increase in share of poll support at Time 1 appears to cause a 4.9 point increase poll support at Time 2. Media share at Time 1 also causes poll support at Time 2. Thus, later poll support is caused by early poll support and early media coverage. The fact that media coverage affects poll support is consistent with the Mass Politics scenario.

Now look at column two, which shows the predictors of Time 2 endorsements. The story here is that the only predictor of Time 2 endorsements is Time 1 endorsements. Nothing else really matters. Thus, party insiders go their own way, regardless of polls, media, and fund-raising. We take this as support for our Free Choice proposition.

Results for fund-raising are shown in column three. The main result here is that fund-raising is well predicted by nothing, not even fund-raising from earlier in the invisible primary. The best predictor is Time 1 endorsements, but the effect is small.

Results for media coverage at Time 2 are shown in column four. Journalists, it appears, also go their own way. The only thing that predicts media coverage is prior media coverage.

Overall, then, the results indicate a good deal of self-caused activity as most groups—the public, insiders, donors, and the media—march to the beat of their own drummers. The most important substantive point, however, is that insider endorsements are essentially unaffected by any other aspect of the process. It is especially notable that support in the polls—the primary means by which a strong candidate might be expected to bully his or her way to nomination over party insiders—has little effect on endorsements. Thus, in terms of our competing hypotheses, endorsers exhibit almost complete "free will" in their choice of nominee.

Before reaching final conclusions, however, we wish to refine our analysis. In our analysis of the restaurant game, we noted that diners trying to coordinate on a common eating place might favor restaurants that attract people of diverse culinary tastes. If fish lovers flock to a fish restaurant, it provides little information to diners who happen not to be fish lovers. But if, in the first group of diners to make a choice, a few vegetarians and families with children chose the fish restaurant, other kinds of diners would take it as a signal that the fish restaurant is a good bet as a common eating place.

We suggest that the invisible primary may work the same way. If the first endorsers to support, say, a liberal candidate are all liberals themselves, it conveys little information to other party insiders who are not liberals. But if the early endorsers of the liberal candidate include some moderates, others will take this as a signal that the candidate is a good bet to unify the party.

With this in mind, we tried to measure the similarities between endorsers and the candidates they supported. We began by coding each candidate on three characteristics, that is, three kinds of groups the candidates might belong to. These characteristics were geographical home base, ideology, and what we called "political group." This political group could be any politically salient group to which the candidate belongs. For example, we coded Jesse Jackson as African American, Patrick Buchanan as a religious conservative, and Richard Gephardt as a member of the House of Representatives. We also coded as many as possible of our endorsers on these same characteristics. We then evaluated each endorsement on whether it came from someone sharing the characteristics of the candidate. If, for example, a strongly conservative party member endorsed a strongly conservative candidate, we counted it as an in-group endorsement. Similarly, a black politician who endorsed Jackson was counted as an in-group endorsement; a member of the House of Representatives who endorsed Richard Gephardt was counted as in-group; all home-state endorsements were in-group endorsements. All endorsements from people with nearly the same ideology were also in-group. We then discarded all in-group endorsements and recalculated insider support based only on endorsements coming from individuals who shared none of the candidate's geographical, ideological, or political group characteristics.

The information to code our endorsers on these three characteristics came from wherever we could get it—electronically searchable databases, media reports, voting records, and, in many cases, the expert knowledge of one of us.[15] Geographical information was, of course, the easiest to obtain. Ideological locations were much harder to measure. We generally estimated them based on information about the endorser, such as organizational affiliation or, for members of Congress, voting record.

Needless to say, making these coding decisions was an arduous and difficult task—and in many cases impossible. Of the 5,629 endorsements in our main data file, we were forced to discard about 60 percent because we could not determine one or more of the characteristics of the endorser. We do not consider these discarded cases a major loss, because if we could not determine the characteristics of the endorsers, few others could probably do so either, making the endorsement less important as a signal in the endorsement game. Or, to put it the other way, we believe we were able to code most of the most important endorsers. But, we must add, there was an element of subjectivity in many of the decisions. Anyone wishing to review our coding decisions can find all of them in the publicly available Web database for this book.

Of the 2,319 endorsements for which we had full information, we found that 800 were from individuals who shared a key characteristic with the candidate they endorsed. These 800 were, in other words, in-group endorsements, and we discarded them as well. This left us with 1,535 from individuals who did not share any key characteristics with the person they endorsed. We refer to these endorsements as out-of-group endorsements. All of these endorsements continue to be weighted according to our measure of political significance, as described in the appendix to chapter 6.

Somewhat to our surprise, the new Time 1 endorsement variable correlated highly with the old one, $r = .94$. Thus, most candidates had similar endorsement shares on both the new out-of-group measure and the old measure that included all endorsements. However, there were some notable differences. Richard Gephardt's endorsement share in 1988 fell from 20 percent of Time 1 endorsements to 2 percent; this was because most of his public support came from the House of Representatives and was therefore omitted from the calculation of out-of-group support. Another big loser in 1988 was Jack Kemp. Most of his endorsements had come from strong conservatives, which we counted as in-group for him, so his share fell from 33 percent to 11 percent. Walter Mondale was the biggest winner. Because he pulled support from all parts of the party, his share rose from

Table 8.3: Causes of success in invisible primary (out-of-group endorsements)

	Polls$_{t=2}$	Endorsements$_{t=2}$	Funds$_{t=2}$	Media$_{t=2}$
10 percentage point change in Polls$_{t=1}$ predicts	**2.9**	0.1	0.1	−0.1
10 percentage point change in Out-of-group Endorsements$_{t=1}$	**4.5**	**8.2**	3.2	4.1
10 percentage point change in Funds$_{t=1}$ predicts	−1.1	0.3	2.4	−2.2
10 percentage point change in Media$_{t=1}$ predicts	0.9	−1.0	−1.6	5.5

Coefficients in boldface are statistically significant at the .05 level, one-tailed.
The dependent variable is total (not out-of-group) weighted endorsement share at $t = 2$.

51 percent of all Time 1 endorsements to 74 percent of Time 1 out-of-group endorsements. In general, stronger candidates did better on the breadth measure and the weaker candidates did worse. But, to reiterate, most of the differences between the two measures were moderate to small.

Our theoretical expectation, based loosely on the logic of the restaurant game, is that out-of-group endorsements will convey more information about acceptability within the party and will, therefore, have greater impact on the dynamics of the invisible primary. Hence, we reran table 8.2 above, except using out-of-group endorsement shares in place of total endorsement shares, as shown in table 8.3.

These results describe a large role for endorsements in the invisible primary. Not only do early endorsements influence later endorsements; they influence everything else as well. No other factor has such wide influence. Nor are endorsements themselves affected by any other variable. Endorsements are also more autonomously stable and hence impervious to external influence during the invisible primary (effect of early endorsements on later endorsements = 8.2) than are polls (effect of early polls on later polls = 2.9)[16] or any other measured component.

Early out-of-group endorsements thus seem to be the unmoved mover of the invisible primary. We do not assert this conclusion strongly, because our data are fragile. The most important limitation of the data is that they involve marginal changes in each variable across only two time periods. As far as they go, however, the results of our statistical analysis are more consistent with the Free Choice scenario than with the Mass Politics scenario.

Another important point: Our theoretical claim in this book is that the political actors who make endorsements in the invisible primary behave as members of a party in the sense that they are concerned to find a candidate who can unite the party. The finding here that their endorsements are more responsive to early out-of-group endorsements, which convey information about breadth of acceptability, than to total endorsements is consistent with that position. Or, to put this point somewhat differently, the candidate who fares best in the invisible primary is not the candidate who can best mobilize early factional support, but the candidate who can best mobilize early out-of-faction support. Or, most simply, the data are consistent with our United Front proposition.

Our analysis of the invisible primary has focused mainly on party endorsements because we believe they are the most important factor in presidential nominations. We must, however, say a few words about the other factors, beginning with public opinion polls.

We saw in figure 8.3 that candidates' standing in the polls is fairly stable over the course of the invisible primary. Only a handful of candidates—Bill Clinton in 1992 is the most important example—are much weaker or stronger at the end of the process than they were at the beginning. Yet some poll movement does occur, and the message from the first column of table 8.3 is that endorsements are the main cause of this movement. In fact, if one wants to predict a candidate's poll standing at the end of the invisible primary, early endorsements predict it more accurately than early poll standing. (The relevant effects are +4.5 and +2.9.) We take this as a testament to the power of endorsements in the invisible primary.

As shown in column 4 of table 8.3, early party endorsements also influence media coverage. Indeed, endorsements seem to influence what journalists write about as much as they influence what citizens say in polls. (The relevant coefficients are +4.1 in column 4 and +4.5 in column 1.)

Money stands out in table 8.3 for its relative lack of connection to everything else. In other words, fund-raising is neither clearly caused by other variables in the invisible primary nor a clear cause of other variables. Some candidates raise a lot of money and some raise very little, but that's about all we can say.

This does not mean that endorsement leaders lack for funding. A look at the raw data shows that endorsement leaders always raise large sums of money. But a fair number of other candidates—for example, John Connally in 1980, Pat Robertson in 1988, Phil Gramm in 1996, and John McCain in 2000—also manage to raise large amounts of money despite low endorsements, scant media coverage, and absence of early poll support. Possibly because of selection bias, fund-raising is not predicted well by our other variables.

For people who fear the influence of money in presidential politics, the relative independence of fund-raising from other aspects of the invisible primary may be encouraging. Money is surely important in presidential nominations, but, by our results, it does not dominate the invisible primary phase of the nomination process.

★ ★ ★

Altogether, these statistical results provide a nice complement to the qualitative analysis in chapter 7, which likewise suggested that the judgments of party insiders are the most important factor in presidential nominations. Neither qualitative nor statistical methods are infallible, but the fact that two quite different kinds of analysis support the same conclusion strengthens our confidence in the validity of that claim.

Yet we are still one big step away from completing our argument. To vindicate the claim of our book—*The Party Decides*—we must still show that the endorsements of party insiders, as made in the invisible primary period, exert a decisive impact on the voter primaries and caucuses that follow.

★

APPENDIX TO CHAPTER 8
MODELS OF THE INVISIBLE PRIMARY

In chapter 8, we presented quantitative evidence concerning the relationships we described qualitatively in chapter 7. In this appendix, we provide the technical details of the quantitative analysis.

The Variables

The variables used are described in detail in the chapter. Table 8A.1 shows basic summary statistics for all of the variables used in the each part of the analysis. Figure 8A.1 shows a complete plot matrix for the primary variables, with the correlations across variables in the lower half of the matrix.

The data in table 8A.1 are in two parts, that for the invisible primary analysis, in chapter 8, and that for the delegates analysis, in chapter 9. We discuss all of the measures here. For the first part, we include seventy-one observations on candidates who were "viable" throughout the invisible primary. That is, they had nonzero measures on multiple invisible primary indicators. Of those seventy-one, only sixty-one actively participated in at least the Iowa caucus or the New Hampshire primary. Those sixty-one

Table 8A.1: Summary of all variables

	When measured	Mean	Std. Dev.	Skew	IQR	Min	25th percentile	Median	75th percentile	Max
Invisible Primary Analysis (N = 71)										
Polls	First half of invisible primary	0.14	0.19	1.76	0.17	0.00	0.02	0.06	0.19	0.78
	Second half of invisible primary	0.14	0.17	1.68	0.14	0.00	0.02	0.07	0.17	0.75
Endorsements (weighted)	First half of invisible primary	0.14	0.20	2.10	0.16	0.00	0.02	0.06	0.18	0.92
	Second half of invisible primary	0.14	0.20	1.75	0.17	0.00	0.01	0.04	0.18	0.74
Endorsements (out-of-group)	First half of invisible primary	0.14	0.23	2.10	0.17	0.00	0.00	0.05	0.17	0.92
	Second half of invisible primary	0.14	0.24	1.91	0.13	0.00	0.00	0.02	0.13	0.86
Funds	First half of invisible primary	0.14	0.15	2.24	0.16	0.00	0.04	0.09	0.19	0.88
	Second half of invisible primary	0.14	0.15	1.31	0.21	0.00	0.03	0.08	0.23	0.61
Media	First half of invisible primary	0.14	0.17	2.23	0.17	0.00	0.01	0.08	0.19	0.87
	Second half of invisible primary	0.14	0.20	1.62	0.21	0.00	0.00	0.05	0.21	0.80
Delegates Analysis (N = 61)										
Polls	End of invisible primary	0.16	0.18	1.53	0.17	0.01	0.04	0.08	0.21	0.69
Endorsements (weighted)	End of invisible primary	0.16	0.21	1.74	0.18	0.00	0.02	0.09	0.20	0.82

Endorsements (weighted out-of-group)	End of invisible primary	0.16	0.25	1.77	0.17	0.00	0.00	0.05	0.18	0.83
Funds	End of invisible primary	0.16	0.13	1.01	0.19	0.00	0.07	0.13	0.25	0.52
Media	End of invisible primary	0.16	0.20	1.26	0.25	0.00	0.01	0.08	0.26	0.75
Final delegate share	Actual end of process	0.16	0.28	1.69	0.15	0.00	0.00	0.00	0.15	0.97
Fat Lady delegate share	Effective end of process	0.17	0.24	1.43	0.25	0.00	0.00	0.04	0.25	0.77
Best delegate share	Candidate's high-water mark	0.17	0.28	1.69	0.15	0.00	0.00	0.02	0.15	0.97
Lagged controls										
Polls	First half of invisible primary	0.16	0.21	1.58	0.22	0.00	0.02	0.08	0.24	0.78
Endorsements (weighted)	First half of invisible primary	0.16	0.25	1.87	0.19	0.00	0.00	0.06	0.19	0.92
Endorsements (out-of-group)	First half of invisible primary	0.16	0.22	1.89	0.18	0.00	0.02	0.08	0.20	0.92
Funds	First half of invisible primary	0.16	0.17	1.89	0.19	0.00	0.04	0.14	0.23	0.88
Media	First half of invisible primary	0.16	0.20	2.02	0.20	0.00	0.02	0.10	0.22	0.87

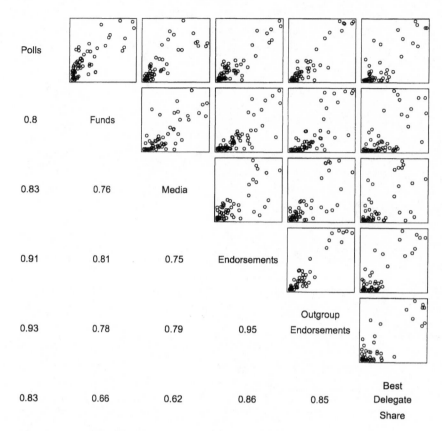

Fig. 8A.1. Summary of all variables.

are the cases in the second part of the analysis, which analyzes delegate shares.

Measurement Error

Several of our variables are measured with error. This is a concern because measurement error on independent variables causes attenuation bias—the effect estimate for the given variable will be too small. One common approach to measurement error is to ignore it, as attenuation bias tends to be a bias against the researcher's hypothesis, and with all of the subtle biases in favor of the hypothesis that work their way into the research design, it can be a good idea to have a thumb on the scale against the hypothesis. However, in a multiple regression, the effects of attenuation bias can be complex, especially when, as in this case, the regressors are correlated with one another.

We therefore undertake to correct for measurement error. The standard "errors in variables" approach is conceptually simple, but difficult in practice because it requires that the degree of measurement error be estimated or assumed for each variable. We shall now describe the steps we took to estimate the reliability of each measure.

For polls and endorsements, reliability is estimated through simulation. In both cases, we simulate data by taking repeated samples from a distribution of, say, endorsement scores that is the same as the distribution of our actual data. The average correlation between pairs of endorsement scores from repeated draws is our measure of reliability. Sample sizes are the same as in the actual data, which for endorsements vary considerably from year to year. For endorsements, we also partially account for the fact that (in contrast to survey sampling) our procedure did not sample endorsements independently of one another; rather, we culled endorsements from newspaper articles, some of which reported many endorsements and others of which reported only one or two. To capture this clustering within the simulation, we drew our endorsement samples not from one large pool, but from many small pools of different sizes and distributions, as occurred in the source-level clusters in our actual data. The resulting estimated reliabilities were higher than we expected. The reliabilities were 0.997 for our measure of polls at Time 1, and 0.999 for polls at the end of the entire period. For endorsements, the respective reliabilities were 0.978 and 0.989.

For media, our data are calculated as shares of coverage in *Time* and *Newsweek* magazine. These magazines are a representative source, but not a perfect one. Aggregated to the level of "first half of invisible primary" and "second half of invisible primary" in each of ten nomination contests, the *Time* and *Newsweek* share variables correlated at nearly unity. As a measure of the relationship between our measure and the actual news flow, this estimate is much too high. However, the *Time* measure correlated with a comparable measure from the *New York Times* at just less than 0.9, which seemed reasonable, so we used 0.9 as the reliability of the media variable.

For fund-raising, we have what we believe to be an essentially error-free measure from the Federal Election Commission. We built the measure from the raw spending data, because the FEC reporting periods do not match the temporal divisions of the invisible primary, which varied by year, as explained in the appendix to chapter 6. Because of spending by independent groups and other reasons (see discussion in closing section of chapter 9), candidates' reported fund-raising is probably a poor measure of total spending by the candidate. However, we take the FEC data to be an essentially perfect measure of what the fund-raising variable purports to measure and therefore do not make a reliability correction for this variable.

It is worth noting that, for all of our attention to measurement error, our substantive conclusions hold up even when we do not correct for it.

Selection Bias

As we discuss in the chapter, the candidates who stayed in the race long enough to get into our data set are not a random sample of all candidates. This creates the problem known as selection bias, as discussed in the text.

A common solution is to use a Heckman selection model to explain how individual cases are selected into the set of cases available for study. A Heckman model requires two things: information about all cases in the initial pool, whether the cases end up in the final pool or not, and a variable that predicts the selection into the final pool.

Survey organizations routinely measure public support for all candidates testing the waters in the invisible primary. Their polls give us both a fairly complete list of names in the large initial pool and a variable (poll standing) for predicting whether cases will "select" to remain in the contest. By this means, we identified 164 candidates in the ten nomination contests we have studied. For each of these would-be candidates, we created variables measuring whether they had ever been elected to office, whether they currently held office, and a few other readily available pieces of information.[17]

As it turns out, none of these variables does a good job of predicting whether a candidate in the initial pool will select into the smaller pool of candidates who compete in the invisible primary and in the state primaries. The best of the predictors is the candidate's best showing in the polls, which has a marginally statistically significant impact ($p < .053$, one-tailed) on entry into the sample. However, the coefficient for the poll variable indicates a moderate substantive effect. A 10 percentage point change in the *best* poll showing the candidate has increases his predicted probability of staying in the race only about 7 percent. A candidate who never had *any* positive poll before the contest still has a 35 percent predicted probability of entering our sample, while the candidate with the highest poll showing of anyone before the invisible primary (Al Gore in 2000) has a predicted probability of remaining in the sample of only 72 percent. This relationship is so weak that when we apply the standard Heckman selection bias to the analyses reported below, the correction effect is unimportant. It may be possible to develop a better selection model with other variables, but we have been unable to do so with anything we can imagine to measure.

Why so weak? There are two fairly obvious explanations. One is that, despite the advantage of strong polls, some candidates lack "fire in the belly" for the arduous contest. Polls may help a candidate decide how well she will do, but no nomination contest is ever a sure thing, so less-motivated candidates may drop out even when they have reasonably high poll scores. Two candidates enjoying strong poll standing but widely considered to have dropped out because of lack of political ambition are Colin Powell (25 percent in polls in 1995) and Mario Cuomo (23 percent in 1991). Meanwhile, dozens of candidates with much lower poll numbers have jumped into the race.

The other likely reason that Heckman corrections based on polls don't have much effect is that polls are not, to begin with, good predictors of success in the invisible primary. By some of our estimates in chapter 9, they do certainly appear to be poor predictors. For example, the average level of support for Ford in the earliest invisible primary polls for the 1980 nomination was 30 percent, which was just ahead of Ronald Reagan's average score, 28 percent. Few, however, would imagine that Ford was really the equal of Reagan as a candidate—and Ford didn't seem to think so either. After 250,000 miles of political travel in the early invisible primary, Ford decided to stay out of the race despite his clear interest in another term as president. Al Gore is another case of this type. As observed in chapter 7, he mounted an intense campaign in the early phase of the invisible primary for the 2004 nomination and led in the polls before dropping out late in 2002. Among several reasons he gave was lack of insider support.

These and a few other cases raise the danger that candidates do withdraw from the invisible primary because they anticipate doing badly—not in terms of polls, but in terms of insider endorsements. No candidate can run a successful campaign without political support, and if, for any reason, that support is not forthcoming, candidates may have no choice but to drop out. Unfortunately, however, we do not have a measure of early endorsement support that corresponds to the early poll standing variable. We therefore cannot correct for selection on expected endorsements. The expected effect of our inability to do so is an attenuation of our estimate of the effect of endorsements. To see this, consider this model:

$$\text{Success}_i = \beta_0 + \beta_1 * \text{Endorsements}_i + \varepsilon_i$$

In this model, the error term ε_i captures unmeasured factors that affect a candidate's success. Candidates only stay in the race when they have resources, measured or unmeasured, that will help them. Our concern is that, among candidates who have few endorsements, those with many unmeasured resources, or a large ε_i, will be more likely to stay in the race than those with a small ε_i. However, among those with many endorsements, those with large *and* small ε_i will both stay in the race. To the extent that this occurs, it will induce a negative correlation between ε_i and Endorsements$_i$ variable, attenuating our estimate of β_1.

Estimation

For both the invisible primary model in tables 8.2 and 8.3 and models predicting delegate share in chapter 9, we use a simple least-squares estimate of a linear model. Because all of the variables are scored as the candidate's percentage share of the measure, interpretation of results is fairly straightforward. The coefficient measures the percent change in the dependent variable associated with a one-percent change in the independent variable.

However, the use of shares creates estimation problems. Shares variables are "compositional variables," in that they all sum to 1 across the candidates in a particular race. This has several consequences. First, the variable is bounded, and yet the linear model might lead to out-of-bounds forecasts. Second, the errors are negatively correlated within each set of contests. Third, our observations are not independent; in each contest, the nth candidate's measures are perfectly determined by all of the others. Finally, we have varying numbers of candidates across nomination contests, which means that candidates' shares might not be directly comparable across races.

The standard solution for compositional data is a log-ratio transformation, but this requires that the elements that add to 100 percent in each group (in our case, each nomination contest) be the same, or at least comparable. Because the fields within contests are completely different from year to year and party to party, this condition is not met. Thus, the standard method is not available to us. Log-ratio transformations create additional complications in the presence of measurement error.

Our solution is to address the various consequences of the compositional variable one by one. To begin with, we use clustered standard errors to account for the correlation in the errors within nomination contests. We adjust the degrees of freedom used in all standard error calculations by the number of candidates in a given year. Thus $n - k$ becomes $n - k - m$, where n is the number of observations in the overall model, k is the number of regressors (including the constant), and m is the number of clusters.

The variation in the number of candidates is addressed through a variable that is the inverse of the number of candidates in a given year. Figure 8A.2 demonstrates why this is the appropriate correction. Suppose the relationship between polls and delegates is 0.5, so that a 1 percentage-point

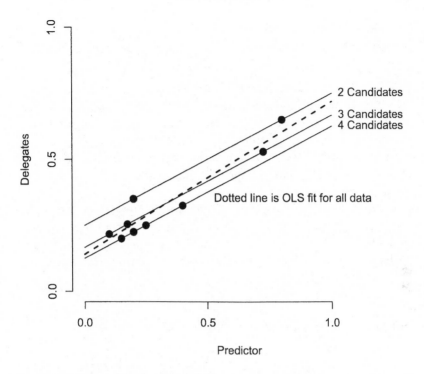

Fig. 8A.2. Hypothetical fit of compositional data.

increase in a candidate's poll share is associated with a 0.5 percentage-point increase in delegate share. If the relationship were perfect, the data would fall along the lines in the figure. The change in the intercept across groups depends on the actual slope, but it is always proportional to the inverse of the number of candidates. (And if separate intercepts are computed, they also tend to differ by the inverse of the number of candidates.)

We believe these adjustments account for the most important special features of our data, but we have spent considerable time exploring alternatives by means of simulation. Use of log-ratio transformations, often favored for the kind of data we have, performed quite badly on simulated data having the characteristics of our actual data. Everything we have tried has either given us substantively similar results or has left us with unstable estimates that neither confirm nor disconfirm the findings we report. There may be better theoretical solutions for the problems we have, but after extensive consultation and experimentation, we feel the combination of techniques we use is well-suited to our problem (see Noel 2005).[18]

The Invisible Primary Analysis

Tables 8.2 and 8.3 in the text of the chapter summarize estimates of the effect of each variable in the invisible primary on each other variable. Tables 8A.2 and 8A.3 show the full models as estimated. In table 8A.2, we estimate the effect of polls, endorsements, media, and fund-raising measured in the first half of the cycle on those same variables in the second half of the cycle. This table uses the candidates' share of all weighted endorsements. In table 8A.3, we instead use the candidates' share of all out-of-group weighted endorsements as an independent variable. Out-of-group endorsements affect every facet of the invisible primary.

Column two of table 8A.3 (in keeping with the results reported in the text), shows the effect of out-of-group endorsements in the first period on total endorsements in the second period. One might also be interested in the effect of out-of-group endorsements in the first and second time periods on each other. This is reported in column five.

Table 8A.2: Invisible primary dynamics: Weighted endorsements share

	Polls, second half	Endorsements (weighted share), second half	Funds, second half	Media , second half
Polls, first half	0.49	0.05	0.04	0.19
	(0.11)	(0.12)	(0.15)	(0.15)
	4.55	0.37	0.28	1.26
Endorsements (weighted), first half	0.08	0.88	0.30	0.03
	(0.23)	(0.28)	(0.41)	(0.44)
	0.34	3.17	0.73	0.07
Funds, first half	0.02	0.03	0.25	−0.08
	(0.25)	(0.28)	(0.38)	(0.48)
	0.09	0.10	0.65	−0.17
Media, first half	0.35	−0.02	−0.11	0.81
	(0.28)	(0.41)	(0.51)	(0.46)
	1.26	−0.05	−0.21	1.77
1/number of candidates, first half	0.05	0.07	0.52	0.04
	(0.14)	(0.13)	(0.22)	(0.14)
	0.38	0.51	2.38	0.30
Constant	0.00	0.00	0.00	0.00
	(0.00)	(0.00)	(0.00)	(0.00)
N	71	71	71	71
Adjusted R-squared	74%	82%	46%	51%
Root MSE	0.09	0.08	0.11	0.13

Coefficient in roman.
Standard error in parentheses.
t-ratio for null hypothesis that $\beta = 0$ in italics.

Table 8A.3: Invisible primary dynamics: Out-of-group endorsements

	Polls, second half	Endorsements (weighted share), second half	Funds, second half	Media, second half	Endorsements (weighted out-of-group), second half
Polls, first half	0.29	0.01	0.01	-0.01	-0.17
	(0.10)	(0.11)	(0.14)	(0.21)	(0.22)
	2.74	*0.12*	*0.08*	*-0.06*	*-0.75*
Endorsements (weighted out-of-group), first half	0.45	0.82	0.32	0.41	1.20
	(0.20)	(0.16)	(0.20)	(0.16)	(0.26)
	2.28	*5.09*	*1.57*	*2.51*	*4.59*
Funds, first half	-0.11	0.03	0.24	-0.22	0.16
	(0.22)	(0.27)	(0.37)	(0.41)	(0.33)
	-0.51	*0.11*	*0.65*	*-0.53*	*0.48*
Media, first half	0.09	-0.10	-0.16	0.55	-0.31
	(0.35)	(0.27)	(0.40)	(0.51)	(0.42)
	0.25	*-0.39*	*-0.40*	*1.09*	*-0.73*
1/number of candidates, first half	0.29	0.24	0.59	0.27	0.12
	(0.21)	(0.13)	(0.20)	(0.25)	(0.26)
	1.39	*1.87*	*2.99*	*1.09*	*0.45*
Constant	0.00	0.00	0.00	0.00	0.00
	(0.00)	(0.00)	(0.00)	(0.00)	(0.00)
N	71	71	71	71	71
Adjusted R-squared	78%	83%	46%	56%	84%
Root MSE	0.08	0.08	0.11	0.13	0.09

Coefficient in roman.
Standard error in parentheses.
t-ratio for null hypothesis that $\beta = 0$ in italics.

The Voters Weigh In

Ordinary voters possess the ultimate power of presidential nomination in the United States. In state-level primaries and caucuses, they choose delegates pledged to particular candidates. Those delegates go on to a national party convention where the candidate with the most delegates wins. This selection process is one of the most open and democratic in the world.

It is also a textbook example of how informal practice can override formal procedure. For as we have seen, an invisible primary occurs ahead of the voter primaries and caucuses. Candidates raise money, chase good media coverage, struggle to raise their poll standing, and compete for the support of party activists and interest-group leaders. Scholars make different claims about which of these factors is most important, but few doubt that the invisible primary is a force in presidential nominations.

One way in which the invisible primary shapes voter choice is through agenda-setting. As described in chapter 8, some ten to fifteen ambitious politicians explore entry into the presidential race, but generally only five or six contestants launch campaigns and make it to the Iowa caucuses and New Hampshire primary. Even if the invisible primary had no influence on presidential nominations beyond this agenda-setting role, its influence would be great.

Another big way in which the invisible primary shapes voter choice—or at least appears to do so—is by endowing the candidates who stay in the race with extremely unequal amounts of media coverage, campaign funds, party endorsements, and standing in public opinion polls. Our question for this chapter is what combination of these endowments matters most for the outcome of the state primaries and caucuses.

The answer is by no means obvious. Voters in the state primaries probably have roughly the same preferences as citizens in preprimary national polls. If so, preprimary poll support would be the most important resource for doing well in the state primaries. Yet if state-level campaigns can reshape opinion, as they well might, state results might be a weak reflection of national polls. Fund-raising is another question mark. By some accounts, the so-called Money Primary is the driving force in presidential nominations. But the effects of money might wash out as state campaigns heat up and take on a life of their own. The influence of party insiders is especially difficult to predict. If voters trust their party leadership, endorsements might have great influence. But if voters are ignorant of leader endorsements, or simply independent minded, endorsements might not make two cents worth of difference.

This chapter examines these and other possibilities. Its main finding is that party insiders are the most important influence on voter decision-making in primaries. This influence is over and above their role in shaping the field of contestants during the invisible primary. A candidate's own popularity and resources also affect voter decision-making, but the preferences of party insiders matter more.

This conclusion does not imply that the outcomes of primary elections are foreordained in some mechanical fashion. We continue to subscribe to the Polsby and Wildavsky maxim that presidential nominations are fought and won in primary and caucus elections. Our important addendum is that the fight takes place on a playing field that tilts in the direction that party insiders want it to.

What Matters in Presidential Primaries

The elections in the 1970s, the first under the McGovern-Fraser reforms, defied political convention in almost every way possible. Ed Muskie, the overwhelming favorite for the Democratic nomination in 1972, quit the race at its midpoint. Chicago Mayor Richard Daley, the boss of bosses in the 1960s, was denied a seat at the Democratic convention in 1972. The 1976 Democratic nominee was "Jimmy Who?" even to party insiders. Ronald Reagan nearly wrested the 1976 nomination from a sitting president of his own party. One scholar compared the nomination process to an Alice in Wonderland adventure (Bartels 1988, chap. 10). The general view was that nominations were "an almost uniquely chaotic and unpredictable enterprise" (Mayer 2003, 84).

That view changed in 1996 with an essay called "Forecasting Presidential Nominations" by Bill Mayer. The 1970s, he argued, were a "transitional period." By 1980, all candidates understood how the game worked, followed the same strategies, and thereby created a system that was quite predictable. To make his point, Mayer showed that the outcome of primaries from 1980 to 1996 could be predicted before they began from just two variables—poll standings on the eve of the Iowa caucuses and, to a much lesser extent, the amount of money a candidate has raised.

After each subsequent nomination, scholars have updated and refined Mayer's model. In recent papers, Randall Adkins and Andrew Dowdle (2004, 2005) argue that the key to the new stability is early fund-raising. In the transitional 1970s, candidates who suffered an early loss could no longer raise money and had to drop out. Even strong candidates suffered this fate, opening the way for lesser ones to succeed. But in more recent contests, strong candidates begin the primaries with full coffers and can therefore withstand an early "bump in the road." Hence Adkins and Dowdle find that "cash-on-hand" at the start of the primaries is an important predictor of who succeeds in contests from 1980 to 2004.

Another scholar, Wayne Steger, argues that party insiders may be the source of the new system stability. Based on a study of the 1996 Republican nomination, Steger wrote in a 2000 convention paper that "by rallying around a single candidate, the party establishments help that candidate become the favorite going into the presidential primaries. Through a combination of cue-giving and proxy organizational support, party elites can help a candidate gain advantages in fund-raising, media coverage, organizational support, and possibly public support in and at the polls. In his most recent paper, Steger (2007) expands his evidence to cover primary election outcomes from 1980 to 2004. He finds that three factors—endorsements by party officials as reported in the media, cash-on-hand at the start of the balloting, and Gallup standing at the end of the invisible primary—affect overall results in the primaries and caucuses.[1] "Elite party elected officials," he writes, "appear to have a potent signaling effect on the partisan electorate as to which candidate should be supported" (97).

Steger's analysis is, in our view, a major step forward in the understanding of presidential nominations. It is the first since the McGovern-Fraser reforms to argue that parties may have regained control of nominations and to present serious evidence in support of that view. Our analysis therefore begins with Steger's. Our first step is to replicate it using our own data and more elaborate methods. The bottom line is that we get the same results he did. We next extend the analysis in two ways: First, we draw in evidence from the entire invisible primary, so as to show how events early in the process affect results at the end. For reasons we explain below, failure to take this step could severely bias our analysis. Second, we bring in state-level voting data, so as to better specify the nature of party influence on voters.

Winners and Losers in the Primaries

True success in the presidential primaries is easy to measure: you win the nomination or you don't. By that measure, the ten nomination cycles we study have produced 10 winners and approximately 160 losers.

Some losers, however, lose a lot worse than others. In 1980, for example, Republican John Connally spent $22 million in the invisible primary (in current dollars) and won only a single convention delegate in the state contests—that's really losing! On the other hand, Democrat Gary Hart finished a very close second to Walter Mondale in the 1984 primaries on the basis of only $3.7 million in pre-Iowa spending (in current dollars). Hart got nothing out of his strong finish, not even a vice presidential nod, but it was still a good showing. More importantly for our purposes, Hart's second-place finish contains useful information about the dynamics of the primary process.

In the analysis that follows, we use all of this information—not only who won, but how well each candidate did. We do not examine the full set of 160 initial candidates, because most drop out very early. Studying the campaign of someone who mounts only half a campaign or one-tenth of a campaign is just not possible. But we do fully analyze the sixty-one candidates who made it as far as the Iowa caucuses.

For our pool of active primary candidates, we still face the problem of how to measure success. Total votes won in the primaries and caucuses may seem like the obvious choice, but it has two problems. First, candidates do not care about votes per se; they care about pledged delegates, and insofar as these two measures are different, they put their energy into winning delegates. Second, in most recent contests, all candidates have suspended operations early on because the outcome was clear, leaving votes in the remaining primaries essentially uncontested.

In light of these complications, we have developed three measures of success in the primary. None is clearly better than any other, but together they address the problem. All three are measures of delegate share, as follows:

- **Fat Lady Share.** This is the total of delegates won at the point at which "the fat lady sings" to indicate that a clear victor has emerged and active campaigning ceases. The 1980 and 1984 Democratic nominations were fought until the last primary, but in other years the "fat lady" has sung before the last scheduled primary, and in recent years she has often sung after only half or fewer of the scheduled contests. Fat Lady Share is close to candidates' share of votes in contested primaries but, for reasons given above, not quite the same.
- **Best Share of Delegates.** The notion of "best share" arises as follows. Some candidates begin to win delegates, reach a high-water mark, but then falter and drop out of the contest before the convention. When this happens, their delegates usually move to another candidate. Ignoring the high-water mark of dropouts would understate the strength of challengers and overstate the margin of victory of the eventual winner. It would also tend to bias the results in favor of our hypothesis of party influence, because the delegates of withdrawn candidates mainly migrate to the candidate of the party insiders. Hence, we permit candidates who drop out of the race to keep the delegates they would have taken to the convention had they stuck it out. But the candidates who do get to the convention are credited with all the delegates they have earned, including those freed up by dropouts. This results in some double-counting of delegates, and therefore percentages do not add up to 100 percent.
- **Final Delegate Share.** The actual shares of delegates each candidate controls at the party convention.

To sort out the relative importance of polls, endorsements, media coverage, and fund-raising in predicting the outcome of the state primaries, we ran a multiple regression. This technique shows the effect of each causal factor, controlling for the contemporaneous effects of the others. To ease comparability, all variables are scored as a candidate's percentage share of support.[2] Thus, for example, Media share is the candidate's percentage share of all media coverage in the last quarter of the invisible primary. Poll share is the share of support in the last pre-Iowa national polls. Technical details appear in the appendix to the chapter.

Table 9.1 summarizes the results, averaged over the Fat Lady, Fair Share, and Final Share measures in a straightforward way. We report separately for our two endorsement measures, Weighted endorsement share and Out-of-group endorsement share. Without going into detail that is available in simple form in the table, we summarize the results as follows. Endorsement share appears to be the most important predictor of success in

Table 9.1: Predictors of success in winning delegates in state primaries (based on all candidates, 1980 to 2004)

	Using weighted endorsements	Using out-of-group endorsements
For each **10 percentage point** increase in a candidate's share of support in a **poll** taken just before the first voter contest in Iowa, his/her share of delegates won in the primaries	Goes up 8.1%	Goes up 2.5%
For each **10 percentage point** increase in a candidate's share of **endorsements** just before the first voter contest in Iowa, his/her share of delegates won in the primaries	Goes up 11.2%	Goes up 8.1%
For each **10 percentage point** increase in a candidate's share of campaign **funds** raised before the first voter contest in Iowa, his/her share of delegates won in the primaries	Goes up 2.4%	Goes up 1.7%
For each **10 percentage point** increase in a candidate's share of **media coverage** in the last quarter of the invisible primary, his/her share of delegates won in the primaries	Goes up 2.2%	Goes down 0.3%

See tables 9A.1 and 9A.3 for more details.

the primaries, with polls next. Media and money matter less and perhaps have no direct effect at all.

Given the small size of the data set, it is impossible to be sure whether apparent differences in the predictive impact of any two variables are real differences. Because there is uncertainty in the estimate of each individual impact, differences between impacts might be simply chance error. However, one variable does outperform others by a margin that is too big to be easily due to chance error. This variable is out-of-group endorsements. Its impact is bigger than that of any other individual variable in its column, including Polls.

These results, which amount to a replication of Steger's results, are an important step in understanding presidential nominations. However, they do not show quite as much as they might at first seem to show. In particular, they do not truly demonstrate the relative importance of the four variables in the nomination process. The reason, as Steger noted in his original paper, is the existence of mutual causation among endorsements, money, and poll support: "A major question for future research involves unraveling the causal arrows between these factors. Do candidates like Bob Dole receive more endorsements because they have higher polling numbers and more money, or do the endorsements come first? . . . Future research will need to focus more on the temporal sequencing between endorsements and fund-raising, media-coverage, and poll position" (2000, 17).

As the reader should recall, we devoted chapter 8 to precisely this problem of the temporal sequence of cause and effect in the invisible primary. In consequence, we are now in a position to build mutual causation among polls, money, media, and endorsements into our analysis of voting in the state primaries, as Steger suggests. In so doing, we endeavor to take the study of primary voting its next logical step forward.

Our approach to mutual causation is summarized in the two schematic drawings in figure 9.1. Assume, for illustrative purposes, that the invisible primary is driven by two factors, media coverage and endorsements, that each factor may cause the other, and that these two factors jointly determine the outcome of the voter primaries at the end of the invisible primary. Many patterns of influence are possible, but we begin by asking the reader to study the diagram shown in the top panel of figure 9.1.

The numbers in the top panel convey the idea that Media at Time 1 (Media$_{t=1}$) entirely causes both Media at Time 2 (Media$_{t=2}$) and Endorsements at Time 2 (Endorsements$_{t=2}$). Media$_{t=2}$ and Endorsements$_{t=2}$ then have roughly equal impact on Delegates in the state primaries. Given this causal story, it could be narrowly correct to say that media share and endorsements have an equal impact on delegate share in the primaries—but also misleading. It would be misleading because both Media$_{t=2}$ and Endorsements$_{t=2}$ have both been wholly caused by Media$_{t=1}$. And given this, it makes more sense to say that Media$_{t=1}$ is the entire cause of Delegates.

Now consider a slight change in the causal story, as shown in the bottom panel of figure 9.1. In this panel, Media$_{t=1}$ is still the dominant variable. It causes all of Media$_{t=2}$ and most of Endorsements$_{t=2}$. However, Endorsements$_{t=1}$ now has some importance, because it can now cause Endorsements$_{t=2}$, which can in turn cause Delegates. Given the numbers in the figure, one can calculate the effect of Endorsements$_{t=1}$ on Delegates as follows: Endorsements$_{t=1}$ causes one-fourth of Endorsements$_{t=2}$, which in turn causes half of Delegates; therefore, Endorsements$_{t=1}$ causes one-eighth of Delegate Share. (Numerically, $1/4 \times 1/2 = 1/8$. The effect of Media$_{t=1}$ may be calculated as $1 \times 1/2 + 3/4 \times 1/2 = 7/8$.)

Our analysis will take the approach in the lower panel. That is, we will trace the influence of variables from the beginning to the end of the invisible

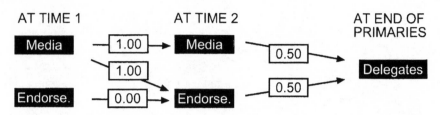

Media at time 1 essentially causes all measurable change in delegates, in part through endorsements.

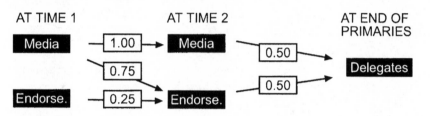

Media at time 1 is responsible for 1.00 × 0.50 + 0.75 × 0.50 = 0.875 change in delegates, while Endorsements at time 1 are responsible for 0.25 × 0.50 = 0.125.

Fig. 9.1. Hypothetical paths among variables.

primary, and from the end of the invisible primary into the state primaries and caucuses. The main difference from the above diagrams is that we will have four variables—Media, Endorsements, Polls, and Funds—rather than just two. These variables are the ones described earlier in this chapter: Measurements of each candidate's percentage share of the *Time* and *Newsweek* coverage, endorsements by party insiders, support as expressed in polls, and campaign donations in his or her contest. More variables complicate the analysis without changing its basic logic. By taking into account how all four variables mutually influence one another during the invisible primary, we can obtain an unbiased estimate of the effect of each variable on delegate share at the end of the process.

Our estimates of these effects are shown in figure 9.2. (Technical details may be found in the appendix to this chapter.) To understand the figure, start with Endorsements$_{t=1}$ on the left. The path from Endorsements$_{t=1}$ to Endorsements$_{t=2}$ is .88. This means that, controlling for the effect of the other variables, each 1 percentage point share of endorsements in the first period (Endorsements$_{t=1}$) causes a gain of .88 percentage points of endorsement in the second period (Endorsements$_{t=2}$).[3] Each 1 percentage point share of Endorsements$_{t=2}$ is then associated with a gain of 1.12 percentage points of delegate share in the state primaries and caucus. From these two

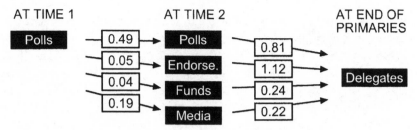

Thus, the effect of a 10 percentage point change in Polls at time 1 is equivalent* to:
$0.10 \times (0.49 \times 0.81 + 0.05 \times 1.12 + 0.04 \times 0.24 + 0.19 \times 0.22) = 0.05$.

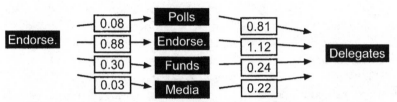

Thus, the effect of a 10 percentage point change in Endorsements at time 1 is equivalent* to:
$0.10 \times (0.08 \times 0.81 + 0.88 \times 1.12 + 0.30 \times 0.24 + 0.03 \times 0.22) = 0.11$.

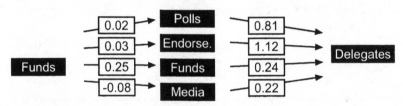

Thus, the effect of a 10 percentage point change in Funds at time 1 is equivalent* to:
$0.10 \times (0.02 \times 0.81 + 0.03 \times 1.12 + 0.25 \times 0.24 - 0.08 \times 0.22) = 0.01$.

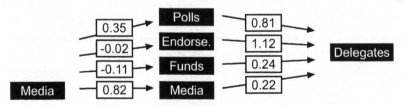

Thus, the effect of a 10 percentage point change in Media at time 1 is equivalent* to:
$0.10 \times (0.35 \times 0.81 - 0.02 \times 1.12 - 0.11 \times 0.24 + 0.82 \times 0.22) = 0.04$.

*The results in table 9.2 use a slightly more complicated method to account for estimation error. For details, see the appendix to chap. 9.

Fig. 9.2. Paths from early variables to delegates.

numbers, one can calculate that a 1 point increase in endorsements early in the invisible primary leads to an additional .99 points of delegate share at the end (.88 × 1.12 = .99). Critically, this estimate is not confounded by the problem of mutual causation by other variables, because those effects have all been accounted for.

But this path—Endorsements$_{t=1}$ → Endorsements$_{t=2}$ → Delegates—is only one of four paths by which early endorsements can affect delegate share. Early endorsements can also affect later polls, later fund-raising, and later media coverage—and each of these can in turn affect delegates won in the state contests. To get the total effect of endorsements early in the invisible primary, one must sum the effects from each of the four paths. Table 9.2 presents these summaries for the Endorsements$_{t=1}$ and for each of the other variables.

This table summarizes the causal importance of polls, endorsements, media share, and fund-raising on delegates won in the state primaries and caucuses. As such, it summarizes the evidence for one of the major arguments of this book. The first column shows results for our simple weighted endorsement variable; the second column shows results for the breadth-weighted endorsement variable.

As can be seen, the effect of endorsements is much larger than the effects of any other variable and the only overall effect that is statistically significant. This gives strong support to our claim that, from the start of the invisible primary to the selection of delegates in the state primaries and caucuses, presidential nominations are dominated by party insiders.

Though consistent with our theoretical position, these results still require careful interpretation. The statistical results do not, first of all, bear directly on our argument that parties themselves are dominated by intense policy demanders. In particular, they do not show which of several kinds of insider actors within the party have the most influence on nominations.[4] The results bear only on the narrower argument of whether parties or candidate-centered factors dominate presidential nominations. Our statistical results also do not show that party insiders strictly determine each winner. They demonstrate only relative success within the whole set of sixty-five candidates. And finally, these results are contingent on whether party members can agree. If they do not agree, as they did not in 2004, they do not determine the winner.[5] Altogether, then, the statistical results say: Whatever exactly a party is, the party and not individually powerful candidates decide nominations—but only if the party can make up its collective mind. This conclusion feeds our general argument even though it does not address all parts of it.

Table 9.2: Effect of early changes on the end of the process

	Using weighted endorsements	Using weighted out-of-group endorsements
Polls	0.05	0.00
	(0.03)	(0.02)
Endorsements	0.11	0.11
	(0.05)	(0.05)
Funds	0.01	0.01
	(0.04)	(0.04)
Media	0.04	−0.03
	(0.06)	(0.05)

Cells are the effect of a 0.10 change in one variable at the beginning of the process on delegates at the end.

The standard deviation of the estimated effect is in parentheses.

Another subtlety: These statistical results also do not show, as they may seem on the surface to show, that media coverage, fund-raising, and public support in national polls have no importance in presidential nominations. As we discuss below, these factors do sometimes make a difference in state-level contests, especially Iowa and New Hampshire. They just do not have an independent impact on the overall process, once we account for endorsements. A good illustration is Steve Forbes in 2000. Spending $43 million of his personal fortune, he hired campaign staff, gave speeches, took out ads on television, and got a fair amount of media coverage. But he got no significant number of political endorsements, and, when citizens began to vote, he didn't get many votes either. He did well enough in Iowa, where he campaigned the hardest and spent the most money, but he dropped like a stone in later races. Forbes is an extreme case, but in many cycles there are one or two candidates who manage to score well on polls, media, or money but not on endorsements, and, like Forbes, they tend to fizzle after the first voter primaries and caucuses.

It would be useful at this point to describe an example of a candidate who won the bulk of insider endorsements but raised no money, got no media coverage, and stayed low in the polls. But there is no such example and probably never will be. Endorsement leaders always have the resources they need to compete; candidates with few endorsements sometimes also have resources, but it does them little overall good in the state contests.[6]

We will discuss further what these results mean at the end of the chapter, but these initial caveats were too important to wait. We turn now to the results of individual state primaries and caucuses to get a better idea of how exactly party endorsements do and do not matter.

First Contests in Iowa and New Hampshire

A limitation of our analysis so far is that it focuses on the effect of national endorsements on the national contest for nomination. But, strictly speaking, there is no national contest. There is only a series of state-level primaries and caucuses. Insofar as endorsements matter, they must matter to voters in state contests.

The question of how exactly endorsements influence voters in state primaries is one we can answer only to a limited extent. The reason is a lack of reliable measures of endorsements at the state level. In the contests of the 1980s, there are several cases in which we have found an average of only three or four public endorsements per state and in some individual states none at all. This could reflect reality, but more likely it reflects limitations in electronically searchable sources. Our endorsement counts are ample in areas covered by national or strong regional newspapers, but suspiciously low in southern, western, and rural states.

The explosion of Internet data sources in the 1990s provides us with much better data from 1996 on. For these years, we have an average of forty endorsements per state (though still skewed toward Iowa and New Hampshire). Even so, we have reason to be suspicious of the results.[7] And in the recent contests we run into another problem: most of the contests entail only a few weeks of primary and caucus competition, sometimes only six or seven (Norrander 1996). This leaves us too few contests and time periods for reliable estimation.

There is, however, one set of contests for which our sources provide us with adequate data for all contests from 1980 to 2004, namely, the first-in-the-nation Iowa caucuses and the New Hampshire primary. This happy situation is partly due to the importance of these contests and the long period in which political reporters have relatively little else to cover.

We begin with Iowa. As shown in figure 9.3, the relationship between endorsements by Iowa insiders and success in the Iowa caucuses is a strong one. The only candidate to break the trend in the data is George H. W. Bush in 1980, whose principal opponent was national front-runner Ronald Reagan. Bush beat Reagan 33 percent to 27 percent in Iowa in 1980, but, as the figure shows, Bush's margin on the vote was much less than his advantage in state endorsements. Figure 9.3 thus shows both the strong overall influence of state endorsements (Bush beats Reagan despite Reagan's strengths

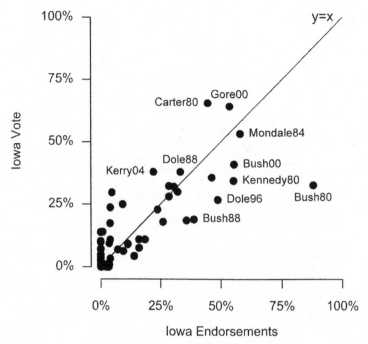

Fig. 9.3. Iowa vote versus endorsements. Iowa Endorsements is the percentage of all politi-cally weighted endorsements by Iowa partisans for each candidate in the year prior to the primaries, up to the day before the caucus.

as a national candidate) and the limits of state endorsements (Reagan does well despite Bush's huge advantage in local endorsements).

Figure 9.3, however, presents the effect of only one variable, Iowa en-dorsements. If we have learned anything at this point in our analysis, it is that multiple factors may affect the outcome of primary races and must be taken into account in analyzing them. We therefore ran a regression that controls for the effects of spending, national media coverage at the end of the invisible primary, national poll results, and national endorsements. This is a strong set of control variables, but the effects of local endorse-ments continued to have large and statistically significant effects. (See table 9A.7.) Most notably, state endorsements give about 17 points of vote share to Mondale in 1984, 16 points each to Bush and Gore in 2000, and a whop-ping 27 points to Bush the elder in 1980.[8]

The effect of Iowa endorsements—most made months before the con-test—is so strong that it holds up even after controlling for an Iowa state poll taken just before the balloting. This is somewhat surprising, because

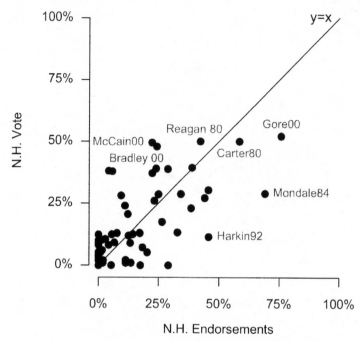

Fig. 9.4. New Hampshire vote versus endorsements. N.H. Endorsements is the percentage of all politically weighted endorsements by New Hampshire partisans for each candidate in the year prior to the primaries, up to the day before the New Hampshire primary.

one might expect endorsements to affect voting only through their effect on candidate support in polls. But in Iowa, where unusual efforts are needed to get voters to participate in caucuses, the candidate with the most local endorsements—and hence the greatest organizational ability to mobilize voters—has an advantage even after taking into account standing in the state polls.

The relationship between endorsements and vote share is weaker in New Hampshire than in Iowa, as shown above in figure 9.4. It is still statistically significant as a bivariate relationship ($t = 4.97$), but lapses to nonsignificance ($t = 1.07$) when Iowa vote share is added as a control variable (see table 9A.8 for more models). Endorsements, however, may still matter. Even by the weaker of these estimates, state-level endorsements netted Gore 12 points and Bush 7 points in New Hampshire in 2000.

These findings take our argument a step forward: It is not simply national endorsements that matter in the presidential primaries, but the endorsements of local officials, activists, and interest-group leaders in Iowa and New Hampshire. These local endorsements shape the results of the first state contests, which, as we shall see below, then shape the results of everything that follows.

Influence of Early Contests

Candidates, pundits, and scholars all agree that the first contests in Iowa and New Hampshire shape the primaries that follow. "The importance of the first-in-nation contests is difficult to underestimate," write William Crotty and John S. Jackson III in a typical assessment (Crotty and Jackson 2001, 16). Many analysts attribute this importance to media overkill. Referring to media coverage of the New Hampshire primary, Donald R. Matthews maintains that "the consequences of media infatuation . . . are obvious—'winners' of the contest receive far more favorable publicity and a far greater boost toward the Presidency than 'winners' of other primaries" (1978, 65). "Were it not for the media," David Paletz and Robert Entman write, "The Iowa caucuses and the New Hampshire primary would be about as relevant to the presidential nomination as opening-day baseball scores are to a pennant race" (cited in Buell 2000, 100).

Attributing so much influence to the media may itself involve an element of overkill. As James Ceaser has noted, "There is simply no way of avoiding the fact that the first tests are bound to be of greater interest, not only to the public but also to the candidates" (1982, 62), and to campaign donors too, as several studies have shown (Hinckley and Green 1996; Hanson 2000; Mutz 1995; Damore 1997). The whole political system—pundits, polls, donors, and the media—responds massively to the first contests, moving toward the winners and away from the losers. Thus, as Polsby, Wildavsky, and Hopkins write, "Candidates ignore Iowa and New Hampshire at their peril. . . . Iowa results, plus media spin, structure the alternatives for the New Hampshire primary. These two events together, plus media spin, structure alternatives for everything that follows" (2007, 111).

This raises the question: Does the influence of the invisible primary—and of the party insiders who dominate it—expire once the results of the Iowa and New Hampshire contest have come in? Can party insiders influence the early contests and nothing else?

The answer to both questions is no. If a measure of candidate success in Iowa and New Hampshire (Early Contests) is added to a standard regression model, we get the results shown in table 9.3. As can be seen, success in Iowa and New Hampshire has a substantial effect on later contests, but insider endorsements continue to have a large impact over and above that

Table 9.3: Predictors of success in winning delegates in state primaries (based on all candidates 1980 to 2004)

	Using weighted endorsements
For each **10 percentage point** increase in a candidate's share of support in a **poll** taken just before the first voter contest in Iowa, his/her share of delegates won in the primaries	Goes up 6.1%
For each **10 percentage point** increase in a candidate's share of **endorsements** just before the first voter contest in Iowa, his/her share of delegates won in the primaries	Goes up 8.2%
For each **10 percentage point** increase in a candidate's share of campaign **funds** raised before the first voter contest in Iowa, his/her share of delegates won in the primaries:	Goes down 3.7%
For each **10 percentage point** increase in a candidate's share of **media** coverage raised before the first voter contest in Iowa, his/her share of delegates won in the primaries	Goes up 1.0%
For each **10 percentage point** increase in a candidate's share of **early contest** votes, his/her share of delegates won in the primaries	Goes up 8.0%

See table 9A.9 for more details.

of the early contests.[9] (Technical details of the estimate may be found in the appendix to this chapter.)

Why Do Endorsements Matter?

It is easier to demonstrate that endorsements affect presidential primaries than to show how exactly they matter. In a sense, it doesn't matter why endorsements matter, as long as we are sure they really do. Still it would be useful to understand the mechanisms by which endorsements operate. In this section, we consider several possibilities.

Endorsements as Campaign Resources

Many endorsements are commitments by a party actor of specific campaign resources. The resources may consist of volunteer labor for phone banks, neighborhood canvassing, rallies, or the distribution of literature. Unions in the Democratic Party and churches in the Republican Party are especially important as sources of volunteers. Groups may help mobilize other citizens in support of the favored candidate, mobilize their own members, or both. The activities of groups do not generally count against campaign spending limits and can sway voters. Governors, some senators, and some local politicians also possess personal organizations they can throw into action behind the candidate of their choice.

Perhaps the best extant study of group influence in a nomination contest is "Do Endorsements Matter? Group Influences in the 1984 Democratic Caucuses," by Ronald Rapoport, Walter Stone, and Alan Abramowitz (1991). The answer to their question is yes, and by quite a lot. In the 1984 contest, the AFL-CIO and related unions, two teacher unions, and the National Organization for Women endorsed Mondale. The authors' first finding was that 52 percent of the caucus attendees in the states they studied were members of one of the endorsing groups. Although they do not provide a population baseline against which to compare this figure, it is clear that members of groups supporting Mondale were substantially overrepresented at the caucuses. The net effect of this overrepresentation, according to the study, was 6 percent more support than Mondale would otherwise have received. This is not a small number. For example, Mondale beat Hart in the Virginia caucuses by a margin of 29 percent to 17 percent. If the group support had gone to Hart instead, the result would have been a 23 to 23 tie.

The 6 percent figure is, moreover, probably an underestimate. Besides mobilizing their own members to attend caucuses, the AFL-CIO and the teachers tried to mobilize nongroup voters. It is plausible to believe this effort netted another 2 or 3 percent support for Mondale. If so, the endorsements of these three groups might have been worth 8 or 9 percentage points to Mondale.

We hasten to add, however, that such large effects are atypical. Unions cannot always agree on a single choice, as they mainly did in 1984, and groups probably cannot have as much impact in primaries as they do in caucuses. Thus, even in Iowa, where organizational support may matter as much as in any state, it can be hard to discern its impact, as Barbara Trish found in a study of the 1996 Iowa caucuses. "[Bob] Dole was considered the candidate of choice for the state GOP establishment," she wrote. Dole did narrowly win in Iowa, but his strength was not concentrated in areas of Republican organizational strength.[10] This and other unexpected findings led Trish to conclude that "it is difficult to determine conclusively whether organization . . . prevailed in the 1996 Iowa Caucus outcome" (Trish 1999, 881, 894).

No academic study has been published on the effect of political organization in the 2004 contest among Dean, Gephardt, Edwards, and Kerry in
the Iowa caucuses, but here is how a *New York Times* reporter saw it:

> Dr. Dean has run as the quintessential political outsider, and his campaign
> here has by far the most workers from outside Iowa. Every weekend since
> Christmas, fresh batches of volunteers have arrived from as far away as Texas,
> Virginia and Mississippi. They get fluorescent orange knit hats, cellphones,
> purple identification wristbands and 45 minutes of training in the nuts-and-
> bolts of caucus procedure, then are sent out to stump as part of what they call
> the Iowa Perfect Storm. . . .
>
> Mr. Gephardt, too, is relying on out-of-state help, but mostly in the form
> of top-flight union organizers with long experience in past campaigns in Iowa
> and around the country, including the political directors of the United Steel-
> workers of America and the International Brotherhood of Teamsters, who
> organize their troops in satiny windbreakers at a "shape-up" each morning, as
> if they were assigning work on a job site. . . .
>
> Neither Mr. Edwards nor Mr. Kerry can claim the same scale of ground
> operation. (Purdum 2004, 1)

Despite their disadvantage, Kerry and Edwards finished well ahead of the
two candidates with the commanding organizations. When, in particular,
Dean got into trouble in Iowa, his organization could not bail him out. Perhaps this was because it was run by out-of-state campaigners. But Iowa and
New Hampshire often attract out-of-state workers. Whatever the reason,
we note that the biggest 2004 ground operations in Iowa are another case
of organization failing to produce much impact.

If Rapoport, Stone, and Abramowitz (1991) give a high-side estimate
of organizational impact, the estimates from 1996 and 2004 are probably
on the low side. The truth, however, may not lie in the middle, but in both
studies together: organizational impacts are sometimes big and sometimes
small—and always potentially big enough to care about. The only really
safe assessment, however, is that more systematic study is needed.

Even the most sophisticated study may have difficulty capturing all of
the ways organization support can affect an election. Consider the following account by Jeff Smith, an activist in the Bradley campaign, on how Al
Gore's union support in Iowa undermined the Bradley 2000 campaign:

> The nat'l media was following BB and so we were excited to have a good
> event—approx 100 rank-and-file [union members] were expected to attend.
> Unfortunately the state chapter got wind of the event and the UAW was one

of the most vehemently pro-Gore blocs of the AFL-CIO in Iowa. . . . State chapter sent hundreds of brawny union guys in black leather jackets from all over South East Iowa to stand outside the UAW hall holding Gore placards and chanting moronic Gore slogan "Stay and Fight," which was an implicit cut at BB for "quitting" the Senate when Republicans took over. This forced BB to "run a gauntlet" of approx 400 Gore guys in order to get into the union hall, and with nat'l media there the visual was looking grim: BB tries to show labor support but there's 4 times more Gore support than BB support at BB's own event.

Postscript: Advance guy called me in the van to tell me what situation was, and advised me to tell the van driver to go around back and have BB enter thru back entrance, or possibly even reschedule the event for later that day. I conferred w/ national staff, state director, and BB about what to do. BB replied, "Are you kidding? We'll drive right up front like we planned to do and I'll deal with it." Everyone advised against that but BB was adamant. So we went and BB got out of the van and all the people were chanting "1–2–3–4 We want Al Gore!" BB walks up to the first guy in line who is about 6'5" and looks him in the eye. He puts his hand out and says, "Hi, I'm Bill Bradley. How you doin?" The guy stops yelling, puts down his sign, and says, "Mr Bradley, honor to meet you. Always been a fan, ever since the Knick days. Good luck." Slowly the chants faded, most of the Gore signs went down, and BB walked up and shook all their hands. (personal communication)

Thus, the candidate managed to hold his ground and battle the Gore forces to no worse than a draw. Not so, however, at the traditional Jefferson-Jackson banquet at which both candidates were to speak. From Smith's vantage as a Bradley backer, this is how it came out:

There were approx 1600 seats so the party gives approx 300 seats to Gore to distribute, 500 seats to the AFL-CIO, 300 to us and 500 to the Democratic Party. Well of course that means 1300 for them and 300 for us. Moreover all the Gore, union, and Dem Party tables were seated up front where C-SPAN would catch them and where they would make most visible noise for their preferred candidate. Our campaign was so pissed, and had so many support- ers who couldn't get seats, that we had an alternative event across the street, which merited little coverage compared to the J-J Dinner.

Most voters in the Iowa caucuses were probably never aware of these gue- rilla struggles for their attention and support. Yet in the end Iowans gave Gore a big victory over Bradley in 2000, probably in part because of Gore's stronger campaign organization.

Endorsements as Cues to Voters

Endorsements may also be viewed as persuasive messages targeted at individual voters who are likely to be receptive to those messages. Many studies demonstrate the persuasive impact of endorsements on voters in various electoral contexts. The most relevant concern endorsements made by state party conventions ahead of primaries for state office. According to two studies, official party endorsements nearly always carry the day in state primaries (McNitt 1980; Kunkel 1988).[11] But nominations for state office are quite different than for the presidency, and no one has examined the effect of endorsements in presidential primaries. In this section, we present three kinds of evidence on this point, one weakly supportive of the importance of endorsements and the other two strongly supportive. We preface this evidence with a brief consideration of the nature of voter participation in the primaries.

Studies of voting in presidential primaries agree on three important points. The first is that presidential nominations do not usually excite widespread voter interest. One indication is the turnout rate in primaries and caucuses, as shown in the table below. Even in the Iowa caucuses and the New Hampshire primary, where the candidates campaign intensely and the results have great influence on the overall process, turnout is much below that in the fall election. One can understand the low figures in Iowa, where participation in a caucus can take two hours or more, but New Hampshire's 44 percent turnout in 2000 is hard to understand except in terms of lack of engagement. The South Carolina primary, at twenty percent turnout in that year, was another early, important contest with an abysmal level of voter involvement.

The second point is that voters—particularly voters in the critical early contests—often have relatively little information about the candidates among whom they choose (Patterson 1980; Keeter and Zukin 1983). The reason, as many scholars emphasize, is the poor quality of media coverage, which covers leading candidates much more than others and stresses, for all candidates, their chances of winning more than the substance of their positions on issues (Patterson 1980; Brady and Johnston 1987; Keeter and Zukin 1983). As Brady and Johnston conclude, "The real problem with primaries is . . . [citizens] learn too slowly about every aspect of the candidates except their viability. And one of the major reasons that citizens learn quickly about viability is the enormous emphasis placed on the horse race by the media, especially right after the Iowa caucuses and the New Hampshire primary" (184).

The third point of agreement among scholars is the importance of voter expectations about which candidate is likely to win. Issues and personal

Table 9.4: Voter turnout rates in primaries and caucuses in 2000

	Primary election or caucus (%)	General election (%)
Arizona	12.7	45.6
California	40.3	55.7
Connecticut	15.6	61.9
Delaware	7.6	59.0
Georgia	17.7	45.8
Iowa	6.8	63.1
Maryland	25.2	55.5
Missouri	18.6	58.2
New Hampshire	44.4	63.9
South Carolina	20.2	47.0

Source: United States Election Project, George Mason University.

characteristics of the candidate matter, but political viability appears to matter about as much. Voters' emphasis on viability may reflect media emphasis on horserace coverage, as suggested by the findings of Brady and Johnston; a psychological wish or need, as theorized by Bartels (1988); expected utility, as emphasized by Abramowitz (1989); or a sophisticated calculation about the most rational use of one's vote, as emphasized by Abramson, Aldrich, Paolino, and Rohde (1992).

All of which leads us to reason as follows: An electorate that is usually not very interested, not very well informed, and attracted to candidates in significant part because they are doing well is probably an electorate open to suggestion about whom to support. If, as we know to be the case, many primary and caucus voters are also strong partisans, what they want in a candidate may be exactly what party insiders want: someone who can unite the party and win in November. Supporting the candidate with the most insider endorsements, who is also likely to be widely viewed as the most viable candidate, may be taken by these voters as a low-cost and reasonable course of action. If so, the influence of informal party endorsements in a presidential primary may be as important as formal party endorsements in primaries for state offices.

With this argument in mind, we turn to a consideration of several ways in which endorsements may act as a cue to voters—the effect of state-level endorsements on state voters, the effect of national party endorsements on party voters, and the effect of group endorsements on voters in that group.

State-Level Endorsement Effects. We have already tested endorsement effects within two particular states, Iowa and New Hampshire. Hence we
are certain that some state-level endorsements are important—indeed,
extremely important. In this section, we will examine state-level endorsements; within all states at once. To do this, we pool all primaries in a given
year and make estimates of the effect of state endorsements and other
factors within each nomination.[12] Thus, for example, we will look at the
effect of state-by-state variation in endorsements in the twenty-two contested primaries and caucuses in the Democratic contest of 2004. Then
we shall do the same for other years. We do not have sufficient density
of endorsements at the state level for the early 1980s, so we shall look at
state-level endorsement effects only from 1988 to 2004.[13]

The results, which we report in a separate technical paper, are mixed.[14]
The average net endorsement effect for the advantaged candidate was about
3 percentage points per state, but its size varied greatly, depending on the
balance of endorsements in the given state. In most years, we found a handful of states—usually states having important contests—in which the favored candidate gained an extra 5, 10, or 20 percentage points of the vote
from endorsements. In 1992, for example, Bill Clinton gained an estimated
19 points in New York from endorsements; in 1996, Bob Dole gained 13
points in the pivotal South Carolina primary. But there were many states
in which no candidate gained much advantage, because—at least in our
data—no candidate had many more endorsements than another.

Thus, while we find clear evidence of endorsement effects across a
range of cases, we do not find consistently large effects. The biggest overall
effect occurs in the 1992 Democratic race, in which endorsements netted
Clinton an average of 6 percent of the delegate share per state, compared
to his expected share if he had no endorsements. This average effect, while
important, cannot explain why Clinton won 45 percent of all delegates in
the contested primaries in 1992, while former Senator Paul Tsongas, who
had many fewer endorsements than Clinton, won only 25 percent.[15] Nor
can state-level effects explain overall results in other years.[16]

These results do not support the view that endorsement effects operate
primarily through state-level officials on state-level electorates. State-level effects are probably somewhat larger than we have been able to recover from
our fallible data, and they are probably very important in Iowa, New Hampshire, South Carolina, and perhaps a few other states. But we find only
limited evidence of widespread state-level endorsement effects.

National Party Endorsements. Endorsements may also serve as a national
party cue and, as such, operate at the level of the nation rather than at the

level of individual states. If so, we should expect endorsements to influence the votes of party members more than the votes of independents.[17]

A test of this expectation is presented in table 9.5 and figure 9.5. The data show the relationship between our measure of insider endorsements (on one hand) and the preferences of partisans and independents in state primaries as measured by exit polls (on the other). The poll data, compiled by William Mayer (2007) for another purpose, are aggregated over all primaries from 1980 to 2004 for which Mayer could find reliable polls.[18] From visual examination of the data, one can see that national endorsements do a good job of explaining the votes of party members but a poor job of explaining the votes of independents. By way of statistical summary, the correlation between national pre-Iowa endorsements and votes of partisans is .77; between endorsements and the votes of independents, the correlation is .18.[19]

We view this pattern as evidence that partisan voters are taking cues from the endorsements of partisan insiders. Because the media do not report summary measures of insider endorsements, it is not clear how exactly the cue diffuses through the population. We suppose that an aura or buzz develops around the insider favorite, as millions of partisans sense that the message from party officials, activists, and interest-group leaders is that, for example, "George W. Bush is our guy in this contest." If voters can, as evidence shows, respond to expectations about who is likely to win, they should also be able to respond to national party cues. Indeed, the two messages may be, in some degree, different frames for the same information.

National party cues of this kind are at once powerful and fragile. They are powerful in that they can lead just about everyone—voters, journalists, donors, volunteers—to regard the favored candidate as not only right for the party but inevitable. And, indeed, this sense of inevitability is not incorrect: No candidate who became the clear endorsement front-runner in the period 1980 to 2004 failed to win nomination. When parties have failed to control nominations, it has been because they failed to agree on a front-runner, not because voters disregarded their cue. But the national cue is still fragile in that, if an insurgent manages to break through in the early primary states, much of the cue's effect may dissipate and the front-runner will suddenly find himself or herself in danger of defeat. This was the case for Walter Mondale in 1984, Bill Clinton in 1992, Bob Dole, and perhaps even George W. Bush in 2000, all of whom faced break-through insurgents who might have beaten them.

Group Endorsement Effects. Few can doubt that the endorsements of group leaders affect the voting behavior of their particular followers in

Table 9.5: Voting and endorsements in contested state primaries, 1980–2000

	Weighted endorsements (%)	Partisan voters (%)	Independent voters (%)
1980 Democrats			
Carter	65	55	50
Kennedy	33	38	35
1980 Republicans			
Anderson	2	18	37
Bush	28	30	30
Reagan	44	57	37
1984 Democrats			
Hart	4	34	46
Jackson	6	20	15
Mondale	55	42	28
1988 Democrats			
Dukakis	27	34	34
Gephardt	23	11	11
Gore	17	18	24
Jackson	13	33	19
1988 Republicans			
Bush	53	57	50
Dole	18	25	28
Robertson	3	12	14
1992 Democrats			
Brown	0	25	43
Clinton	65	56	36
Tsongas	2	15	21
1996 Republicans			
Alexander	6	8	15
Buchanan	2	22	26
Dole	71	54	36
Forbes	2	16	21
2000 Democrats			
Bradley	19	22	43
Gore	81	77	53
2000 Republicans			
Bush	64	64	33
McCain	11	31	60
2004 Democrats			
Clark	12	15	15
Dean	27	10	14
Edwards	10	23	32
Kerry	17	60	43

Source for voter results: Mayer 2007.

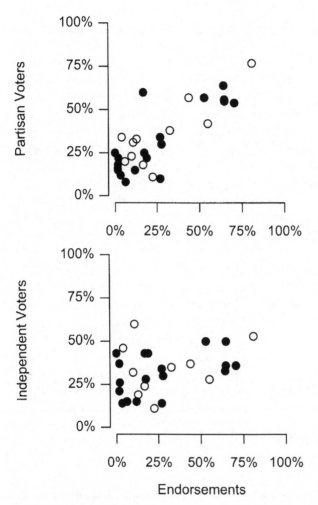

Fig. 9.5. Vote shares versus endorsements. Endorsements is the percentage of all politically weighted endorsements for each candidate in the year prior to the primaries, up to the day before the Iowa caucuses. Primary election vote shares are from Mayer 2007. Solid circles are Democrats. Open circles are Republicans.

primary elections, but such evidence as exists comes mainly from journalistic reports. Most often, these reports focus on evangelical, union, and African American leaders. The only scholarly paper of which we are aware to examine the effect of such cues on voting in primary elections is a study by Vincent L. Hutchings and LaFleur Stephens (2007), "African American Voters and the Presidential Nomination Process."

Hutchings and Stephens argue that African Americans view themselves as sharing a "linked fate" and therefore tend to vote for the candidate—

usually a Democrat—they believe will best promote group interests. The preferences of black voters must then be explained in terms of "how a particular candidate comes to be perceived as best representing black interests." As they write: "the contours of this perception are shaped to a significant degree by prominent and indigenous black leadership elements such as the black press, the black church, black organizations, and perhaps most important, salient black civil rights leaders. Thus, when trusted leaders from the black community endorse a particular candidate most black voters align themselves with that candidate" (2008, 121). Exit polls from primary voting over the period 1976 to 2004 support this view. Hutchings and Stephens note, however, that many black voters ignored the support of black leaders for Walter Mondale in 1984 and voted instead for Jesse Jackson, a nationally known African American civil rights leader.

Our endorsement data shed useful light on this case. Sixty percent of African American leaders in our data set endorsed Jackson for president in 1984, and 33 percent endorsed Mondale. In the primaries that followed, 76 percent of African American voters supported Jackson, and 19 percent were for Mondale, according to Hutchings and Stephens. These figures are usefully contrasted with 1988, when Jackson again ran for the Democratic nomination. In this contest, 91 percent of African American leaders in our data set endorsed Jackson and 3 percent supported the top white candidate, Michael Dukakis. In the primary voting that year, 91 percent of African American voters supported Jackson, versus 4 percent for Dukakis. A plausible reading of these data is that the support of African American leaders for Mondale in 1984 won him about 15 percent of the African American vote.

If 15 percent seems like a small effect, consider this: Among white voters in 1984, Mondale actually lost to his principal opponent, Gary Hart, by 43 to 45 percent; only with the help of African American voters did Mondale achieve an overall win in the exit poll results.

Limited evidence from the 2008 contest between Barack Obama and Hillary Clinton suggests an endorsement effect here as well. Although we do not have actual endorsement counts, media reports make clear that, as in 1984, a significant number of African American leaders supported the leading white candidate rather than the leading black one. In keeping with this, exit poll data after the first primaries in 2008 suggested that 78.5 percent of African American voters supported Obama, versus 17 percent who supported Clinton. Again taking figures from 1988 as the baseline, this analysis suggests that endorsements by black leaders may have helped

Clinton win about 14 percent more black voters than she would otherwise have won.[20]

Given the racial tensions that exist in the United States, the apparent ability of black leaders to swing black voters away from Obama, the first black candidate to be competitive for a major party presidential nomination, is surely a tough test of the power of group endorsements. One must suspect that the effects of endorsements by the leaders of unions and evangelical groups are at least as large.

The theoretical argument laid out by Hutchings and Stephens—that a sense of linked fate leads black voters to support for the candidate they perceive will advance group interests, and that leaders play an important but not monopoly role in shaping that perception—is quite general and may explain the primary voting behavior of other voter groups and their leaders. A problem with testing it, however, is that group endorsements may flow through group channels of communication—newsletters, radio, group assemblies—that are difficult or impossible for outsiders to observe. For example, national media reports of the South Carolina Republican primary in 2000 carried numerous statements that church leaders were supporting Bush over McCain, but our search of major local media found few specific endorsements by church leaders. Apparently, church leaders communicated with their congregations by private means.

A Fabric of Many Threads

The mechanisms by which endorsements affect outcomes are varied, but they have one thing in common: They are all ways in which partisan elites can influence an electoral process that is beyond their formal control. This process is a complicated one, with many moving parts and therefore many opportunities for elite intervention. It should not be surprising if the ways in which endorsements matter reflect that complexity.

A Note on Momentum

The notion of media-driven momentum was a mainstay of analysis of presidential nominations from the late 1970s through the 1990s. The idea, as explained in chapter 6, was that a candidate would do "better than expected" in Iowa and New Hampshire, whereupon media hype would convert early success into unstoppable momentum. According to Elaine Kamarck, an advisor to several Democratic candidates: "The cultivation of momentum is the only real strategy" available to candidates seeking a party nomination (Busch 2000, 73). Donald R. Matthews was the first to broach this argument in his 1978 essay on the "winnowing" effect of the New Hampshire primary. The concept developed into a more general argument about "momentum" in John Aldrich's *Before the Convention* (1980) and was given its canonical statement in Larry Bartels's *Presidential Primaries and the Dynamics of Public Choice* (1988).

If momentum were a strong force in presidential primaries—propelling the chance winner of an early primary to nomination—it would undermine our argument about the importance of endorsements. However, Jimmy Carter in 1976 is the only candidate who ever actually won nomination by this means, and since momentum almost but not quite lifted Gary Hart to the Democratic nomination in 1984, it has seemed a mild force. Even surprise wins in New Hampshire by insurgent candidates over established front-runners—Pat Buchanan over Bob Dole in 1996 and John McCain over George W. Bush in 2000—have failed to set off the expected wave of momentum. As we saw earlier, wins in Iowa and New Hampshire do affect races that come after, but they do not override the effects of endorsements.[21]

The most common explanation for the apparent demise of momentum turns on the combination of front-loading—that is, pushing more and more contests to the beginning of the primary schedule—and early fundraising by the candidates. As Barbara Norrander explains, "The election calendar no longer allows for momentum spawned by unexpected outcomes in Iowa and New Hampshire to be translated into money, name recognition, and future votes. The increasingly front-loaded primary and caucus calendar does not leave sufficient time to garner new resources to be used for the remainder of the nomination season" (2000, 1000). With no insurgent able to ride momentum to victory, Norrander argues that the winner is the last candidate left standing after the others have been forced out.[22] Attrition, rather than momentum, has thus become the principal dynamic of contemporary nomination contests.

The question of what killed momentum is somewhat off our main line of argument. We raise it for the sake of readers who may wonder why we have not presented a more developed treatment of momentum.[23]

Critical Discussion of Results

The question at issue in chapters 8 and 9 has been a narrow one. We have four measures of political activity in the invisible primary—polls, endorsements, fund-raising, and media coverage. These measures do not cover the whole of the invisible primary, because much of the process is truly invisible. The data cover only the period from January 1 of the year prior to the presidential election up to the Iowa caucuses. For these four measures, and for this window of time, we have asked: All else equal, how strongly does each of these variables, as measured in the first half of the invisible primary, predict shares of delegates won by candidates in the state primaries and caucuses that follow the invisible primary? The "all else equal" condition takes into account mutual influence among the four variables between the first and second half of invisible primary.

The conclusion from the statistical analysis is, as we have seen, that early endorsements in the invisible primary are the most important cause of candidate success in the state primaries and caucuses. Initial poll standing is the next biggest, and probably weaker, factor.

In this section, we ask two questions about these statistical findings: How exactly do they bear on our argument about party control of presidential nominations? And how might the findings be wrong or misleading?

The results in chapters 8 and 9 bear on whether nominations are driven by a mass-politics or candidate-centered scenario, or one in which party insiders mainly determine outcomes. We take the key idea for candidate-centered politics to be that candidates are the central actors and advance their fortunes by raising money, getting good press, and building poll support. If measures of success in these activities are the main cause of winning delegates in the state primaries and caucuses, it would be evidence that nominations are candidate-centered. Our alternative view is that nominations depend on party insiders. If, therefore, their endorsements predict outcomes independent of other measurable factors, it would be evidence of a party-centered process. Such evidence would not, however, bear on the question of who party insiders are (top party leaders or policy demanders) or how they coordinate on a choice (via the restaurant game or some other way).

Given this logic and the statistical results we have obtained, we have concluded that presidential nominations are a party-centered process. But where could this argument be wrong? The greatest point of vulnerability, in our view, lies in the thinness of the data that underlie the analysis. The data are thin in three ways. Our main analyses involve sixty-one candidates, but these candidates ran in only ten nomination contests—and ten is not a large number for making inferences about a process as complicated as presidential nominations.[24] Another data limitation is that, in our analysis of mutual causation among the four key variables, we could examine influence between only two time periods.[25] Evidence from a panel analysis having only two periods is not technically flawed, but it is also not very powerful. And finally, because insiders do not begin making endorsements until the year prior to the election, we are quite literally in the dark about what happens in the earliest stages of the process.[26]

A sensible person looking at our statistical results, then, should not feel certain she knows how presidential nominations work. Her assessment should be more like: "It appears that insider endorsements are important, but I want more evidence before I reach any conclusions about exactly how important."

We do, however, present additional evidence in chapter 7. This evidence involves the same ten nomination contests but is methodologically quite different. It uses qualitative (mostly journalistic) observations to construct sketches of the major features of each nomination. These sketches are also open to question, but some of the evidence seems strong. For example, we find it notable that, in the 2000 Republican contest, many insiders began to regard George W. Bush as front-runner as early as 1997, which was before he himself had even decided to run. The resistance of Democratic insiders to Gary Hart—a "lonely front-runner" even when he was the commanding poll front-runner for the 1988 nomination—also seems noteworthy. Qualitative evidence of this kind, showing insiders making up their own minds as quickly or as slowly as they wish, provides a useful complement to the statistical analysis and adds to confidence in it. Still, paucity of cases is a great concern—the Achilles heel of our argument.

We should perhaps also reiterate an earlier caveat. The results in this chapter do not say anything about the likelihood that party insiders will reach consensus on whom to back. They suggest only that, to the extent insiders do reach agreement, they tend to get their way.

The thinness of our data is a major concern throughout our analysis, but if we are interested in the effects of money on the nomination process, it is no longer the greatest concern. The greatest concern is that we have little confidence that official fund-raising reports by candidates accurately reflect the murky world of campaign finance and spending. One part of the problem is that candidates can raise and spend money before declaring their candidacy. This money does not count as campaign spending and yet may affect which candidates survive (Corrado and Gouvea, 2003; Goff 2004). Another is that interest groups have a variety of direct and indirect means of sponsoring television for and against candidates they care about—advertising that runs during state primary campaigns but that does not show up as part of any candidate's campaign spending. For example, the Christian Coalition, National Right to Life, and National Smokers Alliance took out ads against John McCain in the South Carolina primary of 2000. Their attack ads not only directly damaged McCain but, according to two scholars, "allowed Bush to portray himself as taking the high road" in this pivotal state primary.[27] Thus, candidates' official spending reports "are just the tip of [the] electioneering iceberg," according to John Green and Nathan Bigelow. The bulk of this spending, they add, is "submerged from easy view in the form of issue advocacy and traditional grassroots campaigning" (2002, 56–57).

Poor measurement of the flow of money in nominations is bad enough, but there is a conceptual problem as well. In the standard list of functions that candidate-centered campaigns supposedly handle for themselves, fund-raising is always at the top. The idea is that fund-raising is due to the candidate's own skill or connections. This is, we believe, only half right. It is true, on one hand, that candidates have personal networks—among home-state supporters, business relations, and members of their ethnic group or religion—that only they can tap into (Magleby and Mayer 2007, 159). But it may also be true, as we maintained in chapter 7, that a significant fraction of the money candidates raise comes from fairly stable networks of party donors.

The leading study of these networks is *Serious Money*, by Clifford Brown, Lynda Powell, and Clyde Wilcox (1995). As they describe it, fund-raising is organized hierarchically within each party. At the top are a few score professional fund-raisers[28] who organize several hundred middle-level fund-raisers, who in turn do most of the actual solicitation.

> Conventional wisdom holds that in . . . [networked fund raising] the emphasis is truly on the personal. As Ronald Brownstein explains, "For the most part . . . the decision is not whether to support Bush over Kemp or Dole . . . , but whether to reject a direct request from their friend." One wealthy individual who hosted a debt retirement fundraiser for a presidential candidate was even more explicit. He pulled the candidate aside, asked him not to make a long political speech, and added, somewhat ungraciously, "Be brief. These people aren't here for you; they are here for me. Most of them didn't even support you." (61)

How fund-raisers at the top of the pyramid decide whom to support is not clear from existing evidence. By all accounts, they want to avoid activating their personal networks in support of a loser, but this does not imply they want to lead in deciding whom their party should nominate. Indeed, the more fund-raisers care simply about being on the winning side, the more they should hang back and watch what other party actors are doing.[29] If so, much of the money that leading candidates raise should be viewed more as a party-centered resource than as a candidate-centered one.

This argument applies as well to independent contributions. While some groups contribute to their most preferred candidates, others probably have no other wish than to get on board with the candidate best able to unite their party and win in November. Thus, a likely explanation for the support for Bush over McCain by the Christian Coalition and National Right to Life in the 2000 South Carolina primary is that the two groups were going along with the party consensus for Bush. Their true preference, if they had been expressing it, would more likely have been Gary Bauer, president of the Family Research Council.

A third problem is selection bias. As noted in chapter 8, most of the candidates who enter or consider entering the race for president drop out prior to the Iowa caucuses. And the most common reason they give for dropping out is inability to raise money. Thus, what Andrew Busch and James Ceaser report of the 2000 Democratic nomination contest is entirely typical: "Numerous potential Democratic candidates considered a race against Gore, only to back out. House Minority Leader Dick Gephardt, the favorite of organized labor, left the race after the 1998 elections. Senators Paul Wellstone of Minnesota, Bob Kerrey of Nebraska and John Kerry of Massachusetts all explored candidacy, as did perennial gadfly Jesse Jackson. For most, the financial hurdle was decisive—or at least it was the excuse they offered" (2001, 62). If only candidates who can raise money stay in the race, it would make it difficult to tell the true effect of money, because all active candidates will either have money or some unusual trait that compensates for the lack of it.

But before accepting the idea that selection bias is a problem in analyzing the effects of money, let us take the example of the 2000 Democratic race a bit further. Al Gore declared his candidacy unusually early in that contest, on New Year's Eve 1998. The reason, according to journalistic accounts, was that he wanted to sign up the party's principal fund-raisers before other candidates, especially Bill Bradley, could do so. But if Gore knew that other candidates might enter the race, so did fund-raisers. Hence, if Gore rounded up most of them, it must have been because fund-raisers were prepared to support Gore over the other candidates. Our point, then, is that candidates' ability to attract campaign donations is part of the effort to attract political support more generally. Candidates with strong support from party insiders are likely to be able to raise all the money they need; candidates lacking insider support are likely to have trouble raising money and to be forced out of the race. Insofar as this leads to selection bias, it is as likely to be a bias against finding endorsement effects as against fund-raising effects.

We have, then, identified three reasons why our statistical analysis of the effects of money may be misleading. The first is poor measurement of how much money is actually spent in support of candidates, especially the endorsement leader. The second is inability to tell, for purposes of our theoretical argument, how much of the money that supports a candidate is, in reality, party money and how much is candidate-centered money. The third is selection bias. Of the three, we regard the first and second as most serious.

No one doubts that money spent to hire professional staff, put on campaign events, and buy television ads makes a difference in primary election campaigns. But how much money matters independent of the preferences of party players and party interest groups is uncertain. Our judgment, based more on qualitative than quantitative evidence, and perhaps as much on theory as on data, is that candidate-centered money matters somewhat more than it appears from our statistical evidence to matter, but not very much more. Money is more likely to flow to a political favorite than to create a favorite from scratch. In other words, fund-raising is one facet of the more general process of building political support. A useful commentary on the relationship between fund-raising and political support is offered by journalist Jeffrey Birnbaum: "When George W. Bush announced in mid-1999 that he had raised thirty-seven million dollars in increments of a thousand dollars or less and that only one third of that money came from his home state of Texas, what we learned was that he was widely accepted by Republicans across the nation as the man to beat for the nomination" (2000, 19).

We should add that campaign donations may influence what winning candidates do when they get into office, both for particular donors and for the general concerns of the classes of people who make donations. Indeed, there is evidence that it does (Bartels, forthcoming). But this is different from the effect of money on choice of candidates, all of whom are eager for campaign donations.

A final point: In evaluating the role of money, one must bear in mind the extremely uneven way in which it is spent. For example, the top three candidates in each party in 1988 spent an average of $1.16 per voter in Iowa and $2.05 per voter in New Hampshire. But in these two states, the impact of state endorsements and of candidates' own campaign activity was also great, thereby perhaps suppressing the effect of money. In the remaining contested states in 1988, where by our evidence state endorsements mattered less, average spending was only $0.21 per voter, so spending probably mattered less too. Hence, voters in the states in which the large majority of delegates is chosen may be mainly left to vote on the basis of the heavily publicized results of the early contests and the national party cue. This would add up to a large overall effect for local and national endorsements and a small effect for spending.

Finally, a few words about media influence. We have discussed two principal mechanisms by which media coverage may influence presidential nominations. The first is unequal coverage of candidates in the invisible primary, such that some are made to appear viable to voters and others hopeless (see Davis 1997). Our measure of media coverage—each candidate's percentage share of the coverage in the invisible primary—seems a straightforward way of capturing this idea, but we found that the measure had little apparent impact once endorsements and other factors were taken into account. A more focused search could perhaps find such media effects, but for now our null finding seems reasonable. The second hypothesized path of media influence is "overkill" coverage of the winners of early contests, which can build momentum for the favored candidate. Solid evidence of media-driven momentum exists for the 1976 and 1984 Democratic contests (Bartels 1988), but scholars have expressed doubt that it still occurs. Hence, we are again inclined to accept our null finding as reasonable. We do not deny that reporters sometimes influence particular contests, as when, for example, they gave heavy coverage to Edmund Muskie's tearful breakdown in the New Hampshire primary in 1972. However, examples of comparably important incidents since then are hard to think of.

Summing Up Our Argument

The statistical evidence in this chapter completes the argument of our book. Let us review that argument point by point. We promised in chapter 1 to demonstrate that party insiders—a diverse collection of officeholders, interest-groups leaders, activists, and others—have regained major influence in party nominations in the aftermath of the McGovern-Fraser Commission. In chapter 2 we made a theoretical claim that such people could be considered a political party even if officeholders were not the dominant players in the party. By way of validating our theoretical view, we argued in chapter 3 that the most important parties in American history—the Federalists, the Jeffersonian Republicans, the Jacksonian Democrats, and the antislavery Republicans—were founded more by policy-motivated activists than by officeholders acting in response to electoral or career incentives. In chapters 4 and 5, we argued that, despite the decline of the national party convention as a venue of decision-making and the rise of "amateur" partisans, the Democratic and Republican parties remained in control of their nominations down to the end of the prereform period. In chapter 6, we argued that the parties, especially the Democrats, lost control of the presidential nomination process in the 1970s, but we laid out the first evidence that they regained much influence in the 1980s. In chapter 7, we sketched the history of each nomination in the period of resurgent presidential parties to show that party insiders were deciding for themselves whom to nominate and not simply acquiescing to the strongest candidate. Approaching the problem with quantitative evidence, chapter 8 presented evidence that insider decisions on whom to support do not reflect simply the influence of polls, media, or fund-raisers, but represent the autonomous judgments of a relatively small world of party members. Finally, we argue in the present chapter that party support is the most important influence on the outcomes of the voter primaries and caucuses. The reason voters go along with endorsements is not completely clear, but evidence is consistent with the idea that many partisan voters do not have strong feelings of their own and therefore take the recommendations of party leaders.

APPENDIX TO CHAPTER 9
MODELS OF DELEGATE SHARE

Table 9.1 in the chapter shows the relationship of variables from the invisible primary to the primary outcome of interest—the share of delegates to the convention at which the presidential nomination is made. Table 9A.1 in this appendix shows the full models that table 9.1 is based on. As noted in the text, we use three different measures of the dependent variable. They are substantially similar, but each has theoretical justification. Fortunately, the results are robust to which measure we use, and in the text of the chapter, the results we report are the averages of effects from the three different versions of the dependent variable.

The results in table 9.1 show the effects of four variables measured at $t = 2$ on a dependent variable measured at $t = 3$. However, the estimation of each of these $t = 2$ effects includes control variables from $t = 1$. This estimation technique is less familiar than perhaps it should be and therefore requires explanation. Following an example by King (1991), we motivate our estimation approach as follows. Suppose that we wish to explain variation in public opinion on a measure of energy conservation across the fifty American states. Suppose also that we have two independent variables, a measure of the availability of gasoline in the state (Availability) and a mea-

Table 9A.1: Estimated effects of invisible primary on delegates

	Effect of polls			
	Final delegate share	Fat Lady delegate share	Best delegate share	Average reported in chap. 9
Polls	**0.82**	**0.79**	**0.82**	**0.81**
	(0.34)	**(0.22)**	**(0.35)**	**(0.30)**
	2.41	*3.59*	*2.37*	*2.79*
Endorsements	0.96	0.68	0.98	
(weighted), first half	(0.31)	(0.32)	(0.31)	
	3.05	*2.14*	*3.18*	
Funds, first half	0.09	0.20	0.09	
	(0.24)	(0.17)	(0.24)	
	0.39	*1.17*	*0.38*	
Media, first half	−0.65	−0.63	−0.67	
	(0.37)	(0.39)	(0.38)	
	−1.77	*−1.62*	*−1.77*	
1/Number of candidates	−0.22	−0.06	−0.22	
	(0.21)	(0.14)	(0.21)	
	−1.07	*−0.42*	*−1.06*	
Constant	0.00	0.00	0.01	
	(0.00)	(0.00)	(0.00)	
	0.82	*1.17*	*1.52*	
N	61	61	61	
Adjusted R-squared	71%	70%	72%	
Root MSE	0.14	0.12	0.14	

Variable of interest in bold.
Coefficient in roman.
Standard error in parentheses.
t-ratio for null hypotheses that $\beta = 0$ in italics.

sure of media coverage of gasoline availability in each state (Media). If we run a standard model with these two independent variables, we will likely find that Media dominates Availability as a cause of attitudes on energy conservation. However, few would regard the estimate as credible, because actual gasoline availability is likely a major cause of media coverage of gasoline availability and (acting through Media) the most important cause of public opinion toward energy conservation.

Suppose, however, that we have measures of gasoline availability and media coverage at both $t = 1$ and $t = 2$. We might then estimate two regression models, as follows:

$$\text{Attitudes}_{t=3} = \beta_1 + \beta_2 \times \text{Media}_{t=1} + \beta_3 \times \text{Availability}_{t=2}$$
$$\text{Attitudes}_{t=3} = \beta_4 + \beta_5 \times \text{Media}_{t=2} + \beta_6 \times \text{Availability}_{t=1}$$

Table 9A.1 (continued)

	Effect of endorsements			
	Final delegate share	Fat Lady delegate share	Best delegate share	Average reported in chap. 9
Polls, first half	0.37	0.18	0.36	
	(0.13)	(0.15)	(0.13)	
	2.75	1.17	2.72	
Endorsements	**1.13**	**1.06**	**1.16**	**1.12**
(weighted)	**(0.27)**	**(0.34)**	**(0.27)**	**(0.29)**
	4.17	*3.12*	*4.37*	*3.89*
Funds, first half	0.04	0.10	0.04	
	(0.20)	(0.18)	(0.20)	
	0.19	0.56	0.17	
Media, first half	−0.33	−0.39	−0.35	
	(0.24)	(0.28)	(0.24)	
	−1.38	−1.38	−1.49	
1/Number of candidates	−0.21	0.05	−0.20	
	(0.16)	(0.13)	(0.16)	
	−1.33	0.36	−1.27	
Constant	0.00	0.00	0.01	
	(0.00)	(0.00)	(0.00)	
	0.42	1.08	1.48	
N	61	61	61	
Adjusted R-squared	75%	71%	76%	
Root MSE	0.14	0.12	0.13	

Variable of interest in bold.
Coefficient in roman.
Standard error in parentheses.
t-ratio for null hypotheses that $\beta = 0$ in italics.

(continued on next page)

Consider β_3 as a measure of the effect of Availability. The model contains a control for Media, but from $t = 1$. Thus, the Media variable in the model cannot have been caused by Availability at $t = 2$ and is therefore unable to "steal" the effect of Availability at $t = 2$. Thus, we get a "clean" estimate of the effect of Availability while still controlling for Media. ("Clean" is in contrast to "contaminated," as would be obtained from estimates in which only contemporaneous [i.e., $t = 2$] controls were used.) By similar logic, we can use β_5 as the "clean" estimate of the effect of Media. β_5 might well be large if it has effects over and above the effect of Availability on Attitudes, and if it were large, it would not be because it had stolen the effect of Availability. Note that this method requires a separate model to estimate the effect of each variable from $t = 2$.

Table 9A.1 (continued)

	Effect of fund-raising			
	Final delegate share	Fat Lady delegate share	Best delegate share	Average reported in chap. 9
Polls, first half	0.43	0.21	0.42	
	(0.19)	(0.20)	(0.19)	
	2.26	*1.07*	*2.19*	
Endorsements (weighted), first half	0.90	0.83	0.93	
	(0.38)	(0.42)	(0.38)	
	2.34	*1.98*	*2.46*	
Funds	**0.16**	**0.38**	**0.19**	**0.24**
	(0.25)	**(0.16)**	**(0.25)**	**(0.22)**
	0.63	***2.28***	***0.74***	***1.22***
Media, first half	−0.25	−0.35	−0.29	
	(0.28)	(0.37)	(0.29)	
	−0.89	*−0.94*	*−1.00*	
1/Number of candidates	−0.24	−0.08	−0.25	
	(0.28)	(0.21)	(0.28)	
	−0.87	*−0.37*	*−0.90*	
Constant	0.00	0.00	0.01	
	(0.00)	(0.00)	(0.00)	
	0.58	*1.13*	*1.49*	
N	61	61	61	
Adjusted R-squared	70%	66%	72%	
Root MSE	0.15	0.13	0.14	

Variable of interest in bold.
Coefficient in roman.
Standard error in parentheses.
t-ratio for null hypotheses that $\beta = 0$ in italics.

Our estimation of effects of variables in the invisible primary on delegate share is based on this general approach. We have four $t = 2$ independent variables and therefore need four models, each with its own set of $t = 1$ control variables, to estimate their effects. And because we have three versions of our dependent variables—Fat Lady, Fair Share, and Final Share—we need a total of twelve separate regressions. These "clean" estimates are shown in table 9A.1. The reader may be interested to see the results of a more conventional model using contemporaneous measures, which we consider to be contaminated estimates. We show these results in table 9A.2.

In the models in tables 9A.1 and 9A.2, we used our weighted endorsement measures, which are based on all endorsements, rather than the out-of-group measure of weighted endorsements. The out-of-group measure

Table 9A.1 (continued)

	Effect of media coverage			
	Final delegate share	Fat Lady delegate share	Best delegate share	Average reported in chap. 9
Polls, first half	0.50	0.31	0.49	
	(0.21)	(0.20)	(0.21)	
	2.40	*1.56*	*2.35*	
Endorsements	0.62	0.48	0.64	
(weighted), first half	(0.27)	(0.21)	(0.26)	
	2.29	*2.32*	*2.43*	
Funds, first half	0.01	0.03	−0.01	
	(0.29)	(0.25)	(0.29)	
	0.03	*0.14*	*−0.02*	
Media	**0.19**	**0.28**	**0.19**	**0.22**
	(0.18)	**(0.22)**	**(0.18)**	**(0.19)**
	1.08	***1.26***	***1.05***	***1.13***
1/Number of candidates	−0.32	−0.11	−0.32	
	(0.22)	(0.17)	(0.22)	
	−1.49	*−0.65*	*−1.45*	
Constant	0.00	0.00	0.01	
	(0.00)	(0.00)	(0.00)	
	0.51	*1.13*	*1.49*	
N	61	61	61	
Adjusted *R*-squared	71%	68%	73%	
Root MSE	0.15	0.13	0.14	

Variable of interest in bold.
Coefficient in roman.
Standard error in parentheses.
t-ratio for null hypotheses that $\beta = 0$ in italics.

had greater influence on the dynamics of the invisible primary, as reported in chapter 8. We had theoretical reasons to prefer the out-of-group estimate in analyzing the internal dynamics of the invisible primary, based on the idea that party insiders care about a candidate's breadth of support. The logic is not so clear when the analysis focuses on the general public rather than insiders. In view of this uncertainty, results for the out-of-group measure ought also to be reported. Tables 9A.3 and 9A.4 present the analysis of clean and contemporaneous effects for models using the out-of-group measure.

Path Effects

To estimate the size of the effect of a small change at the beginning of the process on the resulting delegates, we simulate how such a first difference

Table 9A.2: Effects of invisible primary on delegates, contemporaneous controls, and weighted endorsements

	Final delegate share	Fat Lady delegate share	Best delegate share	Average
Polls	0.77	0.61	0.77	0.66
	(0.32)	(0.32)	(0.33)	(0.33)
	2.38	*1.92*	*2.32*	*2.00*
Endorsements	0.94	0.61	0.93	0.78
(weighted)	(0.23)	(0.23)	(0.23)	(0.23)
	4.13	*2.60*	*4.06*	*3.35*
Funds	−0.21	0.01	−0.18	−0.11
	(0.34)	(0.34)	(0.33)	(0.35)
	−0.62	*0.03*	*−0.53*	*−0.33*
Media	−0.36	−0.17	−0.37	−0.23
	(0.28)	(0.37)	(0.28)	(0.34)
	−1.26	*−0.45*	*−1.31*	*−0.73*
1/Number of candidates	−0.14	−0.07	−0.16	−0.10
	(0.23)	(0.16)	(0.23)	(0.19)
	−0.61	*−0.42*	*−0.68*	*−0.50*
Constant	0.00	0.00	0.01	
	(0.00)	(0.00)	(0.00)	
	0.73	*1.14*	*1.52*	
N	61	61	61	
Adjusted *R*-squared	73%	71%	75%	
Root MSE	0.14	0.12	0.14	

Standard error in parentheses.
Coefficient in roman.
t-ratio for null hypotheses that $\beta = 0$ in italics.

change runs through both our invisible primary model and our delegate share model (see e.g., King, Tomz, and Wittenberg 2000). For the analysis reported here, we compare a 10 percentage point change in each $t = 1$ variable. We have also explored other measures of a typical change, including the standard deviation of the variable in our sample, but with the same substantive conclusions. We feel that a 10 percentage point change in one resource may be reasonably compared to a 10 percentage point change in another resource, since all are measured as shares.[30]

We wish to estimate the effect of each independent variable (polls, media, funds raised, and endorsements) down each of the paths described in figure 9.2. Following the procedure for computing a first difference, we draw coefficients from the estimated sampling distribution for each coefficient in the invisible primary model and the delegate share model, with a

Table 9A.3: Clean estimates of invisible primary on delegates, out-of-group endorsements measure

	Effect of polls			
	Final delegate share	Fat Lady delegate share	Best delegate share	Average
Polls	0.30	0.13	0.32	0.25
	(0.39)	(0.25)	(0.38)	(0.34)
	0.77	*0.51*	*0.84*	*0.70*
Endorsements	1.19	1.18	1.18	
(out-of-group),	(0.31)	(0.22)	(0.30)	
first half	*3.87*	*5.23*	*3.98*	
Funds, first half	0.05	0.08	0.06	
	(0.35)	(0.20)	(0.35)	
	0.15	*0.41*	*0.17*	
Media, first half	−0.63	−0.72	−0.64	
	(0.44)	(0.36)	(0.44)	
	−1.44	*−2.00*	*−1.45*	
1/Number of candidates	0.09	0.32	0.08	
	(0.27)	(0.18)	(0.26)	
	0.35	*1.76*	*0.32*	
Constant	0.00	0.00	0.01	
	(0.00)	(0.00)	(0.00)	
N	61	61	61	
Adjusted *R*-squared	71%	74%	72%	
Root MSE	0.14	0.10	0.13	

Variable of interest in bold.
Coefficient in roman.
Standard error in parentheses.
t-ratio for null hypotheses that $\beta = 0$ in italics.

(*continued on next page*)

mean at our point estimate and a standard deviation equal to the estimated standard error. For the coefficient in the part of the analysis predicting delegate share, we draw from each of the three versions of the dependent variable, with equal probability. We then compute an expected value of delegate share variable at the mean of the independent variables, and another value of the delegate share variable at the mean plus the typical change (in this case, plus 10 percent), and take the difference. In both cases, we sum across the changes for all four paths from our variable of interest to the dependent variable. The standard error of this estimated difference is the standard deviation of a large number of such estimates.

This procedure averages out the fundamental error, associated with the unexplained randomness in the dependent variable, so that we have only

Table 9A.3 (continued)

	Final delegate share	Fat Lady delegate share	Best delegate share	Average
		Effect of endorsements		
Polls, first half	0.50	0.24	0.49	
	(0.15)	(0.14)	(0.15)	
	3.27	*1.68*	*3.25*	
Endorsements	**0.79**	**0.86**	**0.79**	**0.81**
(out-of-group)	**(0.27)**	**(0.22)**	**(0.27)**	**(0.26)**
	2.89	***3.86***	***2.93***	***3.23***
Funds, first half	0.08	0.10	0.09	
	(0.33)	(0.23)	(0.33)	
	0.26	*0.45*	*0.27*	
Media, first half	−0.25	−0.39	−0.26	
	(0.28)	(0.20)	(0.28)	
	−0.92	*−1.95*	*−0.95*	
1/Number of candidates	−0.12	0.18	−0.12	
	(0.20)	(0.17)	(0.20)	
	−0.62	*1.06*	*−0.62*	
Constant	0.00	0.00	0.01	
	(0.00)	(0.00)	(0.00)	
N	61	61	61	
Adjusted R-squared	74%	73%	75%	
Root MSE	0.14	0.12	0.13	

Variable of interest in bold.
Coefficient in roman.
Standard error in parentheses.
t-ratio for null hypotheses that $\beta = 0$ in italics.

the sampling error for our estimates. But our estimation error is appropriately combined across both models, as well as averaged across all three of our slightly different measures for the dependent variable.

The effect of a change of magnitude δ away from x^* in the ith independent variable at time 1 on delegates at the end of the process thus works out to be:

$$\sum_j (x_i^* + \delta)\beta_{i,j}\alpha_{j,D} - \sum_j x_i^*\beta_{i,j}\alpha_{j,D}$$

where $\beta_{i,j}$ is the estimated effect of the ith variable at time 1 on the jth variable at time 2 (from table 8A.2), and $\alpha_{j,D}$ is the estimated effect of the jth variable on delegates, averaged across all three measures (from table 9A.1).

Table 9A.3 (continued)

	Final delegate share	Fat Lady delegate share	Best delegate share	Average
		Effect of fund-raising		
Polls, first half	0.31	−0.01	0.30	
	(0.13)	(0.12)	(0.13)	
	2.40	*−0.07*	*2.40*	
Endorsements	1.08	1.22	1.08	
(out-of-group),	(0.32)	(0.31)	(0.32)	
first half	*3.33*	*3.97*	*3.33*	
Funds	**0.11**	**0.27**	**0.14**	**0.17**
	(0.32)	**(0.22)**	**(0.32)**	**(0.29)**
	0.34	***1.24***	***0.44***	***0.67***
Media, first half	−0.48	−0.74	−0.50	
	(0.37)	(0.40)	(0.38)	
	−1.30	*−1.87*	*−1.32*	
1/Number of candidates	−0.01	0.25	−0.03	
	(0.26)	(0.18)	(0.26)	
	−0.05	*1.33*	*−0.12*	
Constant	0.00	0.00	0.01	
	(0.00)	(0.00)	(0.00)	
N	61	61	61	
Adjusted R-squared	74%	74%	75%	
Root MSE	0.13	0.10	0.13	

Variable of interest in bold.
Coefficient in roman.
Standard error in parentheses.
t-ratio for null hypotheses that $\beta = 0$ in italics.

(*continued on next page*)

Results based on this calculation are reported in table 9.2 in the text and, with more detail, in table 9A.5. This estimate is correct if we believe that the effect of the internal dynamics of the invisible primary is constant over time and that we have correctly estimated that effect. In which case, the first part of our estimation is the effect, through those dynamics, of small changes at the beginning of those dynamics. The second part takes as its starting point the results of those dynamics.

However, this procedure does not include any direct effect of the $t = 1$ variables on delegate share, but only their effects through the $t = 2$ variables. This estimate is correct for the estimated effects of Polls and Media, whose effects at the end of the invisible primary are the only effects that would be assumed to exist. However, it is arguably the wrong estimate for the effects of Funds and Endorsements, whose values as accumulated over the whole

Table 9A.3 (continued)

	Effect of media coverage			
	Final delegate share	Fat Lady delegate share	Best delegate share	Average
Polls, first half	0.40	0.13	0.39	
	(0.14)	(0.13)	(0.14)	
	2.75	0.97	2.79	
Endorsements (out-of-group), first half	0.82	0.83	0.82	
	(0.21)	(0.23)	(0.21)	
	3.83	3.61	3.99	
Funds, first half	−0.09	−0.16	−0.09	
	(0.28)	(0.24)	(0.29)	
	−0.33	−0.65	−0.32	
Media	**−0.05**	**0.00**	**−0.05**	**−0.03**
	(0.23)	**(0.25)**	**(0.23)**	**(0.24)**
	−0.21	**0.02**	**−0.20**	**−0.13**
1/Number of candidates	−0.08	0.18	−0.08	
	(0.21)	(0.14)	(0.21)	
	−0.36	1.33	−0.38	
Constant	0.00	0.00	0.01	
	(0.00)	(0.00)	(0.00)	
N	61	61	61	
Adjusted R-squared	74%	74%	75%	
Root MSE	0.14	0.11	0.13	

Variable of interest in bold.
Coefficient in roman.
Standard error in parentheses.
t-ratio for null hypotheses that $\beta = 0$ in italics.

invisible primary are what affect Delegate Share. To calculate these total effects for Funds and Endorsements—that is, direct effect from $t = 1$ plus indirect effects through the $t = 2$ variables—we have done another set of estimates for these two variables. For Money and Endorsements, these effects may be calculated as follows:

$$\sum_j \left(\frac{(x_i^* + \delta) + (x_i^* + \delta)\beta_{i,j}}{2} \right) \alpha_{j,D} - \sum_j \left(\frac{x_i^* + x_i^* \beta_{i,j}}{2} \right) \alpha_{j,D}$$

where a change of δ has both an indirect effect on delegates, through the dynamics of the invisible primary, and also a direct effect.

Table 9A.5 shows the results for this alternative method alongside that from the method reported in the text. The estimated effect for Endorsements gets larger, as would be expected given that we allow direct effects

Table 9A.4: Effects of invisible primary on delegates, contemporaneous controls, and out-of-group endorsements measure

	Final delegate share	Fat Lady delegate share	Best delegate share	Average
Polls	0.83	0.48	0.85	0.72
	(0.40)	(0.27)	(0.40)	(0.36)
	2.07	*1.75*	*2.13*	*1.98*
Endorsements	0.75	0.64	0.72	0.70
(weighted out-of-group)	(0.25)	(0.19)	(0.24)	(0.23)
	2.98	*3.37*	*2.99*	*3.12*
Funds	0.04	0.11	0.08	0.07
	(0.39)	(0.33)	(0.38)	(0.37)
	0.10	*0.32*	*0.20*	*0.21*
Media	−0.55	−0.30	−0.56	−0.47
	(0.40)	(0.38)	(0.40)	(0.39)
	−1.37	*−0.79*	*−1.41*	*−1.19*
1/Number of candidates	−0.06	0.07	−0.10	
	(0.26)	(0.18)	(0.26)	
	−0.25	*0.39*	*−0.37*	
Constant	0.00	0.00	0.01	
	(0.00)	(0.00)	(0.00)	
	0.62	*1.14*	*1.52*	
N	61	61	61	
Adjusted *R*-squared	70%	72%	72%	
Root MSE	0.15	0.12	0.14	

Coefficient in roman.
Standard error in parentheses.
t-ratio for null hypotheses that β = 0 in italics.

from the $t = 1$ period, and so does the estimated effect for fund-raising, but the results support the same general conclusion concerning insider domination of the nomination process.

We argue that the effect of Endorsements through the entire process is the largest effect of any of the four variables. Table 9A.6 provides evidence on this point. For each possible pair of independent variables, it reports an estimate of the likelihood that the row variable had a greater effect on the delegate share variable than the column variable. The top panel of the table shows results for the weighted measure, while the bottom panel shows results for the out-of-group measure.

The percentages in this table can be interpreted as one-tailed *p*-values of the null hypothesis that the effects are the same. At the 0.05 level, we can reject the null that the effect of out-of-group endorsements is not larger

Table 9A.5: Effect of early changes on the end of the process

| | Using weighted endorsements | Using weighted out-of-group endorsements | Including direct effects on delegates | |
			Using weighted endorsements	Using weighted out-of-group endorsements
Polls	0.05	0.00	0.05	0.00
	(0.03)	(0.02)	(0.03)	(0.02)
Endorsements	0.11	0.11	0.17	0.11
	(0.05)	(0.05)	(0.04)	(0.05)
Funds	0.01	0.01	0.12	0.06
	(0.04)	(0.04)	(0.04)	(0.04)
Media	0.04	−0.03	0.04	−0.03
	(0.06)	(0.05)	(0.06)	(0.05)

Cells are the effect of a 0.10 change in one variable at the beginning of the process on delegates at the end.
The standard deviation of the estimated effect is in parentheses.

than all other variables. The effect is not clearly larger for the weighted measure, at least at that threshold, but it comes close.

Vote Models for Iowa and New Hampshire Contests

Our analysis of the determinants of success in the Iowa caucuses and the New Hampshire primaries is reported in tables 9A.7 and 9A.8. Both models use state-level measures of endorsements to explain vote share in those contests.

State-level data are harder to obtain than national data, and we have insufficient data to split them into $t = 1$ and $t = 2$ periods. We are therefore unable to make "clean" estimates of the variables of interest, and we are also unable to replicate the analysis in tables 9A.1 and 9A.3. Instead, we offer a variety of specifications to help assess robustness. We use a poll measure at the national level that is measured about three months prior to the Iowa caucuses and also a poll measure at the state level that is, unfortunately, taken immediately before the contest, thus maximizing the contamination problem described earlier. If we believe that something about the natural popularity of the candidate is the real driving force, the early poll measure should capture that effect. However, if we believe that candidate appeal must be measured locally, we should use the endogenous measure.

Table 9A.6: Do some variables have more impact than others?

	Polls	Endorsements	Fund-raising	Media
	Using Weighted Share Measure			
Polls	—	.12	.80	.55
Endorsements	.88	—	.96	.82
Funds	.20	.04	—	.32
Media	.45	.18	.68	—
	Using Weighted Out-of-Group Measure			
Polls	—	.01	.35	.68
Endorsements	.99	—	.97	.99
Funds	.65	.03	—	.74
Media	.32	.01	.26	—

Cells report the probability that the estimated effect of the row variable is greater than the effect of the column variable.

We have attempted to test the effect of state-level spending, but this measure is unreliable, for many reasons. First, for both states, fifteen candidates did not file FEC reports for one reason or another and are thus missing from the data. More seriously, even state-level reports for candidates who do file them are deeply suspect. In New Hampshire, many candidates spend in neighboring Massachusetts, whose media market extends into New Hampshire, and this is only one of several ways in which spending credited to one state may be ultimately directed to another. We have explored these issues, including imputing missing values, but the results were uninformative. We believe that the national fund-raising measure is probably the best indicator of how much money each candidate can spend in Iowa and New Hampshire. Thus, we report results based on that measure. We do not have any state-level measures of media coverage, so we use the national measure.

Many of these concerns center on measurement. We have been careful about measurement error corrections in other models. But for the variables used in the Iowa and New Hampshire models, corrections would not be credible and so we have not attempted them.

Finally, our state-level analysis must account for the unusual role of Iowa in 1992. The major Democratic candidates essentially ceded the caucuses to Iowa Sen. Tom Harkin. As a result, the relationship of the Iowa vote variable to the other variables is muddied in that year, both as a dependent variable, and as a control in predicting the outcome in New Hampshire. Our solution is to drop 1992 from the analysis here. We explored imputing an Iowa result for 1992 and also allowing the slope for the effect of Iowa

Table 9A.7: Predicting the Iowa caucus vote

Dependent variable	Iowa vote	Iowa vote	Iowa vote	Iowa vote	Iowa vote	Iowa vote
National Poll	0.11		−0.05			0.23
	(0.26)		(0.31)			(0.16)
	0.43		*−0.16*			*1.41*
Iowa Poll		0.29		0.34	0.15	
		(0.18)		(0.18)	(0.12)	
		1.64		*1.85*	*1.26*	
National Endorsements	0.07	0.02	0.32	0.13		
	(0.23)	(0.17)	(0.21)	(0.14)		
	0.31	*0.15*	*1.48*	*0.96*		
Iowa Endorsements	0.30	0.28			0.33	0.46
	(0.11)	(0.08)			(0.10)	(0.15)
	2.80	*3.40*			*3.19*	*3.10*
National Funds	0.68	0.62	0.88	0.82	0.45	
	(0.19)	(0.20)	(0.18)	(0.19)	(0.19)	
	3.60	*3.18*	*4.95*	*4.37*	*2.39*	
National Media	−0.24	−0.27	−0.25	−0.35		
	(0.10)	(0.08)	(0.10)	(0.07)		
	−2.50	*−3.46*	*−2.64*	*−4.97*		
1/Number of candidates	0.08	0.06	0.11	0.06	0.07	0.31
	(0.11)	(0.12)	(0.12)	(0.13)	(0.12)	(0.10)
	0.76	*0.47*	*0.88*	*0.43*	*0.59*	*3.24*
Constant	0.00	0.00	0.00	0.00	0.00	0.00
	(0.00)	(0.00)	(0.00)	(0.00)	(0.00)	(0.00)
	0.15	*0.55*	*0.12*	*0.57*	*0.30*	*0.56*
N	56	56	56	56	56	56
Adjusted R^2	75%	77%	69%	72%	74%	68%
Root MSE	0.08	0.08	0.09	0.09	0.08	0.09

Coefficient in roman.
Standard error in parentheses.
t-ratio for null hypotheses that $\beta = 0$ in italics.

results on New Hampshire results to be different in 1992, also with no substantive effect.

Table 9A.7 reports five models of the outcome in Iowa. As noted in the text, the endorsements measure is consistently a strong predictor. It even stands up against contemporaneous poll measures in Iowa.

Table 9A.8 reports ten models of the New Hampshire primary. In addition to the analogous variables from the Iowa models, we add the Iowa outcome. The results in Iowa are strongly predictive of New Hampshire. The endorsements variable does less well in New Hampshire. Polls and the Iowa results dominate. However, in a model without polls or the Iowa

Table 9A.8: Predicting the New Hampshire primary vote

Dependent variable	NH vote	NH vote	NH vote	NH vote	NH vote	NH vote	NH vote	NH vote	NH vote	NH vote	NH vote	NH vote	NH vote
Iowa vote	0.36 (0.10) *3.39*							0.54 (0.09) *5.81*	0.50 (0.17) *2.85*	0.53 (0.13) *4.08*	0.45 (0.20) *2.32*	0.44 (0.17) *2.54*	0.43 (0.21) *2.00*
National Poll		-0.20 (0.25) *-0.82*		-0.11 (0.20) *-0.52*	-0.08 (0.20) *-0.40*		0.26 (0.08) *3.16*		-0.12 (0.19) *-0.62*		-0.13 (0.21) *-0.62*		0.24 (0.07) *3.28*
NH Poll			0.37 (0.12) *3.08*			0.37 (0.12) *3.23*		0.37 (0.08) *4.73*		0.36 (0.07) *5.03*		0.41 (0.11) *3.76*	
National Endorsements	-0.15 (0.16) *-0.94*	0.28 (0.20) *1.38*	0.03 (0.12) *0.22*					-0.13 (0.11) *-1.18*					
NH Endorsements	0.26 (0.16) *1.65*			0.32 (0.17) *1.91*	0.39 (0.12) *3.16*	0.15 (0.10) *1.49*	0.33 (0.15) *2.17*		0.11 (0.19) *0.56*	-0.07 (0.16) *-0.46*	0.10 (0.19) *0.52*	-0.05 (0.17) *-0.29*	0.05 (0.23) *0.22*
National Funds	0.09 (0.19) *0.46*	0.33 (0.35) *0.96*	0.17 (0.22) *0.76*	0.24 (0.37) *0.64*		0.14 (0.17) *0.81*	0.41 (0.12) *3.31*	-0.31 (0.14) *-2.19*	-0.13 (0.41) *-0.31*	-0.35 (0.17) *-2.03*		-0.12 (0.09) *-1.27*	
National Media	0.14 (0.16) *0.91*	0.29 (0.29) *1.00*	0.10 (0.16) *0.64*	0.30 (0.29) *1.06*	0.36 (0.21) *1.69*			0.25 (0.15) *1.62*	0.41 (0.29) *1.41*	0.22 (0.15) *1.49*	0.38 (0.21) *1.82*		
1/Number of candidates	0.30 (0.11) *2.69*	0.30 (0.13) *2.34*	0.34 (0.09) *3.59*	0.25 (0.13) *1.92*	0.34 (0.11) *3.11*	0.33 (0.12) *2.87*	0.41 (0.12) *3.31*	0.28 (0.07) *4.30*	0.22 (0.13) *1.74*	0.31 (0.07) *4.77*	0.19 (0.08) *2.38*	0.31 (0.08) *3.89*	0.28 (0.11) *2.49*
Constant	0.00 (0.00) *(0.00)*	0.00 (0.00) *(0.00)*	0.00 (0.00) *(0.00)*	0.00 (0.00) *(0.00)*	0.00 (0.00) *(0.00)*	0.00 (0.00) *(0.00)*	0.00 (0.00) *(0.00)*	0.00 (0.00) *(0.00)*	0.00 (0.00) *(0.00)*	0.00 (0.00) *(0.00)*	0.00 (0.00) *(0.00)*	0.00 (0.00) *(0.00)*	0.00 (0.00) *(0.00)*
Adjusted R-squared	68%	56%	67%	58%	58%	68%	54%	76%	64%	75%	65%	73%	60%
Root MSE	0.09	0.11	0.09	0.10	0.10	0.09	0.11	0.08	0.09	0.08	0.09	0.08	0.10
N	56	56	56	56	56	56	56	56	56	56	56	56	56

Coefficient in roman.
Standard error in parentheses.
t-ratio for null hypotheses that β = 0 in italics.

results, endorsements have a strong relationship. If we believe that polls are endogenous to party activity, then we have reason to believe that endorsements are important. Finally, because the Iowa results are dominated by Iowa endorsements, it would seem that party endorsements might affect the outcome in New Hampshire indirectly.

Early Contest Analysis

The analysis reported in Table 9.3 in the text is to the same as that of table 9.1 except that it includes a variable for the effect of Iowa and New Hampshire contests. The measure, which we call Early Contests, is the average of the candidates' vote shares in the Iowa caucuses and the New Hampshire primaries, except for 1992, where it is only the New Hampshire results, for the reason given above.

The results in Table 9.3 are based on results in table 9A.9. Of course, it is not possible to measure the Early Contest results prior to the invisible primary variables. It is thus particularly notable that the invisible primary variables perform so well, even after they have had some of their effect through the Early Contest variable.

For estimating the effect of the Early Contest variable itself, we use as controls the other variables measured at the end of the invisible primary, which is by definition before the Early Contests.

Table 9A.9: Clean estimates of invisible primary and early contests on delegates

	Effect of polls			
	Final delegate share	Fat Lady delegate share	Best delegate share	Average
Polls	**0.64**	**0.56**	**0.63**	**0.61**
	(0.42)	**(0.27)**	**(0.42)**	**(0.37)**
	1.51	*2.08*	*1.49*	*1.69*
Endorsements	0.89	0.59	0.90	
(weighted share),	(0.26)	(0.20)	(0.25)	
first half	*3.37*	*3.02*	*3.54*	
Funds, first half	−0.11	−0.07	−0.12	
	(0.27)	(0.21)	(0.27)	
	−0.41	*−0.32*	*−0.46*	
Media, first half	−0.54	−0.48	−0.56	
	(0.37)	(0.31)	(0.37)	
	−1.47	*−1.54*	*−1.49*	
Early Contests				
(average of vote share	0.59	0.76	0.61	
in Iowa and New	(0.34)	(0.26)	(0.33)	
Hampshire)	*1.73*	*2.96*	*1.89*	
1/Number of candidates	−0.46	−0.37	−0.47	
	(0.20)	(0.12)	(0.20)	
	−2.32	*−3.18*	*−2.40*	
Constant	0.00	0.00	0.01	
	(0.00)	(0.00)	(0.00)	
	0.77	*1.16*	*1.49*	
N	61	61	61	
Adjusted *R*-squared	75%	81%	77%	
Root MSE	0.13	0.09	0.12	

Variable of interest in bold.
Coefficient in roman.
Standard error in parentheses.
t-ratio for null hypotheses that $\beta = 0$ in italics.

(*continued on next page*)

Table 9A.9 (continued)

	Effect of endorsements			
	Final delegate share	Fat Lady delegate share	Best delegate share	Average
Polls, first half	0.40	0.22	0.39	
	(0.12)	(0.13)	(0.11)	
	3.36	1.68	3.43	
Endorsements	**0.86**	**0.70**	**0.88**	**0.82**
(weighted share),	**(0.33)**	**(0.31)**	**(0.31)**	**(0.32)**
first half	**2.63**	**2.28**	**2.82**	**2.57**
Funds, first half	−0.12	−0.11	−0.13	
	(0.21)	(0.21)	(0.21)	
	−0.59	−0.54	−0.63	
Media, first half	−0.23	−0.25	−0.24	
	(0.29)	(0.28)	(0.28)	
	−0.79	−0.91	−0.86	
Early Contests	0.60	0.79	0.63	
	(0.29)	(0.22)	(0.27)	
	2.09	3.64	2.31	
1/Number of candidates	−0.52	−0.36	−0.53	
	(0.17)	(0.12)	(0.16)	
	−3.01	−3.08	−3.25	
Constant	0.00	0.00	0.01	
	(0.00)	(0.00)	(0.00)	
	0.43	1.09	1.46	
N	61	61	61	
Adjusted R-squared	79%	82%	81%	
Root MSE	0.12	0.10	0.12	

Variable of interest in bold.
Coefficient in roman.
Standard error in parentheses.
t-ratio for null hypotheses that $\beta = 0$ in italics.

Table 9A.9 (continued)

	Effect of fund-raising			
	Final delegate share	Fat Lady delegate share	Best delegate share	Average
Polls, first half	0.48	0.26	0.46	
	(0.18)	(0.20)	(0.18)	
	2.63	*1.34*	*2.57*	
Endorsements (weighted share), first half	0.69	0.59	0.72	
	(0.39)	(0.37)	(0.39)	
	1.75	*1.60*	*1.85*	
Funds	**−0.42**	**−0.28**	**−0.41**	**−0.37**
	(0.32)	**(0.25)**	**(0.31)**	**(0.29)**
	−1.33	***−1.15***	***−1.30***	***−1.26***
Media, first half	−0.14	−0.22	−0.18	
	(0.30)	(0.33)	(0.30)	
	−0.47	*−0.66*	*−0.58*	
Early Contests	0.84	0.95	0.86	
	(0.28)	(0.22)	(0.27)	
	3.06	*4.39*	*3.21*	
1/Number of candidates	−0.45	−0.31	−0.46	
	(0.21)	(0.13)	(0.21)	
	−2.10	*−2.30*	*−2.17*	
Constant	0.00	0.00	0.01	
	(0.00)	(0.00)	(0.00)	
	0.66	*1.14*	*1.48*	
N	61	61	61	
Adjusted R-squared	78%	80%	80%	
Root MSE	0.13	0.10	0.12	

Variable of interest in bold.
Coefficient in roman.
Standard error in parentheses.
t-ratio for null hypotheses that β = 0 in italics.

(*continued on next page*)

Table 9A.9 (continued)

| | Effect of media coverage | | | |
	Final delegate share	Fat Lady delegate share	Best delegate share	Average
Polls, first half	0.48	0.28	0.46	
	(0.19)	(0.17)	(0.18)	
	2.57	*1.64*	*2.53*	
Endorsements	0.52	0.37	0.54	
(weighted share),	(0.25)	(0.19)	(0.25)	
first half	*2.07*	*1.93*	*2.17*	
Fund-raising, first half	−0.18	−0.19	−0.20	
	(0.25)	(0.20)	(0.24)	
	−0.73	*−0.94*	*−0.83*	
Media	**0.08**	**0.15**	**0.08**	**0.10**
	(0.20)	**(0.18)**	**(0.19)**	**(0.19)**
	0.42	***0.85***	***0.39***	***0.55***
Early contests	0.71	0.86	0.74	
	(0.27)	(0.20)	(0.25)	
	2.69	*4.35*	*2.98*	
1/Number of candidates	−0.62	−0.47	−0.63	
	(0.17)	(0.10)	(0.18)	
	−3.62	*−4.65*	*−3.56*	
Constant	0.00	0.00	0.01	
	(0.00)	(0.00)	(0.00)	
	0.56	*1.13*	*1.47*	
N	61	61	61	
Adjusted R-squared	77%	81%	79%	
Root MSE	0.13	0.10	0.12	

Variable of interest in bold.
Coefficient in roman.
Standard error in parentheses.
t-ratio for null hypotheses that $\beta = 0$ in italics.

Table 9A.9 (continued)

	Effect of early contest wins			
	Final delegate share	Fat Lady delegate share	Best delegate share	Average
Polls, first half	0.64	0.46	0.64	
	(0.32)	(0.18)	(0.32)	
	2.03	*2.52*	*1.99*	
Endorsements (weighted share), first half	0.87	0.52	0.86	
	(0.18)	(0.10)	(0.18)	
	4.92	*5.14*	*4.80*	
Funds, first half	−0.71	−0.61	−0.69	
	(0.31)	(0.26)	(0.30)	
	−2.28	*−2.30*	*−2.32*	
Media, first half	−0.25	−0.04	−0.26	
	(0.24)	(0.23)	(0.24)	
	−1.03	*−0.15*	*−1.08*	
Early contests	**0.73**	**0.90**	**0.75**	**0.80**
	(0.30)	**(0.22)**	**(0.29)**	**(0.27)**
	2.39	***4.02***	***2.59***	***3.00***
1/Number of candidates	−0.28	−0.24	−0.31	
	(0.19)	(0.10)	(0.19)	
	−1.50	*−2.46*	*−1.61*	
Constant	0.00	0.00	0.01	
	(0.00)	(0.00)	(0.00)	
	0.81	*1.16*	*1.52*	
N	61	61	61	
Adjusted *R*-squared	79%	83%	80%	
Root MSE	0.13	0.10	0.12	

Variable of interest in bold.
Coefficient in roman.
Standard error in parentheses.
t-ratio for null hypotheses that $\beta = 0$ in italics.

Political Parties Today

In his diary entry for February 1, 1763, John Adams describes backroom politics in colonial Boston: "This day learned that the Caucas Clubb meets at certain times in the Garrett of Tom Daws, the Adjutant of the Boston Regiment. . . . There they smoke tobacco till you cannot see from one End of the Garrett to the other. There they drink flip, I suppose, and there they choose a Moderator, who puts Questions to the Vote regularly, and Select Men, Assessors, Collectors, Wardens, Fire Wards, and Representatives are Regularly chosen before they are chosen in the Town." The Caucas Clubb did not, however, run Boston by itself. It routinely "sen[t] Committees to wait on the Merchants Clubb and to propose, and join, in the Choice of Men and Measures." The two groups then worked the streets in support of their slate and generally prevailed. The alliance of the Caucas Clubb and the Merchants Clubb had no formal name, but it was in every important way a political party.

Some two hundred fifty years later, we learn from a political blog of another private meeting, this one aimed at choosing a president of the United States:

> After more than a year of fretting, it looks as if many members of the Arling-
> ton Group, an informal roundtable of the country's most influential cultur-
> ally conservative groups, are fast settling around Fred Thompson as their
> presidential candidate of choice.
>
> Thompson is not an evangelical, but he has, evidently, sounded solid
> enough in his private meetings with individual Arlington Group members,
> a series of which have taken place over the past few weeks. (Ambinder,
> 2007)

The Arlington Group, an alliance of some 70 socially and religiously conservative organizations, makes no formal endorsements, but individual
leaders may mobilize their followers in support of the Arlington's group's
collective judgment. But, like the Caucas Clubb, the Arlington Group is
not strong enough to control elections on its own. This, no doubt, is why
evangelical leaders passed over Governor Mike Huckabee of Arkansas, an
ordained minister and a notably stronger advocate of their agenda than
Thompson. As one member explained later, "I think out of respect to the
other members of the coalition, some evangelicals have held back because
[Huckabee] is a challenge to some in the foreign policy ranks and even
some fiscal conservative groups are opposed to him" (Ambinder, 2007;
see also Martin, 2007). In leaning toward Thompson, then, the Arlington
Group was not simply pleasing itself; it was looking for someone who
would be acceptable both to its members and to the larger Republican
coalition.

Despite obvious differences between the Arlington Group and the
crew that met in Tom Daws's smoke-filled garret, much was the same.
Both were diverse groups meeting privately to reach consensus ahead of
the regular elections. Both saw the need to cooperate with other private
groups. And both had means to communicate their preferences to voters.
Thus, our view of politics in these two eras is that, as the French saying
goes, "the more things change, the more they remain the same." Whenever one examines large-scale elections, one finds diverse individuals
coordinating behind the scenes to focus voters' attention on candidates
friendly to their intense policy preferences. This coordination is a defining act of parties and one of the principal means by which intense policy
demanders get what they want out of government. The imperative to such
coordination is as strong today as it was in colonial Boston.

We are writing this chapter after the invisible primary and the first contests in Iowa and New Hampshire, but before either party's nomination
for 2008 has been settled. It is also before we have been able to complete
and analyze our endorsement tally for the 2008 contests. But, despite the

uncertainty, some major features of these races are clear—the development of an epic battle between Barack Obama and Hillary Clinton on the Democratic side, the failure of Republican insiders to coordinate behind any one candidate. The evolving role of the so-called new media in the nomination process is also coming into sharper focus. In this chapter, we shall assess these occurrences in light of the main arguments of the book and then offer a few concluding remarks.

Nominations in the Internet Era

Although coordination is a defining act of political parties, the particular people who work together and the means by which they operate are in continuous flux. The McGovern-Fraser reforms, a central focus of this book, reduced the power of one set of actors and created new opportunities for others. Changes in communication and transportation have had comparably large effects on who plays the party game and how they play it. In the country's first contested presidential election—that between Adams and Jefferson in 1796—activists rode from town to town on horseback passing out handwritten ballots so that like-minded partisans would know how to vote against the Federalist Party. By the next election, a nationwide system of newspapers offered a more effective means of coordination, making it possible for the new Republican Party to win both the House of Representatives and the presidency in the elections of 1800. Improvements in transportation early in the nineteenth century facilitated the birth of regular party conventions to coordinate on presidential nominees, and further improvements in the next one hundred years made it possible for party leaders to do much of the coordination before the national party convention met.

The presidential nominating system of the early twenty-first century may be undergoing another round of communication-driven change. The rise of the Internet—more specifically, political blogs, YouTube, online contributions, and Web-based advocacy groups—has given candidates more ways to mobilize political support and given potential supporters more ways to monitor what candidates are doing. The Internet is, moreover, only one part of the story. The communications mainstays of the 1960s, big-city newspapers and network television news, are notably weaker today than they were. But media that cater to political junkies—cable television news and talk shows; elite national newspapers like the *New York Times* and *Wall Street Journal*; news radio, especially National Public Radio—are all stronger. For political professionals, the routine ease of airline travel for conferences and small-group meetings is another big advance in political communication. In consequence of these advances in communication, no one can say today what T. H. White said of party insiders in the 1960s: "The country is so vast, and its political worlds so many, that these local leaders, groping as they leave their home base, crave contact with one another and are grateful to any man who can give them the sense of strength through multiplication" (1961, 136). The country is as vast today as it ever was, but its political leaders no longer live in separate universes. All are part of a national political community that is far better interconnected than before. This development has been a double-edged sword for parties. On the one hand, internal communication in parties is better than ever. When a candidate does well or badly in a debate, gets a big new endorsement, or alienates a critical constituency, the whole party knows about it within hours and can adjust accordingly. Fox News on the Republican side and the liberal netroots on the Democratic side are evolving as beacons of acceptability for their party rank-and-file. New communication media were especially useful in conveying insider approval of the late emerging candidacies of Wesley Clark in 2004 and, as we shall describe below, Fred Thompson in 2008.

On the downside, however, the pressure of the 24-hour news cycle creates more opportunities for candidates to get in trouble—especially the insider-backed front-runners whom everyone pays most attention to. In the 1980s and '90s, much of the contact between campaigns consisted of candidate entourages passing one another in airports at night. Now campaigns are in constant exchange with one another, with mainstream reporters, and with hyperaggressive bloggers. The campaign is no longer a collection of separate organizations, but a big national debate with multiple candidates and an audience of national news junkies who seem never to sleep.

Besides increasing pressure on front-runners, the new national campaign gives insurgent candidates a public medium in which to act and a ready audience to which they can appeal. Using the Internet, insurgents can also seek out their natural base of support independent of the national campaign. This has, in turn, changed the dynamics of the invisible primary. In earlier years, outsider underdog candidates had to "do better than expected" in Iowa or New Hampshire to generate massive media coverage and come to the attention of a national audience. In more recent campaigns, however, candidates including McCain, Dean, and Huckabee have found their followings and gone from obscurity to the top tier before the first vote has been cast. In the current media-rich campaign, merely rising in the polls in one of the early-voting states is enough to generate buzz and national visibility.

Advances in communication have also brought nomination politics closer to ordinary citizens, making it easier either to follow events or to try to shape them. The party system has always been open to anyone who wanted to do the work of attending party meetings, arranging rallies, and canvassing neighborhoods. The difference now is that the requisite effort has been reduced to mouse clicks and key strokes. Citizens can seek out candidates before the candidates organize locally, make donations and initiate rallies for them, and participate in discussion in the national blogosphere.

It is not clear, however, whether the surge in political communication has in the end made a difference in who wins or comes close to winning. Recall that Eugene McCarthy mounted an effective antiwar insurgency campaign in 1968, and that George H. W. Bush came from national obscurity to beat front-runner Ronald Reagan in Iowa and to capture national momentum briefly in 1980. So there is a chance the campaigns of McCain in 2000, Dean in 2004, and Huckabee in 2008 would have taken off even in the communications environment of the 1980s.

Overall, then, the new communication environment is probably marginally less friendly to front-runners—and the party establishments that help create them—than what existed in the past. But it seems unlikely to change the basic imperative of party nominations: uniting diverse policy demanders behind a candidate committed to their agenda but still able to win the general election.

Hillary Clinton's visit during the invisible primary to the "Yearly Kos," the annual convention of a major liberal blog group, illustrates our point. But first some background. During the 2006 election, liberal bloggers of the so-called netroots were a major force in several elections, pushing Democratic candidates to the left on major issues, especially the war in Iraq. In one notable case, bloggers helped deprive the party's 2000 vice presidential nominee, Senator Joe Lieberman, of the Democratic nomination in Connecticut. The netroots bloggers entered the 2008 presidential nominations with a determination to be similarly effective. Their most preferred candidate was John Edwards, the furthest left and most antiwar of the major Democratic contenders. And their favorite foil was Hillary Clinton, who, like John Kerry in 2004, had voted for the Iraq War Resolution in 2002 and still refused to call for an immediate pullout of U.S. troops. A question much on the mind of Democrats was whether the netroots would play the uncompromising role in 2008 they had played in 2004 and 2006.

The answer appeared to be no. Clinton stood her ground at the Yearly Kos convention, telling the bloggers, "We can't just wake up and say we will move 160,000 troops. That is dangerous." The bloggers let that statement go, but booed when the New York senator said she would continue to take campaign donations from registered lobbyists. Clinton responded nimbly. "I have been waiting [for that]," she said with a smile. "It gives me a real sense of reality in being here. I have a good idea about bringing about change. I wish it were as simple as doing this or that. I will take money from lobbyists, because some represent real Americans like nurses and social workers, and they represent businesses that employ a lot of people. And I ask you to look at my record. I do want to be the president for everybody."

For that set of follow-up comments, which conceded nothing, Clinton got some applause. Afterward, Markos Moulitsas, the group's founder, told a reporter, "[Clinton] did a good job in reducing hostility. Half the battle is getting the proper respect, and she got that. She doesn't have to get total agreement." Moulitsas certainly wasn't endorsing Clinton as his first choice—he later reported voting for Obama—but he was saying, in the standard language of politics, that she was *acceptable* (Simon 2007).

Reflecting on this episode, some commentators praised Clinton's skill in taming the netroots. This would be a candidate-centered interpretation. An alternative view is that, having lost two straight presidential elections, the bloggers realized that, whatever her shortcomings, Clinton might be the best bet to unite the Democratic Party and win in November. This, of course, is the party-centered interpretation.

A Fine Republican Mess

The big story of the Republican invisible primary was that the party found itself in greater disarray than at any time since 1964. Through most of the invisible primary, the party had three top-tier candidates, none of whom was acceptable to all groups in the party. The national poll leader was Rudolph Giuliani, the former mayor of New York City. But Giuliani was pro-choice on abortion, which made him unacceptable to most social conservatives. The second member of the top tier was Mitt Romney, the former governor of Massachusetts, who also had a record of liberalism on social issues. Unlike Giuliani, Romney adopted conservative positions on social issues when he began his run for the presidency, but some social conservatives doubted the sincerity of his conversion. Romney's Mormon faith was also a concern to some religious conservatives. The third top-tier candidate was maverick John McCain, about whom we have already written a good deal. Despite concerted efforts to woo party insiders, McCain was unable to consolidate insider support in the invisible primary.

As the *Economist* (2007) reported: "Mr. McCain is the most conservative of the big three Republicans—pro-life, pro-small-government and pro-projecting American power—but he is also the most loathed among the hard core." McCain's relationship with groups in his party became so strained that, as noted earlier, he skipped the annual conventions of the Conservative Political Action Conference and the Club for Growth. McCain won some important endorsements, but also more anti-endorsements than any other candidate. Each of the big three could claim voter support for the nomination. McCain led in the earliest national surveys of voter preference for Republican nominee, but was overtaken by Giuliani, who led for most of 2007. Meanwhile, Romney took strong leads in polls in the key states of Iowa and New Hampshire.

A central claim of this book is that parties resist candidates who are unacceptable to important members of the coalition, even when those candidates are popular with voters. Our preliminary endorsement tallies from the 2008 Republican race are consistent with this claim: None of the big three won sufficient endorsements to claim the mantle of insider favorite. Both in our data and in media reports on the contest, the story-line throughout the invisible primary was that the Republicans did not have an establishment favorite this year. It is especially notable that a candidate with as many strengths as McCain failed to win over the party's establishment.

At the time of this writing, however, McCain appears poised to win the party nomination. He achieved this position through his prowess as a candidate—beating out the rest of the field in the state-by-state contests. If his success continues, McCain will be the first candidate since 1976 to win nomination despite intense opposition within his party and, as such, a clear triumph for candidate-centered politics. His success would, of course, be a defeat for our notion of party-centered politics.

The defeat would entail some irony. Surveys that ask voters to choose between various candidates in the fall election—for example, McCain or Clinton, Romney or Obama—have repeatedly found that McCain is the Republican party's strongest choice for the fall election. Such surveys are by no means infallible, but they are the best information available. It is therefore quite possible that if the Republicans nominate McCain, they will have nominated their strongest candidate for the general election. But despite this, the logic of our book would require us to count a McCain nomination as inconsistent with our theory of party control. A party, we have argued, should not nominate someone unacceptable to any major faction of the party, even if that candidate is popular with voters, and McCain remained unacceptable to key Republican conservatives through the end of the invisible primary.

But while McCain's nomination would count against our theory, it would also be informative. The failure of Republicans to coordinate on a favorite in 2008 affords an unusual opportunity to observe Republican politics in political vacuum. Who or what took up the slack? How did front-running candidates fare in the absence of party validation? How, if at all, were politics different?

Why McCain?

As we wrote earlier, George W. Bush coasted through the invisible primary of 2000, but he encountered tense moments in the state-by-state contests. John McCain beat him in New Hampshire and seemed well-positioned to beat him again in the next major primary, that of South Carolina. With the vigorous backing of the Republican and religious leadership, Bush rallied and went on to win nomination, but McCain established himself as a formidable national campaigner. Given this, McCain's triumph in the open-field politics of 2008 needs no special explanation. The information in his success relates not to 2008, but to 2000: The candidate that Bush and the Republican establishment beat in that year was no lightweight.

Giuliani Goes South

Giuliani came to national prominence not by building relationships inside the party, but through media coverage of his leadership in the 9/11 terrorist attacks on New York. He parlayed this notoriety into popular support and successful fund-raising. He led the national polls for most of 2007 and raised more money from private contributors than any other Republican.[1]

If polls, fund-raising, and media savvy are indications of candidate strength, Giuliani was the strongest Republican candidate for most of the invisible primary. But if, on the other hand, endorsements from a wide swath of party insiders are the key to success, Giuliani was never strong. Our preliminary counts indicate that he received about a quarter of endorsements, but most came from his home region—New York and New Jersey.

Final results indicate that Giuliani was indeed weak. His campaign went into freefall at the end of 2007 and wound up failing to win a single state contest. Even more striking, Giuliani was unable to mount vigorous campaigns in Iowa and New Hampshire, choosing to use the Florida primary a month later to make his big statement. This strategy has been criticized as shortsighted, but as Jay Cost wrote in *Horse Race Blog*: "Giuliani's Florida [plan] was a strategy born of necessity. Contrary to the conventional wisdom, Rudy competed in Iowa early on. He made 43 appearances there. He spent money there. He pulled out in August—when it became clear he could not win. That goes double for New Hampshire, where he held 87 events (almost as many as he held in Florida) and spent loads of cash on advertisements" (Cost 2008).

Giuliani's lack of success is even more striking in view of the fact that Giuliani began 2007 leading the polls in Iowa and New Hampshire. But popular support is not insider support. Our research turned up almost no insider endorsements for Giuliani in Iowa and New Hampshire, and national media reports indicated he had weak organizations in these states. Much of Giuliani's campaigning in New Hampshire occurred in front of "captive" audiences—workers at a factory whose management was friendly to the candidate—rather than partisans turned out by his organization. "His campaign team appears disorganized and lacks visible 'ground troops' in key states," reported the *Washington Times* (see also Rothenberg 2007).

It is not clear why Giuliani had so little insider support outside the New York area. Our suspicion is that he tried to build campaign organizations but was unable to recruit enough people.[2] As we noted earlier, Giuliani was unacceptable to important elements in the party. But it is also possible that, for some reason, he didn't try. Either way, we see a clear lesson: High poll standing and strong financing are not sufficient for success in the early state contests; the support of "ground troops"—people whom we earlier called regulars—is needed as well.

The Rise of Mike Huckabee

Huckabee was in some ways the mirror opposite of Giuliani: scant support in national polls and little money to spend, but a strong ground campaign in Iowa. With this set of assets, Huckabee finished first in the Iowa caucuses and, for a brief time, edged ahead of Giuliani as leader in the national polls.

Huckabee did resemble Giuliani in that he had few national endorsements. But Huckabee's strongly expressed views on social issues won him the enthusiastic support of religious right groups in Iowa, including conservative home-schoolers. As the *Washington Post* reported: "While early attention focused on Romney and other better-known and better-funded opponents, home-schoolers rallied to Huckabee's cause, attracted by his faith, his politics and his decision to appoint a home-school proponent to the Arkansas board of education. They tapped a web of community and church groups that share common conservative interests, blasting them with e-mails and passing along the word about Huckabee in social settings" (Slevin and Bacon 2007). Some of the activists were new to Republican politics. "We haven't been political before, but we're trying to get there," said a member of the Cornerstone Family Church in Indianapolis, Iowa. "This time, we have to get the Christians out and vote because they really haven't before. And I like Huckabee—he's saying things the nation needs to hear" (von Sternberg 2007; see also Quaid 2007).

The importance of policy demanders like home-schoolers and evangelicals in Huckabee's Iowa success reinforces our view of the nature of party politics. Yet Huckabee's rise in the polls after winning in Iowa is reminiscent of a quite different type of politics—Jimmy Carter's momentum-driven race to the Democratic nomination in 1976 after doing "better than expected" in Iowa. Huckabee did not rocket to the nomination, but his brief stint as poll leader underscores the volatility that still lurks in the nomination process when voter preferences lack the stabilizing influence of a party cue.

The Dark Horse

Perhaps the biggest surprise of 2008 is that the Republican field had no candidate acceptable to all wings of the party. On either the group-centered or politician-centered theory of party, someone should have noticed and tried to fill the void. In fact, someone did. Absence of a "complete conservative" in the Republican field was behind the Arlington Group's dalliance with Fred Thompson, as sketched earlier. These dealings merit a closer look. Efforts to engineer Thompson's late entry to the race show as clearly as any case we have examined (1) how parties in the post-reform period go about trying to coordinate on a candidate with one another, and (2) how modern communication may aid their efforts to do so. We see Thompson as an analog to the so-called dark-horse candidates of the pre-reform system—a candidate who, like Warren G. Harding in 1920, gained strength only after the party had deadlocked on the front-runners.

Thompson began his candidacy on a conservative news show in March, where he allowed that he was "giving some thought" to running for president. Almost immediately, he became the talk of the conservative blogosphere. His record in the Senate, his Internet postings, his radio commentaries, and his folksy persona were carefully dissected by an army of conservative bloggers—and passed muster. To many Republicans, Thompson seemed the white knight the party needed. As columnist Robert Novak wrote:

> In just three weeks, Fred Thompson has improbably transformed the contest for the Republican presidential nomination. It is not merely that he has come from nowhere to double digits in national polls. He is the talk of GOP political circles, because he is filling the conservative void in the Republican field.

> Republican activists have complained for months that none of the big-
> three contenders—Rudy Giuliani, John McCain and Mitt Romney—fits the
> model of a conservative leader for a conservative party. (2007b, 43)

During the next few weeks, Thompson met with party officials, fund-raisers, conservative journalists, and other insiders. Perhaps the most notable event came in May, when lefty filmmaker Michael Moore challenged Thompson to debate the merits of the U.S. and Cuban health-care systems. Thompson responded in a video, posted on his Web site, that attracted 600,000 Internet viewings within a few days and set off a sharp rise in Thompson's stock on Intrade, a Web site where political junkies bet on elections. Two weeks after the video, Thompson displaced Giuliani as the Intrade favorite to win his party's nomination.

Thompson also began to raise money. As with much fund-raising, the money he got was tinged more by partisanship and ideology than benefit-seeking. As Matthew Mosk wrote in the *Washington Post* in June: "Thompson is aggressively pitching himself to conservatives uncomfortable with Giuliani, McCain and Romney, and hoping that he will be seen as a viable—and fresh—alternative to the current Republican field. . . . 'People have been waiting for a candidate who fits their profile,' said Rep. Jeff Miller (R-Fla.), who was a Bush Pioneer in 2004 and recently signed on with Thompson" (2007, A1). Thus, despite Thompson's late entry into the race, party donors still had plenty of money in their pockets. "Of 630 supporters Bush named Pioneers for their ability to raise at least $100,000 or Rangers for collecting at least $200,000, fewer than a third had joined a campaign as of March 31," Mosk wrote.

At about the same time, reports surfaced of private meetings between Thompson and members of the Arlington Group. *U.S. News and World Report* wrote in July, "For months, conservative evangelical activists have been fretting over a Republican presidential field whose front-runners are . . . pro-abortion rights. . . . Now the Christian right is eyeing former U.S. Sen. Fred Thompson . . . but . . . waiting to see how he holds up under increased scrutiny once he officially enters the race. 'There's a deliberate attempt by evangelical leaders to come to consensus,' says [one minister]. [Another] says, 'the leaders I talk to are all really interested in Thompson, but they're waiting to pull the trigger [on endorsements] until later this year'" (Gilgoff 2007).

Many top politicians were also keeping their powder dry. By July 1 of 1999, twenty-three of thirty Republican governors had made an official endorsement, most often George W. Bush. By the end of September 1999, twenty-seven governors had endorsed a candidate. But on July 1, 2007, only six of twenty-two Republican governors had gotten involved in the race, with only one more before October.

After extended testing of the waters, Thompson formally entered the presidential race in September, but he came across less well on the campaign trail than he had on the Internet. "More belly flop than swan dive" was how George Will (2007) described Thompson's formal entry into the race. "Important neutral Republicans decreed privately that [Thompson] had crashed and burned on takeoff," agreed Robert Novak (2007a, 33).

The religious right's interest in Thompson was never more than an effort to spur a party consensus, so when he failed to make headway against Giuliani, who was then the front-runner, some of its leaders tried a new strategy. Following a meeting in Salt Lake City, they floated the idea of sponsoring a third-party candidate in the fall election (Dobson 2007). The point would not be to elect a religious conservative, but to defeat a Republican candidate whom the religious right considered unacceptable. Other social conservatives, however, recoiled from "the nuclear option" and looked to build a consensus for either Giuliani or Romney. For them, either would be better than losing to the Democrats.

The dilemma of the religious conservatives was real. If they quietly accepted a candidate with a liberal record on abortion as the party's presidential nominee, they might come to be regarded as permanent junior partners in the party. Yet assisting or even allowing a Democrat to win would expose them to painful policy defeats. We do not see this dilemma as an indication of party weakness, but as an example of the messy situations that arise in any party coalition that includes diverse members. The history of American parties is littered with such messes. Will Rogers's comment, "I don't belong to any organized political party, I'm a Democrat," still applies—and to the Republicans too.

Yet, on the whole, the GOP's vital signs were healthy in 2008: group leaders trying to coordinate on a candidate; top officials waiting to make formal commitments until the contest has clarified; a pool of party donors motivated by ideology and looking for a candidate able to unify them. Thompson's creative use of the Internet to launch a dark-horse candidacy late in the invisible primary is another positive sign—showing that new communication technology is useful not just for bringing new energy into party politics, as the Dean campaign showed in 2004, but for aiding parties in the difficult business of coordinating on an acceptable nominee. If Republican insiders erred in 2008, it was in failing to recognize sooner and respond more energetically to the deficit of consistent conservatives in their field of potential nominees.[3]

The Democrats: Going for the Big Win

One of the earliest casualties of the 2008 invisible primary was Mark Warner, a moderate Democrat from Virginia. After earning plaudits among party activists in trips to early primary states, he unexpectedly quit the race in October 2006. Warner said he wanted to spend more time with his family, but friends gave a more political analysis. In the aftermath of the party's defeat in the 2004 presidential election, Warner was said to believe that Democratic insiders would accept a moderate in order to recapture the White House. But now he thought they were reconsidering. Bush's popularity was in steep decline, public support for the Iraq War had plummeted, and the party was about to retake Congress in the midterm elections. In these circumstances, insiders would want a presidential nominee closer to their liberal hearts. His sense of this change of mood was, as his friends suggested, Warner's real motive for dropping out (Shear, 2006).

Whether this analysis reflected Warner's views, it did appear to capture the current mood of the Democratic Party. 2008 was not the year to play it safe with a moderate. The party's big question was whether to make history by nominating either a woman or an African American for president. Senator Hillary Clinton appeared at first to be the choice of the Democratic establishment, but far from a universal one. In our initial tallies, she won about half of the weighted endorsements. This was a larger share than Michael Dukakis's 28 percent in 1988, but a smaller share than Bill Clinton's 70 percent in 1992 and Al Gore's 82 percent in 2000. John Edwards, who repositioned himself on the party's left wing after running as a moderate in 2004, ran second in the early endorsements, but was later eclipsed by Barack Obama.[4] No longer on the field of play was the party's 2004 nominee, Senator John Kerry, who quit the race in 2006 after a slow start and a widely reported gaffe.

Obama's late entry and spectacular rise in the invisible primary was the most notable feature of the Democrats' contest. Given the intense support his candidacy later attracted, his lack of early insider support may seem surprising, but it shouldn't. Obama had been in a major office only two years when he entered the presidential race, and he had never faced a tough election outside of the mainly African American section of Chicago he represented in the Illinois statehouse. (His first Republican opponent in his 2004 U.S. Senate bid had been forced out of the race by a sex scandal, leaving Obama to face a weak replacement brought in from out of state.) Thus, Obama's ability to succeed in national politics was almost completely untested at the start of the invisible primary.

Clinton, too, had shortcomings. She was viewed by much of the public as a polarizing figure, and she was not an appealing public speaker. Yet Clinton had fifteen years of national political experience, two senate victories from New York, and an active presidential campaign since at least 2004. Also, like Obama, except much earlier in the contest, she attracted the intense support of Democrats wishing to destroy barriers to equal opportunity in politics. On this combination of strengths and weaknesses, Clinton emerged as the moderately strong insider favorite.

But Obama was by no means shut out. At the level of public endorsements by big-name officeholders, the very junior senator from Illinois got off to a very slow start. But at the level of no-name insider support—the party's regular supporters—Obama ran well from the beginning of the race. Activists, professional staff, and especially fund-raisers joined his campaign in large numbers. When Obama nearly matched Clinton's first-quarter fund-raising, the *Washington Post* correctly forecast that it was now "all but certain that Democrats will face a costly and protracted battle for their party's nomination" (Kornblut 2007).[5] The bulk of Obama's early fund-raising appeared, unlike Howard Dean's in 2004, to flow through established bundlers, many of whom had previously been aligned with the Clintons, in some cases even at the beginning of this cycle. One long-standing Democratic donor, Hollywood mogul Jeffrey Katzenberg, declared himself still "a fan of Hillary's," but added, "I'm supporting Barack Obama. I think he deserves to have a level playing field in which money does not become a barrier" (Solomon and Mosk 2007; see also Sweet 2007). The donor got his wish. Obama matched Clinton's fund-raising in the invisible primary, used his money to build an organization that helped him to prevail in the Iowa caucuses.

What happened after Obama's win in Iowa was unique in the period of our study: The party changed its mind. Or, to be more exact, many important Democrats who had declined to support Obama at the beginning of the invisible primary now came rather late into his camp. Clinton had commanding leads in the national polls and in most early primary states and was still widely favored to win the nomination. Fear of her ultimate success might alone have been expected to keep party members in line, but it didn't. Moreover, the new Obama supporters were a notably broad group, from Kansas Governor Kathleen Sebelius in the moderate center of the party to George Miller on the left. Senator Ted Kennedy, the party's senior leader and custodian of the Kennedy mystique, made a forceful and widely publicized endorsement of Obama. Important Hispanic leaders and the nation's largest Spanish-language newspaper also came out for Obama. Clinton got some post-Iowa endorsements too, but fewer and less notable ones.

Given our argument thus far, the post-Iowa surge of party insiders to Obama is a problem. The party had seemed to back Clinton, but then much of it turned against her. We confess that we did not anticipate this development. When Clinton led in endorsements at the end of the invisible primary, we expected her to prevail fairly handily. But we can, with the advantage of hindsight, offer an explanation for the much tougher fight that developed. Indeed, we have already sketched the three main points. First, the party's prospects for the fall election seemed excellent in the spring of 2008. Many quite reasonably believed that the Democrats could win the White House with either a female or a black nominee. Those who preferred winning with an African American saw no reason to wait for the next such opportunity. Second, Senator Clinton never was, as we have noted, the overwhelming choice of her party. As became more apparent as the contest unfolded, many disliked her take-no-prisoners style of political combat (Packer 2008). Finally, Obama had by the Iowa caucuses demonstrated skills beyond his years and created a kind of excitement more typical of rock stars than presidential candidates.

This last point merits amplification. An insider rally to Obama in the spring of 2007, before he had proved his viability outside of Illinois, would have been daring if not reckless, but after the Iowa caucuses, the picture was different. Obama, a black man, winning in mostly white Iowa was like John F. Kennedy, a Catholic, winning in Protestant West Virginia in 1960—crossing a threshold that needed to be crossed before prudent party insiders could be expected to sign on. As described earlier, John Kennedy himself acknowledged this necessity, telling a reporter on the eve of his nomination, "Could you imagine me, having entered no primaries, trying to tell the leaders that being a Catholic was no handicap? . . . For some men, such as . . . myself, primaries are not only good, they are absolutely vital" (Davis 1997, 64). Of course, winning one or two elections can never fully establish the electability of the first Catholic, black, or woman to run for president. But with Obama's win in Iowa, it became harder to argue that he was more of a risk than Clinton, who was not widely tested or without blemishes. Nor, after the Democratic field had narrowed to just two candidates, could one raise the danger of a surprise outcome. So if, after Iowa, neither politician was clearly more electable or acceptable, the risk of letting them fight it out in the primaries was perhaps not much greater than the risk of sticking with the possibly weaker choice.[6]

Some readers will no doubt see the development of protracted intraparty division over Obama and Clinton as inconsistent with our argument. That view is not unreasonable. A party intent above all on winning the fall election might have stayed with Clinton as the safer candidate—or, more likely, made Warner its nominee. Yet, as we argued in chapters 4 and 5, parties do not care *only* about winning. They want to win with the candidate who will give them the greatest political return. From this perspective, the measured development of insider support for Obama over the course of the invisible primary and early state contests seems a defensible way for a party to decide. He was too untested to warrant insider support at the start of the invisible primary, but by the end, he was a prospect that a sensible party would take seriously. Hence, we do not score his late emergence as an insider-backed challenge to Clinton as importantly inconsistent with our theory.[7] In any event, we view the impending nomination of John McCain as a greater embarrassment to our argument than what has happened in this contest in the Democratic Party.

The Power of Parties

We began the research in this book in a 2001 convention paper, "Beating Reform: The Resurgence of Parties in Presidential Nominations." As we maintained: "Presidential parties are back. Operating as loose but stable networks of elected officials, fundraisers, and other activists, the two major parties control the resources candidates need to compete for delegates in state primaries and caucuses. The result is that the candidates favored by party insiders have won every nomination from 1980 to 2000" (Cohen et al. 2001).

As we have seen, however, parties have not done so well in the three nominations since that time. We see two potential explanations for the three tough nominations that have followed nine comparatively smooth ones. One is that the political environment has somehow changed since 2000, perhaps due to the communications revolution discussed earlier. The other is chance: The parties were never so firmly in command as they seemed in the period 1980 to 2000, nor are they as feckless as they have appeared recently, but are simply encountering different kinds of luck. For example, the inability of the Republicans in 2008 to find a consistently conservative politician with passable campaign skills can be explained as bad luck. It would be hard to argue that this represents a structural weakness in the Republican Party; it is also a situation that is unlikely to repeat itself any time soon. But it was important in 2008.

Chance variation is a constant impediment to valid inference about the nature of the world. In this section, we assess chance factors as the explanation for the pattern of party success and failure we have observed.[8]

We begin with two cases in which chance factors may have been *favorable* to the appearance of party control. President Jimmy Carter was the endorsement leader as the 1980 Iowa caucuses approached, but he looked vulnerable to insurgent Senator Ted Kennedy. Then, as often occurs in foreign policy crises, the Iran hostage crisis gave the president a boost in popular support in November 1979 that carried him through the primaries to renomination. The endorsements of party leaders were surely a boon to the president, but he might not have survived without the foreign policy "rally effect."[9]

In our second example, Gary Hart was the poll leader in the invisible primary for 1988. As we discussed in chapter 7, labor opposed him but had no strong candidate to throw against him. In these circumstances, Hart had difficulty winning party endorsements—a result consistent with our theory—but he might still have prevailed in the state primaries, thus undermining our claim that parties can block candidates they do not want. Yet Hart was forced out of the race by a personal scandal, and Michael Dukakis, with a weak plurality of party endorsements, went on to eke out a win in the primaries.[10]

More recent Democratic contests seem also to have been affected by chance events that are *unfavorable* to the appearance of party control. In 2004, it was the Iraq War. Parties rarely cope well with the intrusion of divisive new issues, and the Democratic Party did not do so in this case. In 2008, party control has been compromised—if it has been compromised—by the emergence of a candidate needing to establish his political viability in the invisible primary rather than, as parties would prefer, ahead of it.

That party control may be affected by events like these is a true testament to its limits. Although chance surely affected choices of nominee in the old system, it could not threaten party control per se, which was assured by the nature of the nomination process. Thus if, for example, Republicans were facing the current field in an old-style nominating convention, they would probably turn with minimal rancor to a "dark horse" acceptable to all of their factions. The lack of such a "consensus-forcing institution" leaves parties more vulnerable to the twists and turns that are inevitable in politics. We thus tentatively conclude that a change in the nature of chance events—favorable to party control in the 1980s, unfavorable in recent cases—may explain the appearance of party stumbling in the most recent contests. Parties themselves seem to be what they have been since 1980.

If there is a systematic factor at work, it may be that the string of successful nominations from 1980 to 2000 lulled the two parties into a complacency they did not feel in the aftermath of the 1970s. Republicans have already gotten their comeuppance—the impending nomination of John McCain, who is unacceptable to many conservative leaders. We will be surprised—and embarrassed—if the Republicans do not try harder to shape the field and arrive at consensus in the next open nomination than they did this time. If the battle between Obama and Clinton turns out to be as bruising as it could be, Democrats, too, will have reason to try harder next time.

Another way to assess party strength in the postreform system is to compare it to the previous era. But how can this be done? Even in the glory days in which parties did have a consensus-forcing mechanism, one of them suffered a major coordination failure in 1860, 1912, and 1924; and in 1896, 1900, 1908, 1928, 1948, and 1964 a nominee failed to rally large segments of his coalition. But any set of handpicked examples is suspect; what is the overall pattern? To get a historical perspective that does not depend on example, we decided to compare first-ballot voting strength of the top candidate in the old system with pre-Iowa endorsement strength of the top candidate in the new system.[11] As can be seen in the left side of figure 10.1, today's reformed parties typically manage about as much internal unity as older parties did. On the right side of figure 10.1, we compare first-ballot strength of the eventual nominee (whether he led on the first ballot or not) with pre-Iowa strength of the eventual nominee—and get similar results.

In view of the differences in the party machinery between the two periods, one cannot attach much importance to these data.[12] But the data suggest at least this: Today's parties do not do better than prereform parties, but they do not, as some have argued, do worse. Of course, the pre-preform parties had plenty of time after the first convention ballot to work out their differences and assemble majority support for a nominee; but, as we argued in connection with the 1988 and 2008 Democratic nominations, postreform parties also have limited opportunity for maneuver and coordination after the first ballots have been cast in Iowa.

An especially important argument of this book is that parties have done a better job of controlling nominations since the 1970s. Here, a strong test is available, as shown in table 10.1. As the table shows, the parties got the outcome they wanted in only one of three contested nominations in the 1970s, or 33 percent. But since then majorities or strong pluralities of endorsers have gotten their way in eight of ten, or 80 percent, of the contested nominations. On a two-tailed test, a difference as large as 33 percent versus 80 percent would occur by chance only about 15 percent of the time. We take this as a reasonable estimate of the strength of the quantitative evidence that parties have achieved greater control of nominations since the 1970s.[13] If, based on our earlier arguments, the nominations

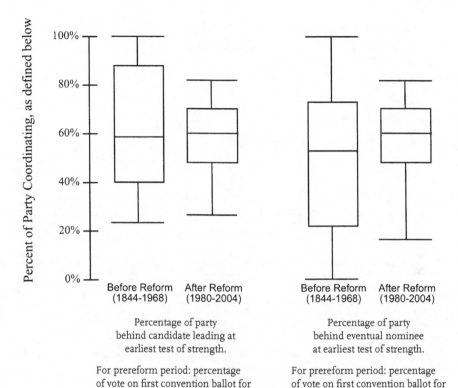

Percentage of party
behind candidate leading at
earliest test of strength.

Percentage of party
behind eventual nominee
at earliest test of strength.

For prereform period: percentage
of vote on first convention ballot for
first convention ballot winner. For
postreform period: percentage of
endorsements before Iowa for
candidate with most endorsements.

For prereform period: percentage
of vote on first convention ballot for
eventual nominee. For postreform
period: percentage of endorsements
before Iowa for eventual nominee.

Fig. 10.1. Party coordination before and after reform.

of 2008 are counted as one party failure and one success, the two-tailed
p-value rises to .196. If both are counted as failures, it rises .326.[14]

If we allow use of qualitative information, the record of post-1980 party
success is better. The wins by McGovern in 1972 and Carter in 1976
provoked harsh remarks within the party and, in McGovern's case, open
defection among some Democratic leaders. Neither was an acceptable
party choice. Dukakis, on the other hand, was the weak plurality favorite of
insiders in 1988, Kerry was the initial front-runner in the invisible primary
in 2004, and neither had trouble consolidating insider support once he
won the primaries. Each, it can therefore be argued, was a more acceptable
party choice than McGovern or Carter had been. Either Obama or Clinton
would also be a more acceptable insider choice than McGovern or Carter.

Table 10.1: Party favorites' track record, 1972–2000

Nomination contest	Party favorite	Outcome
Transition from reform		
1972 Democrats	Muskie	L
1976 Democrats	No favorite	L
1976 Republicans	Ford	W
Postreform		
1980 Republicans	Reagan	W
1980 Democrats	Carter	W
1984 Democrats	Mondale	W
1988 Republicans	Bush	W
1988 Democrats	No clear favorite (Dukakis)	L
1992 Democrats	Clinton	W
1996 Republicans	Dole	W
2000 Republicans	Bush	W
2000 Democrats	Gore	W
2004 Democrats	No clear favorite (Kerry)	L

Only McCain would rank as a clear breakdown of party control. By this reckoning, eleven of the twelve nominees from 1980 to 2008 will be more acceptable party choices than two of three nominees in the 1970s, a result that would be hard to explain on the basis of chance alone.

A Note on Nominations for Legislative Office

The greatest failing of the scholarly literature claiming that presidential nominations are candidate-centered is that it gives parties credit neither for trying to coordinate nor for succeeding much of the time. When a presidential hopeful cruises to nomination, as George W. Bush did in 2000, the story is that the strongest candidate won. The efforts of the parties are simply not noticed. Important politicians who withdraw from competition after failing to get insider support, such as Al Gore in the 2004 race and Bill Frist and John Kerry in the 2008 race, are likewise given scant notice.

The same combination of narrow focus on the activities of candidates and failure to notice parties arises in the literature on congressional elections, where Paul Herrnson sums up the conventional wisdom as follows:

> Candidates, not parties, are the major focus of congressional campaigns, and candidates, not parties, bear the ultimate responsibility for election outcomes. . . . In the United States, parties do not actually run congressional campaigns

nor do they become the major focus of elections. Instead, candidates run their own campaigns.

Candidates are the most important actors in American congressional elections. (1997, 6–7)

This conventional wisdom may be vulnerable to the same challenge we have raised in our study of presidential nominations: that candidates' control of their own campaigns does not necessarily make them the most important actor in the election. If parties effectively control nominations, parties are certainly important too.

Some young scholars (including a member of this team) have written dissertations that take up this issue. Although their work is still mainly unpublished, the findings provide a useful complement to the findings of our book. Here are some in capsule form:

- Seth Masket argues in *Reluctant Partisans* (forthcoming) that groups of elected officials and activists control local, state, and federal offices in their communities by means of an "informal party organization." These IPOs also enforce party-line voting on their officials in the state legislature— but only when institutional arrangements permit them to control nominations.
- Marty Cohen argues in "Moral Victories" (2005) that the Republican takeover of Congress in 1994 was caused, at least in part, by social conservatives who invaded Republican primaries to nominate antiabortion candidates. Far from welcoming social conservatives into the party, old-guard Republicans resisted them until, and sometimes even after, their antiabortion candidates showed their electoral worth. So control of nomination politics is again tantamount to control of the party.
- Casey Dominguez argues in "Before the Primary" (2005) that local party officials assert themselves in congressional nominations mainly in cases in which the general election is expected to be difficult. The purpose is to make sure the party nominates a strong candidate for the difficult race. In districts that are "safe" for their side, parties do not generally intervene, because the natural operation of the primaries turns out a reliable partisan who can win. The important theoretical point here is that, in a stable party system, parties may get what they want out of nominations without doing very much. As in the party system created by Van Buren, where the structure of the party coalitions guaranteed that slavery would be off the national agenda, politics may appear wholly election-centered because the parties have set the terms of candidate engagement.

- In an examination of congressional elections, Mark West (2008) argues that donors from around the country take cues from ideological and party leaders about where to send their campaign donations. This "ideological money" may target incumbent officeholders of the donor's own party who are moderate and from safe seats. Moderate incumbents from nonsafe seats, however, are given a pass. This suggests a strategic purpose: to nominate and elect the most extreme candidate that local conditions will allow. In his larger dissertation project, West aims to show in congressional nominations what we could only speculate about in presidential nominations: that much of the money that candidates raise—especially when they are the party favorites—is party-centered money rather than candidate-centered money.
- Rachel Cobb (2006) collected data on public endorsements for gubernatorial nominations in six states. The dynamics of these contests turned out to be quite different from presidential nominations. Some state parties had institutional means of regulating ballot access and controlled nominations by that means. Where parties lacked institutional means, endorsements played varied roles. Massachusetts and Ohio Republicans, for example, relied on nonpublic endorsements to reach decisions behind the scenes, thus rendering public ones superfluous. Where parties relied mainly on public endorsements, they sometimes controlled nominations and sometimes did not. Overall, Cobb found considerable evidence of coordinated effort, especially when a nomination was worth having, but practices varied.[15]

Because they are still mostly unpublished, these findings must be regarded as preliminary. But they still give an idea of what scholars may learn if, as in our study, one focuses on difficult-to-observe parties rather than the easy-to-see candidates, and on the less visible nomination process rather than the more visible general elections.

Masket's term for contemporary parties, informal party organization, is an excellent one. But the term needn't be restricted simply to modern parties. In some places and times, formal party organization may capture the most important aspects of party behavior. Thus, for much of the nineteenth century, national political parties hardly existed except at their national conventions. Yet we have also seen that, in the final decades of the old system, much of the business of the national parties was conducted by a more informal means, the invisible primary.[16] The work of Dominguez suggests that an invisible primary may also operate at the level of congressional nominations. Understanding the many informal ways by which parties influence nominations may be the key to explaining why the country's officeholders are so much more polarized than the voters who elect them.[17]

What We Have Shown and Not Shown

We observed in chapter 1 that the "two big problems we face in this book" were, first, obtaining good information about party activity at the nomination stage and, second, convincing critics that informal parties could nonetheless be real parties. We did not assert that we would entirely solve these problems and, as the reader surely appreciates, we have not. Having admitted a lack of information about key points in this book, we must be frank to admit that our empirical analysis is uneven. In this section, we will attempt to sum up what we believe we have shown and what we cannot show about parties and presidential nominations, beginning with the former.

Parties in American History

As social scientists, we try to develop general arguments and to demonstrate that they apply to a range of cases. This was one of the main reasons for our extended forays into party formation in early American history and party nominations in the middle decades of the twentieth century. We did not presume our brief analyses of these events to be definitive, but we did hope they demonstrated that the conception of party we believe fits the late twentieth and early twenty-first centuries works as well for other periods and is therefore not overfitted to the current period. As demonstrations of the wide utility of our notion of party, these forays seem reasonably successful. Our hope is that they contain insights useful to specialists in the earlier periods.

Party Control of Nominations in the Current Period

We believe that our analysis has made it credible that party insiders exert a substantial amount of influence over the selection of presidential nominees. Every candidate since 1980 who has pulled clearly ahead on our measure of insider support has managed to make it to the final round of the competition—that is, through the invisible primary and the rocky first contests in Iowa and New Hampshire, and to the stretch of decisive contests that follow. By the same token, no insider favorite has done nearly as badly as Edmund Muskie in 1972, who won 60 percent of endorsements but dropped out midway through the primaries.

Can the insider favorite be beaten? Since Walter Mondale's bare victory in the 1984 nomination contests, we have known that the answer to this question is yes. He was not beaten, but the outcome was close enough that he might have been. If Hillary Clinton is defeated in the state contests of 2008, it will not add much new information to this question since, in our analysis, a substantial part of the Democratic Party turned against her at a time when her prospects for success were still fairly good. Hence, the current state of evidence about the effect of becoming the clear endorsement leader is that it guarantees that the favored candidate will make it to the endgame of the nomination contest, and makes it likely but not certain that the favored candidate will become the nominee.

In contrast, candidates who get clearly out in front in terms of poll support but not endorsements do not make it to the final stretch. There have been only two clear cases since 1980—Howard Dean in 2004 and Rudy Giuliani in 2008—and both fell out of competition well before the endgame. One might also count Gary Hart in 1988. It is true that he was hurt by a sex scandal, but Bill Clinton, with much stronger inside support, suffered a sex scandal in the next invisible primary and survived to be nominated. Thus, as usual, our evidence is thinner and less clean than we would like, but what it suggests is that poll support, by itself, brings no certain benefit. And what is true of polls is even more true of money. Romney raised $88 million in the invisible primary, compared to $41 million for McCain, but was forced out of the race by McCain after the first month of state contests. Giuliani raised $61 million and yet won less voter support than Huckabee, who raised $9 million in the invisible primary. Thus, even in the wide open Republican contest of 2008, money was not decisive. This outcome, on top of similar busts by big spenders lacking insider support—from John Connally to Pat Robertson to Steve Forbes—points to a conclusion: Money, independent of political support, has limited value in presidential nominations.

Our detailed statistical analyses in chapters 8 and 9 provide a systematic statement of the evidence just summarized, including the very important point that insider support is more a cause than an effect of the success of the favored candidate.

Assessing Party Control

According to our analysis of endorsements, the parties have maintained agreement on an insider favorite in eight of twelve contests over the period 1980 to 2008. We assume that, all else equal, they would like to agree in all cases. We are therefore led to ask: When parties have not been able to agree, why have they not? We answer this question, based on previous analysis, as follows:

- 1988 Democrats. The Democrats had a weak field of contenders, the so-called Seven Dwarfs. The field included several who were widely acceptable and no unacceptable candidates in a strong position to win. In this circumstance, leaders waited for the first primaries in order to determine who among the acceptable candidates was the best vote-getter. Thus, inability to agree on electoral viability prevented consensus.
- 2004 Democrats. Party insiders were divided on the Iraq War. Howard Dean, a stridently anti–Iraq War candidate, raised more money and generated more excitement than any contender, but many party insiders were ambivalent about the war and would therefore not rally to Dean, an openly factional candidate. Party division over the war thus impeded consensus.
- 2008 Democrats. Hillary Clinton won enough support to become the party favorite, but Barack Obama established a claim to electability during the nomination process. Both were acceptable to all major party factions, neither was obviously more electable, and each promised a kind of historically important breakthrough. In this circumstance, some party members saw little risk and some potential gain in plunging into a primary battle.
- 2008 Republicans. The Republican field included no candidate acceptable to all major factions in the party. We see this as due to failure to recognize and respond more energetically to bad luck.

These four cases do not yield a clear pattern. The strongest conclusion we can reach from them is that it is inherently difficult for a coalition of diverse policy demanders to coordinate on a candidate who is acceptable to all of them and also electorally viable. We note, however, that Democratic leaders had a reasonable basis for believing in 1988 and 2008 that they might get a better nominee without reaching consensus ahead of the state primaries and caucuses. We therefore view these failures to reach consensus as risky but not a major breakdown. The other two cases, however, were potentially serious. Failure of Democrats to unite on an insider alternative to Dean in 2004 might have saddled them with a nominee who, like George McGovern in 1972, would blemish the party's reputation for decades to come. Whether by luck or skill, the party managed to avoid this outcome and to nominate John Kerry, the candidate to which a more adept party might have rallied at the start. Failure of Republicans to agree on an insider choice in 2008 meant giving—as some would see it, wasting—its nomination on a candidate who cannot be trusted to protect the party's interests if he wins the general election.

Overall, then, the two parties have managed nominations well but not perfectly in the period since 1980, an improvement over the 1970s that, as we noted a moment ago, is too great to be easily explained as due to chance. This assessment is a large departure from existing scholarship on presidential nominations. To the extent it has been credibly established, it is therefore an important accomplishment of this book.

We turn now to our shortcomings.

Where Are the Policy Demanders?

Detailed information about intense policy demanders is in short supply and we have not found nearly as much as we would have liked. We take this to be the most important shortcoming of our study. Still, we have reported some clear glimpses of intense policy demanders in action, usually at important junctures in party history: journalists and democratic club activists in the formation of the first Republican party in the 1790s, abolitionists in the formation of the second Republican party in the 1840s, members of Americans for Democratic Action in the remaking of the Democratic Party on race at the 1948 convention, and economic conservatives in reinvigorating Republican Party opposition to the welfare state at the 1964 convention. Another primary reason for our historical analysis was the incisive view of intense policy demanders that it affords. We attach great importance—more than we wish we had to—to the argument that if policy demanders can make or remake a party alignment, as we have evidence that they can, they have done a large fraction of what they need to do to control presidential nominations.

For the period since 1980, our clearest views of policy demanders have involved religious conservatives in the Republican party. We have observed religious leaders helping to swing key voter support to Bob Dole and George W. Bush in their nomination battles, and we have seen them both trying to shape the party's 2008 nomination and then threatening to bolt when their candidate failed to catch on. Along with some observations of labor activity, this is most of what we have found in this phase of our analysis. Our measure of candidate endorsements turned up some evidence of intense policy demanders, but none that we could turn to systematic use. We must therefore leave it to further research to more firmly establish the role of policy demanders in party politics.

Who Says What to Whom?

A related problem is that the book lacks detailed information about interactions among politicians, group leaders, and activists in the invisible primary. We sketched a restaurant game to show how interactions might work, but could only loosely test its logic (via our measure of out-of-group endorsements). The invisible primary is like a big national conversation, open to anyone who cares to chime in. But we have also described parties as a semiveiled attempt to control government by controlling the candidates from which voters can choose. Given this, some of what is said in the national conversation is likely to remain off the public record. An incident from the 2008 campaign makes this point. In an attempt to make himself acceptable to social conservatives, Rudy Giuliani gave a speech to the Federalist Society in which he promised that he would appoint Supreme Court justices in the mold of Antonin Scalia and Clarence Thomas. His point seemed clear enough, but it left the leader of an abortion rights group startled and confused: "Obviously, judges in the mold of Thomas and Scalia are going to overturn *Roe v. Wade*, no doubt [as the leader afterward told a reporter], adding that her group was uneasy about Mr. Giuliani's recent statements. 'We really feel like, out of the glare of the cameras, we have to sit down with him and his colleagues and ask, which is the real Rudy Giuliani?'" (Cooper 2007). We find it notable that the response of a group leader to a candidate's public speech was to seek a private meeting to find out what the candidate really thought. We further suspect that private commitments and understandings from such meetings are a routine part of the process that leads to the public endorsements that, as our statistical analysis indicates, drive much of the invisible primary. If so, future political scientists are likely to have the same trouble we have had getting reliable information about its inner workings. In the prereform party, observers at least knew who attended meetings in the legendary smoke-filled room; in the postreform system, it is hard to get even that information.

How Do Endorsements Work?

Emmett H. Buell, Jr., maintains that in the Republican contest of 1996, "the eventual nominee owed much of his victory in South Carolina to the votes of religious and social conservatives, who were persuaded by party leaders to choose electability over ideological affinity" (Buell 2000, 99). We are persuaded that his observation is correct and that many other group leaders, including party leaders, often exert similar influence. But we would like to have much better evidence than the stray poll or colorful quote that we and others are often forced to rely upon. The degree to which voters think for themselves in politics, as against following the advice of others whom they trust, is an absolutely central question for political science—a question on which we wish we could have shed more light in this study. It may fairly be said that we relied on past research on leader influence at least as much as we added to it.

A Central Ambiguity in the Theory of Party
Our theory of group-centered parties has important limitations, of which we would like to highlight just two. The first concerns the rational basis for party organization. As the reader should recall, we relied on the logic of Thomas Schwartz's unpublished essay, "Why Parties?" in developing our theory of parties. In this theory, one group of actors forms a minimum-winning coalition and the left-out actors form an opposition party. However, another thread of party theory maintains that rational political actors may form a universalist party that includes everyone and makes an equal division of political benefits. The different theories are, of course, based on different assumptions. A major problem for research on parties is, as we suggested in chapter 2, to delineate the conditions under which politicians and interest groups form one noncompetitive party or multiple competing ones.

The other theoretical ambiguity concerns the electoral blind spot. There can be little doubt that voters do not vigilantly monitor government and that intense policy demanders would like to take advantage of their lack of attention. What is less clear is how much of the advantage groups gain from parties is due to exploitation of voter inattention and how much is due to the advantages of organization alone. Likewise, we have not considered how voters' use of cues, heuristics, and other information shortcuts may ameliorate lack of attentiveness.

Unresolved Normative Questions
We have said little about whether party control of nominations and the kind of parties we have described are generally good for democracy. Obviously, answers to these questions will depend heavily on what one means by democracy, an issue that we do not wish to take on. We can, however, identify some obvious and perhaps nonobvious costs and benefits.

By nominating a president and a team of legislators for office, parties give voters a means of holding some identifiable set of people accountable for their performance in office, which gives officeholders an incentive to do their best. Today's Democratic and Republican parties also give voters a vehicle for weighing in on a range of important issues—abortion, taxes, health insurance, affirmative action, same-sex marriage, and so forth. As Schattschneider (1942) pointed out, the vocabulary of the people consists of just two words, yes or no, but two words are better than none.

One can also argue that if individual parties did not stand accountable for the organization of politics, less accountable private interests would organize it instead. By this argument, an open coalition of group interests is more accountable than a slew of unorganized ones.[18] Indeed, some scholars have presented empirical evidence that the alternative to partisan politics is *not* enlightened government in the public interest, but rather greater domination by lobbies less accountable to voters than parties. Scholars of both American and comparative politics also often argue that strong parties promote participation among lower-income voters.

For these and other reasons, one can readily argue that the benefits parties offer to voters are so important that, as Schattschneider (1942, 1) and many others say, it is hard to imagine democracy without parties.

Still, there is the question of the cost of party services. By the Schumpeter-Downs theory of electorally oriented parties, and the Schlesinger-Aldrich notion of politician-centered parties, the cost may be small. Parties and politicians mainly want just to be elected and therefore do their best to provide voters what they want. Within those theories, parties are, in large measure, the servants of democracy.

Within our group-centered theory of parties, however, the costs of party services may be higher. The parties we have described exist not to serve voters, but to serve their own intense preferences. They will be responsive on issues voters notice and care about, but will take advantage of lack of voter vigilance by pursuing their own agendas when they can. The potential cost to voters of this orientation is obvious, but there may be a not-so-obvious and more important benefit. It is that group-centered parties provide a vehicle for leadership that a myopic and distracted electorate may need. For example, the Federalists who created the United States and the abolitionists who struggled to end slavery both used parties to achieve goals that we now applaud but that might not have been attainable except through a party coalition. Of course, slave owners also used a party to defend slavery, so the record of parties is scarcely perfect. But if we have sufficient confidence in voters to believe in democracy in the first place, we should also believe that, if forced to make rather than avoid difficult choices, voters will ultimately decide rightly. Group-centered parties will bicker and offer more extreme nominees than most voters want; they will take advantage of voter inattentiveness when they can; but they will also, when they sense the public is on their side, force sharp choices in a way that is valuable for the larger society. Parties as organized by intense policy demanders are often sources of insight, energy, and principled leadership in politics that might otherwise be lacking.

We suspect that different readers will judge the value of group-centered parties differently. Those with intense and noncentrist preferences will cherish the opportunity for political engagement that parties afford. Those of moderate or uncertain views—two traits that appear to run together—may prefer weaker parties, or at least weaker group influence within them. "We must be free to organize parties however we wish," the first group will say. "Let's all just get along and do the right thing," the second will counter. We offer no wisdom on which of these views is more correct. Our contribution here is positive and empirical—how best to understand parties and what they do.

Reprise

This book has focused on parties and presidential nominations, but at a deeper level, it is about the efforts of individuals whom we call intense policy demanders to get what they want out of government. Groups of policy demanders focus on nominations because it is easier to achieve their goals by electing politicians who share their views than by winning over truly independent politicians after they have taken office. They form parties because they need to cooperate with one another in order to get their candidates elected.

Policy demanders run the gamut from slave owners to abolitionists to modern liberal and conservative activists. Prominent among them in all periods of American history are officeholders who were nominated for office because other policy demanders trusted them. It has not been as easy for us to get information about non-office-holding policy demanders as about other actors in the party system, but we have nonetheless done our best to keep our theoretical focus on them.

What intense policy demanders want in a presidential nominee is someone whom they can trust to advance their interests and agendas, who is acceptable to other members of the party coalition, and who can be elected in a general election. Many factors affect their ability to nominate such a candidate. Among them are laws that regulate party behavior, the ease of intraparty communication, the compatibility of group demands within a party, and availability of a suitable candidate. Changes in these factors— both across American history and from one election to the next—have affected the institutional form and performance of parties, but not their basic character. From the framing of the Constitution to the present, parties may be fruitfully understood as organized attempts by intense policy demanders to get control of government.[19]

We do not view the McGovern-Fraser reforms as having enfeebled parties. We see them, rather, as having changed the balance of power among actors seeking to control presidential nominations and as having changed how they go about making nominations. In the prereform party system, party leaders could determine nominations through a formal vote at their national convention. Reform deprived them of this power. But well ahead of the McGovern-Fraser reforms, party insiders had begun making the real choice of nominee in the invisible primary, and they have continued to do so in the postreform period. The invisible primary functions today as a national conversation in which each party's intense policy demanders seek to coordinate behind a suitable candidate before the public campaign begins. In some cases, they simply confirm the status of a ranking national leader. In other cases, they resist top leaders—as Gerald Ford, Dan Quayle, Bill Frist, Al Gore, and John Kerry can attest—and pick lesser-ranked politicians instead.[20] And in some cases, insiders are unable to agree on a choice. When they do agree, party rank-and-file, sharing many of their goals, tend to go along with the insider choice.

In focusing on the efforts of intense policy demanders to control nominations, we do not deny the importance of efforts by self-starting politicians to win nomination on their own. To state the obvious: candidates who lack the motivation and ability to mount serious campaigns have no chance of winning presidential nominations. Yet it should also be obvious that political parties can often decide which of many strong candidates actually gets nominated. The intense policy demanders at the core of parties are too committed to stand by, too resourceful to lose very often, and too smart to forget that working through parties to control nominations is often the best way for them to get what they want from government.

Notes

Chapter 1

1. Kennedy entered the race after the New Hampshire primary.

2. See chapter 6 for a discussion of Humphrey's nomination strategy. Humphrey's name appeared on the District of Columbia primary ballot, but only because local officials decided which names to include, and he did not campaign there.

3. In some Republican primaries, the candidate who gets the most votes in a state primary gets all of the delegates rather than simply a proportion related to vote share. These are called winner-take-all primaries. In the Democratic party, about 20 percent of convention delegates are senators, U.S. representatives and party officials who are not chosen by voters in state primaries and caucuses. These so-called super delegates could determine the outcome of a close nomination battle, but the formal role of party officials is nonetheless dramatically less than it was prior to the McGovern-Fraser reforms. Republicans permit three party officials from each state to vote at their nominating conventions.

4. Wayne goes on to note, however, that the role of state parties in general elections has been strengthened by their role in collecting and dispensing "soft money" donations to the party nominees (2000, 121–22).

5. See also Crotty and Jackson 2001, 64; Patterson 1993, 33; Kayden and Mahe, 1985, 195; White and Shea, 2000, 132-133. Howard Reiter (1985) agrees that parties are weak, but believes change was not due mainly to the McGovern-Fraser Commission; we discuss this view in chapter 4.

6. These data are described in chapter 6.

7. See discussion on pp. 352–55.

8. The first to use this phrase appears to be Rhodes Cook (1989).

9. We will not be able to measure cogency, but we can measure resources.

Chapter 2

1. TPOs, as Mayhew characterized them, had five characteristics, including hierarchical organization, control of nominations for a wide set of offices, and reliance on material incentives to motivate workers. When, as may occur, a TPO nominates and elects a majority of local officeholders, it becomes by that fact a political machine. So a TPO is not necessarily a machine but often is.

2. Yet some sort of organization was certainly present. In an intriguing passage, Key describes power relations among party leaders, most of whom were not officeholders, as follows:

> Members of party committees, no matter what the committee's level, usually have a base of power in some geographical area smaller than the jurisdiction of the committee on which they sit. An influential country committeeman is apt to be a power in his precinct, township, or election district. A member of the state committee to be reckoned with is usually a leader of note in his county. And those national committeemen whose word is paid much heed are men who have achieved prominence in their state organizations. Advancement in the political organization tends to be an expansion of influence from a geographical base rather than an ascent up a ladder. (1965, 328)

But what is the basis of this locally based power in the 1960s, when patronage-based organizations have all but disappeared? It is not clear.

3. How exactly preferences are linked to ascriptive characteristics—e.g., why some women become feminists and others do not—is an important subject but is outside of our theory.

4. Chance events, such as a hurricane or market crash, may cause voters to notice what they otherwise would have missed. When voters go to the polls, they vote partly on policies that are visible to them, partly on how much money is spent on the campaigns, and partly on chance events such as booms and busts in the economy.

5. See Bawn andRosenbluth (2006) for an analysis of coalition formation in this case.

6. Ultimately, this will depend on the mix of policy demands and resources that each group has. Groups with low-cost demands on government may have less incentive to bargain with other groups, and those with control of few resources will have little to offer. Groups with severe conflicts may not surmount them. Such groups would typically be in different parties. See Bawn and Noel 2007 for a limited treatment.

7. Parties may even want politicians to "jump ship" at strategic times, but they would want control over who does or does not. (See, e.g., Lawrence, Maltzman, and Smith 2006).

8. As in many principal-agent relationships, the agent may operate from day to day with considerable independence from the principal and yet remain an agent.

9. Politicians are, as noted, also part of the party, so they are principals as well.

10. The Traditional Party Organizations studied by Mayhew and others might be seen as organizations in which party leaders—especially the boss—had the upper hand over groups and, in effect, "owned" the party. These organizations did, however, exert central control over nominations, so they were not politician-centered in the contemporary sense. Also, the leaders of TPOs often had such close relationships with dominant economic interests that the parties may be seen as agents of groups. For example, Duane Lockard provides the following account of a nineteenth-century TPO in New Hampshire:

Railroad interests along with timber barons and a few others had control over the party organizations, and local party barons held their fiefs at the grace of the leadership. Both top and bottom elements of the party performed mutual services in the best feudal tradition—votes from the bottom up and payoffs and patronage from the top down—but there was no doubt that the dominant power rested with leadership. Venality was common as rising economic interests maneuvered to protect and expand their investments. Frequently governors were mere pawns in the hands of party leaders and railroad magnates, although one governor (Charles Sawyer, 1887–1889) vetoed a bill favoring the Boston and Maine Railroad on the grounds that the bill had been bought. He said, "To my mind, it is conclusively shown that there has been deliberate and systematic attempts at wholesale bribery of the servants of the people in the legislature." Shortly after this fiasco, a bill passed to prohibit political spending by such interests as the railroads; it was, however, repealed at the next session! (Lockard 1959, 200)

11. In these same pages, Key describes the rise of what would become known as candidate-centered politics: "to an extent startling in its degree in some jurisdictions, the doorbell ringers have lost their function of mobilizing the vote to public-relations experts, to specialists in radio and television, and to others who deal in mass communication. . . . Of the changes in the manner of organization, perhaps the most striking has been the fractionalization of integrated organization in the states and localities and the substitution of complexes of cliques of professionals grouped about individual leaders" (1965, 343). This breakdown appears quite similar to the breakdown of control of presidential nominations by what Shafer (1988) calls the "official party." However, loss of control by the official party does not imply loss of control by the party in local affairs more than presidential nominations. See Masket 2008.

12. Groups would even want their politicians to compromise on key elements of the group agenda if necessary to maintain party control. When groups and politicians occasionally disagree—as when, for example, politicians favor more compromise on the group agenda than the groups themselves will accept—it may be difficult to say whether the disagreement is due to the politicians looking out for their own reelections or to the politicians having better judgment about how much compromise is necessary to achieve group goals.

13. Karol (2001, 2009) argues that politicians do play proactive roles in shaping party positions on "groupless" issues that are not central to the concerns of components of their parties' coalitions.

14. Aldrich writes that activists exert pressure on candidate positioning through the nomination process, and they may adjust their pressure on politicians to take nonoptimal positions if they judge that electoral conditions require it (1995, 187–93). This is tricky ground. If activists largely determine the positions of candidates through the nomination process on the basis of their reading of the electoral situation, then the politician-centered theory of parties ceases to be politician centered.

15. For a view of politicians as policy demanders, see Van Houweling (2008).

16. Adds another historian, "Chase himself often had difficulty differentiating between his own interests and those of the reform effort he advocated" (Maizlish 1998, 47).

Chapter 3

1. Under the Articles of Confederation, the presiding officer of Congress had the title of president. The office had no real executive power, however.

2. Actually, the Constitutional Convention at Philadelphia may have been technically illegal, since the call for it had not come from established authority. It did, on the other hand, seek the legitimacy of state ratification of its work.

3. The procedure had additional features that are not relevant to this discussion.

4. This calculation omits from the denominator three delegates who opposed the Constitution, two who died too soon after its passage to run for office, and one for whom information is unavailable. Ben Franklin, who died in 1790, is included in the denominator.

5. Fisher Ames (cited in Harlow 1917, 125–26).

6. Fischer 1965, 204.

7. According to Bell (1973, 186), 79 percent of bills supported by Hamilton's core supporters were passed. However, he also emphasizes the instability of the coalitions. See also Cunningham 1957, 71–72.

8. The quote is from Claude Bowers, *Jefferson and Hamilton*, 1925, as cited with approval by Miller (1939).

9. In the 1820s, when party activity was not aimed at displacing an unpopular administration party, voters strongly resisted partisan tickets. See Leonard 2002.

10. This paragraph is based on three examples in Cunningham (1957, 114, 161).

11. In 1808 and 1812, Federalists chose their nominees at secret meetings of party leaders, at least some of whom were not officeholders, rather than by congressional caucus. See Fischer 1965.

12. The Federalist caucus chose its vice presidential nominee on receipt of written instruction of Alexander Hamilton, who was the unofficial leader of the New York Federalists but not an officeholder. But Hamilton's suggestion of Charles Pickney—on grounds that it might lead to a split in the South Carolina delegation that would derail the otherwise unstoppable Jefferson—was so inspired that the caucus could as well have been assenting to sound strategy. See Cunningham's account (1957, 162).

13. Pasley relates an example in 1812 in which an editor concluded that a Republican House member was insufficiently devoted to party issues and worked successfully to get him denominated (see 2001, 340).

14. Van Buren had Calhoun review his letter to Ritchie before sending it.

15. We consulted McCormick's (1966) *Second American Party System* but found that it provided little information on the interest basis of party organization.

16. We say *almost* pure because Van Buren always presented himself as a principled Jeffersonian wishing to revive Jeffersonian principles. He was, moreover, fairly consistent in his adherence to them. However, he also argued, quite persuasively, that Jeffersonian principles offered the best vehicle for party-building, and we take this motive as likely paramount.

17. The party's attempt under President Van Buren to use pressure from the party's organizational base to enforce party discipline on key congressional votes also fits with the notion of a long coalition rooted in local politics.

18. The group was a secret society that instructed its members to say, "I know nothing," when asked about it—hence the popular name.

19. The Whigs had sixty seats, the Democrats eighty-two, and forty-six called themselves Republicans based on state party affiliation. No national Republican Party yet existed.

20. This statement blurs the time line slightly, since some Whigs abandoned their party before the 1854 election, while others managed to return as Republicans.

21. Opponents did finally caucus together late in the process, but little came of the effort (Gienapp 1987, 78–79).

22. Salmon P. Chase was a leader in forming the Free Soil Party, one of three U.S. senators associated with the party and perhaps the most gifted propagandist of the antislavery movement. Senator Benjamin Wade was a Whig-turning-Republican who later emerged as a leading Radical Republican of the 1860s. Lewis Campbell was a respected House member and a leading candidate for speaker in 1855. House member Joshua Giddings was a Free Soiler who opposed the annexation of Texas as a slave state and the Missouri Compromise and was widely known for his egalitarian beliefs. These four were perhaps the most impressive antislavery state delegation in Congress.

23. Gienapp's practice is to give the names of all important politicians. He does not give the names of these three, and we have been unable to discover them.

24. In Pennsylvania's Republican convention at about the same time, Know Nothing delegates elected one of their members as state chair, and he proceeded to sabotage the nascent party.

25. The Free Soil party had three U.S. senators, but all were elected by state legislatures.

26. The Know Nothings were not the only group trying to infiltrate and sabotage the opposition. Antislavery delegates went to Know Nothing conventions with the purpose of using the slavery issue to create discord among northern and southern elements of the party, thus preventing the emergence of a completely national, and hence potentially much more powerful, American Party.

Chapter 4

1. Abraham Lincoln to Samuel Galloway, March 24, 1860, Lincoln Papers, Library of Congress.

2. Or, in Tyler's case, a disaster.

3. The measure of party extremism in figure 4.1 is in units of the NES ideology 7-point rating scale described above in the text. The ratings themselves are from the NES for the period 1972 to 2004, and from Rosenstone (1983) for 1948 to 1968. The details of scale construction are explained in Zaller (2003). The data are available upon request.

4. The slope of the line in figure 4.1 is $-.173$ ($t = 3.13$) and, contrary to appearances, is not much affected by outliers. The slope for Democratic challengers alone is $-.202$ ($n = 8$, $t = 1.46$) and for Republican challengers alone is $-.182$ ($n = 7$, $t = 2.69$). For challengers from 1980 to 2004, the slope is $-.199$ ($n = 7$, $t = 2.78$). Bawn et al. (2006) present evidence that the major parties in Great Britain and Germany are similarly motivated to become less ideologically extreme as they spend more time with the other party controlling the executive.

5. Or, in the Democratic Party until 1936, two-thirds of the delegates.

6. Our account follows Richard Bain's account in *Convention Decisions and Voting Records* (1960, 203).

7. See the first part of chapter 5.

8. The passage cited by Reiter is by Donald Bruce Johnson.

9. The t-ratio on Year in the first model is -2.59. The t-ratio on Year in the second model is $-.31$ and the t-ratio on the 1928 Dummy is -1.71. A more appropriate negative binomial model with Year, a 1928 dummy, and its interaction shows that the number of ballots was increasing before 1928 but fell abruptly in that year and gradually went lower afterward, as suggested in the raw scatterplot. A test of the shift in 1928 shows that it is highly statistically significant ($p < .001$). However, the simpler model shown graphically suffices for our purposes. Experiments with different breakpoints suggest that the change occurred between 1924 and 1928, which is hardly surprising in view of the history of the Democratic

conventions of those two years. But even if those two years are removed from the data, there continues to be evidence of a sharp break in the data at about the same time.

10. He failed in an effort to win the Whig nomination for governor of Illinois in 1854 and, having won the Republican Senate nomination in 1858, failed to defeat the incumbent senator, Stephen Douglas, in the general election.

11. Another term used in this book is *activist*. Activists and regulars are similar, except that the latter works more exclusively for a party's candidates in elections; the former may also work for candidates in elections, but may engage in a broader range of activities. In most contexts, we cannot be certain whether a person is better described as activist or regular, but this note should at least help keep the terms conceptually straight.

12. See note 4 above.

Chapter 5

1. Counting Alaska, Hawaii, Puerto Rico, and the District of Columbia, the APSA study covered 104 separate delegate-selection processes.

2. In other states, the process began with the election of party officers in regular but very low-key mass elections in which only party activists were likely to be sufficiently informed to make meaningful ballot choices.

3. African Americans were not usually permitted to vote in the South, but their numbers still counted in population-based formulas that determined congressional and Electoral College representation. In the north, African Americans could usually vote and naturally favored pro-civil-rights policies.

4. Kennedy applied similar pressure to California Governor Pat Brown, getting some but not all of what he sought. See Rarick 2005, 192.

5. The statement was reported in the November 9, 1959, issue of *Time* magazine and has been widely cited. In a letter to the editor of *Time*, McCarthy denied making it.

6. If Kennedy had lived, he would have faced, at best, an uphill struggle for nomination (Polsby 1983, 23–24).

7. Lingering concern that he might be a crusader was answered by his loyal support of his boss's conservative Vietnam policy.

8. We cannot be certain whether White is using the term *regular* in the same way we do.

9. A small number of conservative delegates favored Goldwater, but the Arizona Senator had taken himself out of the running before the balloting began.

10. These rotten boroughs were so called because they were located in the solidly Democratic South and therefore never elected a Republican to any office, but took party patronage and sent delegates to the Republican convention in support of whoever controlled the patronage. In 1952 they were for Taft.

11. In 1950 Henry Zweifel defeated Jack Porter to become chairman of the Texas Republican party. Their competition, however, continued. When Zweifel committed to deliver the state delegation to Taft in the upcoming nomination contest, Porter went to work for Eisenhower. And Porter, working for a strong candidate, got the better of this fight. Texas rules require each precinct in the state to elect delegates to county conventions, which in turn feed delegates to a state convention, which chooses convention delegates. Following an energetic campaign by Porter-led forces, Eisenhower supporters swamped Taft in much of the state. In a not untypical precinct meeting at Zweifel's home, some one hundred Eisenhower supporters showed up and took over the meeting. "Mr. Zweifel bolted to his own front lawn and both sides elected their own delegations" (David, Moos, and Goldman 1954, 321). The basic procedure seems to have been similar to that of the contemporary

Iowa process, except that campaigns were entirely in the hands of local party activists. Even Taft did not visit the state.

Zweifel condemned the victorious Eisenhower supporters as communist dupes and, under his leadership, the state party sent a predominantly pro-Taft delegation to the national convention, which was then contested by the Eisenhower side.

Like most other challenges to party leaders in this period, the Eisenhower success in Texas grassroots politics is often ascribed to amateur activists. But, given the earlier fight between Zweifel and Porter, it seems more like a party split. David, Moos, and Goldman (1954) make a complementary claim that, in Texas and in a parallel controversy in Louisiana, "the whole affair, from precinct to national convention, was dominated by the problem of party realignment in the south," that is, the attempts of former Democrats and independents to find a place in the Republican Party (167).

12. Rae (1989, 65) writes that Dewey "used the governors' conference in Houston to effectively destroy Taft's prospects for the nomination."

13. That Democrats also sought Eisenhower might appear evidence that his was not a party-centered candidacy. But if read as we do, this is still more evidence that Eisenhower served as a vehicle for the movement that supported him. He no doubt agreed with the Dewey wing of the party, but he was not its principal leader.

14. Absence of strong opposition does not mean the primaries are an unimportant test. Taft lost the 1952 New Hampshire primary to a noncandidate; Goldwater lost the 1964 New Hampshire primary to a write-in, Henry Cabot Lodge; Johnson was bloodied, though not beaten, in the 1968 New Hampshire primary by a weak candidate, Eugene McCarthy.

15. In the "Compact of Fifth Avenue," Nixon had worked most of the night with Rockefeller in his Fifth Avenue apartment to draft principles that could ensure the latter's enthusiastic support for Nixon. On orders from Nixon, the Republican platform was changed to reflect the agreement, but at the cost of great resentment among conservatives (White 1961).

16. John Kessel (1968, 40–42) offers a longer but essentially similar account of the origins of the Goldwater movement.

17. The 1964 convention resembles the 1896 Democratic one, in which the newly dominant majority of silver Democrats made little effort to assuage defeated gold Democrats, and with similar short-run consequences on party performance at the polls.

Chapter 6

1. Many scholars have explored the changes in rules and their consequences. Initially, interest was focused on the McGovern-Fraser reforms, which took effect in 1972, but later studies have included discussion of subsequent rounds of reform. A necessarily incomplete list includes (Cavala 1974, Ceaser 1979, Lengle 1981, Polsby 1983, Shafer 1983, Price 1984, Kamarck 1986, Geer 1989, Norrander 1992, Herrera 1994, Mayer and Busch 2003).

2. Richard Stewart describing his attitude in April 1971 (May and Fraser 1973, 35).

3. Republican operatives planted a phony letter to the editor accusing Muskie of condoning ethnic slurs. This "dirty trick" was a small part of what later became known as Watergate and forced the resignation of President Nixon.

4. It remains unclear whether Muskie was actually crying. His staff claimed that the moisture on his face was from melting snow; however, some close observers claim to have seen tears. Broder (1987) recounts the controversy in "The Story That Still Nags Me." For political purposes, the key is what Broder and others reported at the time.

5. We cannot help wondering whether, if labor had backed Muskie in these races, he would have survived and gone on to be nominated.

6. Norman Miller, "Democratic Reforms: They Work," *Wall Street Journal* (cited in Polsby 1983, 68–69).

7. No major political science work came out of the campaign.

8. Schram (1977) reprints some of these memos in his appendix. Jordan also correctly appreciated that, for an outsider like Carter, it would not be possible (in the later phrase) to "spin" the national media into giving good early coverage to Carter; he would have to earn it through strong performances. At a time when other candidates were picking their primaries, Jordan also correctly appreciated the value of entering every contest.

9. Witcover reports considerable division on Jackson's staff as some thought that "New Hampshire as a psychological media state was overwhelming, that it was New Hampshire or bust" (1977, 191), but Jackson thought otherwise and prevailed. On Wallace's campaign, it was the candidate who apparently wanted to go to New Hampshire and the campaign staff that did not, with the latter calling the shot.

10. At President Richard Nixon's direction, the Republican Party appointed a committee on Delegates and Organization in 1969 to consider reforming the party's nomination process. The committee made recommendations similar to those of the McGovern-Fraser Commission as regards increased openness to public participation in the delegate-selection process, and the party convention accepted them in 1972. However, as Huckshorn and Bibby (1983, 658) note: "although [the committee's] recommendations closely paralleled those of the McGovern-Fraser Commission, they were just that: recommendations. There was no imperative mandate for state parties to follow, nor was there any enforcement or compliance mechanism to see that they were carried out." See also Ranney 1975, 2–3, 195.

11. Al Gore ran a southern regional strategy of waiting until Super Tuesday to enter the 1988 primaries. But Gore chose this strategy from weakness rather than strength, like Polsby and Wildavsky's (1968) "drowning man clutching at straws," and it failed. The same can be said for the abandonment of Iowa by John McCain in 2000, Wesley Clark and Joe Lieberman in 2004, and Rudy Giuliani in 2008.

12. We are adapting this very important idea from Mayhew (1974).

13. For a view more reflective of earlier studies, see Bruce, Clark, and Kessel 1991.

Appendix to Chapter 6

14. Actually, we attempted to interview her but were unable to get contact information via the standard sources.

15. Our weighting protocol was devised with the help of eight political experts associated with the UCLA political science department. We asked our panel to rate a sample of our endorsements on two variables, partyness (how much the endorser is part of the party) and resources (how much the person would be capable of helping the candidate). Our experts had average intercorrelations of .72. We averaged their codes, weighting them by their average correlation with the other coders and their score on a short but difficult test of political knowledge. (This test is available upon request. Do not expect to ace it.) We then multiplied the resultant partyness and resources scales, on the grounds that we are interested in resources from party elites. These results, with a small number of additional modifications described in the text below, gave us our final scale, which groups endorsers in a way that is intuitively satisfying.

16. Use of the weighting scheme does not dramatically affect our results. However, we believe that the results of the weighted variable should generally be given the greatest credence on substantive grounds, whether statistically the strongest or not.

17. Because governors are a known and small universe, we have specifically searched on each of their names to determine whether an endorsement was made.

Chapter 7

1. See Bernstein (2000) for evidence that the world of presidential campaign staff is actually a fairly small and party-loyal rather than candidate-loyal group.

2. In simple models testing the effect of economic performance on the vote, 1996 is a big positive residual for the incumbent. We are inclined to give Clinton half the credit for good performance and the candidate who later became known as "the Viagra man" in television commercials half the credit for poor performance.

3. In simple models testing the effect of economic performance on the vote, 2000 is a big negative residual for the incumbent party candidate, Al Gore. This is often attributed to the effect of the Lewinsky scandal, but could as well be due to Gore's weakness as a candidate. Gore did not even carry his home state of Tennessee in 2000.

4. Germond and Witcover (1981, 48–54) document Kennedy's late decision to enter the race, suggesting late August or Labor Day as the decision point.

5. Representative Shirley Chisholm of New York, who ran in 1972, was the first.

6. Except for Senator Ted Kennedy, who had by then quit the race.

7. Germond and Witcover (1985) also maintain that the Hunt Commission intended to rig the game in favor of Mondale. They write: "To no one's surprise, the new rules encouraged states to move their caucuses and primaries to earlier dates in the hope of having some influence on the result. And it was this 'front-loading' more than anything else that both Mondale and Big Labor depended upon to produce an early decision [favorable to more establishment candidates]" (43). Mayer and Busch (2003) argue that the Hunt Commission's reforms were too mild to have much effect on momentum. As regards 1984, their argument may be largely correct, since Hart did almost ride momentum to a victory over Mondale. On the other hand, Mondale did hang on to beat Hart and might not have done so in the absence of the boost from the Hunt Commission. The Hunt Commission also helped Mondale by adding so-called super delegates—party leaders not chosen through the primaries—to the party convention, and these delegates overwhelmingly favored Mondale.

8. A search on "Gary Hart" plus "Seven Dwarfs" yields forty-seven Lexis-Nexis hits in 1987 and 1988.

9. Hart reentered the race near the end of the invisible primary and led all candidates in the last pre-Iowa poll, but never emerged as a force.

10. "It soon became apparent [to labor leaders] that achieving unity would be impossible in the absence of a candidate who stood out as either a uniquely close friend of labor or an especially electable one" (Dark 2004, 184).

11. This is also in some ways similar to the bandwagon effect common in contested conventions (e.g., Polsby and Wildavsky 1968, 97), in which undecided delegates hasten to support a likely winner once he shows signs of strength.

12. In mid-March, Jackson had won 461 delegates, which was just behind Dukakis's 465; Gore and Gephardt were at 171 and 145.

13. The media- and voter-generated momentum, on the other hand, should have helped Gephardt. He won Iowa on the basis of a Carter-like early organization. He was campaigning in the state for more than a year before the caucus. But after Iowa, he won only South Dakota and his home state of Missouri.

14. In the original article, the final three paragraphs of this quote appeared ahead of the first three.

15. It strengthens our story that one of Bush's initial nominations was unacceptable to the religious right but withdrew once this became clear.

16. See Wilson 1966 on why it is sometimes rational for parties to accept defeat rather than nominate a reformer whose victory might undermine the basis of party support in the long-term.

17. We omit endorsements by top officials of candidates from their own state.

18. Dean won the nonbinding Washington, DC, primary, which was held before Iowa, but lost the binding caucus that was held after Iowa.

19. Many accounts note the possibility that Gephardt and Dean, in mainly attacking each other, opened the way for the rise of Kerry and Edwards.

20. Clark, in particular, skipped Iowa, but was second in the national polls and running a well-funded second in New Hampshire when Dean collapsed; if Dean—the favorite of the large Clinton wing of the party—had won in Iowa as expected, Clark might have become the winning Stop Dean candidate.

21. Based on a study of the career paths of "rising star" campaign workers, Bernstein (2000) finds that top campaign staff tend to be party-loyal rather than candidate-loyal. We take this as a useful corroboration of our general view.

Chapter 8

1. However, the Cato Institute gave Bush a grade of only B.

2. If a politician made an endorsement as a lower level officeholder and as a higher level one, he or she would show up as a top-level repeat endorser at both times. However, many officeholders move to top positions from ones that would be too obscure to attract coverage. For example, D'Amato held a minor county-level office before winning his Senate seat, so that any endorsement he made prior to becoming senator might have gone unreported.

3. In later years, when electronic searches turn up a larger number of endorsements by low-level figures, the number of officeholders in the sample is about 70 percent.

4. Our analysis is similar to that of Emmett H. Buell, Jr. (1996), who used similar indicators to analyze Invisible Primaries in the period 1976 to 1992. The main empirical difference is that he used "straw polls" at party gatherings to measure insider support, a variable he found to be an unreliable indicator of success. For these and methodological reasons, our results and his are difficult to compare.

5. The outstanding exception is George W. Bush. He probably met with as many party activists and leaders as any recent candidate, but he did not have to do much traveling to do this: They flew to Texas to meet with him.

6. The measure for the candidates in 2004 is based on *Time* magazine only.

7. Our magazine data were also coded as the net of positive and negative sentences. The measure of net coverage, however, proved to be a weak predictor of subsequent developments. This was because the media tended to be most critical of the strongest candidates, which led to net positive-negative scores that were close to zero. At the same time, the media also ignored very weak candidates, which led to net scores that were close to zero for them as well. With the strongest and weakest candidates getting similar scores, this measure failed to predict other developments in the invisible primary.

8. Because the number of candidates was different in different years, what constituted fair shares varied by year. Still, there were no races in which shares below 5 percent or above 50 percent constituted fair share coverage.

9. Jesse Unruh of the California State Assembly.

10. Reed, as it happens, was slow to commit. As of April 1998, *USA Today* reported that Reed "is informally advising no fewer than seven men considering White House runs in 2000."

11. Ford also ran competitively with Ronald Reagan in most early polls, so it was not lack of public support that kept him out of the race.

12. Selection bias also arises when someone else boots an actor out of the process because of a belief that actor will not succeed.

13. Dividing the data into two time periods gives us about two hundred endorsements per period in the 1980s. However, for reasons to be explained below, our main analysis is based on fewer than one-third of the endorsements, so finer temporal division of the data would not be feasible.

14. We base this partition on the rate of accumulation of endorsements. If, for example, half of all endorsements in a given invisible primary are made by July in the year before the election, we divided our endorsement, media, and donation data into pre-July shares and post-July shares. We used poll measurements from the midpoint of each period. If, in another year, the midpoint in the accumulation of endorsements was October, we made our two temporal measurements accordingly. As shown in chapter 6, there is much variation in the rate of endorsements in the invisible primary.

Simulation suggested that this approach produced more reliable estimates of variables on one another than basing the temporal cut points on the calendar. In effect, we specify that the invisible primary runs on political time rather than calendar time.

15. Our main expert on this is David Karol.

16. The two-tailed p-value for this difference is .01.

17. This variable was scored 3 if a president or former president, 2 if a vice president or vice presidential candidate or the party leader of either house of Congress, 1 if a holder of a lesser party position, and 0 otherwise.

18. Code in R for estimating all of these models is available at http://www9.georgetown.edu/faculty/hcn4/.

Chapter 9

1. Much of the analysis by Adkins and Dowdle and by Steger examines differences between the two political parties. We do not believe that the six contested Democratic nominations and four contested Republican nominations in the period 1980 to 2004—even though involving a total of about sixty candidates—provide a sufficient base for a statistical examination of party differences.

2. For polls, no preference responses are excluded from the calculation.

3. This is the same effect shown in table 8.3.

4. This is because the analysis lumps all endorsements together and considers only their joint impact. See, however, discussions of relative group influence at pp. 233–34 in chapter 7, and pp. 292–303 in the present chapter.

5. We argued in chapter 7 that Democratic Party insiders helped sway the nominations in 1988 and 2004 despite their inability to create a pre-Iowa consensus, but our statistical results in this chapter do not bear on that claim.

6. Interestingly, the also-ran candidates who have pressed front-runners the hardest in state primaries have not usually owed their success to the invisible primary. Three of the strongest also-rans were Gary Hart in 1984, Paul Tsongas in 1992, and John McCain in 2000, each of whom took off mainly because of strong showings in New Hampshire. Two

others were Jesse Jackson and Pat Buchanan, each of whom owed success more to intense pockets of voter support than to the invisible primary. Two candidates who did owe their strong runs against a front-runner to prior success in the invisible primary were George H. W. Bush in 1980 and Bob Dole in 1988. But in the end, of course, all of these challenges fell short, usually far short.

7. For example, journalistic accounts of the 1996 South Carolina primary made much of Dole's backing from social conservatives in his fight against Buchanan. As would be expected in a hard-fought race, our newspaper search turned up a total of forty-four endorsements, but not one was from an identifiable religious source. This result naturally weakens our confidence in the endorsement measure, especially as deployed at the state level.

8. All Iowa and New Hampshire estimates exclude the 1992 caucus in which Iowa Senator Tom Harkin ran for president. In that year, other candidates refused to campaign in Iowa, leaving Harkin with an overwhelming but politically unimportant win. For more information, see the appendix to this chapter.

9. In his 2007 paper, Steger finds that endorsements affect post–New Hampshire results, but only for Republicans. As stated in an earlier note, we believe that there are insufficient cases to sustain separate estimates for the two parties. However, when we partitioned the cases by party, we found that endorsements had a statistically significant effect within each party. Steger, Dowdle, and Adkins also demonstrate an effect of New Hampshire, but without controlling for party endorsements. See Steger, Dowdle, and Adkins 2004.

10. Iowa caucuses are open only to registered members of the party sponsoring it, but citizens may register on site. For this reason, a party's caucuses may attract many voters from areas in which it has little regular voting strength.

11. Squire and Smith (1988) demonstrate that the insertion of partisan information into formally nonpartisan judicial elections produces very large effects.

12. The average number of endorsements per contest ranges from about ten per state to about forty per state in 2000 and after.

13. The measure of success is the measure of "Chances" used in Bartels 1988. This measure has three parts: prior results as weighted by media coverage, results in the most recent contests, and what Bartels calls objective chances of nomination. We believe that our variable is a close replication of Bartels's measure. Our specification, however, is quite different than that of Bartels.

14. We find significant t-ratios for endorsements in five of eight contests, a t-ratio of 1.2 in the 2000 Republican contests, and a t-ratio of –.7 in the 1988 Republican contests. We had about ten endorsements per state in the 1988 and 1992 contests and about forty endorsements per state from 1996 on.

15. This is based on our "Fat Lady" calculation.

16. The paper reporting these results is available through Cohen's Web site, www.jmu .edu/polisci/faculty_cohen.html.

17. About half of the early state primaries are open only to party members, but about half are effectively open. Iowa, for example, allows only party members to participate in party caucuses, but allows citizens to register with a party at the ballot place.

18. Mayer has data only for the more important candidates, a total of thirty in the period 1980 to 2004. Our regressions are based on sixty-five candidates.

19. The two correlations are statistically different at p < .01, two-tailed.

20. These figures are the medians of fourteen primary exit polls published following the South Carolina and Super Tuesday (February 5) primaries. In 1984 and 2008, black voters who did not vote for the black candidate gave almost all of their support to the white

candidate with the most black endorsements and scarcely any to the other white candidates. Thus, for example, Gary Hart, who had scarcely any black endorsements in 1984, got only 4 percent of the black vote in 1984 (versus 45 percent of the white vote).

21. Other important scholars also believe that momentum is a spent force in presidential nominations. See Sigelman 1989, 35–39; Mayer 2003, 89.

22. For a similar argument, see Haynes et al. 2004.

23. For our analysis of momentum, see Cohen, Noel, and Zaller 2004. For an argument that post-Iowa momentum affected the development of national support for John Kerry in 2004, see Knight and Schiff, 2007.

24. We have, as noted, calculated standard errors clustered by contest.

25. An effort to carve our data into more time periods produced noisy and unreliable results. With a few more cycles, however, finer divisions of the data should be possible.

26. See, however, our discussion of selection bias in chapter 8.

27. The material in direct quotes is from an article by two scholars, Bill Moore and Danielle Vinson, as cited by Magleby and Mayer 2007, 161–62.

28. More today than when Brown, Powell, and Wilcox wrote.

29. We noted in chapter 7 the attempt of a group of Democratic fund-raisers to exert independent leadership in the 1988 nomination; this is the only such effort we know of, and it failed.

30. The variance of the endorsement shares variable in our sample is somewhat larger than that of the poll share variable. If, therefore, our estimates of effect sizes had been based on the sample variance, they would have increased the estimated impact of endorsements relative to that of polls.

Chapter 10

1. Romney raised $88 million in the invisible primary, but $34 million came from his own private fortune. Giuliani raised $61 million from private donors.

2. Some of the workers Giuliani did recruit were bitterly attacked at Republican events in Iowa by conservative Christian activists over their views on abortion.

3. Tennessee Senator Bill Frist and Virginia Senator George Allen were widely acceptable in the party and expected to make runs for the nomination, but they lost viability in 2006 and never formally entered the race. The loss of these two candidates should have been a wake-up call to others in the party.

4. Edwards had a large number of obscure endorsers; we are not certain at this point whether our weighted measure would show him or Obama in second place.

5. Fund-raising for presidential nominations has shot up dramatically since the 1990s, with much of the extra money coming from new sources, including Internet donors. Obama attracted a good deal of the new Internet money—$6.9 million in his April filing, compared to $4.2 million for Clinton.

6. As we argued in chapter 7, Democratic leaders followed a similar course in 1988 when, facing a choice among the so-called Seven Dwarfs, it waited for the results of the early primaries before coming out for Michael Dukakis. In 2008, the choice was between titans, but the principle was similar.

7. If, more generally, parties can use the early state contests to gain information about the strengths of potential candidates without opening themselves to factional, maverick, or otherwise unacceptable nominees, we do not see it as a problem for our theory. The important thing is that parties steer the nomination to a broadly acceptable candidate. We

do, however, recognize that use of the early contests to test candidates makes it harder to see how exactly to falsify our theory, and this we do acknowledge as a problem. Falsifiability, we believe, must be found in the dynamics of the process—for example, the resistance of insiders to popular candidates who are not acceptable to all party groups, the inability of seemingly popular candidates to succeed in the absence of insider support. We also note that the nomination of candidates unacceptable to key party groups—as McCain's nomination in 2008 would be and Dean's possible nomination in 2004 would have been—is inconsistent with our theory and hence tends to falsify it.

8. What we are here calling chance is analogous to the error term in a regression model.

9. The "rally effect," in which presidential approval increases during a foreign policy crisis, was first noted by Mueller (1973).

10. Note that, in both of these accounts, the "chance effect" was a supplement to the efforts by parties to control their nominations, not a substitute. We should also add that Carter might have beaten Kennedy in 1980 without the Iran hostage crisis, just as Ford beat Reagan in 1976. One can also imagine that the continued presence of Hart in the race might have lured in Mario Cuomo, who was a party favorite, or might have provoked the rest of the party to coalesce earlier and more strongly behind Dukakis. So we are not saying that the party would have been beaten in these cases in the absence of favorable luck, only that it got some good luck and it seemed to help.

11. We exclude the 1970s as a transitional period.

12. In particular, party members in the old system could arrive at the convention in disarray and still control the outcome, whereas today's parties risk loss of control if they have not formed a united front ahead of Iowa.

13. We assume a common variance in success across both periods. If the parties nominate one of two favorites in 2008, the two-tailed p-value would rise to .196. If they go 0 for 2, it would rise to .326.

14. We assume a common variance in success across both periods.

15. In her well-executed study, Cobb is skeptical that endorsements alone have much general effect. In many cases, she reports, a candidate sought endorsements only to demonstrate momentum or viability and received no actual resources from the supporter. She further reports that, overall, endorsers were on the correct side only about half the time. However, she also notes that nonpublic endorsements were sometimes very important, and her research may not have turned up all cases of such behind-the-scenes endorsement power by groups or officeholders. Also, in many of Cobb's cases, the nomination was to oppose an incumbent regarded as unbeatable (as was the case for Democrats in 1998, when Republican George W. Bush sought reelection), with the result that no real contest occurred. By our tally, unweighted public endorsements correctly predicted the nomination winner in a large majority of cases in which the nomination was open and worth having.

16. See Ferrell (1994) for a remarkable example of how a small and informal group of top Democratic party leaders—some elected and some not—engineered Harry Truman's selection as vice president in 1944.

17. For evidence that officeholders are more polarized than most voters would prefer, see Fiorina 2005; Adams, Merrill, and Grofman 2005.

18. We argued in chapter 2 that groups also prefer to be organized, which raises a doubt about either our original argument or this one.

19. We view this statement as essentially the same as that of Schattschneider (1942, 22).

20. We refer, of course, to the aborted invisible primary runs by these gentlemen for their party's nomination in 1980, 1996, 2008, 2004, and 2008, respectively.

References

Abramowitz, Alan I. 1989. "Viability, Electability and Candidate Choice in a Presidential Primary Election: A Test of Three Models." *Journal of Politics* 51:977–92.

Abramowitz, Alan I., Ronald B. Rapoport, and Walter J. Stone. 1991. "Up Close and Personal: The 1988 Iowa Caucuses and Presidential Politics." In *Nominating the President*, ed. Emmett H. Buell, Jr., and Lee Sigelman, 72–90. Knoxville: University of Tennessee Press.

Abramson, Paul R., John H. Aldrich, Phil Paolino, and David W. Rohde. 1992. "Sophisticated Voting in 1988 Presidential Primaries." *American Political Science Review* 86:55–69.

Achen, Chris, and Larry Bartels. 2002. "Blind Retrospection: Electoral Responses to Droughts, Flu, and Shark Attacks." Paper given at the annual meeting of the American Political Science Association, Boston.

———. 2004. "Musical Chairs: Pocketbook Voting and the Limits of Democratic Accountability." Paper given at the annual meeting of the American Political Science Association, Chicago.

Adams, John. 1763. Diary of John Adams, February 1763. Adams Family Papers. Massachusetts Historical Society.

Adams, James, and Samuel Merrill III, "The Spatial Strategies of Candidates Facing Both a Primary and a General Election: When Do Primary Elections Help Parties Win Office?" Paper given at the annual meeting of the Midwest Political Science Association, Chicago.

Adams, James, Samuel Merrill III, and Bernard Grofman. 2005. *A Unified Theory of Party Competition: A Cross-National Analysis Integrating Spatial and Behavioral Factors*. Cambridge: Cambridge University Press.

Adkins, Randall E., and Andrew J. Dowdle. 2001. "How Important Is Early Organization to Winning Presidential Nominations? An Analysis of Pre-Primary Campaign Organization in the Post-Reform Era." Paper given at the annual meeting of the Midwest Political Science Association.

———. 2004. "Bumps in the Road to the White House: How Influential Were Campaign Resources to Nominating George W. Bush?" *Journal of Political Marketing* 3, no. 4, 1–27.

———. 2005. "Do Early Birds Get the Worm? Improving Timeliness of Presidential Nomination Forecasts." *Presidential Studies Quarterly* 35, no. 4, 646–60.

Aldrich, John H. 1980. *Before the Convention: Strategies and Choices in Presidential Nomination Campaigns.* Chicago: University of Chicago Press.

———. 1993. "Presidential Selection." In *Researching the Presidency*, ed. George C. Edwards III, John H. Kessel, and Bert A. Rockman. Pittsburgh: University of Pittsburgh Press.

———. 1995. *Why Parties? The Origin and Transformation of Political Parties in America.* Chicago: University of Chicago Press.

———. 2005. "The Election of 1800: The Consequences of the First Change in Party Control." In *Establishing Congress*, ed. Kenneth Bolling and Donald Kenon. Columbus: Ohio State University Press.

Aldrich, John H., and David W. Rohde. 1998. "The Transition to Republican Rule in the House: Implications for Theories of Congressional Politics." *Political Science Quarterly* 112:541–67.

———. 2000. "The Republican Revolution and the House Appropriations Committee." *Journal of Politics* 62:1–33.

Ambinder, Marc. 2007. "Is the Arlington Group Coalescing around Fred Thompson?" *Marc Ambinder: A Reported Blog on Politics*, June 21.

Ambrose, Steven E. 1983. *Eisenhower: Soldier, General of the Army, President-Elect, 1890–1952.* New York: Simon & Schuster.

Ansolabehere, Steven, and James Snyder. 2002. "The Incumbency Advantage in U.S. Elections: An Analysis of State and Federal Offices, 1942–2000." *Election Law Journal* 1, no. 3, 315–38.

Ansolabehere, Steven, Joseph Stewart, and James Snyder. 2001. "Candidate Positioning in House Elections." *American Journal of Political Science* 45, no. 1, 136–59.

Apple, R. W. 1972. "Clues from a Primary; Muskie Hurt, McGovern Aided by Vote, but Big Impact on Florida Is Doubted." *New York Times*, March 9, 32.

Bain, Richard. 1960. *Convention Decisions and Voting Records.* Washington, DC: Brookings Institution.

Balz, Dan. 1995. "Good Work, Good Luck Combine for Dole Success; Pursuit of Governors Pays Off for Campaign." *Washington Post*, December 17, A1.

———. 1999. "Starting Early and Urgently; Presidential Contenders Leave Calendar in Dust." *Washington Post*, April 4, A1.

———. 2002. "Gore Stuns Many by Choosing Not to Run for President in '04." *Washington Post*, December 16, A1.

———. 2003a. "Democratic Rivals' War Dilemma; Hopefuls Must Reconcile Primary Voters' Doubt with Their Own Calls to Act." *Washington Post*, January 31, 1.

———. 2003b. "As Pre-Primary Season Ends, Questions Cling to Dean's Gains." *Washington Post*, December 28, A1.

———. 2006a. "For Possible '08 Run, McCain Is Courting Bush Loyalists." *Washington Post*, February 12, A1.

———. 2006b. "McCain Reconnects with Liberty University." *Washington Post*, May 14, A4.

Balz, Dan, and David S. Broder. 1999. "Many GOP Governors Ready to Back Bush; Early Support Could Be Critical for Race." *Washington Post*, February 23, A1.

Balz, Dan, and E. J. Dionne Jr. 1992. "Clinton: Groundwork and a 'Lot of Breaks'; Attention to Detail Last Year Helped Build Candidate's Strength." *Washington Post*, January 12, A1.

Barnes, Fred. 1998. "The Heavyweight; George W Bush, Presidential Contender." *Weekly Standard*, September 14, 19.

Bartels, Larry. 1988. *Presidential Primaries and the Dynamics of Public Choice*. Princeton, NJ: Princeton University Press.

———. 1996. "Uninformed Votes: Information Effects in Presidential Elections." *American Journal of Political Science* 40:194–230.

———. 1998. "Electoral Continuity and Change, 1868–1996." *Electoral Studies* 17:301–26.

———. 2000. "Partisanship and Voting Behavior, 1952–1996." *American Journal of Political Science* 44:35–50.

———. Forthcoming. *Unequal Democracy*. Princeton, NJ: Princeton University Press.

Bauerlein, Valerie, and Corey Dade. 2008. "Black Leaders in a Quandary." *Wall Street Journal*, January 5, A5.

Bawn, Kathleen, Seth Masket, Marty Cohen, David Karol, Hans Noel, and John Zaller. 2006. "A Theory of Political Parties." Paper given at the annual meeting of the American Political Science Association, Philadelphia.

Bawn, Kathleen, and Hans Noel. 2007. "Long Coalitions Under Electoral Uncertainty: The Electoral Origins of Political Parties." Paper given at the annual meetings of the Midwest Political Science Association, Chicago.

Bawn, Kathleen, and Francis Rosenbluth. 2006. "Short versus Long Coalitions: Electoral Accountability and the Size of the Public Sector." *American Journal of Political Science* 50 (April).

Beck, Paul Allen. 1997. *Party Politics in America*. 8th ed. New York: Longman.

Bell, Rudolph. 1973. *Party and Faction in American Politics*. Westport: Greenwood Press.

Berke, Richard L. 1987a. "Stalking the 1988 Money Hunters." *New York Times*, February 27, A24.

———. 1987b. "Big Fund-Raisers Keep Gore Waiting." *New York Times*, November 16, A30.

———. Berke. 1992. "Big Labor Seeks Ways to Regain Campaign Clout." *New York Times*, January 13, A1.

———. 1996. "Facing Financial Squeeze, Quayle Pulls Out of Race." *New York Times*, February 9, A14.

———. 1997a. "With Eye on 2000, Campaign Begins." *New York Times*, May 11, A19.

———. 1997b. "Governor Bush Becoming One to Watch in G.O.P." *New York Times*, August 25, A19.

———. 1999a. "Bradley Takes Early Party Prize: He Goes One-on-One with Gore." *New York Times*, April 20, 1.

———. 1999b. "Flush Times and Hungry Republicans Generate Bush Campaign Windfall." *New York Times*, July 4, A13.

———. 1999c. "Conservatives Back Bush Abortion Strategy." *New York Times*, November 5, A1.

Bernstein, Jonathan. 2000. "The New New Presidential Elite." In *In Pursuit of the White House 2000: How We Choose Our Presidential Nominees*, ed. William Mayer. Chatham, NJ: Chatham House Publishers.

Binkley, Wilfred, and Malcolm Moos. 1958. *A Grammar of American Politics*. New York: Knopf.

Birnbaum, Jeffry. 2000. *The Money Men: The Real Story of Fund-Raising's Influence on Political Power in America*. New York: Crown.

Blumenthal, Sidney. 1992. *Pledging Allegiance: The Last Campaign of the Cold War*. New York: HarperCollins.

Bond, Jon R., and Richard Fleisher. 2000. *Polarized Politics: Congress and the President in a Partisan Era*. Washington: CQ Press.

Brady, Henry E., and Richard Johnston. 1987. "What's the Primary Message: Horse Race or Issue Journalism?" In *Media and Momentum: The New Hampshire Primary and Nomination Politics*, ed. G. R. Orren and N. W. Polsby. Chatham, NJ: Chatham House.

Broder, David S. 1972a. *The Party's Over: The Failure of Politics in America*. New York: Harper & Row.

———. 1972b. "Muskie Denounces Publisher." *Washington Post*, February 27, A1.

———. 1979. "1980 GOP Presidential Field Is Already Crowded; 8 Republicans Are Girding for '80 Presidential Race." *Washington Post*, January 21, A1.

———. 1980. "Republican Governors Still Sing a Song of Might-Have-Been." *Washington Post*, March 15, A5.

———. 1983. "Democrats' New Calendar, Rules May Produce an Early Winner." *Washington Post*, August 22, A2.

———. 1984. "He Was Supposed to Be the Consensus Candidate." *Washington Post*, March 7, A23.

———. 1988. "Dukakis Has Corralled Few Colleagues; Most Democratic Governors Leery of Endorsing at This Stage." *Washington Post*, February 24, A14.

———. 1990. "Moderate Democrats Trying to Grow Grass Roots; Leadership Conference, Launching New Chapters, Hopes to 'Build a Network' for 1992." *Washington Post*, December 12, A7.

———. 1996. "In the Wings, Future Contenders Position Themselves." *Washington Post*, August 15, A22.

———. 1999. "Showy Bandwagon Is No Free Ride to a Bush Nomination." *Washington Post*, March 8, A1.

———. 2003. "No Way to Choose a President." *Washington Post*, December 31, A19.

Brown, Clifford W., Lynda W. Powell, and Clyde Wilcox. 1995. *Serious Money: Fundraising and Contributing in Presidential Nomination Campaigns*. New York: Cambridge University Press.

Brownstein, Ronald. 1987. "Front-Running Outsider." *National Journal* 19, no. 14 (April 14): 806.

———. 1995. "Quayle Won't Seek GOP Bid for Presidency." *Los Angeles Times*, February 10, 1.

———. 1997. "Setbacks Aside, Gov. Bush May Yet Try to Become Next President Bush." *Los Angeles Times*, March 24, A5.

Bruce, John H., John A. Clark, and John H. Kessel. 1991. "Advocacy Politics in Presidential Parties." *American Political Science Review* 85:1089–105.

Buell, Emmett H., Jr. 1996. "The Invisible Primary." In *In Pursuit of the White House*, ed. William G. Mayer. Chatham, NJ: Chatham House Publishers.

———. 2000. "The Changing Face of the New Hampshire Primary." In *In Pursuit of the White House 2000: How We Choose Our Presidential Nominees*, ed. William Mayer. Chatham, NJ: Chatham House Publishers.

Buell, Jr., Emmett H. , and James W. Davis. 1991. "Win Early and Win Often: Candidates and the Strategic Environment of 1988." In *Nominating the President*, ed. Emmett H. Buell Jr. and L. Sigelman. Knoxville: University of Tennessee Press.

Burka, Paul. 1995. "The Art of Running for President." *Texas Monthly*, April, 128.

Burke, Edmund. 1790. *Reflections on the Revolution in France*. New York: Anchor Books, 1973.

Burnham, Walter Dean. 1982. *The Current Crisis in American Politics*. Oxford: Oxford University Press.

Busch, Andrew E. 1992. "In Defense of the 'Mixed' System: The Goldwater Campaign and the Role of Popular Movements in the Pre-Reform Presidential Nomination Process." *Polity* 24:527–49.

———. 2000. "New Features of the 2000 Presidential Nominating Process: Republican Reforms, Front-Loading's Second Wind, and Early Voting." In *In Pursuit of the White House 2000: How We Choose Our Presidential Nominees*, ed. William G. Mayer. Chatham, NJ: Chatham House.

Cain, Bruce E., John A. Ferejohn, and Morris P. Fiorina. 1984. "The Constituency Service Basis of the Personal Vote for U.S. Representatives and British Members of Parliament." *American Political Science Review* 78:110–25.

———. 1987. *The Personal Vote: Constituency Service and Electoral Independence*. Cambridge, MA: Harvard University Press.

Calmes, Jackie. 2004. "Dean's Difficulties Delay Move to Center." *Wall Street Journal*, January 19. Online.

Calmes, Jackie, and Jacob M. Schlesinger. 2003. "Dean Raises Money, Buzz . . . and Ire." *Wall Street Journal*, July 10, A1.

Canes-Wrone, Brandice, David W. Brady, and John F. Cogan. 2002. "Out of Step, Out of Office: Electoral Accountability and House Members' Voting." *American Political Science Review* 96:127–40.

Carleton, William G. 1957. "The Revolution in the Presidential Nominating Convention." *Political Science Quarterly* 72, no. 2 (June): 224–40.

Caro, Robert A. 2003. *Master of the Senate: The Years of Lyndon Johnson*. New York: Vintage.

Carsey, Thomas, John Green, Rick Herrera, and Geoffrey Layman. 2003. "The New Professionals: An Initial Look at National Convention Delegates in 2000 and Over Time." Paper given at the annual meeting of the American Political Science Association, Philadelphia.

Cavala, William. 1972. "Changing the Rules Changes the Game: Party Reform and the 1972 California Delegation to the Democratic National Convention." *American Political Science Review* 68, no. 1 (March): 27–42.

Ceaser, James W. 1979. *Presidential Selection: Theory and Development*. Princeton, NJ: Princeton University Press.

———. 1982. *Reforming the Reforms*. Pensacola, FL: Ballinger.

Ceaser, James W., and Andrew Busch. 2001. *The Perfect Tie: The True Story of the 2000 Presidential Election*. Lanham, MD: Rowman & Littlefield.

Ceaser, James W., and Neil Spitzer. 1988. "The Parties Take Over." *Wilson Quarterly* 12:49–62.

Chester, Lewis, Godfrey Hodgson, and Bruce Page. 1969. *American Melodrama: The Presidential Campaign of 1968*. New York: Viking Press.

Cobb, Rachel. 2006. "Who Nominates? The Role of Parties in Gubernatorial Nominations in Six States." Paper given at the annual meeting of the American Political Science Association, Philadelphia.

Cohen, Marty. 2005. *Moral Victories: Cultural Conservatism and the Creation of a New Republican Congressional Majority*. PhD dissertation, University of California, Los Angeles.

Cohen, Marty, David Karol, Hans Noel, and John Zaller. 2001. "Beating Reform: The Resurgence of Parties in Presidential Nominations, 1972–2000." Paper given at the annual meetings of the Midwest Political Science Association.

Cohen, Marty, Hans Noel, and John Zaller. 2004. "From George McGovern to John Kerry: State-Level Models of Presidential Primaries, 1972–2004." Paper given at the annual meetings of the Midwest Political Science Association.

Cole, Donald B. 1970. *Jeffersonian Democracy in New Hampshire, 1800–1851*. Cambridge, MA: Harvard University Press.

———. 2002. *Jackson Man: Amos Kendall and the Rise of American Democracy*. Baton Rouge: Louisiana State University Press.

Collat, Donald S., Jr., Stanley Kelley, and Ronald Rogowski. 1981. "The End Game in Presidential Nominations." *American Political Science Review* 75, no. 2, 426–35.

Cook, Rhodes. 1989. "The Nominating Process." In *The Elections of 1988*, ed. Michael Nelson. Washington, DC: CQ Press.

Corrado, Anthony. 1992. *Creative Campaigning: PACs and the Presidential Selection Process*. Boulder, CO: Westview Press.

Corrado, Anthony, and Heitor Gouvêa. 2003. "Financing Presidential Nominations under BCRA." In *In Pursuit of the White House 2004: How We Choose Our Presidential Nominees*, ed. W. G. Mayer. Chatham, NJ: Chatham House.

Cost, Jay. 2008. "The Giuliani Campaign: RIP." HorseRaceBlog. January 31.

Cox, Gary. 1987. *The Efficient Secret: The Cabinet and the Development of Political Parties in Victorian England*. Cambridge: Cambridge University Press.

Cox, Gary W., and Mathew D. McCubbins. 1993. *Legislative Leviathan*. Berkeley: University of California Press.

———. 1999. "Agenda Power in the U.S. House of Representatives." Paper given at the annual meeting of the Conference on the History of Congress, Stanford University.

———. 2005. *Setting the Agenda*. Cambridge: Cambridge University Press.

Crotty, William J. 1985. *The Party Game*. New York: W. H. Freeman.

Crotty, William, and John S. Jackson. 2001. *The Politics of Presidential Selection*. New York: Longman.

Cunningham, Noble E. 1957. *The Jeffersonian Republicans: The Formation of Party Organization, 1790–1801*. Chapel Hill: University of North Carolina Press.

Damore, David F. 1997. "A Dynamic Model of Candidate Fundraising: The Case of Presidential Nomination Campaigns." *Political Research Quarterly* 50:343–64.

Dark, Taylor E. 1999. *The Unions and the Democrats: An Enduring Alliance*. Ithaca, NY: Cornell University Press.

———. 2004. "From Resistance to Adaptation: Organized Labor Reacts to a Changing Nominating Process." In *The Making of the Presidential Candidates 2004*, ed. William Mayer, 161–98. New York: Rowman & Littlefield.

David, Paul T., Malcolm Moos, and Ralph Goldman. 1954. *Presidential Nominating Politics 1952*. 5 vols. Baltimore, MD: Johns Hopkins Press.

Davis, James W. 1997. *U.S. Presidential Primaries and the Caucus-Convention System: A Sourcebook*. Westport, CT: Greenwood Press.

Dine, Philip. 1992. "Clinton Makes Labor Inroads; His Unexpected Support Erodes Harkin's." *St. Louis Post-Dispatch*, January 26, 1A.

Dobson, James. 2007. "The Values Test." *New York Times*, October 4.

Dominguez, Casey. 2005. *Before the Primary: Party Participation in Congressional Nominating Processes*. PhD dissertation, University of California, Berkeley.

Downs, Anthony. 1957. *Economic Theory of Democracy.* New York: HarperCollins.

Economist. 2007. "In Search of the Old Magic." May 31. Internet edition.

Edsall, Thomas B. 1987. "Fund-Raising as Preoccupation; Early Advantage Becomes More Critical." *Washington Post,* April 15, A16.

———. 1988. "Bush Has Upper Hand In Redefining GOP; Reagan's Successes Cut Kemp's Appeal." *Washington Post,* March 10, A29.

———. 1992. "In South, Hope—and Unease—Over Clinton; Democratic Leaders See Arkansan as Electable, but Fear Allegations Could Cripple Candidacy." *Washington Post,* February 11, A8.

———. 1996a. "Christian Coalition Faces Test of Its Place in Republican Party." *Washington Post,* March 2, A11.

———. 1996b. "Christian Right's Political Dilemma: Principle or Pragmatism." *Washington Post,* February 9, A1.

———. 1999. "Conservatives Shield Bush's Abortion Stand from Right Wing." *Washington Post,* March 20, B1.

Edsall, Thomas B., and Dan Balz. 1991. "DNC Poised to Play Role in Late-Starting Campaign." *Washington Post,* September 23, A6.

Ehrenhalt, Alan. 1991. *United States of Ambition: Politicians, Power and the Pursuit of Office.* New York: Three Rivers Press.

Evans, Rowland, and Robert Novak. 1966. *Lyndon B. Johnson: The Exercise of Power.* New York: Signet Books.

Farhi, Paul. 2003. "Tiny but Trusted Inner Circle Surrounds Dean." *Washington Post,* December 6, A2.

Farley, James A. 1948. *Jim Farley's Story: The Roosevelt Years.* New York: Whittlesey House.

Ferrell, Robert H. 1994. *Choosing Truman.* Columbia: University of Missouri Press.

Finnegan, Michael. 2007. "Evangelicals Split on GOP Field." *Los Angeles Times,* October 1, 1.

Fiorina, Morris P. 1980. "The Decline of Collective Responsibility in American Politics." In *Election Law: Cases and Materials,* ed. D. H. Lowenstein. Durham, NC: Carolina Academic Press.

———. 2005. *Culture War? The Myth of a Polarized America.* New York: Pearson Longman.

Fischer, David Hacket. 1965. *The Revolution of American Conservatism.* New York: Harper & Row.

Formisano, Ronald P. 1971. *The Birth of Mass Political Parties: Michigan, 1827–1861.* Princeton, NJ: Princeton University Press.

Geer, John G. 1989. *Nominating Presidents: An Evaluation of Voters and Primaries.* Westport, CT: Greenwood Press.

Germond, Jack, and Jules Witcover. 1981. *Blue Smoke and Mirrors: How Reagan Won and Why Carter Lost the Election of 1980.* New York: Viking Adult.

———. 1985. *Wake Us When It's Over.* New York: Warner Books.

———. 1989. *Whose Broad Stripes and Bright Stars? The Trivial Pursuit of the Presidency, 1988.* New York: Warner Books.

———. 1993. *Mad As Hell: Revolt at the Ballot Box, 1992.* New York: Warner Books.

Gibson, James L., Cornelius P. Cotter, John F. Bibby, and Robert J. Huckshorn. 1985. "Whither Local Parties? A Cross-Sectional and Longitudinal Analysis of the Strength of Party Organization." *American Journal of Political Science* 29, no. 1, 139–60.

Gienapp, William. 1987. *The Origins of the Republican Party, 1852–1856.* Oxford: Oxford University Press.

Gilgoff, Dan. 2007. "Thompson Reaches to the Right." *U.S. News and World Report,* July 23, 25.

Gillon, Steven. 1987. *Politics and Vision: The ADA and American Liberalism, 1947–1985.* Oxford: Oxford University Press.

Glasser, Susan B. 1999. "Bush's Dash for Cash; Family, Friends Join in $50 Million Goal." *Washington Post,* April 7, A1.

Gleckman, Howard. 1988. "In the Fund-Raising Game, Gephardt Is PAC Man." *Business Week.* March 14, 47.

Goff, Michael J. 2004. *The Money Primary: The New Politics of the Early Presidential Nomination.* Lanham, MD: Rowman & Littlefield.

Goldman, Peter, and Tony Fuller. 1985. *The Quest for the Presidency 1984.* New York: Bantam.

Goldman, Peter, Thomas deFrank, Mark Miller, Andrew Murr, Thom Mathews, and with Patrick Rogers and Melanie Cooper. 1994. *Quest for the Presidency 1992.* College Station: Texas A&M Press.

Goodman, Paul. 1964. *The Democratic-Republicans of Massachusetts.* Cambridge, MA: Harvard University Press.

Goshko, John M., and Don Philips. 1994. "The Southwest." *Washington Post,* November 10, A42.

Green, John, and Nathan Bigelow. 2002. "The 2000 Nomination Campaign: The Costs of Innovation." In *Financing the 2000 Election,* ed. David Magleby, 49–105. Washington, DC: Brookings Institution.

Hadley, Arthur. 1976. *The Invisible Primary.* Upper Saddle River, NJ: Prentice Hall.

Hagen, Michael G., and William G. Mayer. 2000. "The Modern Politics of Presidential Selection: How Changing the Rules Really Did Change the Game." In *In Pursuit of the White House 2000: How We Choose Our Presidential Nominees,* ed. William G. Mayer. New York: Seven Bridges Press.

Hall, Richard L., and Alan V. Deardorff. 2006. "Lobbying as Legislative Subsidy." *American Political Science Review* 100:69–85.

Hamilton, Alexander. 1903. *The Works of Alexander Hamilton.* 2nd ed. Vol. 1. Ed. Henry Cabot Lodge. New York: G. P. Putnam's Sons.

Hannity and Colmes. 2007. Fox News Channel, October 8.

Hanson, Gordon S. 2000. "Out of Cash: U.S. Presidential Pre-nominations." *Party Politics* 6:47–59.

Harlow, Ralph Volney. 1917. *The History of Legislative Methods before 1825.* New Haven, CT: Yale University Press.

Haynes, Audrey A., Paul-Henri Gurian, Michael H. Crespin, and Christopher Zorn. 2004. "The Calculus of Concession: Media Coverage and the Dynamics of Winnowing in Presidential Nominations." *American Politics Research* 32:310–37.

Hendrickson, Paul. 1980. "The Long Journey of George Bush." *Washington Post,* January 13, F1.

Herrera, Richard. 1994. "Are 'Superdelegates' Super?" *Political Behavior* 16, no. 1 (March): 79–92.

Herring, Pendelton. 1940. *The Politics of Democracy.* New York: W. W. Norton.

Herrnson, Paul. 1997. *Congressional Elections: Campaigning at Home and in Washington.* Washington, DC: CQ Press.

Hershey, Marjorie Randon. 2005. *Party Politics in America.* 11th ed. New York: Longman.

Hetherington, Marc J., and William J. Keefe. 2007. *Parties, Politics and Public Policy in America.* 10th ed. Washington, DC: CQ Press.

Hinckley, Katherine, and John C Green. 1996. "Fund-raising in Presidential Nomination Campaigns: The Primary Lessons of 1988." *Political Research Quarterly*, 693–719.

Hinderaker, Ivan. 1956. *Party Politics*. New York: Holt.

Hofstadter, Richard. 1970. *The Idea of a Party System*. Berkeley: University of California Press.

Hook, Janet, and Mark Z. Barabak. 2006. "Lone Wolf McCain Cultivates GOP Pack." *Los Angeles Times*, March 12, A1.

Hotline. 2005. "A Pat on the Back." May 2.

Huckshorn, Robert, and John Bibby. 1983. "National Party Rules and Delegate Selection in the Republican Party, *PS: Political Science and Politics*, 16:656–66.

Hutchings, Vincent L., and LaFleur Stephens. 2008. "African Americans and the Presidential Nominations Process." In *The Making of the Presidential Candidates 2008*, ed. William Mayer. Lanham, MD: Rowman & Littlefield.

Jacobson, Gary. 2004. *The Politics of Congressional Elections*. New York: Longman.

Jefferson, Thomas. 1816. Letter to Isaac Tiffany, August 26, 1816. The Thomas Jefferson Papers at the Library of Congress, General Correspondence. 1651–1827, Image 414.

———. 1826. Letter to Roger Weightman, June 14, 1826. General Correspondence. 1651–1827, Image 1133.

Josephson, Matthew, and Hannah Josephson. 1969. *Al Smith, Hero of the Cities*. Boston: Houghton Mifflin.

Kamarck, Elaine Ciulla. 1986. "Structure as Strategy: Presidential Nomination Politics since Reform." PhD dissertation, University of California, Berkeley.

Karol, David. 1999. "Realignment without Replacement: Issue Evolution and Ideological Change among Members of Congress." Paper given at the Midwest Political Science Association, Chicago, April 1999.

———. 2001. "How and Why Parties Change Positions on Issues: Party Policy Change as Coalition Management in American Politics." Paper given at the American Political Science Association, San Francisco, September 2001.

———. 2009. *Party Position Change in American Politics: Coalition Management*. New York: Cambridge University Press.

Kaufman, Robert Gordon. 2000. *Henry M. Jackson: A Life in Politics*. Seattle: University of Washington Press.

Kayden, Xandra, and Eddie Mahe, Jr. 1985. *The Party Goes On: The Persistence of the Two-Party System in the United States*. New York: Basic Books.

Keeter, Scott, and Cliff Zukin. 1983. *Uninformed Choice: The Failure of the New Presidential Nominating System*. New York: Praeger.

Kenney, Patrick J., and Tom W. Rice. 1987. "The Relationship between Divisive Primaries and General Election Outcomes." *American Journal of Political Science* 31:31–44.

Kessel, John. 1968. *The Goldwater Coalition*. Indianapolis: Bobbs-Merrill.

Key, V. O. 1965. *Parties, Politics, and Pressure Groups*. 5th ed. New York: Thomas Y. Crowell.

King, Gary. 1991. "'Truth' Is Stranger than Prediction, More Questionable Than Causal Inference." *American Journal of Political Science* 35, no. 4 (November): 1047–53.

King, Gary, Michael Tomz, and Jason Wittenberg. 2000. "Making the Most of Statistical Analyses: Improving Interpretation and Presentation." *American Journal of Political Science* 44, no. 2, 347–61.

Kirkpatrick, David D. 2008. "Young Evangelicals Embrace Huckabee as Old Guard Balks." *New York Times*, January 13, 1.

Knight, Brian, and Nathan Schiff. 2007. "Momentum and Social Learning in Presidential Primaries." In *National Bureau of Economic Research, Working Paper 13637*.

Kornblut, Anne E. 2007. "Obama's Campaign Takes in $25 Million." *Washington Post*, April 5, A1.

Kunkel, Joseph A. III. 1988. "Party Endorsement and Incumbency in Minnesota Legislative Nominations." *Legislative Studies Quarterly* 13, no. 2, 211–23.

Kurtz, Howard. 1997. "Enough Presidential Hopefuls to Fill Air Force One." *Washington Post*, December 27, C1.

———. 2003. "Dean Assails Bush on Defense." *Washington Post*, December 1, 6.

Lambert, Bruce. 1993. "F. Clifton White, 74, Long a Republican Strategist." *New York Times*, January 10, A34.

Lambro, Donald. 2004. "Is Firebrand Flaming Out? Fueled by Angry Populism, Dean Campaign Got Burned." *Washington Times*, January 25, A1.

Lawrence, Eric. D., Forrest Maltzman, and Steven S. Smith. 2006. "Who Wins? Party Effects in Legislative Voting." *Legislative Studies Quarterly* 31, no. 1 (February 2006): 33–69.

Lengle, James I. 1980. "Divisive Electoral Primaries and Party Electoral Prospects, 1932–1976." *American Politics Quarterly* 8:261–77.

———. 1981. *Representation and Presidential Primaries: The Democratic Party in the Post-Reform Era*. Westport, CT: Greenwood Press.

Lengle, James I., Diana Owen, and Molly W. Sonner. 1995. "Divisive Nominating Mechanisms and Democratic Party Electoral Prospects." *Journal of Politics* 57, no. 2: 370–83.

Lengle, James I., and Byron E. Shafer. 1976. "Primary Rules, Political Power and Social Change." *American Political Science Review* 70, no. 1: 25–40.

Leonard, Gerald. 2002. *The Invention of Party Politics: Federalism, Popular Sovereignty, and Constitutional Development in Jacksonian Illinois*. Chapel Hill: University of North Carolina Press.

Lincoln, Abraham. 1860. Letter to Samuel Galloway, March 24. Lincoln Papers, Library of Congress.

Link, Eugene Perry. 1942. *Democratic-Republican Societies, 1790–1800*. New York: Columbia University Press.

Lockard, Duane. 1959. *New England State Politics*. Princeton, NJ: Princeton University Press.

Luetscher, George E. 1903. *Early Political Machinery in the United States*. Philadelphia: Kessinger Publishing.

Luthin, Reinhard H. 1944. "Abraham Lincoln and the Tariff." *American Historical Review* 49, no. 4: 609–29.

Madison, James. 1791. "A Candid State of Parties." *National Gazette*, September 19, 1792.

Magleby, David B., and William G. Mayer. 2007. "Presidential Nomination Finance in the Post-BCRA Era." In *The Making of the Presidential Candidates 2008*, ed. W. Mayer. Lanham, MD: Rowman & Littlefield.

Maizlish, Stephen E. 1998. "Salmon P. Chase: The Roots of Ambition and the Origins of Reform." *Journal of the Early Republic* 18:47–70.

Martin, Jonathan 2007. "Can Huck Hang On?" Jonathan Martin, *Politico*, December 30. Online publication.

Masket, Seth. 2007. "It Takes an Outsider: Extra-legislative Organization and Partisanship in the California Assembly, 1849–2006." *American Journal of Political Science* 51 (July).

———. In press. *Reluctant Partisans*. Ann Arbor: University of Michigan Press.

Matthews, Christopher. 1989. *Hardball*. New York: Harper & Row.

Matthews, Donald R. 1978. "Winnowing: The Media and the Race for the 1976 Presidential Nominations." In *Race for the Presidency*, ed. F. Christ Arterton. Upper Saddle River, NJ: Prentice Hall, 1978.

May, Ernest R., and Janet Fraser. 1973. *Campaign '72: The Managers Speak*. Cambridge, MA: Harvard University Press.

Mayer, William G. 1996. "Forecasting Presidential Nominations." In *In Pursuit of the White House: How We Choose Our Presidential Nominees*, ed. William G. Mayer. Chatham, NJ: Chatham House.

Mayer, William. 2001. "The Presidential Nominations." In *The Election of 2000: Reports and Interpretations*, ed. E. J. Dionne, W. G. Mayer, M. R. Hershey, and K. A. Frankovic. London: Chatham House.

———. 2003. "Basic Dynamics of the Nomination Process: An Expanded View." In *The Making of the Presidential Candidates*, ed. W. Mayer. Lanham, MD: Rowman & Littlefield.

———. 2007. "Voting in Presidential Primaries: What We Can Learn from Three Decades of Exit Polling." In *The Making of the Presidential Candidates 2008*, ed. W. Mayer. Lanham, MD: Rowman & Littlefield.

Mayer, William G., and Andrew Busch. 2003. *The Front-Loading Problem in Presidential Nominations*. Washington, DC: Brookings Institution.

Mayhew, David R. 1974. *Congress: The Electoral Connection*. New Haven, CT: Yale University Press.

———. 1986. *Placing Parties in American Politics : Organization, Electoral Settings, and Government Activity in the Twentieth Century*. Princeton, NJ: Princeton University Press.

McCain, John. 2000. "Excerpt from McCain's Speech on Social Conservatives." *New York Times*, February 29, A16.

McCann, James A. 2000. "Presidential Nomination Activists and Political Representation." In *In Pursuit of the White House: How We Choose Our Presidential Nominees,* ed. William Mayer, 72–104. Chatham, NJ: Chatham House.

McCarty, Nolan, Keith T. Poole, and Howard Rosenthal. 2006. *Polarized America: The Dance of Ideology and Unequal Riches*. Cambridge, MA: MIT Press.

McClosky, Herbert, Paul Hoffman, and Rosemark O'Hara. 1960. "Issue Conflict and Consensus among Party Leaders and Followers." *American Political Science Review* 58:361–82.

McCormick, Richard P. 1966. *The Second American Party System*. Chapel Hill: University of North Carolina Press.

———. 1982. *The Presidential Game: The Origin of American Presidential Politics*. Oxford: Oxford University Press.

McCubbins, Mathew D. 1992. "Party Decline and Presidential Campaigns in the Television Age." In *Under the Watchful Eye: Managing Presidential Campaigns in the Television Age*, ed. Mathew D. McCubbins, 9–57. Washington, DC: CQ Press.

McNitt, Andrew D. 1980. "The Effect of Preprimary Endorsement on Competition for Nominations: An Examination of Different Nominating Systems." *Journal of Politics* 42, no. 1, 257–66.

Meet the Press. 2006. Transcript of interview between Tim Russert and John McCain. NBC, April 2.

Merriam, Charles. 1922. *The American Party System*. New York: Macmillan.

Michels, Robert. 1915. *Political Parties: A Sociological Study of the Oligarchical Tendencies of Modern Democracy*. Trans. Eden Paul and Cedar Paul. New York: Free Press. (Orig. pub. 1911.)

Mickey, Robert. 2008. *Paths Out of Dixie: The Democratization of Authoritarian Enclaves in America's Deep South, 1944–1972.* Princeton, NJ: Princeton University Press.

Middendorf, J. William, II. 2006. *A Glorious Disaster: Barry Goldwater's Presidential Campaign and the Origins of the Conservative Movement.* New York: Basic Books.

Milbank, Dana. 1999. "Campaign Journal." *New Republic,* October 18, 17.

Miller, John L., and Ramesh Ponnuru. 1998. "Handicapping 2000; Great Wide Open." *National Review Online,* November 9.

Miller, Gary, and Norman Schofield. 2003. "Activists and Partisan Realignment in the United States." *American Political Science Review* 97:245–60.

Miller, William. 1939. "The Fruits of Republican Organization." *Pennsylvania Magazine of History and Biography* 63:41–43.

Mosk, Matthew. 2007. "Defections to Thompson Pose Major Threat to McCain." *Washington Post,* June 8, A1.

Mueller, John E. 1973. *War, Presidents, and Public Opinion.* New York: Wiley.

Mutz, Diana C. 1995. "Effects of Horse-Race Coverage on Campaign Coffers: Strategic Contributing in Presidential Primaries." *Journal of Politics* 57:1019–42.

Nagourney, Adam. 2001. "In the First Mile of a Marathon, Kerry Emerges as Front-Runner." *New York Times,* February 26, A14.

———. 2003. "Centrist Democrats Warn Party Not to Present Itself as Far Left." *New York Times,* July 29, A1.

Nagourney, Adam, and Jodi Wilgoren. 2004. "Dean's Campaign Alters Approach after Iowa Loss." *New York Times,* January 22, 1.

Neal, Donn C. 1973. "The World beyond the Hudson: Alfred E. Smith and National Politics, 1918–1928." PhD dissertation, University of Michigan.

Neal, Steve. 2004. *Happy Days Are Here Again.* New York: William Morrow.

Noel, Hans. 2005. "Smoke Signals: Estimating the Effect of the Invisible Primary with the Data You Have, Not the Data You Want." Paper given at the Annual Meeting of the Society for Political Methodology, at Tallahassee, FL.

———. 2006. *The Coalition Merchants: How Ideologues Shape Parties in American Politics.* PhD dissertation, political science, University of California, Los Angeles.

Norrander, Barbara. 1992. *Super Tuesday: Regional Politics and Presidential Primaries.* Lexington: University Press of Kentucky.

———. 1993. "Nomination Choices: Caucus and Primary Outcomes, 1976–1988." *American Journal of Political Science* 37, no. 2, 343–64.

———. 1996. "Field Essay: Presidential Nomination Politics in the Post-Reform Era." *Political Research Quarterly* 49 (December): 875–915.

———. 2000. "The End Game in Post-Reform Presidential Nominations." *Journal of Politics* 62:999–1013.

Novak, Robert. 1964. *The Agony of the GOP.* New York: Macmillan.

———. 1997. "Bush Makes Full Debut." *Chicago Sun-Times,* August 15, 25.

———. 1998. "George W. Bush's Greatest Worry: Poppy's Pals?" *New York Post,* June 18, 39.

———. 2007a. "Thompson Shuns Top Talent." *Chicago Sun Times,* September 13, 33.

———. 2007b. "Thompson's White House Talk Is No Act." *Chicago Sun Times,* April 2, 43.

Packer, George. 2008. "The Choice; The Clinton-Obama Battle Reveals Two Very Different Ideas of the Presidency." *The New Yorker* (January 28), p. 28.

Pasley, Jeffrey L. 1996. "'A Journeyman, Either in Law or Politics': John Beckley and the Social Origins of Political Campaigning." *Journal of the Early Republic* 16 (Winter): 531–69.

———. 2001. *The Tyranny of the Printers: Newspaper Politics in the Early American Republic.* Charlottesville: University of Virginia Press.

Patterson, Thomas E. 1980. *The Mass Media Election: How Americans Choose Their President.* Westport, CT: Praeger.

———. 1993. *Out of Order.* New York: Random House.

Peel, Roy, and Thomas C. Donnelly. 1935. *The 1932 Campaign: An Analysis.* New York: Farrar & Rinehart.

Polsby, Nelson. 1982. "What If Robert Kennedy Had Lived?" In *What If? Explorations in Social Science Fiction*, ed. Nelson Polsby and Paul Seabury. Albany, NY: Lewis Publishing.

———. 1983. *Consequences of Party Reform.* New York: Oxford University Press.

Polsby, Nelson W., and Aaron B. Wildavsky. 1968. *Presidential Elections: Strategies of American Electoral Politics.* New York: Charles Scribner's Sons.

———. 2000. *Presidential Elections: Strategies and Structures of American Politics.* New York: Chatham House.

Polsby, Nelson W., Aaron B. Wildavsky, and David A. Hopkins. 2007. *Presidential Elections: Strategies of American Electoral Politics.* Lanham, MD: Rowman & Littlefield Publishers.

Poole, Keith, and Howard Rosenthal. 1997. *Congress: A Political-Economic History of Roll Call Voting.* New York: Oxford University Press.

Price, David E. 1984. *Bringing Back the Parties.* Washington, DC: Congressional Quarterly Press.

Prince, Carl E. 1967. *New Jersey's Jeffersonian Republicans: The Genesis of an Early Party Machine, 1789–1817.* Chapel Hill: University of North Carolina Press.

Purdum, Todd. 2004. "Outside Campaigners Flood Iowa, Sharing Their Candidates' Styles." January 13, 1.

Quaid, Libby. 2007. "For Huckabee, Iowa Caucuses Are More Than a Leap of Faith." Associated Press Wire, December 20.

Rae, Nicol C. 1989. *The Decline and Fall of the Liberal Republicans: From 1952 to the Present.* Oxford: Oxford University Press.

Ranney, Austin. 1975. *Curing the Mischiefs of Faction.* Berkeley: University of California Press.

Rapoport, Ronald B., Walter J. Stone, and Alan I. Abramowitz. 1991. "Do Endorsements Matter? Group Influence in the 1984 Democratic Caucuses." *American Political Science Review* 85, no. 1, 193–203.

Rarick, Ethan. 2005. *California Rising: The Life and Times of Pat Brown.* Berkeley: University of California Press.

Ratcliffe, Donald J. 2000. *The Politics of Long Division: The Birth of the Second Party System in Ohio.* Columbus: Ohio State University Press.

Reed, Julia. 1997. "The Son Also Rises." *Weekly Standard*, February 10, 23.

Reiter, Howard. 1985. *Selecting the President: The Nominating Process in Transition.* Philadelphia: University of Pennsylvania Press.

Remini, Robert V. 1959. *Martin Van Buren and the Making of the Democratic Party.* New York: Columbia University Press.

Reynolds, John F. 2006. *The Demise of the American Convention System, 1880–1911.* Cambridge: Cambridge University Press.

Rich, Frank. 2007. "Rudy, The Values Slayer." *New York Times*, October 28, 12.

Robinson, Michael, and Margaret Sheehan. 1983. *Over the Wire and on TV: CBS and UPI in Campaign '80.* New York: Russell Sage Foundation.

Robinson, Michael, Clyde Wilcox, and Paul Marshall. 1989. "The Presidency: Not for Sale." *Public Opinion* 2:51.

Rohde, David W. 1991. *Parties and Leaders in the Postreform House*. Chicago: University of Chicago Press.

Romano, Lois. 1998. "Son on the Horizon; Gov. George Walker Bush Is Running Hard. But Is He Heading in His Father's Direction?" *Washington Post*, September 24, 1998, B1.

Rosenstone, Steven. 1983. *Forecasting Presidential Elections*. New Haven, CT: Yale University Press.

Rossiter, Clinton. 1960. *The American Presidency*. New York: Harcourt-Brace.

Rothenberg, Stuart. 2007. "Iowa Straw Poll: Over Long before It Really Began." *Roll Call*, June 11.

Rutland, Robert Allen. 1995. *The Democrats from Jefferson to Clinton*. Columbia: University of Missouri Press.

San Diego Union-Tribune. 1984. "The Democrats: What Has Rules Reform Wrought?" June 17, C1.

Savage, Charlie. 2006. "Analysts say McCain Wooing Religious Right." *Boston Globe*, May 13, A1.

Schattschneider, E. E. 1942. *Party Government*. Westport, CT: Greenwood Press.

———. 1960. *The Semisovereign People*. Hinsdale, IL: Dryden Press.

Schlesinger, Jacob, and John Harwood. 2004. "Tight Iowa Race Signals Campaign Remains Open." *Wall Street Journal*, A1.

Schlesinger, Joseph A. 1984. "On the Theory of Party Organization." *Journal of Politics* 46, no. 2, 369–400.

———. 1985. "The New American Political Party." *American Political Science Review* 79:1152–69.

Schram, Martin. 1977. *Running for President 1976*. New York: Stein & Day.

Schumpeter, Joseph A. 1942. *Capitalism, Socialism, and Democracy*. New York: Harper & Row.

Schwartz, Maralee. 1987. "Deukmejian Declares Neutrality." *Washington Post*, June 12, 1987, A5.

Schwartz, Thomas. 1989. *Why Parties?* Research memorandum, Department of Political Science, UCLA.

Shafer, Byron E. 1983. *Quiet Revolution: The Struggle for the Democratic Party and the Shaping of Post-Reform Politics*. New York: Russell Sage.

Shafer, Byron E. 1988. *Bifurcated Politics: Evolution and Reform in the National Party Convention*. Cambridge, MA: Harvard University Press.

Shear, Michael D. 2006. "'Family' Reasons? Theories Abound on Warner's Exit." *Washington Post*, October 19, PW02.

Sigelman, Lee. 1989. "The 1988 Presidential Nominations: Whatever Happened to Momentum?" *PS*, March, 35–39.

Simon, Roger. 2007. "Hillary Booed (but Only Twice)." *Politico*, August 5. Online publication.

Sinclair, Barbara. 2000. "Do Parties Matter?" In *Essays on the History of Congress*, ed. David W. Brady, and. Mathew D. McCubbins. Palo Alto, CA: Stanford University Press.

Sitkoff, Harvard. 1971. "Harry Truman and the Election of 1948: The Coming of Age of Civil Rights in American Politics." *Journal of Southern History* 37, no. 4, 597–616.

Slevin, Peter, and Perry Bacon, Jr. 2007. "Home-School Ties Aided Huckabee's Iowa Rise; Early Backers Rallied Conservative Network." *Washington Post*, December 17, A1.

Smith, Robert Norton. 1982. *Thomas E. Dewey and His Times*. New York: Simon & Schuster.

Smothers, Ronald. 1984. "Alabama Black Leaders Are Urging Pragmatism in Supporting Mondale." *New York Times,* March 12, B9.

Solberg, Carl. 1984. *Hubert Humphrey: A Biography.* New York: W. W. Norton.

Solomon, John, and Matthew Mosk. 2007. "New Loyalties for Old Fundraising Networks." *Washington Post,* April 17, A6.

Southwell, Patricia. 1986. "The Politics of Disgruntlement: Nonvoting and Defection among Supporters of Nomination Losers, 1968–1984." *Political Behavior* 8:81–95.

Squire, Peverill, and Eric R. A. N. Smith. 1988. "The Effect of Partisan Information on Voters in Nonpartisan Elections." *Journal of Politics* 50:169–79.

Steger, Wayne. 2000. "Candidate Endorsements: The Under-Appreciated Role of the Political Party Establishments in the Presidential Nominating Process." Paper given at the annual convention of the Midwest Political Science Association, Chicago.

Steger, Wayne P. 2007. "Who Wins Presidential Nominations and Why: An Updated Forecast of the Presidential Primary Vote." *Presidential Research Quarterly* 60:91–97.

Steger, Wayne, Andrew J. Dowdle, and Randall E. Adkins. 2004. "The New Hampshire Effect in Presidential Primaries." *Political Research Quarterly* 57:375–90.

Stolberg, Cheryl. 2005. "Senate Leader Criticized and Praised for Stem Cell Shift." *New York Times,* July 30.

Stone, Walter J. 1986. "The Carryover Effect in Presidential Nominations." *American Political Science Review* 80:271–79.

Stone, Walter J., and Alan I. Abramowitz. 1983. "Winning May Not Be Everything, but It's More Than We Thought: Presidential Party Activists in 1980." *American Political Science Review* 77:945–56.

Sundquist, James L. 1983. *Dynamics of the Party System: Alignment and Realignment of Political Parties in the United States.* Washington, DC: Brookings Institution.

Sweet, Lynn. 2007. "Obama Talking Small Bucks, Thinking Big; 'Ordinary' Donors No Match for Elite 'Bundlers.'" *Chicago Sun-Times,* April 15, A6.

Taylor, Paul. 1987. "Politicians Refuse Rides on Hart's Bandwagon; Coloradan a Lonesome Front Runner." *Washington Post,* March 13, A4.

———. 1988. "For Gephardt, No Payoff Yet in Iowa Strategy." *Washington Post,* March 24, A1.

Thee, Megan. 2004. "Preferences of Super Delegates." *New York Times,* January 18, 20.

Time. 1980. "But Can Reagan Be Elected?" March 31. www.time.com/time/magazine/article/0,9171,921912-1,00.html.

Toner, Robin. 1991. "In 'Waiting for Mario,' Only the Plot Goes On." *New York Times,* October 16, B7.

Trish, Barbara. 1999. "Does Organization Matter? A Critical-Case Analysis from Recent Presidential Nomination Politics." *Presidential Studies Quarterly* 29, no. 4, 873–96.

Trounstine, Jessica. 2008. *Political Monopolies in American Cities: The Rise and Fall of Bosses and Reformers.* Chicago: University of Chicago Press.

United Press International. 1968. "Humphrey to Avoid Speeches in States Due for Primaries." *New York Times,* May 16, 22.

U.S. News and World Report. 1980. "It's Reagan vs. Bush; A Survey of Republican Leaders." January 28, 57.

U.S. News and World Report. 2004. "The New Shoe Leather Politics." January 19, 36.

Van Houweling, Robert P. 2008. "Legislators' Personal Policy Preferences and Partisan Legislative Organization." Unpublished MS, University of California, Berkeley.

VandeHei, Jim. 2004. "Dean Puts a New Face on His Candidacy." *Washington Post,* January 21, 1.

VandeHei, Jim, and Dan Balz. 2003. "As Anti-Dean Forces Shrink, Their Battle Becomes More Urgent." *Washington Post,* December 12, 1.

Verhovek, Sam Howe. 1999. "Republican Governors, Wanting One of Their Own, Decided Early on Bush." *New York Times,* November 23, A22.

von Sternberg, Bob. 2007. "How Iowa Found Faith in Huckabee." *Minneapolis Star Tribune,* December 31, 8A.

Warren, Charles, 1931. *Jacobin and Juno.* Cambridge, MA: Harvard University Press.

Wattenberg, Martin P. 1991. *The Rise of Candidate-Centered Politics: Presidential Elections of the 1980s.* Cambridge, MA: Harvard University Press.

Wayne, Stephen J. 2000. *The Road to the White House 2000: The Politics of Presidential Elections.* Boston: Bedford/St. Martins.

West, Mark. 2008. "Congressional Primaries, the Internet, and Ideological Money." Paper given at the annual meeting of the Midwest Political Science Association, Chicago.

West, Paul. 2006. "McCain Adopts Insider Strategy; Maverick Retools for '08 Campaign." *Baltimore Sun,* March 20, A1.

Whitcomb, John, and Claire Whitcomb. 2002. *Real Life at the White House: 200 Years of Daily Life at America's Most Famous Residence.* New York: Routledge.

White, John Kenneth, and Daniel M. Shea. 2000. *New Party Politics: From Jefferson and Hamilton to the Information Age.* Boston: Bedford/St. Martin's.

White, Theodore H. 1956. "Kefauver Rides Again." *Colliers,* May 11, 28.

———. 1961. *The Making of the President 1960.* Cutchogue: Buccaneer Books.

———. 1965. *The Making of the President 1964.* New York: Atheneum.

———. 1969. *The Making of the President 1968.* New York: Atheneum.

———. 1973. *The Making of the President 1972.* New York: Atheneum.

———. 1982. *America in Search of Itself: The Making of the President 1956–1980.* New York: Harper & Row.

Wildavsky, Aaron B. 1965. "The Goldwater Phenomenon: Purists, Politicians, and the Two-Party System." *Review of Politics* 27:387–413.

Wilentz, Sean. 2005. *The Rise of American Democracy: Jefferson to Lincoln.* New York: W. W. Norton.

Will, George 1986. "The Sound of a Lapdog." *Washington Post,* January 30, A25.

———. 2007. "A Rocky Rollout for Thompson." *Washington Post,* September 13, A25.

Wilson, James Q. 1966. *The Amateur Democrat: Club Politics in Three Cities.* Chicago: University of Chicago Press.

Witcover, Jules. 1977. *Marathon: The Pursuit of the Presidency, 1972–1976.* New York: Viking Press.

Wollman, Jonathan. 1987. "Endorsements Don't Mean Much, but Every Delegate Counts." AP Wire, November 30.

Wunderlin, Clarence E., Jr. 1997. *The Papers of Robert A. Taft.* Vol. 1, *1889–1938.* Kent, OH: Kent State University Press.

Zaller, John. 2003. "Floating Voters in U.S. Presidential Elections, 1948–2000." In *Studies in Public Opinion: Attitudes, Nonattitudes, Measurement Error, and Change,* ed. Paul Sniderman and Willem Saris, 166–213. Princeton, NJ: Princeton University Press.

Index

Page numbers in italics refer to figures and tables.

Made in the USA
Lexington, KY
06 August 2015